W9-BCX-678

JOHN REED

Portrait of John Reed painted by Robert Hallowell and presented to
Harvard University by the Harvard Alumni John Reed Committee.

John Reed

The Making of a Revolutionary

By

Granville Hicks

With the Assistance of
JOHN STUART

BENJAMIN BLOM
New York/London
1968

First Published 1936
Reissued 1968 by Benjamin Blom, Inc., Bronx, N.Y. 10452
and 56 Doughty Street, London W.C. 1

Library of Congress Catalog Card Number 68-21220

Printed in the United States of America

To

LINCOLN STEFFENS

CONTENTS

CONTENTS

JOHN REED

I

BOYHOOD IN PORTLAND

JOHN REED was born, October 20, 1887, in his grandmother's mansion, Cedar Hill, and there was another celebration in a house that had come to be known for its festivities. It was a large house and possibly the most pretentious Portland could boast. Henry D. Green, who had not lived to see the birth of his first grandson, had built it ten years before on a spur of the hills west of Portland, the first of the first citizens to move away from the little cluster of wealthy homes on the flat land near the river. Cedar Hill was the show-place of the city, a real French chateau, people said, with formal gardens, stables, green-houses, and a glass grape arbor.

The child was christened John Silas in fashionable Trinity Episcopal Church, and, while Mrs. Green entertained her friends and the friends of the father and mother, Lee Sing, her cook, celebrated in his own way in his cellar room. He lit joss sticks, burned paper prayers, and gave a feast of dried shark-fins, seasoned chicken-gizzards, and sam-shui to his Chinese friends. Later that evening his mistress found him alone in the pantry, very drunk, with twelve of her Royal Worcester cups lined up before him, drinking whiskey out of one after the other.

The chateau on Cedar Hill was the outward mark of Henry Green's eminence among the pioneer builders of Portland. He was not quite among the first settlers, for the city had been established in 1845, and the foundations of its first fortunes had been laid in the early fifties by Henry W. Corbett, Henry Failing, William S. Ladd, and Simeon G. Reed. These were the builders of the steamship lines, the banks, and the railroads. But

Green had his share of the profit and the glory. He had rounded the Horn in 1853 to join his brother in Astoria, where John Green and H. C. Leonard had, three years earlier, established the only competitor of the Hudson Bay Company's trading-post at the mouth of the Columbia River. And in 1856 he and his brother had moved their business from Astoria to Portland.

Three years later the Greens founded the Portland Gaslight Company and built the first gas works in Oregon—the third, they boasted, to be constructed on the Pacific Coast. In 1861 they purchased the Portland water works from the original grantee, whose plant consisted of one mile of wooden pipe and a pump located on a small stream. Soon afterward they promoted the Oregon Iron Works Company, the first company on the Coast for smelting iron ores and manufacturing pig iron. With these three enterprises, all highly successful as Portland grew, Mr. Green had reason to compete with the city's best in the splendor of his home.

All Portland was proud of Cedar Hill and proud of its builder. Though it was common knowledge that Henry Green drank to excess, everyone pointed out that he never appeared in public when intoxicated and that, whatever his condition, he was a charming gentleman. He had died in 1885 in New York City, whither he had gone on business after visiting the New Orleans exposition and attending the inauguration of President Cleveland. A friend, who had been with him in Washington, wrote a fulsome eulogy for the Portland paper. "In all the countless throng of distinguished men that walked those streets, embracing the aristocracy of both continents," he said, speaking of the inaugural ceremonies, "there was no more graceful figure nor flashing presence than the tall and sinewy figure of this representative Oregon man, who moved through those courtly throngs with the aplomb of Alcibiades himself. . . . He will be missed by the hard-faring poor, whose sufferings he relieved and kept his munificence a profound secret. He will be missed by the rich, who know the value of that charity which gives no alms but pours out tender words in hours of grief and mental suffering. He was a self-poised character, a man who rose to wealth without resorting to oppression and one whose courage was only equaled by his modesty."

This was John Reed's grandfather. His grandmother, like her husband, was born in New York State. She was the granddaughter of Christian Wilmerding, a German merchant whose descendants had married into the richest families of the East. Charlotte Jones Green was quite as proud of her cousins—Paynes, Fields, and Wilmerdings—as she was of her husband's success in pioneer Portland. Her two daughters were educated in a finishing school in New York City, and she was the first woman in Portland to have a carriage, and with a coachman and a footman too.

After Mr. Green's death, Cedar Hill became more famous than ever for its hospitality. Portland was both delighted and shocked by Charlotte Green's parties. In the summer the guests danced on the lawn, which was lighted by flaring gas-jets that had been piped to the tops of the pointed firs, and in the winter the ballroom on the third floor was crowded and gay. Everyone wanted to be included in these parties, and almost everyone was. The next day those who had been shocked had plenty to discuss; those who had not were usually recovering.

Portland was overwhelmingly conservative. Its early settlers had come either from New England or the older southern states, and it believed that it was less raw and western than other coast towns. On the surface, at least, it was an orderly city, proud of its churches, restrained in its manners, suspicious of gayety and color. It obliterated as quickly as possible all traces of the frontier and cultivated the decorum of a Massachusetts town. Social snobbery quickly developed, and a sense of what should and what should not be done. Charlotte Green—whom everyone affectionately called Sudie—refused to conform. Exuberant, the best of good company, liked even when not approved, she went her own rather boisterous way, but at the same time insisted upon and held her position of social prestige. It was an achievement that Portland marveled at.

Mrs. Green's children were almost as popular as she. There were four of them, two boys and two girls. One of the sons, Ray, was often away in far corners of the world, but returned to tell hilarious stories. Both of the daughters were married soon after their father's death: Katherine to an army officer, Lieutenant Edward Burr, who was transferred not long afterward to the East, and Margaret to C. J. Reed, a promising young business man, newly come to the city.

The young C. J. Reeds thought of themselves, without immodesty, as belonging to Portland's best. Margaret Reed, though less unconventional than her mother, was quite as gifted a hostess, a well-bred, charming, rather dainty woman, fastidious and a little proud. Charles Jerome Reed—always called C. J.—had, during his few years in the city, won a reputation both as a sound business man and as a wit. He had come to Portland as the representative of the D. M. Osborne Company of Auburn, New York, which was his birthplace, and he supervised the sale of their agricultural implements throughout the Northwest. The business was prosperous, and he was personally so well liked that he was made a member and then the president of the exclusive Arlington Club. Presiding at the daily lunch table of the club, he jeered at all comers, and his sallies at the expense of the city's dignitaries were quoted for many years. Indeed, his fame traveled up and down the Coast, and he became a member of the Bohemian Club of San Francisco and a great favorite at its meetings.

John Reed was born, as he was eventually to realize, into a position of privilege. Throughout his youth, though his father's fortunes varied, there was never a time when he was conscious of deprivation of any sort. Without being wealthy, his mother and father were able to give him anything that a rich man's son in the Portland of that day was likely to have. They could give him, too, the sense of being well-born, respected, superior to the mass of people. The desirability of wealth and social position was taken for granted by the Reeds. But at the same time there was a feeling that nothing could justify the sacrifice of independence. John Reed had the example of his grandmother, who insisted on living her own life as she saw fit. More important was the example of his father, a business man and a successful one, who never hesitated to say what he thought, a born fighter, though as yet he had found no cause worth fighting for. There were traditions of conformity and traditions of rebellion. In their generation Jack's younger brother Harry became the conformist and Jack the rebel. "Harry is a lamb," Mrs. Green once said, "but Jack is a lion. I prefer lions."

WHEN the young Reeds moved to a house down in the city, there were still gay parties and many guests, and they maintained an establishment appropriate to their position. Jackie had a nurse, of course; in fact, there was a succession of them, for Mrs. Reed was not easy to work for. One of them, who remained for ten days, always remembered the little boy as affectionate, lovable, and bright. She left because Mrs. Reed rebuked her for letting a little girl from a poorer section kiss Jackie, and because she was required to wear a cap and apron.

The servants John Reed best remembered were Chinese. There was a cook whom his father particularly liked, and with whom he discussed business and politics. The Chinese fascinated the little boy with their tales of ghosts, their superstitions, and the rumors of their bloody feuds. He was curious about their food and drink and all their customs. And later he attributed to his intimacy with them his easy acceptance of what was different from himself, his zest for foreign food and strange customs, his happy sharing in other ways of life than his own.

The Chinese seemed romantic to John Reed. He felt, looking back, that there was something a little fantastic about his whole boyhood: pigtails and gongs and fluttering red paper, and his grandmother's glamorous chateau with dancing under the flaring trees, and the carriage with the blooded horses and the footman. Then there was his Uncle Ray, who was interested in coffee plantations in South America, and came home with strange tales of revolutions, battles, and treasures. Once he told how he had been a leader of a successful revolution in Guatemala, and had been made secretary of state. His first act, he said, was to appropriate the funds of the national treasury to give a grand state ball; his second was to declare war on Germany because he had flunked his German course in college.

When John Reed discovered books, he surrendered to romance. From fairy tales, he went on to the stories of King

Arthur, and then to history. The histories of the crusades—noble kings, knights in armor, brave crossbowmen—gripped him. He began to invent stories of his own, telling them to the children of the neighborhood, whom he terrified with his accounts of the monster called the Hormuz—and terrified himself too. And in time he wrote his stories down, planned a comic history of the United States, and wrote and staged his own plays.

He began to discover Portland. The Willamette River divided the city, though the area on the eastern side was largely ignored by such people as the Reeds. Its streets were muddy; some of its houses poised uncertainly on the edges of gulleys; it could be reached only by ferry. C. J. Reed, in common with other sagacious business men, predicted that East Portland was destined to grow with the city, and he talked about the wisdom of investing in its real estate; but he would not have thought of living there.

The principal stores and office buildings—some of them six and seven stories high—were crowded together on the west side of the river. John Reed could not help noticing that most of them bore the names of his playmates—Ladd, Failing, Corbett. To the north, towards the junction of the Willamette and the Columbia, were the grain elevators and the store houses, symbols of the commerce that had given Portland its fifty thousand inhabitants. To the south were the lumber mills and the woolen factories and the other industries that were beginning to change the nature of the city. Often John Reed heard his father talk about these businesses and about the great railroads and their makers, Henry Villard, E. H. Harriman, and, as time went on, James J. Hill. Not everything that C. J. Reed said about these men and their local associates—W. S. Ladd, Simeon Reed, and the others—was flattering, but his pride in Portland was unmistakable.

If John Reed wanted to go from the apartment hotel in which he spent part of his boyhood to his grandmother's mansion, he walked up from the river-bank towards the fir-clad hills on the western horizon. From the narrow streets and the low, compact buildings, he mounted to the region of churches and middle-class homes. Portland was proud of its churches, dozens of them, representing almost every denomination in the country. Churches, schools, hospitals—the marks of the culture the city coveted. And at last Reed would come to the West End, where some of the wealthy lived in decorous Queen Anne houses, and above them all his grandmother's house.

Now, looking back, he gazed over the city to Mount Hood, Mount St. Helens, and Mount Adams, their white peaks always dominating the city on the east and the north. The whole city spread before him, neat roofs, green lawns, proud spires, sloping down to the curving river. And to the north there was the Columbia, bearing the boats of the Pacific trade. It was a beautiful city, though it touched John Reed's imagination far less than other cities he was to know.

His mother and father sent him and his brother to the Portland Academy, a private school with a good reputation. For the first two or three years school excited him, for he seemed to be learning so much that he had wanted to know, but then it grew dull, and thereafter only an unusual subject or a rare teacher aroused John Reed's interest. He was bright enough to pass, but he would not be bothered to get good marks. Later on he marveled that he had tolerated the dull routine of the educational system as well as he had. "Why should I have been interested in the stupid education of our time?" he asked. "We take young, soaring imaginations, consumed with curiosity about the life they see all around, and feed them with dead technique: the flawless purity of Washington, Lincoln's humdrum chivalry, our dull and virtuous history and England's honest glory; Addison's graceful style as an essayist, Goldsmith celebrating the rural clergy of the eighteenth century, Dr. Johnson at his most vapid, and George Eliot's *Silas Marner;* Macauley and the sonorous oratings of Edmund Burke; and in Latin, Caeser's Gallic guide-book and Cicero's mouthings about Roman politics. And the teachers! Men and women—usually women—whose chief qualification is that they can plough steadily through a dull round of dates, acts, half-truths, and rules for style, without questioning, without interpreting, and without seeing how ridiculously unlike the world their teachings are. I have forgotten most of it, forced on me before I was ready; what I do know came mostly from books I had the curiosity to read outside school hours. And many fine things I have had to force myself to explore again because school once spoiled them for me."

In those early years Reed was small for his age and not altogether well, and he could not take an effective part in the games that went on around the school. He had neither the physical equipment nor the temperament for organized sports. But when he could make his own rules, he was a good companion, and he often led his schoolmates in fighting Indians or hunting bears in the woods back of town. The more scope a game gave to his imagination, the better he liked it, and his imagination was audacious. After his first reading of Roman history, he was inspired to give a banquet in the imperial manner. Arranging couches about the table, he invited his friends to recline and eat. The Chinese cook had given place by now to a Negro, and Reed, clapping his hands, called, "Ho, slave, bring on the repast!" Outraged, the cook gave notice and left.

The summer that he was ten, his mother took him and his brother to the East. The Osbornes had sold their business to the International Harvester Company, and for a time the Reeds had very little money, but C. J. Reed had established himself in the insurance business, and once more they were people of means. Mrs. Reed wanted the boys to know their grandfather and grandmother Reed, and to meet the Jones and Wilmerding cousins. And after the round of visits had been made, she took them to Plymouth for a month at the seashore. They went on to Washington, and were there when the *Maine* was blown up. Soon Uncle Ray was off for the Philippines, and came back with a fine new story about how he had been made King of Guam.

The trip to the East set a date that stood out in the timelessness of childhood memories, but John Reed had another reason for remembering his eleventh year. He had never been very well, and now he began to speak of a severe pain in his left side. The doctor traced the trouble to the kidney, but could find no cure. For the next six years Reed was periodically visited by attacks of the pain, and often he was kept in bed for a week or two at a time. His mother's friends spoke of him as a delicate child.

At school it was generally recognized that he was brilliant but likely to be difficult. In the last year of the lower division of the academy he came under Miss Addison Jewell, most illustrious and most feared of its teachers. Piqued by her reputation as a disciplinarian, he refused to study, refused to pay attention, refused to keep order. Knowing that he was the brightest student in the class, she cajoled, commanded, and disciplined, but with no result. One morning Harry, who was deeply concerned by his brother's behavior, came to school without him. Questioned, he reported that Jack had said to him, "Don't disturb me; I'm composing a melodrama." Jack found ways of bothering Miss Jewell: one day, when some point about civics was raised, and he was called upon to recite, he used as illustration his grandmother's smuggling of silks from Japan. Miss Jewell, despairing of overcoming his hostility, had no choice but to give him the low grades he deserved. He took them with indifference. Then one day a visiting authority on education announced to the class that he had a new kind of test, one that actually tested intelligence. Miss Jewell noticed that Jack's eyes were shining, as he wrote furiously. This was his opportunity for revenge, and he took it.

Gradually he found it easier and easier to get on with his fellow-students. He seldom took part in baseball or football, but he excelled in swimming. All summer long he would go to the beach in the Willamette River, swimming farther than any other boy, diving from greater heights, doing tricks they could not do. But what made it easier for him to mingle with his associates was that physical prowess no longer seemed all-important. He and Harry built a theatre in their attic, and there were always a few boys who were willing to come and take part in the plays that Jack composed. He was business manager as well as playwright and producer, carefully calculating the profits of the enterprise. The parents of the actors attended, often with their friends. Once a man came who was professionally interested in the theatre, and he suggested that the plays and the actors were amusing enough for public performances. The boys were excited by the prospect of making a fortune, and their fathers and mothers had trouble in dissuading them.

Much of the time Jack did not care whether he had playmates

or not. He could always read, and he read everything he could find, from Marie Corelli to Scott, Stevenson, and Sir Thomas Mallory. Reading and writing were occupation enough. From the age of nine he had been determined to be a writer, and he never wanted to be anything else. Nothing interested him so much as the editing of newspapers; at fourteen or fifteen he had theories of publishing, financing, and advertising. He began to write poetry, and to look up to Colonel Charles Erskine Scott Wood, with whose sons he played, because Wood was a poet.

All this, though he seemed to get on well enough with his schoolmates, set him apart from them. "I wasn't much good at the things other boys were," he explained, "and their codes of honor and conduct didn't hold me. They felt it, too, and had a sort of good-natured contempt for me. I was neither one thing nor the other, neither altogether coward nor brave, neither manly nor sissified, neither ashamed nor unashamed. I think that is why my impression of my boyhood is an unhappy one, and why I have so few close friends in Portland, and why I don't want ever again to live there."

"I was a good deal of a physical coward," he wrote, "I would sneak out over the back fence to avoid boys who were 'laying' for me or who I thought were 'laying' for me. Sometimes I fought, when I couldn't help myself, and sometimes even won; but I preferred to be called a coward than fight. My imagination conjured up horrible things that would happen to me, and I simply ran away. One time, when I was on the editorial board of the school paper, a boy I was afraid of warned me not to publish a joking paragraph I had written about him—and I didn't. My way to school lay through a sort of slum district called 'Goose Hollow,' peopled with brutal Irish boys, many of whom grew up to be prize-fighters and baseball stars. I was literally frightened out of my senses when I went through Goose Hollow. Once a Goose Hollowite made me promise to give him a nickel if he didn't hit me, and walked up to my house with me while I got it for him. The strange thing was that when I was cornered, and fought, even a licking wasn't a hundredth time as bad as I thought it would be; but I never learned anything from that—the next time I ran away just the same, and suffered the most ghastly pangs of fear."

Often he felt that his mother and father must be ashamed of him. Neither was opposed to his reading and writing, and his mother rather rejoiced in his quietness, but both of them wanted him to be a leader, and his father had only contempt for a coward. John Reed, more intimate with his parents than were most boys of his generation, was sensitive to their opinions. They rarely coerced him in any way, and the friendliness and gratitude that he felt towards them made him eager to justify their hopes. He would have liked to be the self-assured, fearless boy that his father wanted him to be, and the gracious, respected young gentleman that was his mother's ideal, and it grieved him to fall so far below their expectations.

ALMOST certainly John Reed exaggerated the disappointment of his parents and the disapproval of his fellows. His mother and father were proud of his achievements, and it was easy—and not far wrong—to attribute his shortcomings to his bad health. His schoolmates noticed, of course, that his tastes were not always theirs. When Mr. Ladd gathered a group of boys to go hunting, John Reed was not likely to be among them. Colonel Wood's sons discovered that Jack was happier talking with their father than he was playing football with them. Sometimes when he did join in some game, he would quietly walk off in the very midst of it, and no one could tell whether he was in pain or merely bored. The boys knew that he was different from them, certainly, but they attached less importance to the fact than he suspected.

As he grew into his teens, curiosity and high spirits often overcame timidity. The vivid interest in places and people that was to dominate his life sent him into every corner of the city. Beneath the surface of respectable business enterprise, he found that some of the turbulence of frontier days remained. One did not have to go far from Portland to see cow-punchers and prospectors, and there was always the romance of lumbermen in their spiked boots, brakemen walking swaying freight trains, and rangers fighting forest fires. Chinatown still fascinated him, and he loved to lead a crowd of whooping boys through the red-light district. Occasionally his father took him to the ocean, and the blazing sunsets over the Pacific set him to writing verses. Sometimes they went to the mountains, and, hearing the wail of a cougar, he imagined himself back in the pioneering days of his grandfather.

The summer that he was fifteen he and four other boys went on a camping trip, and Reed, competing for a prize offered by a local newspaper, wrote an account of the expedition. If one can judge from this, he not only seemed more normal than he thought himself but actually was a good deal like other boys. "On Tuesday, June 24, 1903," the essay begins, "five boys, Cliff, Sox, Bates, Pat, and myself, to use their popular names, set out on a camping trip. Cliff had a sailboat, and we had determined to go camping somewhere along the Willamette with the boat to carry our provisions and other equipment. Our parents' permission having been secured, we embarked on Tuesday morning at half-past nine from Portland. We were a tough-looking crowd, Cliff wearing a soft felt sombrero, a blue cotton shirt with an old bandana knotted around his neck, and old trousers, with a revolver in his hind pocket and a murderous-looking bowie-knife hanging from his cartridge-belt. . . . For equipment we carried a canvas wagon-sheet for a tent, five rolls of blankets, six valises of duds, and provisions enough to last us about a day, with a frying pan, sauce pan, lard can, and three coffee pots, because Cliff, Sox, and Pat drank coffee, Bates cocoa, and I cereal coffee."

The wind died down soon after they started, and they had to take turns paddling with the only oar on board. "This work," he observed, "soon made us cross and sulky, and when we had eaten our lunch we went in swimming from the boat." "Much refreshed," they went on until they came to an island, about twelve miles from Portland and two miles from Oregon City. Here they pitched their camp, which they christened, "with three rousing cheers," High Five's Camp. After dinner, they "sat around the camp-fire and sang and told stories until way into the night."

They spent more than a week, exploring the island, shooting

at rabbits and grouse, swimming, fishing, and sailing on the river. Twice they had to go to Oregon City for provisions. There was one day when "the rain came down like everything," and they stayed in bed, playing cards, eating cold meals, and trying to keep dry. Two of the boys had to leave the first of the following week. On the Wednesday after they left, the other three went sailing. "There was a very high wind, almost like a gale," Reed wrote, "and we expected any moment to be tipped over. As it was, when I was pulling at the center-board rope, it broke, and I hurt my back against the side of the cock-pit."

The next day his back pained him and he felt sick to his stomach. His mother arrived, a day earlier than she had been expected, and he was glad to see her. "She said right away that she thought the river water which we drank had made me ill, because the river was going down, and she said I had to go right home, which I did. . . . And thus ended the memorable outing of the High Five's Camp. The cost of this expedition, besides of course what we took from our homes, was between $8.50 and $9."

The following autumn Reed entered his last year at Portland Academy. His family had decided that the two final years of college preparation should be spent in the East, and already they were studying the catalogs of the various schools. In the course of the year, apparently as a result of a diet that had been ordered for him, the attacks of pain in his left side ceased, and for the next ten years his kidney gave him no trouble. He felt stronger than he ever had before. The restless energy that drove him for the remainder of his life welled up within him, and, without losing his interest in books and in writing, he began to crave more active forms of expression and a more vigorous part in the life of his contemporaries. But the habits Portland had formed and the attitudes of others towards him could not easily be changed. It was in a different world, among new friends, that John Reed, the leader, fighter, playboy, would be born.

The change would be great, but the influence of the seventeen Portland years would persist. Memory of past cowardice would always encourage recklessness in defying danger. Independence would become his highest ideal because he had known too well the protecting care of a devoted mother. He would demand not merely power but also recognition because for so long he had felt cast out and scorned.

His boyhood, however, would shape his manhood positively as well as negatively. He would always be romantic, eager for the unknown, chivalrous and even quixotic. He would always be sensitive, feeling the suffering of others and easy to hurt. That sensitiveness he would try to conceal, succeeding well enough so that many would think him ruthless, but it would endure and be potent in molding his life. With sensitiveness went sympathy. No amount of recognition could make him forget the unhappiness of failure or alter his conviction that success came at the hands of fortune to the very few. He would never be in danger of complacence, nor would egotism harden into callousness.

He was potentially a poet. It was not merely that he had romantic dreams and had learned to play with words. There was a kind of singleness in his nature, despite all its many contradictions. Thought, feeling, and action were fused in him. He went from experience to experience, seizing what belonged to him and eventually rejecting all else. Of conscious purpose he had little, but he acted without hesitation, obeying impulse with a loyalty that might temporarily lead him into folly but was nevertheless wise.

So, in the winter of 1904, he went about the streets of Portland, a nice-looking boy, grown tall now, well-dressed, orderly except for his hair. His face was taking shape, rather long, the upper half of it uncommonly symmetrical: a good broad forehead; greenish brown eyes, well set, by turns friendly, curious, and intense, with a little scar, the result of a swimming accident, in the corner of one of them; an even, intelligent nose. Symmetry vanished, however, below the nose: the mouth was large and irregular, and the heavy chin did not belong to the rest of the face. But at sixteen, before his cheeks filled out, it was the delicate eyes and forehead one noticed, and the boy seemed singularly handsome.

Everybody knew him. The son of C. J. Reed, the famous wit; C. J. Reed, the insurance man who was always talking about Teddy Roosevelt and saying too much about trust-busting for his own good. The son of Margaret Reed, one of Portland's accomplished hostesses, a favorite at teas and card parties. The grandson of old Mrs. Green, who still gave hilarious dances and was always traveling about the world. Everybody knew him, and knew he was going away to school. Good Portlanders always sent their children east for their education.

All through his last year in Portland, John Reed looked forward to the time when he would be leaving. Not that he disliked the city or was acutely unhappy; but he had a sense that life would begin when he got away from it. In spite of the failures he could not ignore, his adolescent sense of glory to come was strong, and he was impatient for something to happen. After seventeen years of marking time he wanted to march.

II

RELEASE

C. J. REED, who had seen his schoolboy friends go away to college and been unhappy because he could not join them, was determined not only that his sons should be educated at Harvard but that they should enter college with the prestige that a respectable preparatory school could give. Morristown, in New Jersey, which he and Mrs. Reed selected, was a school of fifty or sixty students, rather expensive and a little pretentious. Founded under Episcopalian auspices, it had subsequently been taken over by three young Harvard men, class of 1888, Butler, Woodman, and Browne. For the most part, only boys from well-to-do families came there, boys with strong opinions about micks and rowdies and high school students.

Jack Reed, tense with curiosity and the zeal for achievement, caught at once the atmosphere of the place. "The ordered life of the community interested me," he afterwards wrote; "I was impressed by its traditional customs and dignities, school patriotism, and the sense of a long-settled and established civilization." He might have been too much impressed. By no means sure of himself with boys of his own age, even in his native Portland, he could easily have withdrawn in solitary consciousness of his inferiority to the stolid complacence of eastern breeding. The boys were not uncommonly brilliant in studies or gifted in sports, but they belonged together, and Reed had always hated to be an outsider.

What saved him was the seething energy that good health had released. He was so driven to action that he could not stop to distrust himself. The first day of football practice found him on the field, plunging about with a kind of inept but irresistible fury. The coach laughed at the gawky boy—he was almost six feet tall and weighed only one hundred and thirty-four pounds —but commended him. The other players were too concerned with their own difficulties to pay much attention to the new-comer. Reed suddenly discovered that he could play football and that he wasn't afraid of being hurt. Before the first game, he was regularly playing at left guard, and he took part in all seven of the team's games with other small schools. "Reed, L. G.," wrote the critic in the *Morristonian*, "has played for the first time, and has made great progress in knowledge of the game. He is a good tackler, runs well with the ball . . . and ought to make a fast man. He is a little slow in starting, but can easily remedy that fault." Reed marked the paragraph when he sent the paper home to his mother.

The happiness that he felt in the rough physical combat of the game and the recognition that came with his mild success gave John Reed all that he needed to become not merely one of the Morristown boys but a leader. In the compact little life of a small, isolated school, it took him only a few weeks to win the respect, whole-hearted or grudging, of the sixty boys. When a few of them gathered in some one's room, it was Jack Reed who uttered the boldest, most crushing arguments in the discus-sions of sex, religion, and politics. It was Jack Reed, too, who could tell the most spectacular stories, building fantasies around the Green chateau, describing raids into forbidden streets, imi-tating Indian war-whoops and the cries of a wounded cougar.

His ingenuity and fearlessness in mischief added to his reputa-tion. There was nothing particular to do in the village of Morris-town, a mile or two away, but, because pupils were permitted to go there only on Wednesday and Saturday afternoons, he or-ganized expeditions that left the dormitories, after the retiring hour, by fire escapes and ropes, and returned before dawn in the same clandestine way. More exciting were the secret visits to country dances. There would be the smirking surprise that went around the hall when the three or four boys, whom the dancers immediately identified as aliens from the school, swaggered in,

and then the supreme audacity of walking up, before resentful
eyes, and asking some girl to dance.

"His powers as a boy," one of the three masters remembers,
"were turned too much toward mischief and disorder. He was a
difficult and rather disturbing influence in the school." "He was
free from ordinary restraints," says another, "but was amiable
and had no serious disciplinary trouble." There was one time, it
is true, when he offended against Morristonian canons of good
taste. An entertainment was going on to which only members
of the sixth form and their guests were invited. Between the first
and second floors of the main building stood a suit of armor, and
on its helmet Reed set a chamber pot—in full sight of the women
guests. He was put on bounds, lost all privileges, and was deprived of his room in the Harvard dormitory and given an al-
cove in the Columbia dormitory under the charge of the teacher
he liked least.

Football and mischief were all very well, but Reed could
never be happy long unless he was writing. The school had a
monthly magazine, the *Morristonian*, to which he immediately
contributed. He wanted nothing less, however, than a magazine
of his own. The school had once had a comic paper, suppressed
because its humor was too personal. Reed revived it, a thin little
paper, published twice a month, the *Rooster*. It avoided personalities well enough to survive the year, but that was its principal
achievement. Twelve issues of dismal schoolboy humor were
enough, and the paper was not continued the next year. It had
served its purpose as a vehicle for John Reed's urgent need not
so much to create as to organize.

Creation, such as it was, found outlet in the *Morristonian*. His
first contribution was a labored piece of exaggeration, a type of
humor to which for more than a decade he frequently recurred.
His other two stories were purely romantic, one of them the
story of the destruction of Atlantis. His verse, no more original
than could have been expected, tried to say what was going on
within him, that private life of surging hope, vague desire, occasional despair, that persisted underneath the agitated public life
of schoolboy activity. He strove to be literary in describing a
storm and ended:

An atom in this world of might and night
I stand alone.

He wrote of a violin:

> Sobbing through the still night places,
> Like a little child a-weeping,
> Singing happily, and laughing,
> Laughter like the bells of silver
> Which are rung in Paradise.
> Then it dies away and leaves us
> Something wanting in the night.

The year went by. He spoke on behalf of Alton B. Parker in a mock election campaign. His mother visited the school. He went home with a classmate, Frank Damrosch, for Thanksgiving Day. In the spring he was elected to the board of the *Morristonian*, made vice-president of the athletic association, chosen manager of the football team. He won the Scribner prize for the best historical thesis. He began to call on girls in the town and to think of himself as a "fusser." "Busy, happy, with lots of friends I expanded into self-confidence. Without trying I found myself; and since then I have never been very much afraid of men."

WHEN he returned to Portland, he found his father entering upon his duties as United States Marshal. The appointment had come in a strange way. Several years earlier, Ethan Hitchcock, Secretary of the Interior, had come to suspect the existence of land frauds in the West. A preliminary investigation by William J. Burns showed that the public land in Washington, Oregon, and California was being seized by lumber companies and railroad interests. To be granted a section of public land, a claimant swore that he had occupied the land for five years and had improved it. A ring of politicians, with the aid of government officials, including the Commissioner of the Land Office himself, had systematically falsified the records and taken the land. Lumber interests, railroads, and insurance companies were all involved.

Francis J. Heney, who had fought graft in Arizona, was made special prosecutor. When he went to Portland, he called on C. J.

Reed, whom he had known in the Bohemian Club in San Francisco. Mr. Reed, with a kind of good-natured cynicism, took him around the city, introducing him to the leading men and letting him learn what he could from their gossip. Heney soon realized that the lumber companies controlled the land office, the senators and representatives, and even the federal judges. Although his first cases were against men and women with criminal records, respectable citizens of Portland came to him and tactfully suggested that conviction would be unwise. The frauds affected the politics and business of the entire state, and Heney saw that he would have to fight the good men as well as the bad.

One of the principal obstacles to Heney's success was Jack Matthews, United States Marshal and Republican boss of Portland. Matthews, in impaneling juries and in whatever other ways were possible, obstructed Heney's course. Heney appealed to Roosevelt, and Matthews was ousted. When Heney asked C. J. Reed to take his place, Reed could scarcely believe he was serious, but Heney argued, and Reed caught fire. He had always been shocked by the calm predacity of his associates, but he had been satisfied to make the discrepancies between pretense and practice the butt of his wit. Now cynicism vanished, and he became a crusader.

It was a new experience to John Reed to find his father so full of conviction and passion, and he responded to the air of excitement that swept through the house. He loved to go to the office and see his father poking fun at William J. Burns' solemn hawkshaw manners or talking strategy with Frank Heney. C. J.'s enthusiasm entered the boy, who began to talk hotly of busting trusts and jailing grafters. But the impression that lasted longest was of his father's fearlessness, for there was actual physical danger in this crusade and there was the intense pressure of respectable opinion. The Arlington Club elected a new president, and some of its members would not speak to the man they had so often applauded. As the prosecution went on, reaching a United States Senator, touching the Northern Pacific Railroad and the Southern, leading to the death in New York of the president of an insurance company, Portland saw Frank Heney as an enemy of society and C. J. Reed as a traitor. And all the time the man grew bolder, stronger in his convictions, sharper in his wit.

John Reed went back to Morristown with a new admiration and a new friendship for his father, and with even greater confidence in himself. He had been chosen to the committee of seven, a harmless concession to the theory of student democracy. He was manager of the football team as well as a player. The boys called him Rooster and Farmer, the first because of the now defunct paper, the second because of his gangling body, his round, unfirm face, and his unkempt hair. The masters found him more troublesome than ever, for defiance of discipline had become instinctive. For two months he was removed from the school committee, and later he was made to resign from the editorial board of the *Morristonian*. The latter action brought an indignant, self-righteous petition from Reed and Damrosch, his fellow-offender, and they were restored to the board.

His own experience and his admiration for his father strengthened his belief that concessions were wrong, that he must always do exactly what he wanted and say exactly what he thought. He would win recognition, but only on his own terms. He began to associate with an older boy in his class, a southerner who subsequently flunked out. Reed liked the boy because he was so completely honest, and he made up his mind to emulate his candor. They went to New York together for a weekend, fabricating some sort of excuse. "I'm going to get a girl," his friend said, and he did, and brought her to his room and slept with her. Reed, though not quite ready to emulate him, admired his audacity. And when they were coming home, crossing on the ferry to take the Morristown train, the boy said, "I feel good. I feel like singing." So he sang, sitting on the rail, paying no attention to the passengers who gaped at him. Candor, audacity, unself-consciousness—Reed placed them at the top of his hierarchy of virtues.

Candor and audacity he could cultivate and the appearance of un-self-consciousness, but he was too complex a person to be entirely free from awareness of what other people were thinking about him. He became, instead, something of an actor, casting himself in roles that he admired. And all the time he led an intense emotional life that he revealed to no one except insofar as he clumsily hinted at it in his poetry. The growth of strong sexual impulses fostered his romanticism, and each girl that interested him was a Guinevere or an Elaine. Though he craved every form of eminence, he was at heart convinced that he was to be a great poet, for he thought of himself, in spite of all his activity, as a dreamer. There was a strange experience one Saturday afternoon, when, in the midst of a game, he looked up and for a moment believed he saw a vision of Galahad and the Holy Grail. He remained the romantic boy whose early years had been so much a matter of solitary dreaming. His new confidence in himself was expressed in warm-hearted sociability and constant action, but he continued to dream.

He did not know how to convey the intensity of his feelings, even if he had been willing to attempt it. He was prolific, however, in his writing. He liked the spectacular; one of his stories in the *Morristonian*, "The End of the World," closes with New York City falling into a pit and the prophet from the desert, who had announced the disaster, leaping in after it. Of his verses none has more than personal significance, and only two or three have that. There is a poem called "Twilight" that suggests a nostalgia for the West:

> That wind has stirred the mighty pines
> That cling along Mt. Shasta's side
> Has hurled the broad Pacific surf
> Against the rocks of Tillamook;
> And o'er the snow-fields of Mt. Hood
> Has caught the bitter cold and roared
> Across the prairies, piling high
> The huge white drifts of swirling snow.
> . . . .
>
> And yet, although the bitter wind
> Bites deep into my shrinking flesh,
> I seem to see against the sky
> The mountains of the white cascades;
> And grandly through the mighty range
> The vast Columbia flowed down
> Unto the sea forevermore.

There is also a rather extraordinary poem to Tennyson:

> Singer of the kingly Arthur,
>   Deathless song which cannot die.
> To thy truth I'd fall a martyr,
>   Truth from lips that will not lie.
>
> Give to me thine inspiration,
>   Let thy soul my soul immerse
> Till through sweetest meditation
>   I can sing my soul in verse.

He was not very different from other prep school boys. Like most pre-college students who have any literary inclinations at all, he wrote in imitation of the author he had most recently read and was capable of the most naive enthusiasms. He was below the average as a scholar, and he barely passed his entrance examinations to Harvard. In athletics he was only fairly good, though he won his letter two years in football and one year in track. He made the masters miserable with his tricks, but he was neither an incorrigibly bad boy nor a thoughtful rebel.

Yet Reed is remembered by the masters of Morristown School and by the boys who were there with him, more than thirty years ago. A tremendous explosive energy was released on that stodgy little campus, and, though it accomplished nothing, it left its mark. Reed made himself felt as a force. And he succeeded, even then, in dividing his associates into two camps, those who loved him and those who hated him. Thirty years later two men who were in the class below Reed's wrote about him. "He seemed to delight," said one of them, "in showing his authority over the new boys. I happened to be a new boy and I suppose that may have prejudiced me." "At that time there was a certain amount of hazing in the school," said the other, "and I remember Jack particularly because he was especially friendly to me as a new boy and refused to take part in any of the hazing activities." Whether he bullied the new boys or not, they did not forget him.

III

"Pain of Growing, Ecstasy of Unfolding"

In September, 1906, John Reed entered Harvard. Harvard,
Cambridge, Boston were romantic names to the boy from
Oregon. There was the Yard, open and spacious, laid out
with elm-shaded paths. There were the old halls, built a century
and more ago, Massachusetts, Harvard, Hollis, Stoughton. There
was Bulfinch's administration building, University Hall. There
were Sever and Emerson, where classes met. There were Gore
Hall and the squat-spired, incongruous little chapel. This was the
Yard, the old, the essential Harvard. To the north were museums, the gymnasium, the law and divinity schools; to the
south, one block away, on Mt. Auburn Street, the private dormitories, the Gold Coast.

This, Reed confidently believed, was to be the scene of his
new triumphs. In his good-natured, casual way he was ambitious,
wanted the best that Harvard offered, and could see no reason
why he should not have it. After the conquest of Morristown,
the conquest of Harvard seemed inevitable. There was nothing,
certainly, that he was afraid to try. A day or two after college
opened, he walked up to Bob Hallowell. "I hear that you draw,"
he said. "Why don't we do a book about Harvard? I'll do the
text and you do the pictures."

"But," Hallowell objected, "we don't know anything about
the place."

"Hell," Reed replied, "we'll find out doing the thing!"

It was only one of thousands of ideas that momentarily swept
Reed off his feet and then came to nothing. If, however, he had
set out to discover what kind of institution it was in which he

planned to spend four years, he might have understood why its conquest was not going to be easy and why, to the end, his victory would be equivocal.

Harvard was the oldest, largest, richest, and by general consent the greatest university in the United States. The man who had presided over it during its rise to greatness was Charles W. Eliot, who was seventy-two when Reed entered college and who retired before he graduated. During the forty years that he was president Harvard changed from a provincial college with barely a thousand students to an internationally famous university with a faculty of more than five hundred, an undergraduate body of more than two thousand, and a graduate enrollment in its half-dozen professional schools of sixteen hundred. Its endowment increased from two million to twenty-two, and its annual expenses from a quarter of a million to two million and a half.

Charles W. Eliot was not a minister, and to that extent his appointment in 1869 was revolutionary. He was a chemist. But he was also a Boston Eliot. His paternal grandfather, a merchant, was probably the richest man in Boston when he died in 1820. His mother's father had made a considerable fortune in the northwestern fur and East India trades, a fortune augmented by investment in the infant textile industry. His father, thus endowed, had devoted himself to public service, first as Mayor of Boston and Congressman from Massachusetts, then as philanthropist. The family fortune was materially diminished by disastrous investment in 1857, but the family position was never threatened. At a time when his academic future seemed dubious, Eliot seriously considered becoming superintendent of the Merrimack Company's textile mills. There were always opportunities for an Eliot.

Eliot was a democrat and a liberal. He spoke cordially to garbage collectors and brusquely to ambassadors. He never consciously bowed down before wealth, and he honestly believed that America was a land of opportunity. He criticized trade unionism because it restricted individual freedom; a scab might, he said, be a hero. He favored segregation for Negroes, but he desired equal treatment, in their separate compartments, for black

and white. The processes of colonial expansion should be hu-
mane and educational. He was carefully fair-minded, graciously
tolerant, and he preserved intact the prejudices of his Beacon
Street birthplace.

President Eliot brought to Cambridge some of the finest minds
in America. There were James, Royce, Santayana, and Palmer
in philosophy; Münsterberg in psychology; Kittredge, Neilson,
Wendell, and Baker in English; Channing and Hart in history;
Taussig in economics. Since the undergraduate, once he had
passed the required freshman course in English and had satisfied
the authorities that he had a reading knowledge of French and
German, was free to take any courses that suited his fancy, he
could, if he chose and if other considerations such as convenient
hours and reputations for leniency did not weigh too heavily
with him, listen to men who had no superiors in America.

John Reed could have learned all this; indeed, in a vague way
he knew it already. He knew what Eliot stood for, and he approved. The liberalism of Charles W. Eliot was the creed in
which C. J. Reed had been raised, though at the moment he was
engaged in belligerent enforcement rather than abstract affirmation of middle-class rights. John Reed would not even have objected to the fact that the Corporation, the governing body of
Harvard University, was dominated by Henry Lee Higginson,
Boston's leading financier and patron of the arts. It was only the
predatory business men, the malefactors of great wealth, as C.
J. Reed's new idol called them, that the Reeds condemned. They
believed in business itself, in competition, in capitalism.

In fact, the way in which the university was run must have
seemed so natural and so unimportant to John Reed that, if he
had written about Harvard, he would not have bothered to
mention it. He was impressed when Eliot told the class of 1910
that the purpose of the university "is to allow each man to think
and do as he pleases, and the tendency is to allow this more and
more." And when Eliot asked the freshmen if they were afraid
of this liberty, Reed could have answered with a ringing "No!"
That was all that really concerned him: he was free to think and
do as he pleased, and he did not care to whom he owed the
privilege.

Much more interesting to him than the official administration of the university was the world of the college undergraduates. So far as John Reed was concerned, the great men Eliot had brought to Harvard and the millions of dollars he had added to its endowment were simply a background for the exploits of some two thousand young men like himself. What he did not realize, in those early days when he made his audacious proposal to Hallowell, was that the undergraduate world was quite as complicated as the world of academic officialdom, and just as alien from anything he had ever known. He saw scores of opportunity for achievement: the various sports, the managerships of the various sports, the magazines, and all the clubs. He did not see that Harvard had its own ways of judging fitness for the prizes of its little world. Morristown had taught him more about class distinctions and social hierarchies than he had known in Portland, but it had also convinced him that they were only of secondary importance. Harvard was to teach him how important they could be.

As soon as his first ebullience had died away, he found that he was extraordinarily lonely. "In 1906," he afterwards wrote, "I went up to Harvard almost alone, knowing hardly a soul in the university. My college class entered over seven hundred strong, and for the first three months it seemed to me, going around to lectures and meetings, as if every one of the seven hundred had friends but me. I was thrilled with the immensity of Harvard, its infinite opportunities, its august history and traditions—but desperately lonely."

Without much thought, he elected Latin, English literature, elementary French and German, history, and philosophy. There was nothing in the insipid routine of freshman courses to arouse his imagination, and he quickly learned how little work was necessary to win a passing grade. In the classrooms he made acquaintances, and perhaps walked with them across the Yard, but they never asked him to their rooms, and, indeed, they scarcely recognized him if he met him at some undergraduate gathering. So many of the men seemed to have been together at one of the larger preparatory schools, St. Mark's or Groton or

Exeter or Andover. They knew each other, and they knew upper-classmen, whose familiarity with college traditions they soon absorbed. And they found Reed's impetuous cordiality a little embarrassing. If this man was some one they wanted to know, they would soon enough find out; meanwhile he would do well not to thrust himself forward.

Loneliness would have driven Reed to engage in as many undergraduate activities as possible, even if ambition had not pushed him on. He had to show these fellows. Football, crew, managerial positions, the magazines—he went out for them all. He was not good enough for the freshman football team, though he now weighed twenty pounds more than he had at Morristown, and he was soon eliminated. Disappointed, he began to spend more of his time in writing for the magazines.

The *Lampoon*, he was excited to discover, accepted his jokes. He was not aware that they were as inane as the jokes he had written in abundance for the *Rooster*; he only rejoiced that they found favor with the exacting, if not precisely discriminating, young editors. Success with the *Lampoon* was important to him because the magazine represented the essential Harvard, the Harvard of the chosen few. It belonged to and defended the complacent, self-assured, superior Harvard that vaguely distressed John Reed and yet of which he wanted to be a part. If his inventiveness did not carry him beyond the classroom exploits of a student called "Mr. Grinda," his work was acceptable and was, indeed, on a level with most of the jokes that, stupid as they individually were, made the *Lampoon* a bulwark of the Harvardian *status quo*.

His work also proved acceptable to the editors of the Harvard *Monthly*, which represented a different Harvard tradition, the tradition of serious literary effort. Hermann Hagedorn was editor-in-chief Reed's freshman year, and John Hall Wheelock and Lucien Price were on the board. George Santayana, Edwin Arlington Robinson, M. A. DeWolfe Howe, and William Vaughn Moody had written for the *Monthly* in the past. The *Monthly* affirmed nothing except the right of undergraduates to be as mature as they could be. It offered no formal opposition, at least in 1906, to the prejudices of the *Lampoon*, but its values were not the *Lampoon's* values. It summoned from John Reed the best prose he had thus far written—a short, romantic, poetic story called "Bacchanal"—and the best poetry, a sonnet, "Guinevere."

The fact that he wrote with equal enthusiasm and success for both the *Lampoon* and the *Monthly* indicates the inner confusion that made Reed unhappy in his first year at Harvard. Wiser men were content with what they could have, and Reed could have a literary career. He wanted that, but he wanted more too; he wanted popularity, acclaim, the glittering prizes that Harvard offered. He thought longingly of his triumphs at Morristown, and despaired because he could not immediately duplicate them at Harvard.

In the spring he made a valiant try for a position on the freshman crew, staying in Cambridge through the vacation to work at a rowing machine in the empty boathouse. And when he was dropped from the list of candidates, he entered the competition for the assistant managership of the varsity crew, working day and night to collect subscriptions. When the appointed date came, it was found that Reed had easily won, but the manager said that Reed was not the right sort of man, and he extended the competition, permitting Raymond Belmont to go to New York and get his father, a Morgan man, to help him. Belmont was given the position.

Reed experienced other kinds of discrimination. One of the social leaders of the class promised to room with him sophomore year, and then, warned that Reed was not quite sound, drew away from him. And Reed became snobbish himself: "I, too, hurt a boy who was my friend." The boy was a New York Jew, "a shy, rather melancholy person," Reed called him, but a boy with a brilliant mind. Reed liked him and learned much from him. But he began to reflect: "We were always together, we two outsiders. I became irritated and morbid about it—it seemed I would never be part of the rich splendor of college life with him around—so I drew away from him. It hurt him very much, and it taught me better."

IT WAS a rather troubled, distrustful boy who returned to Oregon in June. But C. J. Reed, who had himself learned something about snobbishness, told him to keep on fighting. And, it became clear the next fall, the defeats were less serious than they had seemed. He was elected an editor of the *Monthly*, and, in February, of the *Lampoon*. His old audacity, which even in his despair he had maintained as a pose, returned in full ebullience. At the *Monthly's* initiation ceremony, when each of the prospective editors was required to recite an original poem, Reed suddenly gave voice to a parody of one of the sea poems John Hall Wheelock, now editor-in-chief, had written:

> Long have I longed about Longacre Square
> For the sound of the sea and the loud yellow plunk
> Of the breakers beating against the moonlight
> And the desolate horizoned spaces.
>
> O voiceless, murmurous sea,
> Full of salt water and the great sad crabs. . . .

Wheelock interrupted, and Reed's election was unanimously confirmed. It was perhaps a greater audacity that led Reed's fellow neophyte and friend, Edward Hunt, to read, on such an occasion, a serious and moving poem on death; but that was a kind of audacity John Reed had yet to learn.

Of course there were still defeats. Not satisfied with being on two of the magazines, Reed joined the competition for the staff of the *Crimson*, the college daily. Though even then he was a good journalist, he was not elected. Such defeats did not come because he was socially ineligible. He did not belong to one of the best Boston families, nor had he attended St. Mark's or Groton, but he did have behind him some money, a reputable ancestry, and two years at an expensive preparatory school. With his ability, which nobody doubted, he was precisely the sort of person that the aristocracy would have been glad to adopt, as two years later, it adopted his brother Harry, who knew how to play the Harvard game. But there was something in Jack that the social leaders feared. He wanted to be accepted, but it had to be on his own terms, and his terms simply were not theirs. Much as he longed to conform, he could not do it. He remained, in spite of himself, defiant, belligerent, mocking. When good manners would have counted most, his manners were the worst he could contrive. In dealing with contributors to the *Lampoon* and the *Monthly* he was rude to men of influence and considerate to nonentities. There were times when it seemed to the more sober men of his class, men who went their own ways indifferent to the aristocrats, that he was bootlicking. There were times, perhaps, when he would have been willing to lick boots; but he did not know how.

It was no wonder that he was not elected to any of the clubs with social prestige. The complicated club system of Harvard remains a mystery to thousands of undergraduates, who spend their four years in satisfied unawareness of it, except when, at various periods, the men chosen to the Institute go running through the Yard in gray pants and blue shirts. Reed, however, knew every detail of the club system and described it: "In sophomore year, the Institute of 1770 selects one hundred men from the class, presumably fit social material, who thereafter regard themselves as the socially elect. The waiting clubs, which are final to one another (that is to say, a man can belong only to one waiting club) elect a few more, and further refine the original hundred. This group of what is supposed to be the best men in the class composes the material with which the final clubs fill their ranks in junior and senior years."

It is a complicated system for the achievement of a simple object. The majority of final club members are men whose families have always controlled Harvard. These men as undergraduates dominate, under ordinary circumstances, college activities. After they graduate, they supply the university with directors of the Alumni Association, Overseers, and members of the Corporation. They admit outsiders to their ranks, but only such outsiders as they are sure they can assimilate.

John Reed, not being assimilable, remained outside. Even the literary clubs, after his success in the magazines, blackballed him. It probably would have done him no harm if he had been taken into the clubs, for, once the prizes had been won, he would have seen how trivial they were. Nevertheless, as he remarked, "the effect of the system on its own members is deadly," and it perhaps was as well that he was not exposed.

He remained outside the Harvard of the clubs, and thus he was forced to discover another Harvard, the Harvard that was undergoing what he later, with pardonable exaggeration, called a renaissance. He himself dated the renaissance from an essay that Lee Simonson, a hitherto obscure member of the class of 1909, published in the *Advocate* for January, 1908. "I am an outsider," Simonson said, "as that term is understood in college. ... The particular problems of college activity so often discussed in these columns are not vital for me." He was concerned with "the tepidity, the inertia, the listlessness of our life here." "The idea of gentility," he said, "soothes us like a warm blanket . . . For us, life (spelled with a capital) is neither very serious nor very urgent. . . . The virtues here are the contented, unassertive virtues of middle-age, tact and deference, easy comradeship and slipshod kindliness. . . . But there is no effective sign here of the boisterous virtues of youth, of those for whom life is tense with secret surprises—revolutions, rejuvenations and catastrophes."

Simonson did not speak for himself alone, and within four months after his article appeared three new clubs had been formed that made some attempt to foster and to express the boisterous virtues. With two of these, the Cosmopolitan Club and the Dramatic Club, Reed became closely associated. The Cosmopolitan Club, the direct outgrowth of President Eliot's liberalism, was a semi-official attempt to facilitate the international exchange of ideas. It might have been almost purely formal, but, responding to the new insurgency, it encouraged controversy, and debated executions in Spain, syndicalism in France, revolution in China. The Dramatic Club, an indirect product of Baker's course in playwriting, presented original plays by graduates or undergraduates. In its choice of plays and its methods of production it aimed at maturity, intelligence, and vitality. "It should be a club," Simonson said in an article in the *Monthly*, "primarily for the playwright, the enthusiast, the theorist."

The third of the new organizations, the Socialist Club, Reed did not belong to, though in his senior year he occasionally attended its meetings. Its stated purpose was "the study of Socialism and all other radical programs of reform which aim at a better organic development of society." Walter Lippmann joined it, became its president, gave it influence and prestige in the life of the college. Harvard had always believed in philanthropy, and there were committees, to one of which T. S. Eliot belonged, for the distribution of clothing to the poor. ("We are very systematic about dispensing our shabby clothes," Simonson had written.) But the Socialist Club made fun of charity. It had social legislation introduced into the Massachusetts legislature; it attacked the university for not paying its servants living wages; it led to the formation of a league for woman suffrage, a single tax club, an anarchist group; it petitioned the faculty for a course in Socialism. "All this," Reed later wrote, "made no ostensible difference in the look of Harvard society, and probably the club-men and the athletes, who represented us to the world, never even heard of it. But it made me, and many others, realize that there was something going on in the dull outside world more thrilling than college activities, and turned our attention to the writings of men like H. G. Wells and Graham Wallas, wrenching us away from the Oscar Wildian dilettantism which had possessed undergraduate litterateurs for generations."

Although he did not as an undergraduate sufficiently recognize the importance of the Socialist Club to want to join it, and though his whole appreciation of the "renaissance" really came after graduation, he did feel, when he returned for his junior year in the fall of 1908, that he was part of something more important than the unimaginative, narrow, showy life of the waiting and final clubs. He became assistant manager of the Dramatic Club, which staged as its first play Allan Davis' *The Promised Land*. Under the direction of Hans von Kaltenborn, the manager, Reed solicited advertisements for the program, raised funds from patrons and patronesses, sent publicity to the press, worried about properties and scenery, and bulldozed the cast into attending rehearsals. It was hard work, but the glamor of first nights was sufficient reward.

He was too sure of himself now to care much about the aristocrats, though lack of recognition occasionally made him uneasy. He joined and later became president of the Western Club, an informal organization resulting from the realization that men from the West were slow in making friends at Harvard. It was an eating club, and Reed presided at meals, making personal jokes, as his father had done at the Arlington Club in Portland, and apostrophizing each arrival at the table. Once, when Walter Lippmann came to the club as a guest, Reed leaped to his feet, made a sweeping bow, and cried, "Gentlemen, the future President of the United States." But sometimes his humor was on a lower level: once he threw a handful of beans and said, "Where have you been?" In fact, a good deal of raucous horseplay went on at the Western Club, in more or less conscious defiance of the Harvard that prided itself on having outgrown schoolboy tricks. There were practical jokes, sometimes of a painful sort, and there were burlesque operas, such as "The Girl of the Golden Toothbrush," of which Reed wrote the words and Joe Adams the music.

Now that he was no longer troubled by failure, he was full of an energy that neither his courses nor his undergraduate duties could exhaust. "Let's find some excitement," was his characteristic phrase. He was involved more than once with the Boston police, and he occasionally picked a fight with Cambridge loafers, who were given to jeering at Harvard boys. He could find amusement even in a graveyard: one Sunday afternoon, when he and Alan Gregg were walking in Mt. Auburn cemetery, Reed took out his calling cards, wrote on a dozen or more, "Sorry you weren't in when we called," and left them at the tombs with the most illustrious Boston names. And one midnight he led a group of his classmates through Lexington, shouting, "The British are coming."

In the spring of his junior year he and Joe Adams and W. T. Pickering went together to New York. Adams, a delicate, small, fair-haired boy from Mason City, Iowa, was one of Reed's closest friends. Though Adams was completely conservative and they never agreed, they were constantly together. Both had become friendly with Pickering during several weekends that they spent with him in a log cabin in Sharon to which he had access. In the city they devoted three or four days to attending the theatre and drinking at the Harvard Club bar. Reed took them down to Morristown, where he led the students in singing school and college songs, and pointed out the scenes of his erstwhile glory. But five days of vacation remained, and there seemed to be no excitement left in New York. They decided to go to Bermuda.

They had money enough, they estimated, but there were no boats that would bring them back in time for the beginning of classes. Pickering, a senior and therefore faced with the possible loss of his degree, refused to go, in spite of violent abuse, and Reed and Adams left without him. Their financial calculations had, not surprisingly, underestimated their capacities, and they found themselves desperately short of cash. Reed wrote out all the poems he had contributed to the *Monthly*, and succeeded in selling them to a newspaper. Adams raised his share by playing the piano in a resort of dubious reputation.

They caught the boat and got back to Cambridge. The authorities could not overlook a tardy return from vacation, especially when it resulted from such an escapade, and they revived a form of punishment that had been common in the nineteenth century, rustication: Reed and Adams were sent to Concord for the remainder of the term. Absence from Cambridge in the spring was not wholly unpleasant, and Reed found time, while supposedly pursuing his studies under the direction of a terrified schoolmaster, to make the acquaintance of Concord's more interesting citizens. He also found time to send to the Western Club a daily bulletin in the form of a Sunday school lesson. Number seven, for example, bore the "golden text for the day": "Where rolls the Oregon and hears no sound save his own smashings," which was attributed to Bryant's "Thanatopsis." The bulletin read: "Last night Mason City and the Oregon rolled around a good deal in a hunt for the elusive moth miller. In the scrimmage two windows were broken, one electric light globe, and the lid to the slop jar. A large moth was severely injured about the neck and ears. Two old ladies who room below us and are Seventh Day Adventists thought that Christ had come again, and prayed violently all night. The hotel cat was so horrified by the unexpected tumult that the next morning she was found to have given birth to a litter of pups in the cash register."

There was only one of his classes that Reed would have regretted during his rustication, and that was English 12, Charles

Townsend Copeland's course in composition. During his first two years at Harvard Reed had found occasional stimulus in the classroom, but he had not met any teacher who deeply affected him. There had, it is true, been one chance meeting that he always remembered. During his lonely days as a freshman he had found himself standing beside an elderly man in front of a bookstore window. They fell into conversation about the books exhibited, especially the works of O. Henry, which both admired. The man invited him home to dinner, and they talked until midnight of Harvard, undergraduate clubs, how to become popular, and comic operas. As Reed left, his host asked his name, and, being told, gave his own: William James.

But that was a single, casual contact. Copeland became not merely a teacher but also a friend. The little man, with his absurd dignity, his amusing poses, his pretended ferocity, and his ironic courtesy, did most of his teaching in his room in Hollis Hall, for he was too wise to suppose that the art of writing could be adequately treated in classroom lectures. He taught his students what he knew about writing in generous private conferences, and he taught them what he knew about life in friendly talks in the evening. On Saturday evenings students were always welcome, and sometimes there was a famous writer or actor to talk to them, though Copey was attraction enough. Precisely what he did for his students no one has ever managed to say, though dozens of his famous pupils have publicly paid tribute to him. "He has stimulated generations of men," Reed wrote, "to find color and strength and beauty in books and in the world, and to express it again." Copey gave of himself, refusing to set up a barrier against his students in order to preserve time for productive scholarship. And out of his friendship came a deep sense of the power and importance of the written word.

Copeland selected the students who could take English 12, and at first he did not want Reed, for he had heard that he was contentious and troublesome. But Reed begged and begged to be allowed to enter the course, promising to be well-behaved, and at last he was admitted. Copey soon knew that the boy had something like genius, and did all that he could to bring it to fruition. Reed was profoundly grateful. He liked the little man, liked him because he was human and made no attempt to conceal human weaknesses, because he was a superb showman and knew how to dramatize himself, because he was such an affront to academic tradition and had been punished by being kept an instructor while diligent nonentities rose to professorial rank. They became friends, and Reed went in and out of Hollis 15 as he would have gone in and out of the room of a classmate. He ran errands for Copey and accompanied him when he went away to give one of his famous readings. He told him his troubles and his ambitions.

On a Saturday evening only a swimming meet could keep Reed away from Hollis 15. He liked the room with its walls solidly lined with books, the fireplace, the autographed pictures, and Copey sitting in an armchair under the single light, smoking and talking. He liked the crowd, the boys sitting close-packed on the floor, athletes, scholars, aristocrats, radicals, editors, and the obscure, the unknown. He liked the talk: "Everybody talks of the thing nearest his heart; everybody finds himself alert, quick, almost brilliant." This was romance, drama, greatness, life. "There are two men," Reed wrote in 1917, "who give me confidence in myself, who make me want to work, and to do nothing unworthy." One of them was Copeland.

Copey gave him confidence in himself, for Copey knew that, whatever aristocratic opinion might hold, John Reed was destined to success. And towards the end of his junior year Reed found some confirmation of Copey's trust in him. He was elected Ibis of the *Lampoon*, which meant that he was second in command. It was true that, traditionally, the outstanding artist was chosen Ibis and the outstanding writer was made president. In reversing the order, making Hallowell president, the board was expressing a certain residuum of its old attitude towards Reed. But Reed, in his friendship for Hallowell, could not resent the slight, and he was satisfied with his share of the power and the glory. He liked the work on the *Lampoon*. The magazine has always had a glamor for undergraduates, though many of its editors have grown up, as Reed did, to become a little ashamed of it. He worried about each issue, spent nights at the printers, deliberated solemnly over the selection of bad jokes and fair

cartoons, wrote and re-wrote the editorials, battled with his colleagues, and sent copies, with his contributions carefully marked,
to his mother and father.

The *Monthly*, though he knew even then that it was more
important, was less exciting, perhaps because it was less his.
Edward Hunt had become editor-in-chief, and Reed, who
would have liked the position and was a logical candidate for it,
was not displeased. He respected Hunt, for he had come to Cambridge penniless and with a mother and two sisters to support,
and had found time not only to organize a stenographic bureau
and do other work to meet his and their needs, but also to become an honor student, president of the Dramatic Club, and the
most praised of the *Monthly's* poets. And there were others on
the staff whom Reed respected: Walter Lippmann, whose clear
logic he vaguely distrusted and yet admired, and Alan Seeger,
whose irritating aloofness from mankind and painful, rapturous
devotion to beauty made him seem to Reed the perfect romantic
poet. Nothing was more satisfying than to get an issue of the
Lampoon safely on the press, but a meeting of the *Monthly*
board was a foretaste of manhood.

By the end of his junior year Reed held responsible positions
on two magazines, was manager of the music clubs, was vice-
president and president-to-be of the Cosmopolitan Club, and
was captain of the water polo team. In swimming he had found
his one opportunity to win athletic distinction, and especially
in water polo. It was a brutal game, and Reed loved it. Since the
only rule was that a man could not be tackled unless he was
within four feet of the ball, there was opportunity for the rough-
est type of combat. Men sometimes were held under water so
long that they had to be pulled out and resuscitated, and members of the team were often sick for a day or two after a game.
The absence of rules and the purely physical conflict delighted
Reed, and the fact that the game was played in the water per-
fected his pleasure. This minor sport, soon to be abolished at
Harvard, gave him joy, if not honor.

AT THE end of Reed's junior year President Eliot retired, and
the next autumn Abbott Lawrence Lowell was inducted into

office. He was descended from Francis Cabot Lowell, who had founded the textile industry in New England. His father and both his grandfathers were successful manufacturers. Lowell had practiced law for seventeen years and then taught government at Harvard. No better man could have been found to consolidate the gains that Eliot had made. A pure New Englander, member of a family that could boast of greatness in literature and in business, he knew how to cement the alliance between culture and industry.

Lowell immediately sought to curb the "anarchistic spirit," as Reed called it, that Eliot had fostered. Atomic individualism, Lowell perceived, had served its purpose, and now, if business was to achieve an era of stability and order, there must be trained, responsible leadership. Under Eliot, according to John Reed, Harvard was not "a brooder for masses of mediocrely-educated young men equipped with 'business' psychology; out of each class came a few creative minds, a few scholars, a few 'gentlemen' with insolent manners, and a ruck of nobodies." That was precisely what Lowell wanted to change; he wanted to give to each of Harvard's thousands of students a measure of culture and to impose certain minimum standards of civic behavior.

He moved against the individualism of the Eliot era by modifying the elective system and by putting all the freshmen into one set of dormitories. Reed disapproved. He liked the Harvard in which "men could live pretty much where they pleased, and do as they pleased," and "there was no attempt made by the authorities to weld the student body together, or to enforce any kind of uniformity." He believed that whatever he owed to Harvard was the result of the freedom that was now to be abridged, and he attacked Lowell's plans in *Lampoon* editorials.

Yet Reed became in a sense an instrument of the new policy of conformity. Harvard had never excluded sports from its theory of indifference. Some men took an ardent interest in the teams; others paid no attention to them; either attitude was permissible. But in the fall of 1909 there was talk about school spirit; pressure was exerted to bring men to pre-football game mass-meetings; the importance of cheering, which had always been slightly desultory, was preached. And John Reed, being eligible as the captain of a team, was appointed song-leader. He knew and resented the ridiculousness of college sentiment, but he could not resist "the supremely blissful sensation of swaying two thousand voices in great crashing choruses." He wrote a football song called "Score," with music by Joe Adams, in which he proposed to "twist the bull-dog's tale" and to "call up the hearse for dear old Yale." With Hamilton Fish, Jr., leading the team, Reed pranced before the stands, the most inspired song-leader Harvard had known. In practice meetings, Robert Hallowell wrote, "he would stand up alone before a few thousand undergraduates and demonstrate without a quiver of self-consciousness just how a cheer should be given. If he didn't like the way his instructions were followed, he cursed at the crowd, he bullied it, sneered at it. But he always captured it." Of course he knew he was being absurd, and once, when he saw a girl he liked in the stands and she was laughing at him, he threw down his megaphone and walked off the field. Usually, he did not care; power and drama combined were enough to make him forget himself, A. Lawrence Lowell, the aristocrats, and even girls.

Cheer-leading was the most exciting activity of the autumn, but not the only one. The clubs and the magazines demanded plenty of time, and, as the football season was ending, rehearsals began in earnest for the production of Percy MacKaye's *The Scarecrow*. Though Reed was only on the business staff, he took a strong interest in the play, and he and Kenneth MacGowan, Robert Edmond Jones, and Sam Eliot often went to MacKaye's home to talk with the author. There they usually met Percy MacKaye's brother, James, who was giving a series of lectures at Harvard on the politics of utility, and the discussions were as likely to be political as literary. Indeed, these gatherings at MacKaye's were evidence of the alliance between politics and literature that was the foundation of the renaissance. The same men were active in the *Monthly*, the Dramatic Club, and the Socialist Club, and the same impulses dominated the three organizations. Reed was equally glad to talk with Percy MacKaye about the role of drama and pageantry in awakening a new civic consciousness and with James MacKaye about the psychological causes of political action. Walter Lippmann was more directly affected than Reed by James MacKaye's utilitarianism, but Reed began to catch glimpses of realms of ideas he had not known.

It is difficult, of course, not to feel that Reed would have been happier if he had been satisfied with the magazines and the Dramatic Club, with the world of ideas and literary expression. But he could not help craving political and social position in the college. Since he did want eminence in undergraduate affairs, it is, in view of his deep-rooted distaste for the aristocrats and the rebelliousness that later became so strong in him, rather strange that he was not a leader in the opposition party that developed in his class. From the fall of its freshman year, the class of 1910 was divided. What began as a kind of private feud of a student named Bob Brown against the aristocrats grew into a fight between the Yard and the Street. The Street was Mt. Auburn Street, where the richer men lived in private dormitories, leaving the relatively poor, relatively inconspicuous students to occupy the college dormitories in the Yard. Under Brown's somewhat demagogic leadership, the unrepresented majority rose against the traditionally dominant minority.

Reed's sympathies should have been and perhaps were with the Yard, though he lived on the Street. During his first three years, without being committed to the Brown faction, he gave it some support; but he made no attempt to use his talents in leading it. He did not want to identify himself with the outsiders. And when, in his senior year, the insiders, the aristocrats, gave him a modicum of recognition, he embraced their cause. The nominating committee, after some hesitation, offered his name and G. W. Martin's for ivy orator. Both were the Street's candidates, and the Yard, nominating Frank W. Sullivan by petition, elected him. Reed was defeated in company with Hamilton Fish, Jr., the aristocrats' candidate for first marshal, and a half dozen of the class's choicest snobs.

Reed could justify himself, as others did, by insisting that Brown had resorted to the tactics of a ward politician, but the clearer thinking men in the class, without deceiving themselves about Brown, supported what they knew to be essentially a democratic revolt. Reed not only turned his back on the democratic cause; he developed a hot-tempered indignation against his successful opponents. On *Lampoon* stationery he scratched down a parody of Tennyson's "Charge of the Light Brigade." Neither witty nor wise, it disclosed a bitterness that, once he understood the triviality of the whole affair and the wrongness of his own position, he was ashamed of. The last stanza read:

> "Charge the Committee then!"
> Three hundred stalwart men,
> Traitors to Nineteen Ten
> Broke the class spirit, while
>   All the world wondered.
> Swayed by false argument,
> Urged to the polls they went,
> Scoundrels and ignorant,
>   Worthy three hundred!

The defeat by the rank and file was followed by another grudging recognition from the aristocracy. The Hasty Pudding Club, though its most conspicuous function was the annual production of a musical comedy, selected its members not for their ability as writers, composers, or actors but for their social distinction. As a result, it found itself in the spring of 1910 without a member qualified to write lyrics for the forthcoming production. Reed's verses in the *Lampoon* gave clear enough indication of his talent, and, without enthusiasm, the club offered him membership. Though he knew well enough why he was chosen, he was delighted with the chance to do the lyrics, and he felt some pride and considerable malicious satisfaction in the honor bestowed upon him.

Reed's fellow-victim of the Yard avalanche, George Martin, had already written the book, and Walter S. Langshaw was composing the music. Martin's father, Edward S. Martin, long editor of *Life*, had known and rather liked C. J. Reed in Auburn, New York. Young Martin did not dislike Jack Reed, but he did not like him; he thought him brilliant but unsafe; the trouble, he felt, was that he did not know the difference between cricket and not-cricket; there was no telling what he might do. They made somewhat unfortunate collaborators, especially since

Martin could not help realizing that Reed should have written the entire libretto.

What Reed did was to take full advantage of the few opportunities for satire that Martin's book provided. They were not many, for *Diana's Debut*, as Martin had conceived it, poked only the politest kind of fun at Boston society. Reed's most popular song, still sung at class reunions, was exceedingly simple:

> At the Somerset
> Things were rather wet,
> Big exclusive affair—
> From the lack of heat
> All of Beacon Street
> Surely must have been there.

Slightly more pointed is the song in which one of the characters gives advice on the achievement of social distinction:

> Just insist that your aunt was a Cabot,
> And your grandmother's real name was Weld.
> Try hard to make rudeness a habit,
> And be careful with whom you're beheld.
>
> . . . .
>
> Be familiar with Ibsen and Wendell
> And learn to be lazy with grace;
> But if you are driven to work, why
> Lee Higginson's really the place.

It was not the first time that Reed had expressed his impatience with Back Bay society. In a *Lampoon* editorial he had written: "The selection of a properly qualified father and mother is an operation which demands a tact and finesse seldom possessed by children so young. . . . Hyphens are of immense value—remember that anyone will always be glad to lend money to an Endicott-Sears-Cabot, a Wendell-Wendell, or a Trumbull-Peabody. . . . If the child is too late to corral a Back Bay Brahman for a progenitor, let him seize upon a self-made man who has made a good job of it. Money will finally land any one among the Captains of Society."

Mild enough, it is true, but unconventional for a Harvard man, especially a Harvard man who was Ibis on the *Lampoon* and a member of the Hasty Pudding Club. Reed, even as a senior, had no clear convictions about the aristocrats in the college and their relatives in the Back Bay. At first he envied them, but he refused either to imitate or to cultivate them. He had brought letters from Portland to a certain number of Boston's finest families, but, after his first dinner party, he tore them up in disgust. When he was invited to Back Bay dances or dinners, perversity drove him to behave as badly as possible. His roommates his senior year, Carl Chadwick and Francis Davis, were constantly receiving invitations to social affairs, and sometimes Reed felt a little sorry for himself because he was so consistently left out. If, however, one of them had taken him to visit some society leader of the town, he would have started—and won— an argument on anarchism or free love. He knew that it would please his mother if he made the right kind of friends, and he was himself made a little uneasy by the insolent indifference and open hostility of persons of power and prestige; but he could not curry favor, and he remained defiant.

Defiance was not a principle with him; it was an instinct. He could detect snobbishness and pretense with unerring accuracy, and could affront them with unfailing precision. His seething energy, his love of excitement, his joy in making himself conspicuous, all blended with honesty and courage, made him a terror to the complacent. It was pure love of excitement that led him and Jack Kelley, when they became bored during a week at Nantucket, to steal a boat and sail it to the mainland. It was mere playfulness that encouraged him to attend spiritualist meetings and build up quietly from one serious question to another until finally he had exposed the medium to ridicule. But he could go after bigger game and go after it in all seriousness. Professor Schofield had revived an old club, the Symposium, and tried to turn it into a gentlemanly affair with beautifully served stand-up suppers. Reed and other members very quickly converted polite discourse into serious and sometimes violent discussion. The climax came when Schofield, to let the boys meet a successful business man, invited President Mellen of the

New York, New Haven and Hartford Railroad, to speak. Mellen began with a baby-talk description of the locomotive as it was when he was a boy and how it had grown. Reed interrupted, and began a series of questions about the financing of the New Haven. Armed with facts and deadly earnest, Reed, backed by Alan Seeger and one or two others, pounded at Mellen until he writhed. William Roscoe Thayer, who was present, tried to restore the discussion to the level of fatuous gentility, but his efforts merely made Reed more savage, and he pushed relentlessly on until Mellen collapsed in silence. It was a defense of the principles of C. J. Reed, but, more important, it was a victory over the pompousness and hypocrisy that Jack Reed hated.

Reed liked the Cosmopolitan Club because it made room for both seriousness and horseplay. To meet the men of twenty nations seemed to him a significant part of his education. To prefer their company to the company of the men of the Institute was a sound gesture of defiance. To find opportunities for leadership and excuses for merrymaking was a joy. He wrote and staged a play, called "Tit for Tat," built around the legend of the Tower of Babel. He organized an international track meet. He taught the members songs. He and Wheeler Sammons, the secretary, gave a demonstration of hypnotism, in the course of which Reed climbed in a professorial lap and played with distinguished whiskers. But at the annual banquet he presided with dignity, ceremoniously introduced the speakers, Melville E. Stone and Prince Selim Senudah among them, and said with feeling that the presidency of the club was the highest honor that had been bestowed on him at Harvard.

The Cosmopolitan Club banquet was one of the events that marked the end of John Reed's college career. He and Hallowell had, with relief and regret, turned over the *Lampoon* to Gluyas Williams and Alan Gregg. The *Monthly* was in new hands. All the managerships and captaincies, all the presidential and vice-presidential duties had been surrendered. Only commemorative exercises remained. The *Monthly* held a dinner, to celebrate its twenty-fifth anniversary, at which Santayana, MacKaye, Baker, and others spoke, and Reed read a poem. There was a farewell class party. The Hasty Pudding Club held its "strawberry night," presenting a one-act play, "The Last of the Pirates," which Reed had written, with music by W. B. Barker, and with Hanford MacNider in the cast.

Very proud of their son's achievement, Mr. and Mrs. Reed came east for his graduation. He was pleased to be able to introduce his father to certain classmates who, he knew, would appreciate his wit and courage. The prosecution of the lumber thieves had ended with an unusual number of convictions, and for the moment the public land was safe. C. J. Reed had offended the Taft administration, and he knew that, since it could no longer be argued by Heney and other friends that he was needed for a special purpose, he was certain to be ousted from the marshalship. He did not particularly care, for the position held no interest aside from the attack on the lumber trusts. What he now wanted to do was to carry on the battle of Roosevelt progressivism on other fronts, and he was planning to run for Congress. Since he had so frankly expressed his opinion of the regular Republicans, even to the extent of literally throwing the local boss out of his office, he had no chance but to make his campaign as an avowed insurgent. Friends in Portland believed that his chances were excellent, but they were distressed at his leaving just when the struggle for nomination was getting under way. He insisted, however, that he was going to see his son graduate, no matter what it cost. Both Jack and his father were in high spirits and happy in each other's company.

Class Day was on June 24. Edward Hunt recited the class poem, and T. S. Eliot's ode was sung. In the stadium Reed had to listen to F. W. Sullivan's ivy oration, consoling himself, perhaps, with the thought that he could have done better. His own part in the ceremonies was purely informal. There was a moment when the class was gathered together, and he leaped upon a table and began to speak. The speech was a tribute to Bob Hallowell. Reed grew eloquent, but seriousness did not last long. Clarence Little, crawling beneath the table, lifted it on his back and toppled the speaker over.

One thing saddened commencement week. A Negro in the class had been seriously ill. Not many classmates knew him, for only the hardest labor had got him through college, but Reed, always sensitive to the handicaps of men of other races, knew and liked him. Now, in the boy's illness, Reed was one of two or three who found time to nurse him. And, as it became appar-. ent that the Negro could not live, Reed felt the tragedy of effort and self-denial that had been cheated of their reward.

JOHN REED had been graduated from Harvard College. He had won no academic distinction, and certainly he would have regarded his courses as almost the least important elements in his education. Not that he had disliked his studies: Copey's course had been a pleasure and satisfaction; William Allan Neilson had helped him to discover Chaucer; Baker's course in the Elizabethan drama had fed his old love of plays and playwriting. He had learned a little bit about art, music, and philosophy. Deliberately choosing a purely literary education, without a single course in either physical or social science, he had also deliberately chosen from his courses in literature the men and the books that interested him. He could write an acceptable paper on the novel of terror or the drama after 1642, because he found something that he wanted to talk about, but he had none of the diligence in dull details that brings good grades. He did not care about the grades, and he got what he wanted.

Most of what he wanted had to be got outside the classroom. Early in his college years Reed tried to formulate the philosophy that guided his conduct at Harvard. He divided students into three groups: the athletes, the scholars, and the activity men. The first he dismissed, not perhaps without envy, as lifeless, purposeless machines. The second he condemned as narrow. The third he described as "the realest expression of what Harvard means today." "They are dreamers and often poets," he said, and he spoke of Theodore Roosevelt, Owen Wister, and Edward Sheldon as activity men. John Reed, twice an editor, captain of a minor sport, manager of the musical clubs, president of the Cosmopolitan Club, vice-president of the Dramatic Club, a leader in the Western Club, writer of lyrics for Hasty Pudding, member of Oracle, Round Table, and Symposium, was an activity man. And all these activities seemed to him exciting and important. He was flattered by every office and eager in the performance of each new set of duties. He was an activity man partly because he deeply craved recognition and power, but chiefly because he had to be active.

He was also a literary man. It would be foolish to pretend that he was a distinguished writer as an undergraduate. He was not one of the rare individuals—perhaps less rare at Harvard than elsewhere—on whom a precocious brilliance descends midway in college, so that their undergraduate work is not less mature than whatever they do in the next ten years. Lee Simonson was rather like that, bringing out of aloofness a sophistication that dazzled his classmates. And Walter Lippmann, suddenly emerging from three years of silence, became a lawgiver; "a Manhattan Zeus," Edward Hunt called him, "steady, massive, impassive, hurling his thunderbolts judiciously among the herds of humankind." Even Alan Seeger, who also came startlingly out of obscurity, was no more juvenile as a Harvard senior than as the embattled poet of France, and had the same facility. Other men, too, though less amazingly developed, were nearer manhood than Reed: Van Wyck Brooks, who had been an editor of the *Monthly* when Reed first wrote for it; Kenneth MacGowan, who was one of his successors; Conrad Aiken, who wrote for the *Advocate*.

Reed was closer to the college norm. His ambitions had no bounds; he wrote one-act plays, short stories, innumerable poems, and occasional essays; he planned a novel and a full-length play. His best prose was in the poetic and imaginative short stories of the type he had written at Morristown. When, as in "The Red Hand" and "In England's Need," he sought to combine fantasy and satire or fantasy and realism, he was purely sophomoric, but the romanticism of "The Pharaoh," the inventiveness of "The Singing Gates," and the allegorical unity of "The Winged Stone" are not unimpressive. His one serious attempt at realism, a description of a trip with friends in Oregon, smothers in poetic verbiage a sound feeling for the mountains and the sea.

As for his poetry, it was no more commonplace than most of the poetry in the Harvard magazines, than T. S. Eliot's, for example, and considerably less conventional. The sonnet, "Tchaikowsky," which was reprinted in the anthology with which the *Monthly* celebrated its twenty-fifth anniversary, compares well enough with the poems in the volume by men with distinguished names. "The Desert" and "Coyote Song," which he chose to preserve in *Tamburlaine*, suggest the two principal influences on his work: Swinburne and the esthetes, Kipling and the poets of action. "A Winter Run," which is rather in the Kipling vein, has the merit of deriving some fine poetic imagery from actual Cambridge experience. Of the more literary poems, "Melisande" is probably the least banal.

Reed had the sensibility of a poet, but he was not dedicated to poetry in the way that Alan Seeger was. He loved power and the exercise of his executive ability quite as much as he loved poetry. Moreover, he was so eager for experience that he could not be bothered to assimilate it. He never lacked things to say, but he was likely to choose an easy way of saying them. And the influences on his poetry—for any undergraduate poet is bound to be influenced—were not healthy. It was a pity that he should be imitative, but doubly a pity that he should imitate poets who were also imitators. Real poets were in the making, but either they had not appeared or were not known.

Fortunately there were three men who could say to John Reed things that needed to be said. There was Copey, who said again and again that writing was important because life was important, and who never let a man forget that he had eyes. There was Lincoln Steffens, not yet a close friend of Reed's but a friend of his father's and of Walter Lippmann's. Steffens could tell him that there was not the great chasm between journalism and poetry that he imagined: "It's all a matter of expression, which is journalism, and which may be literature—if the writer is striving not to make a work of art, but simply to tell his story for you and me and the man on the street." And there was his old friend in Portland, Charles Erskine Scott Wood, who took the trouble to write the Harvard senior a long letter about poetry. Wood could tell him that poetry must be made new: "The poetry of the future must not be a re-vamping of the past, no matter how beautiful it may be in form. Whitman, who sacrificed form and is full of excrescences, comes nearer being the

American genius, nearer being a *new* man than all of them."
And Wood could tell him, too, that poetry could not live without the spirit of revolution: "The poetry of the future must not
be a moral essay nor an economic tract, but it positively must
have the pulsing thought of the modern man. If it be full of the
surge of the ocean and the wet south wind of an ever-recurring
spring, it must also be full of the surge of human lifeblood and
wet with the tears of humanity."

Thinking of these things, Reed left Harvard. As at Morristown he had made bitter enemies, who would talk for twenty-
five years of his "showmanship and craving for notoriety," and
call him "a grandstand player, utterly selfish, a publicity seeker,
basically unsound on fundamentals of religion, government, and
society in general." "His death," they would say, "was the only
piece of good fortune he contributed to the United States," or,
more mildly, "I always thought he was a most offensive man."
He also had made friends, who believed in and admired him as
strongly as his enemies condemned him. As at Morristown he
had learned self-confidence, but now it was a confidence that
had triumphed over discrimination, disappointment, and defeat.
Harvard had done him some good and much less harm than it
does most of its graduates. It had not robbed him of his energy
and hope, had not diminished his courage, had not made him
ashamed of either his gayety or his seriousness. Most important
of all, it had not closed him up, shut him away from life. He was
only beginning to grow.

IV

To See the World

AT ELEVEN-THIRTY on the morning of July 9, 1910, the S.S. *Bostonian* left Boston with seven hundred steers on board. Copey had given his invariable advice: do something, see the world, have experience, find something to write about. And John Reed had listened and obeyed. He planned to work his way not only to Europe but around the world. His father approved the plan, though he insisted on modifying it by drawing heavily on sparse resources and giving the boy, despite his protests, one hundred dollars and a letter of credit.

Reed had persuaded Waldo Peirce to accompany him. Peirce was a Maine man who had revolted against the close-figuring caution that had made his grandfather a power in Bangor. His more than two hundred pounds of solid strength had inevitably put him on the football team, though he disliked the long afternoons of dreary practice. He disliked anything that partook of the nature of discipline. He could not be bothered to work at drawing, though his cartoons in the *Lampoon* had more originality than the sleek pictures of its cleverest artists. He could not be bothered to work at writing, though one or two realistic stories in the *Monthly* had exposed the empty imitativeness of the ruck of undergraduate tales. He could not be bothered to work at his courses, and the university had more than once penalized him. Towards the aristocrats, who had to accept him, he felt the careless indifference that Reed wanted to feel and couldn't quite. Reed said he admired Peirce because he wore the kind of clothes he wanted to wear. He also admired him because he was one man who was more daring, more irresponsible, more adventurous than John Reed.

Peirce planned to go to Paris to study painting, but he planned to go in the comfort of the *Mauretania*. Reed wanted him on the cattle boat, and, though he failed to get definite consent, gave his name to the officer when he himself signed up for the voyage. On the morning of departure Peirce went with Reed to the dock to explain that his name had been given by mistake and that he was not going. But Reed pleaded with him so eloquently that he at last agreed to let chance settle the dispute; he would go to the bank for money and, if the boat was there when he returned, he would sail with her. Though the boat should have departed at once, and though he spent as much time at the bank as decency would permit, he lost the bet.

It was an uncommonly hot day, and the stench of the cattle filled the forecastle and hung heavy on the deck. Even out in the harbor the fierce heat was unrelieved. Peirce began to think of a girl he had wanted to see, of messages he should have sent his family, of the luxury of the *Mauretania*. He told Reed he had half a mind to slip overboard and swim back. Reed said it was ridiculous. But would it be all right with him, Peirce asked. "Certainly not," said Reed.

The dozen college students gathered on the deck and signed the ship's articles. Then each was given a tin plate, tin cup, and spoon, and they went below to eat. There was boiled meat and some sort of vegetable soup with white worms in it. Peirce went up on deck. The water looked singularly cool and pleasant. He went back to the forecastle and laid his watch and wallet on Reed's bed. On deck he looked carefully around. The men were still below, and the captain was out of sight on the bridge. He dove overboard.

The water was as pleasant as he had expected. He slipped off most of his clothes, and swam slowly away from the vessel, trying hard to keep out of sight. His one concern was that he had signed the ship's articles. He was committed to ten days or more on board that stinking ship, and he was convinced that, if the captain saw him, he would turn about and capture him. Reed might tell the captain. He watched the ship, but it moved steadily away from him. Swimming a few miles in water as calm as the Dunster House pool was pure pleasure on such a day. Besides, there were plenty of fishermen's boats within hail, too near indeed for comfort, since, he was almost ready to believe, one of them might pick him up and pursue the *Bostonian* and perhaps claim a reward for the return of a fugitive cattleman. At last, when the *Bostonian* was almost out of sight, he called out to a pair of startled lobster fishermen, who took him aboard. They left him at one of the islands in the harbor, where he borrowed a pair of pants and a shirt from a soldier. Back in Boston, he hurried to Cambridge and told the story to his friends.

On board the *Bostonian* no one, except John Reed, paid any attention to Peirce's absence, and even Reed, though he suspected the truth, thought he might be asleep in the hay. But next morning the captain mustered all hands and discovered that Peirce was gone. Reed told his story and produced Peirce's wallet and watch. The captain expressed some skepticism, and the crew was convinced that Peirce had been murdered. Reed maintained that Peirce would meet him at Liverpool. "God help you," said the captain, "if he doesn't."

But Reed was confident, and the threat of a hearing before the Board of Inquiry in Manchester did not disturb him. There was enough to worry him. The food was bad and the sleeping quarters unbearable. Reed wanted experience but not in so intensive a form. The college men got together, and discussed ways of making themselves more comfortable than the common bull-pushers. With a few bribes, they arranged for better food, and got permission to put up a tarpaulin tent on deck. Most of them were Harvard and Yale men, and they excluded two "middle-western muckers from the University of Illinois" from their "university club."

Reed and a man named Walker got themselves appointed night-watchmen. They had to look after the steers from eight-thirty to four in the morning, when they turned out all hands to feed the cattle. In the afternoon, when they awoke, they helped haul up the hay. As night-watchmen they were entitled to an extra meal, and when tips and small favors had awakened the second steward to a proper appreciation of the consideration due college boys on cattle ships, even Reed's appetite was sated. He made friends with the dry, quick-witted chief engineer, who gave the university club the privilege of turning on the salt water pumps every afternoon and taking sea-baths on deck.

As the men on board grew to like him, they became concerned over his fate. There were three Irishmen who begged him to slip overboard when the ship was nearest to the coast of Ireland. If he would go to Cork, they said, they would meet him and take care of him. But he laughed and declared that Peirce would be at the dock. They reached Liverpool, and the tug came out. Reed looked everywhere for Peirce, but he did not come, though the *Mauretania* had been in for two days. The captain and mate frowned. Finally the mate slipped on a pair of leg-irons and locked him in a little cabin. The ship moved slowly up the canal to Manchester.

Peirce, in the meantime, had taken the *Mauretania* and had arrived in Liverpool. There had been some talk in Cambridge of his swimming out to meet the ship and pretending he had followed it all the way over. But the thought of the ship's articles dispelled any humorous plans. His imagination played with the various forms of punishment an offended captain could employ. At Liverpool he kept out of sight and made inquiries. He wanted to see Reed alone; once he caught a glimpse of him, but he was talking with the captain. Peirce fled and went to a lawyer, who scoffed at his fears.

As the *Bostonian* made dreary progress through the locks, John Reed lay awake and worried, not so much because of what might happen to him as because of what, he was now convinced, had happened to Peirce. He wished he had never asked Peirce to go with him, wished he had taken his suggestion seriously and dissuaded him, wished he had told the captain as soon as his suspicions stirred. When, preceded by the captain, flanked by two British bobbies, followed by the mates, the steward, the cook, the crew, and the cattlemen, he marched to the Board of Trade building, he was almost willing to believe that he was a murderer.

Before eleven stolid Britishers, with the officers and men of the *Bostonian* filling the room, Reed began his testimony. Peirce, fortified by legal advice, walked in. Reed called his name, and, unperturbed in the tumultuous room, Peirce identified himself. The captain rose: "Do you remember," he shouted, "that you signed the vessel's articles and that you are liable for breaking your contract."

But Peirce had been well instructed. "Yes," he said, "but you are liable for criminal negligence. I was seasick. I went aft to lean over the rail. I slipped, I cried for help, I fell overboard. You yourself were on the bridge at the time and paid no attention to me."

When it had been established that the captain was on the bridge, the chairman, after some reflections on Peirce's sanity, ordered Reed released and Peirce's property returned to him. The only punishment came when, as he left the *Bostonian* with his watch, his wallet, and his bags, the sailors and cattlemen lined up to express their opinion of him. Several of them shook hands with Reed and advised him to get rid of his partner as quickly as possible.

As a matter of fact, they did separate immediately, though with plans to meet in London. Reed had set his mind on a walking trip through England, and Peirce was not interested.

Reed went first to Chester, and at the Duke of Westminster's estate he saw "a pageant so beautiful it fairly made you ache." Equipped with rough clothes and stout shoes, he started off through the Welsh mountains. "And still," he wrote his brother, "the example of American pluck, democracy, and independence pursues his way through these devastated reaches." He split his little toe, and had to stay over for a day and a night in a little village, where "the people came from miles around to see the fool American who walked when he could ride."

He went on and the next night found himself with sore feet a long way from the nearest town. He saw an old Tudor mansion, and near the stables there was a haystack. He crawled in, took off his shoes, and lit a cigarette. Before he could finish it, a liveried servant appeared and cursed at him for smoking in the hay.

"Whose house is that?" Reed asked.

"Mrs. Vanderbilt's."

"Not Mrs. Alfred Vanderbilt's?"

"Yes, sir—why, sir—"

"But surely she doesn't mind *my* sleeping in the hay?"

"No, sir, I don't suppose so—gentleman-like, sir."

Reed continued to rub his feet with Elliman's embrocation.

"Will that be all, sir?" asked the servant.

"Yes, for the present. But see," and he jingled coins in his pocket, "if you can't get me a bucket of water, soap, and a towel in the morning; and call me at seven-thirty."

"Yes, sir; be careful of the hay, sir."

"That will be all."

"Good night, sir."

Reed slept well, and was awakened by a respectful touch at seven-thirty. After he had washed, he gave the servant sixpence and his card. "Present this," he said, "with my compliments to Mrs. Vanderbilt, and say that I am very sorry not to have seen her."

And he went on, to Shrewsbury, to the Royal Oak, and, taking a train to avoid Birmingham, into Worcester. At Stratford he stayed at the Harvard House, saw a performance of Josephine Preston Peabody's *The Piper,* and contrived to see Shakespeare's tomb on Sunday by entering with the church-goers and avoiding the beadle. He rented a bicycle and went to Kenilworth, where he invaded the estate by the Duke of Leicester's private gate, and where, finding Mervyn's Tower closed, he broke into it. He went to a village festival at Chipping-Norton, and thought the men and women "lots cleaner and happier than our farming and village people." On his way to Oxford he stopped at Woodstock and stole a swim in the Duke of Marlboro's private pool.

Finally he reached London and met Peirce. A creditable proportion of his hundred dollars had survived the walking trip, but in London he began to draw on the letter of credit. He bought not only a heavy suit and a light tweed suit, but also a cutaway, a dress suit, and a tuxedo. He saw most of the sights, but he failed to meet Wells and Chesterton, as he had hoped to do.

Liking London and having sold two or three articles to the London *Daily News,* he contemplated remaining in England, but Peirce was eager for Paris, and at the end of August they walked to Canterbury, attended service in the cathedral, and went on to Dover. No ordinary method of crossing the channel would suit Reed. He proposed that they smuggle themselves across on a fishing boat, but Peirce would have nothing of it, and in the end Reed had to be satisfied with the rather tame exploit of stowing away on the Calais boat. Of course they were caught, and there was nothing for them to do but lamely tell the purser that they had found a friend on board and now could pay their fares. Peirce was irritated and at Calais he suggested that they separate. Reed walked alone down the coast towards Paris.

In Paris he met Carl Chadwick and Joe Adams. After dressing in tuxedoes, with canes, gloves, and all appropriate finery, they had dinner at the Café de la Paix and went the rounds of Montmartre, ending at Maxim's at four o'clock. From Maxim's they drove to Grez, where Chadwick's family lived. There were brothers and sisters and brothers-in-law and sisters-in-law, and they all "did something," painted pictures or wrote poetry or composed music. Reed was delighted.

He was delighted, too, with the freedom he found. Chadwick drove him and Adams to the Norman coast at St. Pierre, where he knew three or four French girls. "You can't imagine the freedom of young girls in France," Reed wrote his father. "They go without a chaperon everywhere, even on long eight-day trips in the auto; everybody turns in at the same hotel, or we all sleep together in a haystack by the roadside. Everybody makes jokes about the most delicate subjects, and everybody roars with laughter." The three young men took two of the girls to Havre for the aviation meet, had dinner on the porch of the casino, played *petits chevaux*, and got back to St. Pierre at two in the morning, "when we all went into the ocean without anything on, the girls on one side of the beach and we on the other."

They found Peirce at Grez on their return, and Reed, Peirce, Adams, Chadwick, and Alden Brooks, Chadwick's brother-in-law, motored to San Sebastian to see a bullfight. Reed tried to be tough-minded about the fight. "The bull tosses the horse, at the same time goring him, so that his guts hang out. Then they flog the horse to his feet again, and make him fight with his bowels hanging out." Bullfights, after all, were experience. But what really excited him was Spain. They had all planned a walking-trip, but the others were lazy or had things to do in Paris or had been unfortunate at San Sebastian's gambling tables, and Reed, without knowing a word of Spanish, started off alone.

He bought a peasant's corduroys and, with his camera over his shoulders, marched through the green fields and along the lively rivers of the country of the Basques. That night he watched the dancers in the plaza of Tolosa and listened to the music of a band of blue-bloused peasants. In the third-class coach —"the last survival of the Inquisition," he called it—of the train to Burgos, he was the object of argumentative curiosity and lavish hospitality. In Burgos he followed a solemn procession to high mass in the cathedral, and saw a witch hunt. On the way to Valladolid he made the acquaintance of a sailor who could say "godam." The sailor happened to be lousy, and the keeper of the inn he chose tried to charge Reed, at the sailor's suggestion, double the normal amount for lodging for the two. But he bought Reed a beer and saw him to the train.

Changing trains at Medina del Campo, where a royal visitor was expected, he was arrested on suspicion of being an anarchist. Once he had satisfied the authorities, he wanted to stay in the warm examination room, but he was sent back to the bare, unheated station. Salamanca delighted him and roused him to speculation on religion and art. En route to Toledo, again third-class, he was once more pointed at and questioned, but this time, when it emerged that he was a North American, he was attacked, to the delight of everyone in the car, by a biting, scratching woman who had had a son killed in ninety-eight. Two days of Toledo—"the most wonderful of Spanish cities, more regal than Madrid, more gloriously disdainful than Burgos"—were not enough: he wanted weeks to study the cathedral, look at the El Grecos, wander in the streets. But he went on to Madrid, where he slept for two nights in the park under a borrowed blanket, spent a day at the Prado, and looked in vain for the exotic glamor *Carmen* had taught him to expect. The third-class ticket for Paris took the last of the money he had with him.

IN PARIS Reed began to take stock. He began to question a little the wisdom of trying to go around the world, though he was still willing to make a try if he could find anyone to go with him. The dash into Spain, glad as he was that he had made it, had taught him a lesson: "It's no fun," he wrote his brother, "to bum your way alone in this beast of a continent, because if you haven't anybody to laugh with, there isn't a hell of a lot of humor in it." Paris would suit him for the fall and early winter, and then perhaps a trip through Italy, Greece, Austria, and Germany. He would return home in the spring.

He took a room at the Hotel des Deux Anges and covered the walls with posters. Sleeping late, he usually met Waldo Peirce at a café for breakfast. In the afternoon he tried to write or worked on his French. In the evening he and Peirce and anyone they happened to meet wandered around Montmartre or dropped in at the Bal Bullier. He was occasionally invited to polite dances, and Professor Schofield, who was exchange professor at the Sorbonne and sought to become the mentor of all Harvard youths in France, had him for dinner and lectured him on his behavior.

His behavior invited rebukes, though he was quick to resent them. He and Peirce competed in the invention of new ways of shocking the American colony. They broke into respectable parties dressed in bizarre clothes. They welcomed brawls in cheap cafés. They not only frequented low resorts, but boasted of their exploits, adjusting the degree of exaggeration to the horror of the listener.

"This is the greatest place in the world," he wrote his family and his friends. It was a great place because it was free. "You never imagined such utter freedom," he informed Alan Gregg. "Freedom from every boundary, moral, religious, social." Reed wanted freedom for its own sake and because in freedom lay romance. In college he had avoided, in large degree and perhaps completely, the kind of sexual exploits that undergraduates with a little money were likely to engage in. In Paris he thought he was not buying a woman; he was taking a mistress. One night it occurred to him that he must bring her flowers. He bought a cabful, and he and his friends went to the girl's room and heaped them over her on her bed. This was romance. But there was a night when she stroked his hair and said, "Tell me; how do you make your money?" Throwing on his clothes, he ran downstairs, and walked and walked until the bad taste was out of his mouth.

His education continued. He was very glad that he had gone to Harvard, and, when he discovered that most of the Harvard men in Paris had belonged to the Hasty Pudding, he was inclined to forget the way in which he had been taken into the club. Harvard was a good deal in his thoughts. He cabled congratulations to Copey when he was made an assistant professor. He proposed to Waldo Peirce that they take a tramp steamer back to America and turn up on the eve of the Yale game. "It would be," he said, with an appreciation of his own legend that Copey could not have bettered, "such a characteristic thing for us to do." He laid bets with the Yale men in Paris on the outcome of the game, went to the annual Harvard dinner, and was downhearted when the news came that the best Lothrop Withington's team could achieve was a tie. He was affectionately concerned about the *Lampoon*, pleaded with Alan Gregg to send him copies, and wrote detailed criticisms of the issues he saw. He even wrote a serial for the *Lampoon*, describing the mythical adventures of Dean Hurlbut and Regent Stearns in Paris.

Harvard, four months after graduation, was still the most important thing in John Reed's life. "You hear lots of graduates telling how small things are at collage, now that they are out," he wrote Gregg. "That makes me foam at the mouth, because college always looms tremendous to me. The foolishnesses I did there smart just as much, the good things have more of a glamor than ever." There are two ways, he went on, of taking college: "one as a school, where nothing really counts but what applies materially to your after success—or that it is a separate life. I took the latter and I'm not sorry." Now, he felt, he was beginning something new, which had no continuity with college, and for which college had been a preparation only insofar as it had given him a chance to find himself through victory and defeat.

But he sometimes wondered whether he had found himself or not. He had been so absorbed in college life that he had seldom considered what lay outside the bounds of Harvard. Four months in Europe had shown him so much that Harvard had not prepared him for that he was a little frightened. "The first effect of being over here," he told Gregg, "is a pretty full real-ization of all you have ever dreamed of. This is followed by a sort of top-heavy exhilaration, when you want to be arrested, or join the Foreign Legion, or tear off a bizarre party in the Apache district. And then one morning you wake up just five years older than you were the night before. Every bit of self-confidence you got in college leaks out, or at least mine did. I'm just emerging from a period of shakiness and doubt in myself that was pretty morbid for about two weeks."

One thing that shook Reed's self-confidence was the utter lack of self-distrust in his fellow-alumni in Paris. He was associating, on fairly intimate terms, with men who had snubbed him in col-lege. Paris, which had so excited him and changed his ideas, did not deflect them an iota from the complacent pursuit of the way of life they had followed in Cambridge. Except that they took full advantage of the opportunities for promiscuity, they lived lives that differed scarcely at all from those they had lived on Mount Auburn Street. They knew what they wanted, and he did not. He was tempted to conform to their standards, but every concession he made seemed disastrous. Finally he told him-self, "If you try to pretend you are wise, you're a goner; some-body'll get you sooner or later. Therefore say your mind on everything, no matter how stupid it seems. If someone talks high philosophy, and you think low, out with it, and be despised if necessary."

"I find myself at outs with all the world," he exclaimed, "and it must be my fault." He wished he could be "a lazy philosopher, like Waldo, who can sit on his tail, at friends with all the world, and suck the sweetness of things." He wished he could settle down, like Gluyas Williams, who had come to Paris to study art, and, though baffled and disappointed, was driving himself every daylight hour in his studio. He did not know what to think or what to do. He began to wonder if his father, who had been defeated for Congress and was having to return to the selling of insurance, could afford the luxurious and leisurely education of his two sons. The realization grew that he must return to Amer-ica and find a job.

John Reed's remedy for melancholy was, of course, action,

and the kind of action that proved most effective was travel. He began the exploration of as much of France as lay within easy reach of Paris. In the intervals between his trips, he wrote short stories and accounts of his journeys. As Christmas drew near, and the thought of the sacrifices his mother and father had made became sharper, he wrote a poem for his mother. Gluyas Williams, who had always thought of Reed as uncommonly free from sentiment and even ruthless, was amazed to find him, one afternoon, hand-lettering and decorating the poem, a task to which he had devoted himself for days.

He planned one more trip before he returned to America. He set off alone to the south of France, to Orange, Avignon, Tarascon, and Marseilles. Avignon he thought the most beautiful city he had ever seen. "I went to a Medieval theatre last night, slept in a Pre-Raphaelite bed, and am now eating an early Renaissance lunch." He became excited about the Provençal poets, especially Mistral, whose "Mireille" he tried to translate into English verse. "Marseilles," he wrote his father, "is a great city. I imagined such a place, once, where all the nations meet and jostle on the Cannabière, where there is a port that beats anything I ever saw, and a restricted district that has Hell lashed to the mast; but I never hoped to see it." He arrived at night, chose a hotel "as is my custom, right off the bat, without inquiries or the consultation of guides or other holy writs," and immediately sought out the district that Baedeker described as "dangerous after dark." He stayed there until one, "talking with all the motherly old prostitutes, and childish young prostitutes, and Lascar sailors." He went over the ground of *Monte Christo*, spent hours on the quais, and climbed the mountain to the Church of Notre Dame de la Garde to look down over the city to the Mediterranean.

"Marseilles," he wrote, "is a much more *romantique* city than Paris, if you know what I mean. For instance, you see the sun go down over the Louvre, and you know it's going down over the English channel and the Hebrides. You see it set at Marseilles, and it goes to bed behind the Pillars of Hercules, with the nations tacking out to sea from Marseilles to fish in their red-sailed feluccas. In Paris, the Seine flows into the Manche, where the fast mail-boats tear across from Havre to Southampton; at Marseilles, the turquoise water leads your eyes gently out through the jungle of masts to the blue horizons—beyond them are Italy and Greece, Asia and Egypt, Algiers and Spain! The wind comes down from Germany at Paris—the mistral brings to Marseilles a sound of solemn bells from Avignon and guitars from Arles, and the smell of Provence. At Paris, Notre Dame and the Louvre are elegant, spic-and-span; at Marseilles, there is a Greek inscription on the walls of the Chateau St. Jean, at the entrance of the Old Port, which the waves of the Phœnician Sea have worn thin for centuries and centuries. Paris is fine and insidious and chic—Marseilles is bluff and masculine."

He left Marseilles to go to Toulon, where he met Waldo Peirce and Harold Taylor. With them were three friends of the Chadwicks, Madeleine and Marguerite Filon, nieces of a famous scholar, and Mme. Beaurain. The six of them walked together along the coast to Monte Carlo, taking their time, turning aside now and then into the mountains, staying in little hotels, swimming whenever they felt like it. The men bore the packs, and they all carried long bamboo canes. They visited Roman ruins, laughed back at the wondering people of the seaside resorts, went fishing in a hired boat on the Mediterranean. Reed chose the routes and the inns, and managed the money. After nine days they came to Nice, spent an evening at the Casino, and went on to Monte Carlo.

The first evening Peirce, having lost all that he could afford, went back to his room. Reed came in much later, so excited that his roommate was sure he had won heavily at the tables. He was engaged to Madeleine Filon. The trip had been "a dream of joy from beginning to end," and anything less than a grand romantic gesture would be anti-climax. As soon as he could get his things together, he left for America "to make a million dollars and get married."

V

PROUD NEW YORK

MAKING only one stop—at Cambridge—John Reed returned to Portland. Family finances he found rather worse than he had expected. Although the real estate owned by the Reeds and the Greens theoretically represented a comfortable sum, it was so burdened with mortgages and the ownership was so divided that his father could realize little money from it, and was having difficulty in meeting daily expenses. There was no doubt that the son would have to find a job as soon as possible.

His mother and father tried to be pleasant about the engagement, but he could see that they were distressed. Their friends were dismayed at his planning to marry a French girl, and his friends were dismayed at his planning to marry at all. They asked him how he planned to support a wife on rejection slips, and he had no answer except to set his jaw and consign the whole city to hell.

If he had to find a job, he had no intention of looking for it in Portland. Despite his mother's objections, he hastened back to New York, where the first thing he did was to join the Harvard Club and the second was to get in touch with Lincoln Steffens. Steffens said, "I guess you will have your chance." He had always regarded Reed and Lippmann, whom he had already placed on *Everybody's*, as his boys. He secured Reed a temporary position on the *Globe* and then set him to work on the *American Magazine*.

Reed had been a little afraid of Steffens when he met him at Harvard; he seemed too serious, too wise, too difficult to talk to. But now the man's kindness swept all reserve away. "You can do anything you want to," said Steffens, and Reed believed him. From then on Reed took all his difficulties to Steffens, who smiled and understood and let the boy solve his problems for himself. From then on Steffens stood with Copeland—the two men who made Reed want to do nothing unworthy. And Steffens had something to give Reed's mind.

The job on the *American*, Steffens warned, was merely a springboard; it would do for the time being. The magazine was changing. It was still publishing the work of the muckrakers who had taken it over in 1905, the old *McClure's* crowd, Steffens himself, Ida Tarbell, Ray Stannard Baker, William Allen White. Miss Tarbell was writing on the tariff and Baker on the revolt against Taft. Albert Jay Nock, who was on the staff, expounded the single tax, and Frederick Taylor wrote on scientific management. But the proportion of fiction grew larger and larger, serials by W. J. Locke and Frances Hodgson Burnett, stories by Samuel Hopkins Adams, Neith Boyce, Edna Ferber, and Dorothy Canfield. And John Siddall, developing the methods that were to make the *American* so profitable an organ of the gospel of success, had introduced a department called "Interesting People."

Reed's work was purely routine: correcting proof, reading manuscripts, and, later, helping to make up the magazine. To supplement the meager salary he took an additional job as business manager of a quarterly, *Landscape Architecture*, which was soon buried beneath a pile of bills. The million was a long way off.

He could afford to forget the million, however, because in June he broke his engagement. In February he wrote an eloquent letter to Waldo Peirce from Portland, beseeching him to forsake his vagabond ways, to find his true love and settle down with her. In July he informed Peirce: "A man does not meet his predestined mate—never. He could love and be married and be happy with any one of a thousand." "The nightmare of this spring!" he cried. "To have to write—to have to be passionate every other day." Besides, he said, "I was sentimental about it, and remained chaste up to the other night." Five months was a long time for the enchantment of the Mediterranean to last. His family was very glad.

There was more time for literary work now, though he had been prolific enough before. He saved each rejection slip, and the number grew. Out of his six months in Europe came an essay, "A Dash Into Spain," which went from magazine to magazine and always came back, and half a dozen short stories. "Overboard" was taken in hand by Julian Street and finally appeared in the *Saturday Evening Post*. "The Man from the Seine" found its way to the *Century* office, and appeared, with some revision, a year after it had been written. "Showing Mrs. Van" was, after many delays, taken by the *Smart Set*. Other stories were less fortunate.

The first pieces he had published were an editorial, "Immigrants," which *Collier's* took, and an essay, "The Involuntary Ethics of Big Business," which a magazine called *Trend* accepted and printed but did not pay for until Reed had brought suit. Steffens liked "Immigrants" well enough, but the essay, he gently suggested, was a little dubious. It tried to prove that the big business man, who seeks only efficiency and profit, miraculously achieves beauty, liberty, and justice. Reed called it a fable; Steffens—but it was not his way—could have found a better word.

Other essays, including a facetious discussion of the quick lunch and an elaborate satire on the theatre, went the way of so many of the short stories, but within a year after he arrived in New York Reed had had work accepted by *Collier's*, the *American*, the *Saturday Evening Post*, the *Forum*, and the *Century*. Arthur Foote had set one of his poems, "The Wanderer to His Heart's Desire," to music. He had been elected to the Dutch Treat Club. Robert Benchley had asked him for advice on how to become a writer, and Copey had requested him to speak to English 12. The editors of the *American* were beginning to value him as a contributor as well as a colleague: they had printed three brief articles by him, including a tribute to Copey which it had been a satisfaction to write, and a number of poems. The successful men at the Dutch Treat Club, the Irwins, Tom Masson, Rupert Hughes, James Montgomery Flagg, Irvin Cobb,

Julian Street, the men who knew what the public wanted and how to get paid for supplying it, said that John Reed was a coming man.

LONG before he could regard it as the scene of his success, John Reed loved New York. It was the enchanted city.

> O let some young Timotheus sweep his lyre
> Hymning New York. Lo! Every tower and spire
> Puts on immortal fire!
> This city, which ye scorn
> For her rude sprawling limbs, her strength unshorn,—
> Hands blunt from grasping, Titan-like, at Heav'n,—
> Is a world wonder vaulting all the Seven!

Rome, Babylon, Athens, and Troy were gone. Romance was here:

> This spawning filth, these monuments uncouth
> Are but her wild, ungovernable youth.
> But the sky-scrapers, dwarfing earthly things,—
> Ah, that is how she sings!
> Wake to the vision shining in the sun!
> Earth's ancient, conquering races rolled in one,
> A world beginning,—and yet nothing done!

The vantage point from which he began his affectionate, untiring explorations of the city was Greenwich Village. The Village, with its vestiges of ancient respectability and its neighboring slums, grew slowly towards Bohemian notoriety. At 42 Washington Square, Reed and three Harvard friends, at Reed's suggestion, rented rooms in the fall of 1911. Robert Andrews and Alan Osgood had been on the *Lampoon*, Robert Rogers on the *Monthly*. Andrews, who had gone through college in three years and was now working in the advertising department of Lamont, Corliss and Company, was tart and critical, quick to ridicule excesses or expose fallacies. Osgood, perhaps the least mature of the quartet, Reed liked for that very reason. He was always gay, good-natured, ready to play. When the four of them started out together for an evening, Reed and Osgood, running ahead, would alternately hide in doorways and leap out at each other. Even the Village gaped at them, and waiters at the Brevoort trembled at their arrival. Rogers, who had gone to work on the Brooklyn *Eagle*, with Hans von Kaltenborn, Samuel Duff McCoy, and Don Marquis, was, already, a little too thick-set for street races, and he and Andrews joined in sardonic commentary on the behavior of their roommates.

Usually there was some other Harvard man with them. Joe Adams, working for an investment house in Chicago, would stay for a week or two. Alfred Kuttner joined them for part of the year. Alan Seeger, who had come down from New Hampshire to take a position at the Spanish Museum, gave up his job out of sheer emotion when he fell in love, and spent most of his time at 42 Washington Square. He would walk in with his white, mask-like face and his stony eyes, and stand about until somebody fed him. If no one was at home, he would leave his poems under the door, with a note asking Reed to sell them if by any chance they could be sold. Then he would go and lie on the wharves.

But the most important resident of the house, so far as Reed was concerned, was Lincoln Steffens. Reed had persuaded him to come there, and he had rooms underneath theirs. Whenever he was in town, Reed would come banging into his room, any time after midnight, and tell him in excited superlatives what he had seen or done. Steffens would listen, without impatience, whether the talk was about girls or revolutionists, but in time it occurred to him that Reed was losing good literary material and he was losing sleep. "Write it down," he said. Reed did, and the next day Steffens would criticize what he had written and make him re-write it. And he was as ready to deal with personal problems as literary ones. "You're not in love," he wrote Reed from one of his trips out of town, "or you'd never put it that way. 'Damn it! I'm afraid I've fallen in love again.' You're not and you weren't before. So watch out."

Steffens was even ready to lend money on the proper occasions. Reed was hard up a good deal of the time, and at first he tried to borrow from Steffens to pay his rent and other expenses.

Steffens refused. "No regular bills, Jack," he said; "but whenever you want money for some wasteful, idiotic affair that nobody else would think of, then you can come to me."

Reed took him at his word, and in the Christmas holidays he suddenly demanded a considerable sum. Edward Hunt had come down from Cambridge at Christmas, worn out by eighteen months in the dean's office after four exacting years in college, and prostrated by the sudden death of his brother in South America. Reed decided he must have a vacation: he would take him to Bermuda. Without telling Hunt, he wrote Dean Hurlbut and President Lowell, both of whom heartily consented. He wrote Hunt's mother and got her approval. Then he obtained leave of absence from the *American,* and bullied Robert Rogers into asking the *Eagle* for a vacation. Finally, when every other provision had been made, he borrowed the money from Steffens.

Hunt, suddenly informed of the project, thought of a dozen reasons why he could not go. Reed confronted him with a letter or telegram to meet each objection. Lowell had wired, "Take Hunt by all means," and, Reed threatened to follow this injunction if it meant the use of knock-out drops. Hunt gave in.

They left on the coldest day of the winter of 1911-12. The steam pipes froze. There were six berths in the stateroom, and one was occupied by an aged actor who was dying of tuberculosis, and another held a groaning convalescent from blood-poisoning. Hunt became seasick, went on deck, and just escaped when a heavy sea wrenched off an iron ladder and sent it crashing through the rail. Reed wrote:

> Each steward marked his helpless prey
> And Hunt became a leetle gray
> As Coney Island fell away
> Across an ocean bleak.

But once they were in Bermuda, it was extraordinarily pleasant. Reed, of course, was their guide. Hunt, slight and wan, eagerly followed his impetuous lead, and Tubby Rogers smiled and chuckled as he bobbed along beside them. Hamilton was too expensive, and they went to St. George's, where Reed immedi-

ately made friends with the garrison and found entertainment
for them. Hunt's natural charm expanded in the benevolent
warmth, and he returned to Cambridge with an ebullience that
made Reed and Rogers rejoice. They felt that the money had
been well expended, and began to pay it back to Steffens, wrap-
ping bills as they could spare them around his door knob. After
this had gone on for a few weeks, Reed announced that he didn't
intend to go on paying for the rest of life and demanded a statement. When Steffens realized that neither he nor they had kept
any account, he canceled the debt, and Reed danced with joy.

There was always some kind of excitement at 42 Washington
Square. When Rogers was leaving town for a time, Reed insisted
that there must be a farewell party at the Brevoort, and, after
the half-dozen of them had had enough of eating and drinking,
he led the whole party to the Grand Central. Rogers said good-
bye, got on the train, found his berth, and prepared to retire.
Andrews and Reed waited until he was partly undressed, and
then rushed into the car and brought him out onto the platform.

Hilarity made it seem foolish to go home, and so, when the
train had finally left, they went into a saloon. A man came up
and spoke to them, mentioning his name, which they pretended
not to understand. Reed called him Box, Andrews addressed him
as Cox, McCoy named him Sox. They tired of the game, and wandered over to Times Square. While they were in Child's, the
same man appeared, and they again hailed him as Box, Cox, and
Sox. Angered, he stated with dignity his full name and address.
Reed remembered them, and, as soon as they left the restaurant,
led the others to a telegraph office, where each of the trio sent the
gentleman a long collect telegram.

By now Reed was determined to show his friends what Fulton
Street Market looked like in the early morning. They must go
and see "the red and green and gold sea things glisten in the blue
light of the sputtering arcs." They did, stopping now and then
for another drink, and Reed realized that he was unlikely to be
equal to the day's work. He sent a telegram to Phillips: "Having
spent last night in a barrel of squid will not be at work. Reed."
The idea pleased him, and subsequently he either did try sleeping with squid or convinced himself that he had, for he wrote:

I have watched the summer day come up from the top of a pier of
    the Williamsburgh Bridge,
I have slept in a basket of squid at the Fulton Street Market.

To his roommates he seemed a mad playboy with a streak of
poetry, but to strangers he was a very puzzling young fellow.
A popular illustrator, who was under contract to do a series of
sketches of European celebrities, was looking for some one to
write the accompanying interviews. A friend suggested Reed.
She found him breezy, nice-mannered, smiling, broad-shoul-
dered but a little flabby, good-looking in a pale-eyed, round-faced
way. He was very confident that he could do what she wanted
done, and his assurance amused and irked her. Deciding to test
his qualifications, she suggested that he do an imaginary interview with an elderly duchess who had recently arrived in New
York. In the course of his article he described how his card was
sent up to the duchess, speaking of the pneumatic tubes as the
guts of the hotel, and saying that the card was evacuated. He
liked the phrases, and, when the illustrator criticized them, took
offense. He was not, he said, going to play second fiddle to a
fussy female, and they separated. She thought him vain, theatrical, and superficial.

He was vain, perhaps, and a little theatrical, but he was not
superficial. However unsettled and immature his ideas, his feelings were deep and sound. Strongest of all his feelings at the
moment was his love of New York, his city. "Within a block of
my house," he wrote, "was all the adventure in the world; within
a mile was every foreign country." Night after night he wandered the streets from his beloved skyscrapers downtown to the
obscurest corners of the city. He was never tired of the alien
towns of the East Side, loved the shrill markets under the roaring bridges and the clamorous pushcarts with their smoky flares.
"I know Chinatown, and Little Italy, and the quarter of the
Syrians; the marionette theatre, Sharkey's and McSorley's saloons, the Bowery lodging houses and the places where the
tramps gather in winter; the Haymarket, the German Village,
and all the dives of the Tenderloin."

The girls that walked the streets were friends of his, and he talked with drunken sailors off ships from the world's ends. He found wonderful restaurants where he could try the foods of all the nations. Chance acquaintances told him how to get dope, where to go to hire a man to kill an enemy, what to do to get into gambling rooms and secret dance-halls. He found the old, beautiful, leisurely squares and streets that were being submerged by the advance of the slums. He went to gangsters' balls at Tammany Hall, took part in an excursion of the Tim Sullivan Association, joined the surging crowds at Coney Island.

He knew as well the houses along Fifth Avenue and Riverside Drive, the fashionable hotels, the festive first-nights at theatres. The theatre always stirred him. He saw everything that came to the city: John Barrymore in *Uncle Sam* and Ethel Barrymore in *The Witness for the Defense*, Margaret Anglin in *Green Stockings*, Otis Skinner in *Kismet*, Mrs. Fiske in *Lady Patricia*, David Warfield in *The Return of Peter Grimm*, Weber and Fields in *Hokey-Pokey*. He saw the Irish Players do *Riders to the Sea* and *The Rising of the Moon* and the Little Theatre do Galsworthy's *Pigeon*. He stood in line for hours to see the opening game of the World's Series, sat in the cheering section at the Harvard-Yale game, took his friends to Barnum and Bailey's circus at the Garden.

Though he had never admitted it to himself, John Reed had been looking for romance only in the past; that was why he had written his short stories about the end of Atlantis or the decline of the Pharaohs, and his poems about Guinevere and Melisande. In New York he learned to love and to write about the things he saw. "There I got my first perceptions of the life of my time. The city and its people were an open book to me; everything had its story, dramatic, full of ironic tragedy and terrible humor. There I first saw that reality transcended all the fine poetic inventions of fastidiousness and medievalism. I was not happy or well long away from New York."

Lincoln Steffens listened with joy to Reed's stories of the city. He wanted Reed to let his eyes do everything for him that they could. He introduced him to radicals of every variety, Socialists, anarchists, single-taxers, labor leaders, and "all the hair-splitting Utopians and petty doctrine-mongers who cling to the skirts of

Change." Occasionally he recommended books, which Reed would buy at Frank Shay's bookshop, and perhaps finish. But Steffens knew that ideas alone didn't mean much to Reed, who said, "I have to see." He did see, and, with Steffens' unobtrusive help, felt and understood what he saw: "I couldn't help but observe the ugliness of poverty and all its train of evil, the cruel inequality between rich people who had too many motor-cars and poor people who didn't have enough to eat. It didn't come to me from books that the workers produced all the wealth of the world, which went to those who did not earn it."

This was what Socrates Steffens wanted. Reed began to realize that he had been privileged. Through no merit of his own, he had been given opportunties that had enabled him not merely to escape from poverty but also to learn to enjoy the color and drama of life. He had always sympathized with underdogs, revolting equally against the little injustices of snobbish society and the major injustices that were done to Indians and Chinese on the Coast and to the poor of New York. He began to feel more than sympathy, however; intimacy with the more rebellious underdogs brought liking and respect. He hated uplifting reformers, but he admired men who fought for their rights.

Slowly he began to take cognizance of the changes that were taking place in him. He did not sit down and try to formulate a philosophy, but he did experiment in revaluation. Before he had come to New York life had offered nothing more important than Harvard, and his four years there still seemed exciting and significant. He went to Cambridge as often as he could, was delighted to discuss with his successors the problems of the *Monthly* and the *Lampoon*, was proud to be invited to speak to English 12. But he knew that his values were changing. To record and clarify these changes he wrote an essay, never published, called "The Harvard Renaissance."

The essay praised Harvard for its long line of rebellious individuals, its "army of independent thinkers," and went on to describe, in detail, the sudden surge of rebellious activity that had come in his undergraduate years. Perhaps aware that, if his own nature had permitted, he might have belonged to the tradition of conformity rather than the tradition of revolt, he paid tribute to the men who had never been tempted by the glamor of the final clubs. He gave most credit for the renaissance to the Socialist Club, to which he had never belonged.

In the fall of 1911 the undergraduate radicals had clashed with the administration, which had refused to permit Mrs. Pankhurst to speak in a college building, and Reed made his article an attack on the authorities and a plea for free speech. The respectable alumni had come to Lowell's support. A person calling himself "an ex-Editor of the Harvard *Advocate*" had produced a booklet, "The Harvard Radicalettes," in which he described the Socialists "with gawky, ill-fitting clothes hanging badly on their puny figures." Samuel A. Eliot, Jr., grandson of the former president, had presided at a meeting for Emma Goldman, whom he had addressed as comrade. The ex-editor of the *Advocate* wrote:

> We hang our heads in shame
> To speak his grandson's name
> Unhonored, who by dint
> Of yellow journal's print
> Has spread his name abroad
> To win the worthless laud
> Of those who go about
> With clamor and with shout
> In high unselfish guise
> To flout the good and wise
> And ravish for their spoil
> The fruit of others' toil,
> With social dynamite
> More base than open fight.

In answering such abuse Reed was making clear to himself what had been important in his four Harvard years and what had not. He was far from feeling indifference to the university, but at least he could discriminate.

He was also beginning to discriminate in literary matters. He had come to New York with the same desire he had had when he entered Harvard, the desire to win all possible prizes. When he had thought of himself as a writer, he had thought of the widely-circulated magazines, the magazines that paid big prices. But in a year marked by unusual success he had begun to understand how the prizes were paid for. In an essay called "Art for Art's Sake," apparently written for the clarification of his own mind, he recorded that the men he respected, such as Lippmann and Steffens, all agreed that their best work could not be published in the popular magazines. On the other hand, John Siddall, whom he liked and whose shrewdness he acknowledged, pointed out that, if a writer did not write as these magazines demanded, he had no audience. The writer, Siddall said, should be humble. Failing to recognize the full insidiousness of this defense of the *status quo*, Reed impulsively rebelled against it. "The trouble with all the American mediocrities," he exclaimed, "is that they want individuals to all be worms and grovel on the ground." Shelley, Nietzsche, Emerson, and Whitman had not been humble, he declared, and added Shaw, Ibsen, and Rodin to the list. As for him, he would write what he wanted to write: "A real artist goes on creating for art's sake whether he achieves publication or not."

BEFORE John Reed could discover what happens to the real artist who goes on creating for art's sake, there came a sudden and painful break in his literary progress. At the end of June his mother wired that his father was dangerously ill and he must return to Portland.

Reed had been constantly drawing closer to his father. His mother wrote him lively letters, and he replied with long accounts of what he was doing. But his father, out of his own bitterness, could understand the boy's gayer but not less intense dissatisfaction with convention. His mother wanted him to meet the right kind of people in New York, and she had been able to supply him with letters of introduction. She did not care for society, she told him, any more than he did, but he might some day be grateful—and his wife, when he had one, certainly would be—for friends with position and prestige. His father wasted no time on such advice. He was naively delighted when Steffens introduced Reed to Theodore Roosevelt: "I was so pleased to have you meet Teddy as you did. He is all man and the greatest American alive." But his main concern was that Jack should be free to live his life as he chose. He was delighted by his successes: "I think and talk of you every day and love and am proud of you every hour." And he was not sorry that his son was thinking for himself and was interested in even bolder plans for the emancipation of mankind than he and his fellow-progressives had dared to dream.

Both Mr. and Mrs. Reed had become deeply concerned about money. "Debt is an awful burden," Mrs. Reed wrote; "try to keep out of it." "Do try to keep out of debt and save a little," her husband added. "I have been cursed with debts all my life and one of my greatest griefs now is that I cannot afford to make you an allowance." Speaking of his brother-in-law, he said, "He has no sense at all any more than have the balance of the Green family about money matters." There was reason for his bitterness: Tod, as the Reeds called Mrs. Green, had started off, with the last of the Green money, on a trip around the world. Mr. Reed commented with the savagery that had made him feared at the Arlington Club: "Yesterday came a large photograph of Tod mounted on a camel, holding with a death grip to a Bedouin sheik, who looked as if he could cheerfully chop her with a scimitar. Another son of the desert, remaining carefully out of reach, looks as if he had the best of his partner. In the background stands the Sphinx with a nauseated expression. . . . Surely the long line of Pharaohs were in luck to have become only a memory before Tod invaded Egypt. If Moses could have subsidized her there would have been eight instead of seven plagues."

Because he knew how much generosity lay behind such extravagant diatribes, just as he knew how much deep feeling for mankind went into the enthusiasm for Teddy, Reed loved and admired his father. But only after he was back in Portland, in the last few days around the deathbed, did he realize how much had been sacrificed for him and his brother Harry. Harry had just been graduated from Harvard, where he had lived, as Jack had lived, like a rich man's son. Perhaps Jack, thinking of Harry's kind of success, his election to the right clubs won by unimaginative conformity, won by doing nothing, by merely making an infallible distinction between the right people and the wrong, and thinking, too, of the conclusions he had already reached about Harvard, may have wondered if the results justified the strain under which his father had at last broken. But such doubts could not diminish his appreciation of the spirit, not merely uncomplaining but even ardent and gay, in which the sacrifices had been made.

C. J. Reed died on the morning of July 1, 1912. John Reed, who had thought of him as a friend as well as an indulgent father, felt for the first time a bitter grief. The city of Portland, though some of its leading men, as Jack knew, were secretly glad, paid official tribute. Reed's friends wrote him, Steffens, the men at 42 Washington Square, the men on the *American.* He was restless and tortured and would sometimes walk all night. He tried to write down what he felt and was shocked at the inadequacy of his verse. At last, sometime during the summer, he wrote:

> Calm he lies there,
> In the brave armor he alone could bear,
> With a proud shield of Honor at his side,
> And a keen sword of wit. And when the tide
> Mysterious—when the swift, exultant Spring
> Thrills all this hillside with awakening,
> Wild-flowers will know and love him, blossoming.

It would have been easier if he could have returned immediately to New York, but the complexities of the family's affairs kept him three months in Portland. There were old friends, of course, to visit, but they quickly lost their savor for him. As the first shock of his father's death passed, he longed more and more for his city, New York. Even a trip to the headwaters of the Amazon, which Harry Kemp suggested, seemed less exciting than the wanderings about the East Side he so deeply missed. Finally, out of his nostalgia for 42 Washington Square, came a poem, humorous but tender, *The Day in Bohemia.*

The book is dedicated to Lincoln Steffens—"one of us; the only man who understands my arguments":

Steffens, I hope I am doing no wrong to you
By dedicating this doggerel song to you;
P'raps you'll resent
The implied compliment,
But light-hearted Liberty seems to belong to you.

. . . .

Even in artists I notice a tendency
To let old Daily Bread gain the ascendancy,
Making that petty boss
Sort of a Setebos
'Stead of a useful but servile dependency.

How can an artist create his Utopia
With his best eye on the World's cornucopia?
See, for example;
There's recompense ample
In just writing this—let us call it—*epopæa*.

. . . .

Well, if these numbers recall a good year to you,
And, as to me, certain things that are dear to you,
Take them, you're welcome,
I'm with you till Hell come,
Friend Steffens, consider me quaffing a beer to you!

The poem describes a day: the morning at 42 Washington Square, then the office of the *American*, then a literary tea, and finally an evening of argument and revelry. It introduces a number of parodies, some of which had been published earlier, but for the most part it is a faithful reflection of what Reed loved in the life of the Village:

Yet we are free who live in Washington Square,
We dare to think as Uptown wouldn't dare,
Blazing our nights with argument uproarious;
What care we for a dull old world censorious
When each is sure he'll fashion something glorious?

He does not forget the tenement back-yards:

There spawn the overworked and underpaid
Mute thousands;—packed in buildings badly made,—
In stinking squalor penned,—and overflowing
On sagging fire-escapes.

But he is chiefly concerned with the rooms "where the immortal four spent many a blissful hour."

Apollo's beams our humble house adorn,
And wake th' immortal four on Tuesday morn;
Coincident, while still our ears we pound,
The loud alarm-clock gives a horrid sound.
With one bound, orient Osgood hits the floor.
(Cerberean timeclocks guard his office door.)
Reed, with a countenance whence joy has fled,
Drags the resisting Rogers from his bed.
But Andrews still the downy pillow presses,
While every feature deep disgust expresses;
And ere he once forsakes his virgin couch
Accumulates his early morning grouch.

At the *American* office he introduces Siddall, "the high-brow low-brow of the Magazine"; Albert Boyden, "the one who makes the wheels to go," "great editor, great hustler through and through"; J. S. Phillips, "poet a third and two-thirds editor"; Albert J. Nock, "an anarchist in everything but art." He describes an editorial conference on poetry, with Nock quoting Matthew Arnold against his quotations from Whitman, and the other editors calling for the police.

The party is at the studio of the great Umbilicus:

When young he studied on the Continent,—
Eleven years in galleries he spent,
Copied the Masters with minutest care,
Learned what they ate, and how they wore their hair

. . . .

At last he knew so much, he was so deft,
That neither vision, fire, nor self was left.

There we find the poet who produces one verse a year, the imitation Celt, the sedentary vagabond, the girl whose "job in

life is simply to inspire," the rich man "who tried to be Mae-
cenas and is Midas," the artist who talks about vice, the artist
who exists in dirt, and a dozen females—"the mild, the violent,
the stout, the thin." They talk—

> Cranks, cranks, cranks, cranks,—
> Blanks, blanks, blanks, blanks,—
> Talk about talking and think about thinking,
> And swallow each other without even blinking.

When some one rises to recite a sonnet, Reed retreats, and
arrives at 42 Washington Square in time to join the other three
of the immortal four for dinner. Bob Hallowell arrives, and
they meet Sam McCoy and Wolf, a young German engineer,
on the street:

> Balloon-like, Rogers bounces on ahead,
> Then slothful Samuel, less alive than dead,
> Ozzy and Herr, with one unmeaning grin,
> Talk gibberish you'll find no meaning in.
> Reed following, elated and erect,
> Bob Hallowell—gloves, hat and all correct.
> Old Andrews singing harshly,—music wrong,—
> Last, like a wounded snake, drags his slow length along.
> Paglieri's self directs us, with a leer
> To the round table waiting at the rear.

After they return to their rooms, and Hallowell lends them
money with which to placate their landlady, friends arrive:

> Lippmann,—calm, inscrutable,
> Thinking and writing clearly, soundly, well;
> All snarls of falseness swiftly piercing through,
> His keen mind leaps like lightning to the True;
>
> . . . .
>
> Our all unchallenged Chief! But . . . one
> Who builds a world, and leaves out all the fun,—
> Who dreams a pageant, gorgeous, infinite,
> And then leaves all the color out of it,—
> Who wants to make the human race, and me,
> March to a geometric Q.E.D.
>
> . . . .

A timid footstep,—enter then the eager
Keats-Shelley-Swinburne-Medieval-Seeger;
Poe's raven bang above Byronic brow,
And Dante's beak,—you have his picture now;
In fact he is, though feigning not to know it,
The popular conception of a Poet.

.   .   .   .

The unkempt Harry Kemp now thumps our door;
He who has girdled all the world and more.
Free as a bird, no trammels him can bind,
He rides a box-car as a hawk the wind.

They argue until midnight, and finally adjourn to the Lafay-
ette. There is the last and best of the incidental songs:

O let us humbly bow the neck
To George Syl-ves-ter Vi-er-eck
Who trolled us a merry little Continental stave
Concerning the Belly and the Phallus and the Grave—

It would have almost raised the hair
Of Oscar Wilde or Bau-de-laire
To hear Mr. Vi-er-eck so frank-ly rave
Concerning the Belly and the Phallus and the Grave—

And in the last an-al-y-sis
He says it nar-rows down to this:
A fig for the favors that the high gods gave!
Excepting the Belly and the Phallus and the Grave—

If you have drunk Life to the lees
You may console yourself with these;
For me there are some things that I do not crave
Among them the Belly and the Phallus and the Grave—
What ho! for the Belly and the Phallus and the Grave
The Belly and the Phallus
And the ballad very gallus
          And the Grave!

LATE in September, Reed finally started back to New York.
Sam McCoy, who was then in Indianapolis, had repeatedly

urged him to stop for a visit on his way across the continent. Reed sent him a card from Chicago, explaining that his financial condition would not permit any side-trips. "I've ridden the rails so far," he wrote, "and have stayed my belly for the past three days with a bunch of bananas." Whether that was literally true or not, Reed was quite penniless when he reached 42 Washington Square.

Some of the group had left. Seeger was in Paris, Lippmann, though he was soon to return for the founding of the *New Republic*, was at the moment assisting Schenectady's Socialist Mayor Lunn. Rogers was leaving for Cambridge. And Alan Osgood, blithest of the roommates, was dead. "He had genius," Reed wrote Alan's mother, "quite beyond us, and more than he himself realized. . . . It was always a joy to be with him. . . . We used to marvel at his unfailing laughter and kindness." Reed and Osgood had planned to sail before the mast, around the Cape of Good Hope to China. Now that, like so many other plans, could never be carried out. McCoy wrote a poem, "Youth," in tribute to Osgood and to the life that, he felt, could not be recaptured, and Reed, liking it, persuaded Phillips to publish it in the *American*.

Reed, too, felt that youth was slipping by, but for the moment he was happy at being back in New York. Edward Hunt was now working on the *American* and living at Number 42, and in the winter Reed was startled to run across another classmate, Robert Edmond Jones, thin and hungry, wandering from impresario to impresario. He and Hunt took Jones in, called upon Hallowell and other friends for assistance, and armed him for the conflict with New York.

Reed kept a card catalog of the manuscripts he sent to the magazines, labeled "Posthumous and Juvenile Works of J. S. Reed, Bart." There were fewer rejection slips now. Even some of the earlier stories, brought out and refurbished, were taken by editors who had learned to know the name of Reed. On the whole he had reason for satisfaction, but, after the elation of being back in the city dwindled away, he was more discontented than he had been since the morning in Paris when he woke up and found himself five years older. Steffens encouraged him:

"You haven't yet found your form, your 'lay,' your 'line,' as you wish to express it." When he did find his line, Steffens assured him, nothing could stop him. Reed was not so certain.

There was not much that he had published that seemed to him representative of what he had wanted to do. His articles for the *American* had, with the exception of the reminiscence of William James and the tribute to Copey, been routine exercises. The pair of short stories in the *Century* about the stupid but lucky M. Vidoq were mechanical, though he had enjoyed elaborating the humorous details and even made a third attempt with the same formula. He had exploited the same tricks of facetiousness in the two stories Willard Huntington Wright, who had been a classmate in their freshman year, had taken for the *Smart Set*. "Overboard" had been given the stamp of Julian Street's deft *Saturday Evening Post* manner. "The Swimmers" was derivative melodrama.

He felt better, of course, about the poetry. "The Wanderer to His Heart's Desire" and "Deep-Water Song," were, it is true, a little too much after the fashion of Richard Hovey and Bliss Carman, but they were firmer and fresher than anything he had written in the same vein in college. Certain occasional poems he had done for the *American*—"April," "A Song for May," and "June in the City"—were clean and pleasant. He had grown oratorical in "Revolt," which Viereck's *International* had taken:

> Oh, there is peace in wrong-doing,
>   Joy in the blasphemous thing,
> Sweet is the taste of a prodigal waste,—
>   Lawless the songs that we sing.
> And you, who are holy, have made it,—
>   Have ticketed men and their ways,—
> Have taken the zest from all that was best
>   In these contemptible days.

In a few poems he had gone beyond Vagabondia and Bohemia. The love of New York, city of enchantment, almost inarticulate as yet, had reached partial expression in "A Hymn to Manhattan" and in "The Foundations of a Skyscraper":

Clamor of unknown tongues, and hiss of arc
Clashing and blending; screech of wheel on wheel,—
Naked, a giant's back, tight-muscled, stark,
Glimpse of mighty shoulder, etched in steel.

Even his romanticism achieved maturity in the new and re-sourceful resonance of his lines. "Tamburlaine," which he called "an organ prelude," begins:

A voiceless shaking of the air . . .
Then a low shuddering of sound,
Vibrant, thunderous, like the profound
Pulsation of great wings. O rare—
In the high-vaulted transept's gloom
Wakes sonant echoing, and the deep
Tone-breakers gather ponderously and leap
From beam to beam, like sullen boom
Of lazy summer thunder. *See!*
On the bare rock-rimmed Scythian plain
The swarthy shepherd Tamburlaine . . .

And it ends:

Falls like a sea-wind at sundown
The full-toned sonorous battle-chant;
Yet the sound-surf reverberant
Rolls the dim-springing nave adown,
Rolls thunderous—subsiding—low—
In a burnt, treeless land where loom
The world's high mountains, lies a tomb—
Vibrant the shuddering tremolo—
A tomb half-hid with drifting sand,
Nameless—in Samarkand.

In "Sangar" romanticism served the purposes of allegory. The poem, which Lincoln Steffens insisted on regarding as "a fierce poem denouncing me," was meant as a tribute to his settlement of the MacNamara case. In the midst of battle—

> leaps one into the press—
> The Hell 'twixt front and front—
> Sangar, bloody and torn of dress,
>   (He has borne the brunt.)
> "Hold!" cries, "Peace! God's Peace!
>   Heed ye what Christus says—"
> And the wild battle gave surcease
>   In amaze.

Sangar tells the men on both sides that they are brothers. He is called a blasphemer by the priest, and is slain by his own son, and the war goes on.

> Oh, there was joy in Heaven when Sangar came.
> Sweet Mary wept, and bathed and bound his wounds,
> And God the Father healed him of despair,
> And Jesus gripped his hand, and laughed and laughed.

His poetry was praised by poets he respected, Edwin Arlington Robinson, Louis Untermeyer, Sara Teasdale, Harriet Monroe. Albert Jay Nock, though he might quarrel with Reed on esthetic principles, had no doubt that his colleague was a poet. Percy MacKaye wrote warmly about "Sangar," and Reed replied: "I can't tell you how much I appreciate your note appreciating my 'Sangar.' No one has ever before written me so about anything I ever did. It opens up vast possibilities and stimulates my imagination to conceive a time when I shall be able to tell people a little part of the glorious things I see. Every day of my life I see more of them."

Reed was in dead earnest about his poetry, and it distressed him to realize that poetry could never win for him the kind of success that he was determined to achieve. The practical men of the Dutch Treat Club told him that poetry was dead. He knew that they were wrong. He had read nothing as yet of Frost's or Sandburg's, but he realized that Robinson was trying to say something that had not been said, and he picked up and read with curiosity and satisfaction Vachel Lindsay's *Rhymes to be Traded for Bread*. And he was beginning to understand what was wrong with poetry. "I have found," he wrote Harriet Monroe, "that among men of whatever class, if they are deeply stirred by emotion, poetry appeals; as, indeed, all the arts appeal. The apathetic, mawkishly-religious middle class are our enemies. . . . Art must cease, I think, to be for the esthetic enjoyment of a few highly sensitive minds. It must go back to its original sources."

The magazine editors were degrading poetry. That, he discovered, was not all they were degrading. In the spring of 1912 he had written a little sketch of New York life called "Where the Heart Is," the first of many such sketches he was to write, born out of his nocturnal adventures and the love and exaltation that the city roused in him. It was not a neat empty tale with a surprise ending; it was just a story of Martha, who had left the Haymarket, where she was a dancing partner, to see Europe. She had done much respectable sight-seeing, and then, when her funds were low, had become the mistress of an amorous and wealthy Portuguese, who had taken her to Rio de Janeiro and kept her in luxury. But she could not forget New York, and back she came to the Haymarket.

One editor after another rejected the story. Finally one of them explained: "A magazine is bought by the year. The father of the children, counting on its past record of avoiding the treatment of sex problems, allows the magazine to come into the house and to lie carelessly on the library table. His children read it, even before he looks it over himself. He counts on us to be the censor. And that is the main reason why magazines must be very careful about the points of view they present in their stories. You have been working at the *American*; you ought to know their point of view. You can't over-ride such a proposition." Such a theme, he concluded, could be treated only by a Daudet, a Flaubert, or a de Maupassant: "The very delicacy of the problem renders necessary the highest form of literary skill."

Reed understood. "Where the Heart Is" was his first contribution to the *Masses*.

BUT John Reed loved success. He was flattered by being mentioned in F. P. A.'s column. He was very proud of being a member of the Dutch Treat Club. Irvin Cobb and James Montgomery Flagg called him by his first name. He talked about literary markets and prices with Julian Street and the Irwin brothers. He listened to the jests of Tom Masson and Charles Hanson Towne. He knew how much Owen Johnson was paid per word and Charles Dana Gibson per picture. They represented success, tangible, measurable, demonstrable success.

When he had a chance to do a play for the Dutch Treat Club, to be produced at its annual dinner at Delmonico's, he was as excited as he had been when he made the football team at Morristown or the *Lampoon* at Harvard. Bill Daly, one of the editors of *Everybody's*, composed the music. Reed wrote the words, and, despite the impressiveness of their reputations, would not allow the professional humorists of the club to alter a line. He hectored the performers as disrespectfully as he had bullied the Harvard cheering section. It was his show, and he insisted on doing it his own way. But he was very proud that he had been asked to do it, and he invited many of his friends to the dinner at which it was produced.

Everymagazine, an Immorality Play was the fruit of two years in the *American* office, two years of acceptances and rejections, two years of Dutch Treat Club luncheons. Much of what Reed wrote about the magazines was what every Dutch Treater felt. No one, for example, could be anything but jubilant when Charles Hanson Towne, dressed in bombazine with drooping curls and knitting needles, representing *Century*, *Scribner's*, and *Harper's*, sang:

> You are mistresses of Mammon;
>   I'm a literary virgin—
> All the warmness of a salmon,
>   All the passion of a sturgeon.
> I'm aristocratic, very,
> I'm a live obituary
> Of the giants literary
>   Who have given up the ghost.
> In illuminating snatches
>   Since the spring of Sixty-one
> I've been publishing dispatches
>   From the battle of Bull Run.

With life I do not bother,
    I'm caviar to most;
In fact I am the Father,
    The Son, and Holy Ghost.

Of refinement I'm a symbol
    On your literary table;
All of culture in a thimble
    By the new Atlantic cable.
And though Congress does not heed me,
And the public does not read me,
I'm convinced the people need me
    From the Hudson to the Coast.
O when Trollope kicked the bucket
    And when Dickens was no more
I had half a mind to chuck it
    Till I found the Civil War.
Aristocratic rather,
    Exclusiveness my boast;
In fact I am the Father,
    The Son, and Holy Ghost.

And the wits of New York must have relished the *Outlook's*
song:

I'm a moderate reformer
Just because reform's the thing.
I've a practical religion
And my hat is in the ring.
I'm a catch-as-can uplifter
With a strong belief in jail.
It's a policy that gathers in the kale.

I'm the blooming Christian Herald
With the Christian part in hock.
I'm the Homely Ladies' Journal
All excepting Mister Bok.
I'm the Rev'rend Doctor Parkhurst,
I'm all that sort of chaps.
In fact, I'm Hamilton W.—Perhaps!

It was amusing when *McClure's* complained that it had "raised so much hell" and "done it so well" that there was nothing left to say, or when the *American* explained how to blend reading matter and advertisements. The *Cosmopolitan* was fair game:

> Every month I'm full of spice
> And naughty Robert Chambers makes it nice.
> Some lingerie, a glimpse of stocking.
> Lips unlocking, nothing shocking.
> And Gibson hints at hidden beauty,
> Lovers' booty, tutti frutti.
> Read me once and I'll bet I can
> Refresh the tired business man.

It was a little more pointed to sing:

> An honest magazine
> Needn't tremble to be seen
> Abowing to a business man
> And taking off his hat.
> And it isn't so surprising
> That we chase the advertising
> But alas we've got a secret worse than that.

The grand finale was entitled "The Freedom of the Press." There are such lines as

> A silly tale I've heard
> That round the town is flying
> That every monthly organ
> Is owned by J. P. Morgan.
> Now isn't that absurd?
> Somebody must be lying.

And again—

> We're all agreed, I guess,
> In this ourselves we flatter,

No influence external
Controls the monthly journal.
It is our great success,
Unbiased reading matter.

The chorus goes—

It must not be inferred
That wealth is what we're after.
We greet that gibe absurd
With supercilious laughter.
The criminal and grafter,
From wickedness deterred,
Revere the printed word,
Revere the printed word.

Of course none of it was taken as serious satire. Everybody congratulated Reed, who sold copies of *The Day in Bohemia* and grew shrill-voiced and happy as the liquor and the praise went to his head. But the suspicion persisted in the minds of some members of the club that they had somehow been betrayed. Samuel Merwin was to grumble for twenty years, "The trouble with Jack Reed was that he wasn't housebroken." And Julian Street would save his venom until, ten years after Reed's death, the *Saturday Evening Post* would pay him well for putting it down on paper. Just as, in college, Reed had irritated the men his ambitions should have counseled him to please, so, among the high-paid hacks of New York, the eagerness for success clashed with some impulse of defiance, and defiance won.

VI

PROFESSION: POET

IT TOOK John Reed a surprisingly long time to discover that paying magazines get what they pay for. He could not learn from the experience of others; he had to find out for himself. What he had wanted on his arrival in New York in the spring of 1911 was success, in terms of both money and recognition, and he wanted it so badly that some of his friends were worried. But he wanted it on his own terms. His integrity was not a matter of articulate·principles; it was, rather, a deep-rooted stubbornness, an almost physiological necessity to be himself. When he had learned to fashion salable commodities, and the lust to see his name in print had been gratified, he began to wonder if this was all he wanted; and what people called his vanity was strong enough to tell him that it wasn't. There was no satisfaction in winning applause for conforming to the standards of others, he once more discovered; the only recognition that counted was recognition for what he really was. Two years of experimentation were necessary to convince him, but in the end he was convinced.

Even after he had learned his lesson, he did not abandon the idea of the sort of success that the Dutch Treat Club appreciated. He adopted the simple and familiar compromise of doing two kinds of writing: the kind the editors liked and the kind he liked. He knew the dangers of such a division of purpose: he had once written a story called "Success" about a young man who, beginning with a consecrated determination to write an epic in his spare time, ended by rejoicing in the adaptation of lines from his masterpiece to the purposes of a pink pill advertisement. But he could not believe that these dangers existed for him.

For the publication of what he wanted to write, there was, fortunately, the *Masses*, which Piet Vlag had founded in January, 1911, as "an outgrowth of the cooperative side of Socialist activity." Thomas Seltzer, the first editor, drew heavily on the fiction of Europe, printing stories by Tolstoy, Chirikov, Sudermann, and Bjorkman. Many of the muckrakers and Socialist intellectuals contributed—John Spargo, Gustavus Myers, George R. Kirkpatrick, W. J. Ghent, and Eugene Wood—and Art Young, Charles Winter, and Maurice Becker did cartoons.

During 1911 and 1912 the magazine limped aimlessly from left to right. Horatio Winslow succeeded Seltzer as editor and filled the magazine with his own stories. Piet Vlag injected heavy propaganda for the cooperatives. All sorts of persons contributed occasional articles or stories: Thomas L. Masson, Inez Haynes Gillmore, Samuel Hopkins Adams, Will Irwin. Except for attacks on the direct action theories of the I.W.W. and defenses of parliamentarianism by Eugene Wood, Ellis O. Jones, Victor Berger, and Walter Lippmann, the *Masses* was indifferent to economic and political struggles, and even in literature it was a long way from the vanguard.

Piet Vlag, whose sacrifices had kept the *Masses* alive, became discouraged. Though the magazine sold for five cents a copy, the circulation remained low. Finally, in the autumn of 1912, he proposed to merge it with a suffragist paper in Chicago. But the magazine, despite all its wavering, had succeeded in creating a group of writers and artists that had some sort of common purpose. Of the founders, Eugene Wood, Hayden Carruth, Ellis O. Jones, Thomas Seltzer, Horatio Winslow, Art Young, and Charles and Alice Winter remained loyal. Inez Haynes Gillmore and Maurice Becker had become firm supporters. Mary Heaton Vorse and John Sloan had begun to contribute. Two of the workers in the Intercollegiate Socialist Society, Leroy Scott and William English Walling, were interested. A number of these men and women met in the Winters' studio and decided, at Art Young's suggestion, to invite Max Eastman, until recently an instructor in esthetics at Columbia, to become responsible editor of a rejuvenated *Masses.*

The magazine sought to be the expression, on the highest literary and artistic level, of the insurgent spirit in American life. Out of the middle-class revolt at the turn of the century. with its muckraking and its trust-busting, its progressive governors and its single-tax mayors, had come a great hope. The renaissance that John Reed had observed at Harvard had been only one seething crest on a great wave. The new insurgency was marked neither by unity nor clarity, but it had vigor and it was ubiquitous. Scarcely a writer or artist who was to have importance in the twenties was untouched by it. It found political expression in anarchism as well as Socialism, and single-taxers were allied with suffragists, free-lovers, and birth-controllers. It owed much to the discovery that urban life made possible the escape from provincial Victorianism, and yet it was in no small part a revolt against the standardization that was supposed to have been wrought by the machine and the city. Vachel Lindsay and Sherwood Anderson, dreading industrialism, were as much a part of it as Carl Sandburg, who sang the beauty of industry. It welcomed any attack on convention, and the same men and women wrote for the *Masses* and for Mencken's *Smart Set;* but it made room for the Puritanism of Upton Sinclair and the piety of the Christian Socialists. It subscribed to the principles of realism in art, but its politics tended towards the romantic. It had the seriousness of strong convictions and the gayety of great hopes.

John Reed was more a part of this than he knew. He did not suspect how many people shared his belief that literature must be emancipated from the stupidity and triviality of the bourgeoisie and from the commercialism of the profit-making magazines. The spell that New York cast upon him in his midnight adventures was felt by other young writers. He was not the only one who loved the bravery of the poor and grew indignant at their suffering. Nor was he the only son of a Bull Moose father who laughed at the trumpetings of Teddy and pledged his allegiance to Eugene Debs and Big Bill Haywood.

When he heard of the new plans for the *Masses,* John Reed

wanted to help. Eastman told him that stories were needed, and he immediately thought of the little sketches he had written with so much affection and pleasure and had had so persistently rejected. Eastman praised his stories, selected "Where the Heart Is" for the January issue, and urged Reed to send something every month. The realization, at the very beginning of the new venture, that there were men like Reed, men who wanted and needed the *Masses,* was one of the things that made the board of editors willing to take up the burden of debt and go on.

With the March issue he was listed among the contributing editors. In the meantime he had drafted a statement of purpose. "We refuse to commit ourselves to any course of action," he said, "except this: to do with the *Masses* exactly what we please. No magazine has ever done that in this country and preserved a wide influence. The *Masses* is neither a closet magazine nor a quarterly philosophic review. But we have perfect faith that there exists in America a wide public, alert, alive, bored with the smug procession of magazine platitudes, to whom What We Please will be as a fresh wind." It was the Reed note, with just a touch of swagger in such phrases as, "We don't even intend to conciliate our readers." He paid his respects to the *American* and the other magazines for which he had written: "Poems, stories, and drawings rejected by the capitalistic press on account of their excellence will find a welcome in this magazine." Defiance was the rock on which the *Masses* was to be built.

But the defiance was not to be a meaningless gesture. "The broad purpose of the *Masses,*" he wrote, "is a social one: to everlastingly attack old systems, old morals, old prejudices—the whole weight of outworn thought that dead men have saddled upon us—and to set up new ones in their places. Standing on the common sidewalk, we intend to lunge at spectres—with a rapier rather than a broad-axe, with frankness rather than innuendo. We intend to be arrogant, impertinent, in bad taste, but not vulgar. We will be bound by no one creed or theory of social reform, but will express them all, providing they be radical. . . . Sensitive to all new winds that blow, never rigid in a single view or phase of life, such is our ideal for the *Masses.*" It was a statement to which all the young radicals of 1913, all those who wanted more than Woodrow Wilson's New Freedom, could subscribe. "And if," John Reed added, "we want to change our minds about it—well, why shouldn't we?"

Although the statement was somewhat altered before it appeared in the magazine, Reed had expressed the spirit of the enterprise with considerable exactness. It called itself "a revolutionary not a reform magazine," but except for Max Eastman's editorials under the heading "Knowledge and Revolution" and William English Walling's page of news about the Socialist movement, it devoted little space to discussion of radical principles. What boiled up on its pages was exactly the kind of chaotic revolt that John Reed felt inside himself, a powerful dissatisfaction and an unformulated hope. At first the artists— Art Young, Maurice Becker, and John Sloan—gave more effective expression to this insurgency than any of the writers, but gradually, in poems by Arturo Giovannitti, Louis Untermeyer, and Harry Kemp, in Reed's sketches, and in Howard Brubaker's paragraphs, there was a literature that matched the art.

The editors, especially the younger ones, enjoyed their work. Untermeyer and Reed had been entrusted with the responsibility of selecting the poetry, and they shared their discoveries. Untermeyer wrote Reed: "Victor Jorbert is a find, a gem of the first water and a poet of purest ray serene. He is of the Elect, the Cognoscenti. I hail him and thank you for introducing him to me. There are lines in his stirring ode (or is it a march) that seem influenced by J. Gordon Coogler, but this is petty carping. I believe Mr. Jorbert is worthy of a place next to that Mr. Kennedy whose noble lines to 'Bergson of Dynamic Mind' are (to me) immortal:

> Read Ida Tarbell's words; all noble deeds record;
> Learn of Dr. E. B. Davis in New York at Bedford.

What a couplet! I applaud the sentiment no less than the music —and gnash my metaphoric bicuspids in awful envy."

By the time *Everymagazine* had been produced and the great men of the Dutch Treat Club had had time to reflect on its implications, John Reed was associated with a group of men and women who were interested in something more than markets. It had taken him two years to do it, but at last he was looking straight towards the future.

MABEL DODGE came home from Florence, where she had spent three years in expensively remaking a villa. "Remember, it is ugly in America," she sobbed to her son. "We have left everything worth while behind us. America is all machinery and money-making and factories—it is ugly, ugly, ugly!" But she decided to make the best of it. She devoted her energies and her showmanship to staging the famous exhibition that introduced post-impressionist and cubist art to America, and, in her home at 23 Fifth Avenue, she created a salon, to which artists, actors, anarchists, Socialists, I.W.W.'s, celebrities, eccentrics, and nonentities came. Hutchins Hapgood, Arthur Lee, Andrew Dasburg, Marsden Hartley, Lee Simonson, Lincoln Steffens, Charles Demuth, Jo Davidson, Helen Westley, Emma Goldman, they all were her guests. There was food and drink and cigarettes, and sometimes lively arguments, and always there was Mabel Dodge, possessive, adroit, sensitive.

Of course John Reed went to Mabel Dodge's. Half of the editors of the *Masses* and all the members of the Liberal Club were regular attendants. He went and enjoyed the show. His life had become almost as full as it had been at Harvard. There was his paid work at the *American* and his volunteer work on the *Masses*. He had written a three-act play and had a novel in hand. He was called upon at regular intervals to try to straighten out the financial difficulties of the Reeds and Greens. In the early spring he and Bobby Jones took a walking trip, and, being caught in the rain, found shelter in an empty house. Reported by neighbors to the police, they were saved from jail only because Reed remembered that an old Portland friend, Benjamin Wistar Morris, the architect, lived nearby.

In such a life an evening at Mabel Dodge's was only an incident. But then one night Big Bill Haywood was there and talked about the Paterson strike, telling why the silk-workers had gone out, and what had happened to them. Reed liked the calm and unaffected way he talked to the strange gathering of society women and Bohemians. This was the candor, the in-souciance, John Reed admired.

He wanted to see Haywood in action, and he wanted to see the strike. He went to Paterson early in the morning of April 28. It was cold, and there was a light rain. At first the streets were empty, but a score of policemen soon appeared. Workers began to gather on the porches of the company houses that lined the street across from the mill. To escape the rain Reed went onto one of the porches, and used the excuse to begin talking with the three or four men who were standing there. He was amazed at the calmness with which people went about the eating of breakfast.

Policemen broke up a group of men who had taken shelter under the canopy of a saloon. Two detectives arrested a striker, and there was some booing. Some boys yelled at the detectives, and a policeman kicked them. An officer came to the porch on which Reed was standing and ordered the men to disperse. They said that they lived in the house, and the officer, order-ing them to get inside, turned to Reed and told him to move on. Reed informed Officer McCormick that he was there by permission of the occupants and had a right to stay there.

"Never mind," said the officer. "Do what I tell you. Come off of there, and come off damn quick."

Reed said that he wouldn't. McCormick seized him by the arm, and jerked him to the sidewalk, where another policeman took his other arm. "Now you get to hell off this street," he said.

"I won't get off this street or any other street," Reed an-swered. "If I'm breaking any law, you arrest me."

McCormick didn't want to arrest him, and said so profanely. As politely as he could, Reed said, "I've got your number. Now will you give me your name?"

"Yes," McCormick bellowed, "and I've got your number. I'll arrest you."

Reed was taken to the jail and put in a cell, about four feet by seven, in which eight pickets had recently been kept for twenty-four hours without food or water. In a few minutes forty pickets were brought into the jail, and Reed could hear them singing and cheering. Before long he was led into the court of Recorder Carroll, a man "with the intelligent, cruel, merciless face of the ordinary police court magistrate." He was permitted to tell his own story, and then McCormick recited a tale that, Reed felt, he was by no means smart enough to have invented himself. Carroll asked Reed his occupation.

"Poet," said Reed.

"Twenty days," said Carroll.

Carlo Tresca, the fiery Italian strike-leader was in one of the cells of the Passaic County jail, and was explaining the class struggle to his Negro cellmate, when John Reed was brought in. He was so obviously respectable that Tresca was suspicious. He told Reed who he was, but he would not respond to the warm greeting with which the stranger hailed the name of Tresca. When Reed persisted in asking questions about the strike, Tresca's suspicions were confirmed, and he refused to talk. The three of them spent the night in bewilderment and hostility, Reed lying awake and smoking one cigarette after another.

The next morning Bill Haywood, who had been arrested and was being held without any charge, discovered Reed, thought he was there as a reporter, and asked him what his assignment was. He was amused and pleased when he learned the truth, and he took Reed around to introduce him to the strikers, including the apologetic Tresca. Quinlan, Haywood, and Tresca were all in jail at the time, and there were some fifty strikers.

Reed was particularly interested in the silk-workers, but he did not fail to study the normal functions of a county jail—"a place," he wrote, "that takes in weak men and turns them out weaker." The food was worse than that on the *Bostonian:* the bread stale and soggy; the salt and pepper boxes full of insects; the soup rank with decayed vegetables, spoiled meat, and dead vermin. ("You just gotta be careful they don't get in your spoon," the prisoners told him.) Fourteen hours out of every twenty-four were spent in the verminous cell, and there was no escape from the noise of the prison or from the stench of the open toilets.

Except for the strikers, the men in the jail seemed hopelessly debauched. There were men who, reduced to begging, had been sentenced to six months or a year for first offenses. An insane man and a man far advanced in venereal disease were locked up with the others. An idiot boy of eighteen was kept in the jail after his father's arrest because nobody knew what to do with him. A normal, intelligent boy of seventeen, who had been convicted of stealing a bicycle, was associating with confirmed criminals. Many of them were sick men, and the treatment the doctor gave, on his rare visits, was farcical. Crap games and cockroach races were the chief forms of amusement. The guards and the trustees were eager to be bribed, and men with a little cash could get whatever they wanted, from decent food to cocaine.

It would have been wholly depressing if it had not been for the silk-workers, who, in their variety of languages, educated John Reed in the events of the strike. It was the second strike in two years, and it had been going on for more than two months when Reed heard Haywood talking about it at Mabel Dodge's. Within two weeks after the strike call, more than twenty thousand men and women were out. The picket lines stood firm in the face of organized terror. There were daily arrests; picket lines were charged and strikers clubbed. On April 19 Valentine Modestino was shot, and fifteen thousand strikers attended his funeral. Elizabeth Gurley Flynn, fresh from the victories of Lawrence, stirred the workers of Paterson to passionate loyalty and indomitable courage. Haywood's calm, masterful leadership gave them confidence. When school-teachers spoke against the strike, the children picketed the schools. The leaders were arrested again and again, but the picket lines stood firm.

Reed was in jail only four days. The New York papers made more fuss about one reporter, Police Captain McBride said bitterly, than they had about the scores of strikers he had jailed. Robert Rogers, writing with condescending humor to Edward Hunt, was, for all his facetiousness, quite accurate in saying that the judge was a fool and that Reed would be twenty times the menace to Paterson law and order he had been before he was arrested. Hunt, in the meantime, was not only looking out for Reed's comfort in the matter of food and cigarettes; he was working for his release. Somewhat regretfully, John Reed left Sheriff Radcliff's hotel.

He had been there long enough to learn a great deal. He really saw and felt what for a long time he had theoretically known: "that the manufacturers get all they can out of labor, pay as little as they must, and permit the existence of great masses of unemployed in order to keep wages down; that the forces of the state are on the side of property against the propertyless." He also intensified his feeling that the Socialist Party was "duller than religion and almost as little in touch with labor." When an Italian weaver wanted to know why the Socialists were not helping in the Paterson strike, Reed, already a partisan, told him that "a good share of the Socialist Party and the American Federation of Labor have forgotten all about the class struggle, and seem to be playing a little game with capitalistic rules, called 'Button, button, who's got the vote?' "

Most important of all, he discovered the gayety and courage and fineness of militant workers. "When it came time for me to go out," he wrote, "I said good-bye to all those gentle, alert, brave men, ennobled by something greater than themselves. They were the strike—not Bill Haywood, not Gurley Flynn, not any other individual. And if they should lose all their leaders, other leaders would arise from the ranks, even as they rose, and the strike would go on! Think of it! Twelve years they have been losing strikes—twelve solid years of disappointments and incalculable suffering. They must not lose again."

REED could think of nothing but Paterson. Though he was as yet a hesitant and embarrassed public speaker, he addressed meetings on behalf of the strike. He not only went again and again to Paterson, but he insisted on his friends' going—Mabel Dodge and Hunt and Bobby Jones and Walter Lippmann. Haywood got him to speak to the strikers. He found, however, that there was something he could do that was more effective than speaking: he could teach them to sing. With all the tricks he had learned as cheer-leader, and with the perfect self-abandonment of which he was capable, he led them in singing their own songs, and he taught them new songs, Harvard songs with Paterson words. He took particular pleasure in teaching them the song that the Institute of 1776 had adopted as its own. It had originated, he discovered, in the French revolution, and it tickled him to be giving it back, after the snobs had had it for more than a century, to the people to whom it belonged. Sometimes as many as thirty thousand people would follow Reed in shouting out "The Marseillaise" or "Solidarity Forever." They loved the singing, these warm-blooded men of Paterson, and they loved John Reed. One Italian said to him, "You make us to be happy."

He could talk of nothing but the strike. When F. P. A. had lunch with him, our own Samuel Pepys recorded: "He told me how great a man is Bill Haywood, and it may be as Jack saith. Also he told me that the Industrial Workers of the World are sorely misjudged and that the tayles in the publick prints of their blood-thirstiness are lies·told by the scriveners. And out of it all I wish I did know how to appraise what is true and what is false, but I am too ignorant, and ill-fitted to judge truly."

Reed wanted to do more than talk. Police terror was becoming fiercer. During a striker's trial one girl in the audience was given sixty days for smiling, and another thirty days for gasping at the sentence. There were more and more heads battered, more and more arrests, longer and longer sentences. At last, in the middle of May, the idea of the Paterson pageant was born. Percy MacKaye, whose experience with pageants Reed respected, enthusiastically urged him to go ahead.

For three weeks Reed worked at nothing else, sleeping little and then with his clothes on. The leaders were divided: Haywood favored the plan, but Tresca at first thought it was impossible. The strikers were delighted. Reed met with a large group of them, and, though they spoke at least a dozen different languages, managed to understand and be understood. Out of a single sentence came the theme of the pageant: "We were frightened when we went in," said one of the girls, describing the first day of the strike, "but we were singing when we came out." Out of other such hints the pageant grew.

Reed plunged back and forth between Paterson and New York. In Paterson the rehearsals promised success. Responding to Reed's enthusiasm, the strikers evolved the details of each scene, lost their self-consciousness, and felt themselves re-enacting the stirring events of their own drama. In New York plans moved too slowly. Mabel Dodge, Jessie Ashley, Hutchins Hapgood, Edward Hunt, Ernest Poole, and others set about the raising of funds, but only enough could be secured to rent Madison Square Garden for one night. They did what they could, but preparations were slow.

Reed, paying little attention to practical details, concentrated on plans for production. Bobby Jones was drafted to design the scenery, a panorama of Paterson factories, and he did a poster of a crouched, shouting, challenging workman that was to appear year after year on I.W.W. publications. A runway was built so that the strikers could march on and off the platform. On the afternoon of June 7, a thousand strikers were brought to New York for the final rehearsal.

New York was tense. The cry of sabotage had been raised against the I.W.W., and the newspapers were raging against what Sheriff Julius Harburger called "sedition, treasonable utterances, un-American doctrines, advocating sabotage, fulmination of paranoiacal ebullitions, inflammatory, hysterical unsound doctrines." Harburger sat in a box near the stage. He wanted to forbid the playing of "The Marseillaise," but, as he regretfully told reporters, a judge had ruled that it was legal. He had to content himself with declaring, "Just let anybody say one word of disrespect to the flag, and I will stop the show so quickly it will take their breath away."

An hour before the pageant began, the streets on every side of the Garden were full. The cheaper seats were all taken, but the rows that were priced at a dollar or two dollars a seat were largely vacant. A hurried conference decided that the crowd would be admitted at a quarter apiece. It was nearly an hour, filled with the shouting of sellers of pamphlets and the confusion of the entering crowd, before the pageant could begin.

"The pageant," said the program, "represents a battle between the working class and the capitalist class conducted by the Industrial Workers of the World. . . . It is a conflict between two social forces." The first scene showed the mills at six o'clock on a February morning. The mill whistle sounded the call to work. Bent and shivering, the workers entered the mills, and the sound of the looms began. Then there was silence, followed by the mounting passion of "The Marseillaise" as the striking workers marched from the factories. In a second episode brutal police clubbed pickets, and Modestino was hit by a hired gunman's bullet. At Modestino's funeral, after the strikers placed evergreen twigs and red carnations upon his coffin, Flynn, Tresca, and Haywood spoke. A great mass meeting at Haledon and a May Day procession followed. The hungry strikers sent their children away to be cared for by the workers of other cities. Finally the strikers shouted their support for Haywood's demand for an eight-hour day and sang "The Internationale."

The audience, many of whom had wept at the funeral of Modestino, rose and sang with the strikers. It was, to a greater extent than any one had anticipated, a workers' audience, and they went out from the Garden with a new faith in themselves and their class. The intellectuals saw visions. Susan Glaspell dreamed of what the theatre might be. Hutchins Hapgood felt the promise of a new order in which "self-expression in industry and art among the masses may become a rich reality, spreading a human glow over the whole of humanity," an order "from which we shall all be gainers—in real life, in justice, in art, in love." Even the reporters were impressed, and the next day's papers spoke of the pageant with respect, though editorials subsequently pointed out that it was produced "under the direction of a destructive organization opposed in spirit and antagonistic in action to all the forces which have upbuilded this republic," and that its motive was "to inspire hatred, to induce violence which may lead to the tearing down of the civil state and the institution of anarchy."

Only the thousands in Paterson were disappointed, for, three weeks later, Jessie Ashley and Fred Boyd made their report and announced, not the huge profit that everyone who had seen the crowd in the Garden expected, but a deficit. Profits can not be made from single performances when scenery costs hundreds of dollars and other expenses are in proportion. But the strikers could think only of the dwindled funds that the pageant should have replenished. What Paterson had lost the working class had gained, but that could not be apparent to men and women entering the fifth month of a bitter, bloody strike.

JOHN REED, at the time when the Paterson strikers learned the truth, was on his way to Europe. A month after the pageant he was irritating Gertrude Stein by telling her stories about witches in Spain which she, having spent months in Spain, did not like and did not believe. A fortnight later he, Robert Jones, and Carl Van Vechten—Mabel Dodge's *jeunes gens assortis*, in Miss Stein's phrase—were domiciled among the grandeurs of the Villa Curonia in Florence.

Paterson seemed to be merely an episode in an active life. The pageant was something to be talked about with Gordon Craig and other visitors at the villa. Muriel and Paul Draper arrived one evening with Arthur Rubinstein and John McMullin. There were triangular arguments between Mrs. Draper, Jones, and Van Vechten about painting. Van Vechten quarreled with Rubinstein and Mrs. Draper about Bach. John Reed, hitching up his pants and impatiently pawing curly hair, called them all fools. Mabel Dodge sat quietly, missed nothing, enjoyed everything.

There was a ghost: "It doesn't appear or anything. It simply smothers you. You wake up suffocating, and always almost out of bed. The story is a simple one. It was an Italian woman who died there, and who loved the place and Mabel Dodge, so that she doesn't want any one else to stay. We weren't told anything specific about it. But afterward, we found out that lots of people had been actually driven away by it. And all had the same symptoms. So tonight we had a couple of priests down from the monastery on the nearby hill, with acolytes and censers, and little horse-hair rattles to sprinkle holy water with, and they put on their vestments and went through the service of Exorcism of Devils, parading through the house, chanting, intoning, and carrying on like all get out."

He loved the villa, "an ancient Medici affair, with contours supposed to be by Michel Angelo, and a great courtyard by Brunnelleschi." Living there, overlooking all Florence and the whole Arno valley, he felt "like the fisherman caught up by the genie's daughter and carried to the mountain-top." The room in which he slept was hung with strips of crimson damask, edged with gold, which came from an old church in Venice, and there were great fourteenth century armoires reaching to the ceiling. From the terrace on which it opened, he could look out over cypresses and oleanders and grapevines and olive trees to the rolling Tuscan hills, and could hear a peasant on the road to Siena singing "a song that must have come out of the East with the Etrurians before Rome."

When Mabel Dodge organized a motor trip, and they visited the old towns to the south of Florence, sleeping one night in a monastery on a bleak mountain and the next upon the shore of Lake Trasimeno, he was excited by the palaces, delicate but barbaric, of Siena, by the high towers of San Gianiguano and its view over vineyards and mountains, by the Sodoma frescoes at Monte Olivetto and the Giottos at Assisi. Each town as he came to it seemed to him the perfect place in which to live.

And back in Florence there was swimming every day in a tank at the Villa Bombichi. Always a place to swim meant happiness for Reed, but this was a tank built by Michel Angelo, set in an olive grove and backed by a hill of cypresses. Swimming and talk—and Mabel Dodge kept the house full of "smart, clever, hard Londoners, very *raffiné* and effete," and the flower of "ultra-modern, ultra-civilized Continental society." She took care that each of the visitors heard about the pageant and read *The Day in Bohemia*. She knew not only how to capture lions but also how to show them off.

Mabel Dodge had become rather more than John Reed's benefactress. She attracted him as she had attracted and was to attract many other men. She, too, had revolted against the deathly dreariness of the bourgeoisie. She, too, wanted life, though, as he was to discover, she wanted it only for herself. Her immovable calm and her kind of naive wilfulness seemed soft and feminine, but she was ruthless and could be terribly exacting. She liked John Reed because he was alive. "I have never known a great man or woman," she wrote, after she had known many, "who did not first of all give one a feeling of realness, true livingness." Her fondness for Reed flattered him. She was experienced enough so that her affection could be construed as a tribute to his virility, as it was undoubtedly a tribute to the promise of genius. Flattered and fascinated, Reed was perfectly willing to have her for his guide into a world of new experience, of which Italy was merely the geographical locale.

"I never was so happy in my life," he wrote Hunt. And yet, having heard from Hunt how much disappointment the financial failure of the pageant had brought and how that failure had been used to attack the I.W.W. and weaken its leadership of the strike, he felt, he said, like a coward. He had known that he was running away. There were not merely the details of the pageant; there was the strike itself. When he led the singing for the last time, the strikers had said, "We been so lonesome for to sing—you come tomorrow?" And there was a sense of disloyalty to his family as well, for Harry had had to settle down to a dull, routine job, and Mrs. Reed was struggling with the dreary tangle of dubious assets and unmistakable liabilities.

But Reed had had to go. More was at stake than the glamor of Italy. "I'm really tired," he wrote his mother, "for the first time in my life, and I know I can do finer work if I can rest." Of course he was tired, after the three breathless weeks of preparation for the pageant, but not merely tired. What he felt, perhaps none too clearly, was that he was being impelled to make a choice. He had been attracted to Bill Haywood, Gurley Flynn, and Carlo Tresca: "I liked their understanding of the workers, their revolutionary thought, the boldness of their dream, the way immense crowds of people took fire and came alive under their leadership. Here was drama, change, democracy on the march made visible." He could not forget "the exultant men who had blithely defied the lawless brutality of the city government and gone to prison laughing and singing." It was by no means the first time that he had become conscious of injustice, but he had never known how intense the struggle against injustice could be and how great the stakes. He had felt the beauty and glory of that struggle, and had seen that he was fitted for a part in it. After the pageant it seemed inevitable that he should be drawn into it further and further.

He was not afraid. What made him hesitate was the recognition that any commitment sheared away some part of life's possibilities. He wanted to hold to everything that he had found good. It was typical of him that, in the fortnight between the pageant and his sailing for Italy, he was not too busy or too tired to attend the triennial reunion of the class of 1910. When he wrote his mother that he was not tying up with the I.W.W, he was, of course, trying to reassure a conventional, harassed, aspiring woman of the middle class, but the reasons he gave her were the reasons he gave himself: "I am not a Socialist temperamentally any more than I'm an Episcopalian. I know now that my business is to interpret and live Life, wherever it may be found—whether in the labor movement or out of it. I haven't ever been patient with cliques any more than Paw was, and I won't be roped in, any more than he was, in some petty gang with a platform."

The problem was many-sided. Bobby Rogers wrote him, "Cut out the quick-lunch, emotionally effective propaganda dope, such as the jail story in the *Masses*. You can either do that, or you can try to do literature without strings tied to it. The latter for the sake of art, or the first for the sake of Big Bill. You can't do both." Reed could not foresee that Rogers, having won notoriety by advising his students at Massachusetts Institute of Technology to be snobs and marry their bosses' daughters, would do his "literature without strings tied to it" for a Hearst newspaper. What he did realize was that all he had ever said about art for art's sake, in revolt against the kind of literature that propagandized for bourgeois morality and capitalist economics, could be applied to literature that propagandized for proletarian justice and I.W.W. principles. He felt there was a difference, but he could not define it.

Definition was never his way of solving any problem. Intellectual analysis might have saved him long delays, much confusion, and some unhappiness; on the other hand, it might have betrayed him. In any case he was both incapable and scornful of rational solutions. He had an opportunity to go to Italy, and he went. Except on one occasion, when he walked into a Socialist meeting and presented the greetings of the American

Socialist movement—"Signor Reed, a tall, robust, and blond youth, completely won the sympathies of the audience"—he thought little about the labor movement. He took what the moment gave, with confidence that, when the moment was over, he would know what he wanted to do.

At the end of the summer he and Robert Jones, who was bound for Germany to study under Max Reinhardt, started on a walking-trip. At some point they discovered an old cistern, thick with green scum, which local legend associated with Leonardo da Vinci. Reed plunged in. There or elsewhere he caught diphtheria. He recovered rapidly, and in the middle of September sailed for America.

VII

THE ROMANTIC REVOLUTION

THE genie's daughter brought Reed back from the castle on the mountain-top. He had given up his job on the *American* when he went to Italy, and now, in October, 1913, he became managing editor of the *Masses*. The cartoons and pictures were becoming better and better. To Young, Sloan, and Becker had been added K. R. Chamberlain, George Bellows, Glenn Coleman, and Stuart Davis. They drew the life of New York that John Reed had learned to love: crowded streets, night courts, Coney Island, the markets, saloons, and alleys. Young, always thrusting at capitalism, had provoked a libel suit by the Associated Press with his cartoon, "Poisoned at the Source." Sloan did a devastating back cover on the Binghamton factory fire. Other artists attacked the evils of capitalism or satirized the absurdity of middle-class pretensions. But for the most part they were discoverers, awakening, just as John Reed had awakened, to the rich variety of Manhattan, never indifferent to the injustice and cruelty that were part of that variety, but equally excited by the fate of a political prisoner, the woes of a prostitute, and the misadventures of rowdy boys.

Reed's own contribution reflected as catholic a taste as the drawings. He wrote a simple, restrained sonnet on a farmer's woman, and the editors of the *Masses*, in the midst of political upheavals and economic warfare, devoted a full page to the poem and the drawing by Sloan that accompanied it. He satirized philanthropy in "Another Case of Ingratitude." He wrote a one-act played called "Moondown" about the romantic dreams of working girls. Whatever he found that was fresh and alive was material for the *Masses*.

The sense of discovery was everywhere, and it was always joined, though sometimes by fragile ties, to the spirit of protest. Henrietta Rodman, a high school teacher, had fostered the Liberal Club to give some sort of unity to the diverse expressions of the new insurgency. She knew teachers, settlement workers, and Socialists, as well as artists, poets, and hoboes. When the Liberal Club and Polly Holladay's restaurant were established in the same building on Macdougal Street, the Village had not merely a social but an intellectual center. Newcomers, such as Floyd Dell or Alfred Kreymborg, could meet the giants of the Village, Horace Traubel or Thomas Seltzer or, if he happened to be in town, Big Bill Haywood. And they could readily find their places in the turbulent activity that grew out of the surging rush of emotions and ideas.

To the new arrivals in the Village, Jack Reed, already a legendary figure at twenty-six, seemed a thoroughgoing radical. And, by the standards of the Village, he was. He was contemptuous of organized religion, the institution of marriage, and what is called law and order. His sympathies were on the side of labor. He was romantic, but not sentimental. He was gallant, even reckless, but he could count the cost of recklessness, and he never complained at having to pay the price.

And radicalism was beginning to go a little deeper. He had not forgotten his friends of the Paterson strike. In particular there was F. Sumner Boyd, under indictment in Paterson for violating New Jersey's anarchy statutes. Boyd was an Englishman and the son of radicals. His first memories were of the refugees from the Continent who stayed for days or weeks in his parents' home. He became a Socialist, a street speaker, an organizer of the unemployed. He led demonstrations, and went as a delegate to the International Socialist Congress in Copenhagen. In 1910 he came to America. The Socialists he met seemed dry and professorial or suave and opportunistic, but from the first he liked Bill Haywood as a person, and during the Lawrence strike he accepted his principles and became a member of the I.W.W. Thus it happened that he was called into the Paterson strike when Haywood was arrested, and in its bitterest days delivered a speech on sabotage.

Boyd was perhaps the first thoroughly informed Marxist Reed had known. Though he was only two years older than Reed, he had been brought up in the radical movement, had been an active revolutionary for more than a decade, and had read and re-read the classics of Marxism. They had met at strike headquarters in Paterson, had liked each other, and had worked together on the pageant. Soon after Reed left for Italy, Boyd was arrested, and was awaiting trial when Reed returned. He had at first supported himself in this country by radical journalism, but his connection with the I.W.W. had ended all possibility of employment by Socialist papers. Reed found work for him, and they were constantly together. Boyd was poet enough to appreciate Reed; Reed was radical enough to appreciate Boyd.

Mabel Dodge did not like Boyd. In fact, she liked only those friends of Reed's who would submit to her domination or add to her glory. Reed found her demands a little trying. When he wanted to explore the East Side, she would propose that they go together in her limousine. If he neglected her for the *Masses* or the Liberal Club or for other friends, she might threaten to take poison, and at least once she took it. As on a similar occasion in Italy, the dose proved less than fatal, but the incident was rather embarrassing for Reed. He ran away in desperation to Boston and Cambridge, leaving Hapgood and Steffens to cope with Mrs. Dodge's hysteria. But he had to return, and nothing had been accomplished.

The whole situation was distressingly complicated. The flight to Italy had solved no problems. The demands of radicalism, so eloquently presented by Boyd, clashed just as relentlessly as ever with the poet's craving for all experience. The defeat of the Paterson strikers and the consequent weakening of the I.W.W. robbed him of the satisfaction he had taken in the pageant. For both financial and temperamental reasons, the managing editorship of the *Masses* could only temporarily serve his purposes. It was a satisfaction to bring out such an issue as the one that celebrated Christmas, with its coruscating cartoons against religion, but Reed knew that he had little executive ability, and he could not contemplate an indefinite future as Max Eastman's right-hand man. He was depressed, though his friends seldom suspected it. He had lost confidence in himself and in the convictions he had arrived at. So far as he could see, he had reached an impasse.

SUDDENLY a way opened for him. Francisco Villa, crossing the border from El Paso in March of 1913, had raised an army in his native mountains, and driven the Federal troops from Jiminez and Torreon. With the capture of Chihuahua City in November, and his sudden raid on Juarez, he became the sensation of the American press, and the war-correspondents rushed down into Mexico. The *Metropolitan* asked Reed to go. He had done two articles for the magazine; Carl Hovey, managing editor, had been a pupil of Copey's; Lincoln Steffens said he could do the job.

The *Metropolitan*, changing owners in 1912, turned to Socialism as, a decade earlier, *McClure's* and *Everybody's* had turned to muckraking. Like its muckraking predecessors, it gave most of its space to fiction, and the generous subsidy of Harry Payne Whitney permitted it to publish works by Rudyard Kipling, Arnold Bennett, Joseph Conrad, Booth Tarkington, Rupert Hughes, Fannie Hurst, and a good many others whose names sold copies on the newsstands. At the same time, it sought the intellectual prestige of the new radicalism. George Herron, victim of a famous academic scandal, Walter Lippmann, and Morris Hillquit expounded Socialism. Frederic C. Howe wrote on the labor movement abroad, Israel Zangwill on the militant suffragists of England, Bernard Shaw on equality, Lincoln Steffens on corruption. The wiser radicals were skeptical and amused, but they were bound to feel that, when hard-boiled editors backed by a sporting millionaire took up Socialism, the movement was growing.

The editors suggested that Reed would have more prestige in Mexico, as well as greater profit, if he could also act as the representative of a daily newspaper. The *Tribune*, he discovered, was sending Richard Harding Davis. He hurried to the *Sun*, where Don Marquis, whom he had known as a friend of Robert Rogers', was working. Reed's necktie was untied, his shoestrings flapping, his hair uncombed. Marquis took him to see the owner, a fat little man, conventional and smug, who shrank behind his desk as if he expected a bomb to be thrown, and barked out a refusal. Finally the *World* gave Reed the assignment he desired.

Three days later he was at the border. At Presidio, on the American side of the Rio Grande, he climbed to the flat mud roof of the post office and looked across low scrub and the shallow yellow river to Ojinaga, headquarters of Mercado's beaten army. General Orozco had forbidden reporters to enter the Mexican city, but Reed waded across the river and found Mercado, who blubbered and blustered about his defeat. The houses of the town, which had been lost and taken five times, were roofless and the walls riddled. Along the main street hordes of sick and starving people passed, driven from the interior by fear of the approaching rebels. Refugees poured across the river, challenged by rude inspectors. Asked what she carried beneath her voluminous shawl, one woman placidly answered, "I don't know, señor. It may be a girl, or it may be a boy."

Presidio, with its dozen adobe shacks and its two-story frame store, was overrun with war-correspondents, secret agents of both armies, representatives of American interests, drummers for munition companies, and rangers, sheriffs, cow-punchers, and customs officials. The store-keeper spent half his time profitably outfitting refugees and supplying provisions to the Federal army, and the other half trying to protect his three daughters from amorous Mexicans and cowboys. An agent for a portrait company was getting thousands of orders for colored enlargements from photographs. The High Sheriff of Presidio County periodically bustled into town with a revolver on each hip, a knife in his left boot, and a shotgun over his saddle. Then there was "Doc," who played Wagner and Beethoven on a castrated melodeon, charged twenty-five cents for setting a limb or delivering a child, was always drunk, and dimly remembered days in London with Frederick Watts and William Morris.

Up the river to El Paso Reed went, and again there were correspondents and agents and salesmen. Across the river, at Juarez, he had his first sight of the Constitutionalist army—two thousand horsemen and five hundred infantry, most of them wearing blue denim suits but a few in khaki, each of them with a bright-colored handkerchief about his neck and a gay sarape on his saddle. The general arrived: "Two thousand nondescript, tattered men, on dirty little tough horses, their sarapes flying out behind, their mouths one wild yell, simply flung themselves out over the plain. That's how the general reviewed them." Already Reed was taking sides: "These were wild men, well fed, clothed, armed, and mounted, volunteers instead of conscripts like the Federals. A great bunch, believe me." "What pageant material!" he added.

On Christmas Day he was at Villa's headquarters in Chihuahua, in the middle of a brown, savage desert, with great jagged mountains in the distance. "More wonderful than Italy," he thought, as he saw the mosque-like white churches and the soft yellow-brown cathedral, with its arabesques and its primitive angels and popes. He followed Villa to the opera house. Thousands of people stood along the street shouting "Viva Villa." Bands played, and the theatre, into which women and children poured, was gay with Mexican flags and colors in bunting and lights. Villa called the children to the platform in a long line, and gave each a suit of clothes and a dollar and a half in the new currency. Reed noticed that more than once, as the ragged children passed before him, there were tears in Villa's eyes.

The next morning Reed was taken into Villa's room by his private secretary before the general arrived. Soon there was a fanfare of bugles outside, and a fairly tall, thick-set man in a brown suit entered, followed by a throng of peons. The room was with difficulty cleared, and Villa sat down at his desk. Benavides, his secretary, read his letters, and he swiftly dictated his answers. Then there was a conference with Terrazas, Secretary of State. Meanwhile Reed watched. Villa's movements, it seemed to him, were like an animal's. When he stood up, he was awkward and stiff below the knees, from much horseback riding. Above the waist, with hands and arms and trunk, he moved with the sureness and swiftness of a coyote. His mouth hung open, and his face seemed good-natured, almost simple. Only his eyes, dark, perfectly round, and steely, were terrible.

When he had finished his work, Villa turned to Reed, and the first of a score of interviews began. The stories, circulated by the *Metropolitan*, of Villa's deep affection for Reed, and of his making him a Brigadier General, Reed took pains to deny. "It is not true," he wrote, "that 'a remarkable friendship' existed between General Villa and myself. I doubt if I should even call it a friendship." Nevertheless, Villa, who was capable of dismissing newspaper men without ceremony, did permit Reed to accompany him about the city, to spend hours in his office, and, two months later, to go with him into battle. As for Reed, though he stood in awe of Villa—"He is a terrible man"—he became his staunchest supporter in the American press.

He was attracted to Villa by his romantic story. He had heard all the legends: of the government official murdered in revenge, of the raids on rich *hacendados*, of the distribution of spoils among the peons. He knew the ballads of reckless and romantic bravery that had grown up around the Mexican Robin Hood, "the friend of the poor." He had read of Villa's loyal support of Madero in 1910, and he had been told by Federals and Constitutionalists alike of the incredible campaign that, in eight months, had given Villa control of Chihuahua and most of northern Mexico.

Moreover, Villa was democratic. One day, as a troop train stood on a siding in Chihuahua, loading men and cannon and supplies, Reed noticed the general, his brown suit dirty, his shirt open at the neck, driving mules into a car. The sweat poured down his face as he cursed and kicked the balking animals on the narrow gangplank. Finally, when the car was loaded and the doors closed, he turned to a soldier and seized his canteen. Despite the man's protest, he emptied it, and, returning it, said, "Go over to the river and say you have my permission to fill it." The man grinned and left. Villa, Reed found, trusted nobody, but he liked everyone except his enemies, and the soldiers worshipped him for his bravery and his coarse, blunt humor.

Finally, Villa had a generous vision of what Mexico might become and a considerable ingenuity in devising rough-and-ready means for serving the needs of the peons. Almost his first act as Governor of Chihuahua had been the creation of a controlled currency. He issued two million pesos in paper, guar-

anteed by nothing but his name, distributed them to the army
and to the poor, and ordered the acceptance of the money at par
throughout the state. He then fixed the price of beef, milk, and
bread. When the merchants began posting two sets of prices, he
proclaimed Mexican silver and bank-bills counterfeit after a
stated day. That day came, and the hoarders, doubting Villa's
word, had not exchanged their Mexican money for his currency.
A few arrests sufficed: the silver piled up in his treasury and his
pesos circulated everywhere in the state of Chihuahua.

He used the army to run the electric light plant, the street
railways, the telephone exchange, the water works, and the Terrazas' flour mill and slaughter house. "The only thing to do
with soldiers in time of peace," he said, "is to put them to work.
An idle soldier is always thinking of war." He planned, once
the revolution had been accomplished, to establish military colonies for the veterans. Instead of a standing army that might
become the bulwark of tyranny, there would be vast agricultural and industrial enterprises. Here the veterans would work
three days a week. The other three days they would drill and
give military instruction to all the people, to create a citizens'
army for the defense of the fatherland.

He believed that education would solve the problems of
Mexico, and he established schools throughout Chihuahua. He
was willing to talk about Socialism, remote as its ideas seemed
to him. Startled by the proposal that women should vote, he
could at least contemplate the possibilities of woman suffrage,
especially when his wife, in a test Reed suggested, exhibited the
sternness of mind he had thought was purely masculine. He
repeatedly declared that he had no desire to be president. He
would like to live, he told Reed, in one of the military colonies
he planned to create, where he and his comrades could find useful work to do. "I think I would like the government to establish a leather factory there, where we could make good saddles
and bridles, because I know how to do that; and the rest of the
time I would like to work on my little farm, raising cattle and
corn. It would be fine, I think, to help make Mexico a happy
place."

Ultimately Reed's admiration for Villa rested on the fact that

he, too, wanted Mexico to be a happy place. Despite his love for
the urban life of an industrial civilization, he had a deep, persistent distrust of industrialism, and he dreamed, as have so many
of the radicals who have followed him to Mexico, of an agrarian
paradise. What he knew of Marxism told him that Mexico could
not escape the advance of science and technology, and, indeed,
his own eyes showed him the constant progress of the machine.
But he hated the American business men who were bringing
the machine and machine-slavery to Mexico, and he loved the
peons. He hoped that they might escape from bondage to the
land-owners without falling into the hands of Wall Street exploiters. At least the immediate step was their liberation, and it
was their battle that Villa, himself a peon, was fighting.

Reed did not understand all the issues, but that did not dis-
tinguish him from other newspaper correspondents or even from
the majority of experts. Lincoln Steffens carefully reasoned his
way to the belief that Carranza was the man to save Mexico.
Reed let his feelings guide him to unquestioning endorsement
of Villa. Steffens should have been right, but it is still, more than
twenty years later, not absolutely certain that he was. Villa,
Steffens told Woodrow Wilson, was "a grossly illiterate, unscrupulous, unrevolutionary bandit." That Villa was ruthless,
Reed knew well enough; but he had seen that Mexico was a
country of ruthless men. That Villa could be bought, as Steffens
was convinced after his investigations in Wall Street, Reed did
not believe. Steffens had a hundred arguments to support his
claims; Reed had only his acquaintance with Villa and Villa's
men, but for him that was enough.

DURING his week in Chihuahua, Reed had the opportunity to
strengthen his convictions by talking with some of the American business men who hated Villa. He went one day out through
the chaparral and around great brown mountains to the Hacienda Robinson, whence he rode, on the engine of an ore-train,
to a mining-camp controlled by American capital. The manager,
though cool in his welcome, provided him with a horse, and they
climbed over the mountain, past hundreds of deserted shafts, to
some of the active lead and silver mines. Profits, he found, were

excellent. Even in these unsettled times, it was a poor company that could not pay seven percent. Wages were low. Much of the work was let out to native contractors, who paid less than two dollars a day in Mexican money. Despite the manager's insistence that the miners were a bad lot and hated all gringos, Reed went into their houses, and was treated with courtesy. They were wretchedly poor—"the poorest people I've seen in Mexico, underfed, bare-footed, physically degraded"—but they offered him coffee. The houses one of the companies had built were cheerless "contractor's boxes," all alike in their square, dreary bareness, but even so they were better than the houses the laborers in other mines made out of mud and boards and Standard Oil cans.

"Those are pretty dirty places to live in," Reed said to the manager, who replied, "Yes, and a pretty filthy lot of people live there." The manager took him to a mountain crest, whence they could look forty miles in any direction over plains and mountains and valleys. "It's the greatest climate in the world," the manager said. "These damned Mexicans don't deserve it. They ought to quit fighting and settle down and enjoy it." Enjoy it by working ten hours a day in a mine, Reed thought. "It's a rich country," the manager went on, waving his arm at the rolling mountains. "Why it hasn't even been prospected yet. All we want is peace, and a chance to work. We could turn over a pretty piece of change."

He continued his lecture. American capital, he said, had made Mexico. All the skilled workmen in the mines were Americans. It might be true, as Reed interrupted to point out, that Mexicans had had no chance to learn skilled trades, but they wouldn't be any good anyway. The 1910 revolution had changed the peon, made him more uppish, spoiled him. There were strikes all the time. The only thing to do with strikers was to shoot them down. Nothing could save Mexico but American intervention. Reed began to argue, and the manager checked his expansiveness. "If you write anything to discourage intervention," he warned, as Reed left, "we'll get you."

The better Reed understood Villa's enemies, the more eager he was to mingle with Villa's men and to come to know his country. And he wanted to see action. Nothing was happening in Chihuahua, and he began to think about going south. Torreon, poorly garrisoned, had fallen to the Federals, and, while Villa made preparations for an organized attack, his supporters in the mountains fought a guerrilla warfare with the skirmishing parties of the enemy and held the Durango passes. Reed wondered if he could find any one to go with him.

On New Year's Eve, stopping at Chee Lee's for a Tom-and-Jerry, he found three Americans engaged in conversation about the immorality of Mexican women and the purity of the American home. He sat down with them. A half-dozen drunken officers arrived, looking for gringos to shoot, but they were pacified with Tom-and-Jerrys, and the Americans resumed their talk. One of them was Mac, who, though he was younger than Reed, had been a railroad foreman, a plantation overseer in Georgia, a cow-puncher, and a deputy sheriff. He was now boss mechanic in a mine in Durango, to which he was soon to return. After the fourth Tom-and-Jerry, Mac told with relish about hunting a Negro with bloodhounds in Georgia. The trouble with Mexicans, he explained after the fifth or sixth drink, is that they haven't got any Heart.

But Mac was going south, and would be glad to have Reed go with him. The troop train on which they left the next morning had five freight cars, filled with horses and carrying soldiers on top, and one coach, in which Reed and Mac sat, together with two hundred noisy non-combatants. The windows of the coach had been smashed, and the walls were full of bullet holes. The rails that had hastily been laid after Orozco's destructive retreat trembled and bent. There was a rumor that bandits had planted dynamite. The peons sang and talked, organized a cock-fight, drank tequila, and fired at coyotes. When they stopped at ruined stations, women got out, started fires, and made coffee.

Late in the evening the train reached Jiminez, and Reed and Mac went to the Station Hotel, kept by an eighty-year-old American woman, who opened a side window and squinted at them through steel-rimmed spectacles. "Well, I guess you're all right," she said, unbarred the door, and let them in. She explained: "There's so damned many drunken generals around today that I've got to keep the door locked." Two of the generals had come with their women and asked for rooms. "Sure I got rooms," she told them, "but this ain't no whorehouse. Beat it."

In the bar Mac met an acquaintance, Captain Antonio Garcia, a man with a reputation throughout Villa's army for his savage temper and cold-blooded cruelty. It was said that, after Tierra Blanca, he shot forty-five prisoners with his own revolver. He was polite enough to the Americans, and offered to show them the city. There were no lights on the dilapidated street that led from the station to the plaza. The night was dry and cold and full of a subtle excitement; guitars twanged; snatches of song and laughter and low voices, and shouts from distant streets, filled the darkness. Occasionally little troops of foot-soldiers on guard-duty or horsemen in high sombreros and serapes came by. Officers passed in surreys, girls in their laps. In the plaza a regimental band played, without protest, a counter-revolutionary song. On one side of the plaza they found five ragged American boys, soldiers of fortune driven from the army by Villa's order against American enlistments. The square was full. Men, mostly soldiers, promenaded on the outside; girls on the inside. When a man saw a girl he liked, he passed her a note—at the risk of a gun-fight if she happened to be some other man's favorite. If she liked him, she smiled, and they met at church, or he came and talked to her through the window.

Back at the hotel Mac and Captain Garcia stopped for another drink, and Reed went to his room to make notes. When the others came up, Garcia noticed Reed's wrist-watch and admired it so frankly that Reed urged it upon him. When he could finally be prevailed upon to accept it, the ferocious captain embraced Reed, pledged eternal friendship, and poured forth a hundred plans for serving the generous American.

The next afternoon Mac and Reed and a soldier on leave named Fidencio, who served as muleteer, turned west to Magistral in Durango. Into a one-seated buggy, with patched harness and wobbly wheels, they piled six suitcases and two large boxes. They drove through a hot, quivering land, smothered in gray dust, between mesquite and chaparral bushes. Irrigating ditches ran everywhere, overshadowed by long lines of great alamo trees, leafless and gray as ashes. They came first to the village of San Pedro, where Reed stopped to admire a low building of exquisite pink plaster, set back from the road in a grove of green willows. It was a flour mill, and across the street there was another, with strange heads of angels carved above the door. They bought corn for the mules, and drove on.

The sun went suddenly down behind the western mountains that traced a faint, waving line across the sky. Blood-red clouds flamed in the sky, and the mountains became curtains of blue velvet. They had hoped to reach the Hacienda San Isidro that night, but they found that they had lost their way. They drove on for a time in the dark, odorous with sage, Mac beating the mules and cursing them, while Fidencio sang. Finally they camped for the night and began to cook their supper.

There was a crackling of footsteps and a hail. "Is it permitted to come out?" a voice inquired, and two figures appeared from the mesquite. The strangers doffed their hats politely and shook hands. Both wore floppy straw sombreros and were muffled to the eyes in tattered sarapes. One was a tall, black-bearded, slender man, with great eyes and a kind, smiling mouth. The other was very old and deeply wrinkled. They were poor rancheros, owning a small farm where they raised a flock of goats and a little corn. They offered the travelers hospitality, but Mac refused, knowing that the prescribed ceremonies of leave-taking would delay their departure by several hours. They brought dry wood for the fires, and, refusing food, drank coffee, smoked, and talked politics. They were *pacíficos*, non-combatants, weary of war and revolution. "Why do the rich want so much?" the old man asked. "The poor man is contented with so little. It is a mystery known alone to God. And now the United States wants Mexico." They led the mules into their corral, and bade the travelers good-night.

When Reed awoke, the others were up, and the farmers were harnessing the mules to the wagon. Poor as they were, they refused to accept money until Mac said, "Please do me the favor to take this and buy some aguardiente with it to drink my health." Then the two Americans and Fidencio drove away in the sharp chill of early morning. The sun rose, like metal pouring out of a furnace, and at noon they reached San Isidro, with its ancient Spanish church and the white bare wall of the hacienda.

They left their mules at one of the stables and walked into the large square, round which stood perhaps a hundred one-story adobe houses. These were the homes of the men who worked the miles of field and cared for the great herds that belonged to the owner of the hacienda. In the square life teemed. There were thousands of pigs, chickens, burros, dogs, piles of ordure, pieces of harness, scraps of iron, children of all ages, from naked two-year olds riding pigs to swaggering boys and flirtatious girls of fourteen or fifteen. Diagonally across the square, women, with jars or cans on their head, walked to and from the river, a mile away. Other women squatted outside the white-washed doors, mashing wet corn in stone mortars. Horsemen, wearing tight leather trousers with silver buckles, and great straw hats, three feet wide and two feet high, lavishly ornamented with silver braid, rode madly after a bunch of young horses they were preparing to brand. Reed felt that he was beginning to know the Mexicans: "The most humble peon has a delicacy of tact and a quick intelligence that are not found among any class of any race that I know. There are no people I have seen who are so close to nature as these people are. They are just like their mud houses, just like their little crops of corn."

The decrepit buggy and the cadaverous mules brought them at last to Magistral, and Mac went his own way into the mountains. Reed, though he disliked the man's bullying ways and his cruel prejudices, realized that in leaving him he was cutting himself loose from his own land. He was frightened: "I was afraid of death, of mutilation, of a strange land and strange people whose speech and thought I did not know. But a terrible curiosity urged me on; I felt I had to know how I would act under fire, how I would get along with these primitive folks at war." "He is twenty-six," the *Metropolitan* had said in its advertisements, "and does not know fear."

Fidencio urged him to visit his home in Valle Allegre before he went on to join General Urbina. The young soldier swaggered into the tiny village, and every one made of him—every one except Pablito. Pablito, who had been courting Fidencio's Carmencita, drew a revolver, and Reed thought his companion would be killed. But Pablito did not shoot, and Fidencio, having demonstrated his right to Carmencita, went off to drink aguardiente.

It was Fidencio who took Reed to Santa Maria del Oro for *Los Pastores*. El Oro, where there were dances almost every night and the girls were the prettiest in all Durango, was famous for the miracle play produced on the Feast of the Santos Reyes, the Magi. Reed sat for three hours, as the story of Lucifer's attempt to seduce a young shepherd's wife unfolded, and led to the revelation to the shepherds of the birth of Jesus and their journey to the manger in Bethlehem. "It flashed upon me," he wrote, "as Fidencio and I went home with our arms about each other's shoulders, that this was the kind of thing which had preceded the Golden Age of the Theatre in Europe—the flowering of the Renaissance. It was amusing to speculate what the Mexican Renaissance would have been if it had not come so late. But already around the narrow shores of the Mexican Middle Ages beat the great seas of modern life—machinery, scientific thought, and political theory. Mexico will have to skip for a time her Golden Age of Drama."

AT LAST he joined General Tomas Urbina at Las Nieves. An Arab peddler carried him the two days' journey from Magistral in a two-wheeled gig. The general was sitting in the patio of the great hacienda that had become his through the fortunes of war, feeding tortillas to a tame deer and a lame black sheep. He gave Reed a limp hand and bade him eat. The next day he suggested that he would like to have some pictures taken, and Reed photographed General Tomas Urbina on foot, with and without a sword, on three different horses, and with and without his family. He also photographed, separately and in groups, his mother, his mistress, and his three children.

Urbina thought it might be ten days before he would go into battle, and Reed, knowing he could not escape from Mexican hospitality, resigned himself to a prolonged stay at Las Nieves.

But suddenly the general changed his mind and came out of his room, roaring orders. In five minutes troopers were saddling horses, peons were rushing to and fro with armfuls of rifles, and five mules were being harnessed to the general's coach. And then La Tropa appeared—the troop, in whose constant company Reed was to spend the next few weeks, in whose ranks he was to find many friends, in whose battle he was narrowly to escape death. They came on the dead run, shouting and firing their revolvers, one hundred of them, some in overalls, most in peons' jackets, a few in tight vaquero trousers.

After an hour's delay, the general rode off on a gray charger. Reed entered the coach with the cases of dynamite, which rolled about and crashed ominously as the rough trail dipped sharply into arroyos. Late in the afternoon they came to the Hacienda of Torreon de Canas. The general, it was announced, was sick. The troop settled itself among the corrals and stables, and Reed ate with the officers in one of the lofty, barren halls of the Casa Grande. The next morning the general bade them farewell, and they started off, Reed in the coach with a jealous officer and his amorous mistress.

After lunch at another hacienda, Reed secured a horse and joined the troop. "Now you are with the men," said one of them. That was what Reed wanted. They welcomed "meester" with jokes and liquor and songs. That night, on the floor of a stone storehouse, despite the snoring and the songs of the guards and the fleas, Reed slept better than he had before in Mexico. "Those weeks," he wrote three years later, "of riding hundreds of miles across the blazing plains, sleeping on the ground with the *hombres*, dancing and carousing in looted haciendas all night after an all-day ride, being with them intimately in play, in battle, was perhaps the most satisfactory period of my life."

Steadily the troop pushed south, and at last they came to La Cadena. Though Reed had some money and his outfit was highly desirable, nothing was ever stolen. Indeed, the troop, unpaid for six weeks, would not accept money for the food and drink and cigarettes they supplied in abundance. When the troop went to another post, and a new garrison came to La Cadena, there were new friends. Sometimes the traditional hatred of gringos flared up, but always there was some one to explain that Juan Reed was different. He felt closer and closer to these men, and some of them became his brothers by the Indian ceremony of blood.

For some days there was nothing for the soldiers to do but amuse themselves. Then, one morning, an officer announced that a thousand *colorados*, the irregulars of the Federal army, had come through the pass while the guard was asleep. "Now meester's going to see some of those shots he wanted," said a soldier. "How about it, meester? Feel scared?" Reed didn't feel scared. The whole business didn't seem real. He said to himself, "You lucky devil, you're actually going to see a fight. That will round out the story." And he loaded his camera.

He had no horse, and stood by the Casa Grande as the commanding officer sent out small detachments to meet the bands of *colorados* that, from different sides, swept towards the hacienda. Suddenly he became conscious that for some time he had been hearing shooting—far off, like a clicking typewriter. But it was coming nearer, and soon the sound was almost the roll of a snare-drum. Hundreds of little black figures appeared, riding furiously through the chaparral. There were savage Indian yells, and bullets thudded against the adobe walls. A soldier dashed up with a message for the colonel, and his jaw was shot away before he could speak. Then came the rout, a wild huddle of troopers lashing their terrified horses. "Come on, meester," said Juan Vallejo, and they began to run.

Straight through the desert Reed ran, dropping his camera, casting aside his coat. He ran until he was sobbing instead of breathing and awful cramps gripped his legs. He was still in plain sight, and groups of irregulars were riding everywhere after the fleeing troopers. He saw friends killed. As breath permitted, he ran. "I wasn't very frightened," he wrote. "Everything still seemed so unreal, like a page out of Richard Harding Davis. It just seemed to me that if I didn't get away I wouldn't be doing my job well." He kept thinking to himself, "Well, this is certainly an experience. I'm going to have something to write about."

Other men were running, too, and suddenly he saw a boy, no

more than thirteen, closely pursued. The Federal troopers ran him down, jumped their horses on him, and killed him. Reed, while the *colorados* dispatched the boy, ran on. He stumbled into an arroyo, and lay there, half-hidden by mesquite as the party of guerrillas rode by. Afraid to move, he fell asleep. When he woke, there were still scattered shots, and not far away an Indian with a rifle crouched on his horse. Reed waited for half an hour after the Indian rode out of sight, and then walked, stooping low, towards the mountains. The sun burned fiercely; chaparral tore his clothes and face; cactus, century plants, and the spikes of the espadas slashed his boots. At last the hacienda was dim in the distance, and only a thin line of dust marked the troop of *colorados* taking their dead back to Mapimi.

At noon he reached a ranch that he had visited with one of his comrades, Gino Guereca. Guereca's parents, despite their dread of the Federal troops, gave Reed food and water, and showed him the way to the Hacienda del Palayo. All afternoon he hurried on, hiding as well as he could from every horseman that appeared on the horizon. Safe at last among the peons of Palayo, who marveled more at the distance he had walked than at his account of the skirmish, he bathed and slept, and the next morning set out in a two-wheeled cart for Santo Domingo.

As he came late in the afternoon to the hacienda, some peddlers whom he had seen the day before at La Cadena crowded about him. "The meester!" they cried. "Here comes the meester. How did you escape?" And from them he learned the list of fatalities: "Blithe, beautiful Martinez; Gino Guereca, whom I had learned to love so much; Redondo, whose girl was even then on her way to Chihuahua to buy her wedding dress; and jolly Nicanor." Reed felt sick, "sick to think of so many useless deaths in such a petty fight."

As the rest of the troop came back from burying their dead, he learned more of the story and found that most of his friends who survived had been wounded. And it was then that he met Elizabetta, who was trudging behind Captain Romero's horse. Her lover had been killed in the battle, and Romero had become her man, but for that night she revolted, and sought refuge with Reed. "Without the least embarrassment," he wrote, "Elizabetta lay down beside me on the bed. Her hand reached for mine. She snuggled against my body for the comforting human warmth of it, murmured 'Until morning,' and went to sleep. And calmly, sweetly, sleep came to me."

REED returned to Chihuahua, and waited for Villa to march on Torreon. Villa, instead, went to Juarez to supervise the arrival of supplies that, now President Wilson had lifted the embargo, were pouring into Mexico. Reed followed him, interviewing him after his secret conference with General Scott on the international bridge between Juarez and El Paso. He covered the Benton case for the *World*, and interviewed Maximo Castillo. Benton, a Scotch land-owner in Juarez, a multi-millionaire, had protested against the stealing of his cattle, and had, the Constitutionalists charged, threatened Villa with a revolver. His execution was celebrated by the interventionists in El Paso. Castillo, a follower of Zapata, had crossed the border, closely pursued by Villa's men, and was interned in Fort Bliss. Villa asked to have the chance to execute him, and charged that he was responsible for the Cumbre tunnel disaster. His life threatened both by Americans and by Villa's followers, he was closely guarded by United States troops. To Reed, he gave a long statement, asserting his innocence and describing Villa as a man of no principles. Villa, when Reed told him over the telephone, said, "What do you think, *amigo?*" and announced that, if the United States would turn Castillo over to him, his principles would become clear enough.

Meanwhile, Reed had established contact again with his friends in New York. Hovey of the *Metropolitan* wired on February 17, "Battle article received. Nothing finer could have been written. You are sending us great stuff. We are absolutely delighted with your work." And a few minutes later he sent a second telegram: "Rush us good picture of yourself. Local color stuff, uniform if possible." And on the twentieth Max Eastman telegraphed: " 'Mac—American' is a peach."

Reed remained a fortnight in El Paso, and the more he saw of his fellow-citizens, the more warmly he felt towards the Mexicans he had lived with in Durango. He had lunch one day with a man who claimed to be a special agent for William Randolph Hearst's Mexican possessions. "Madero," he said, "sure I knew Madero. Why, I'll tell you. He was a dreamer. He was a crazy man. He wanted to let the Mexicans govern themselves. He believed that everybody was good. Ain't that a hell of an idea for a man to have in Mexico?"

"It's a quaint enough idea in El Paso," Reed answered, looking about the lobby. There they were: a former butcher who did the work for the Terrazas land ring; the man who, in the Diaz regime, had debauched the state of Chihuahua; a German merchant who had given $30,000 to Villa's enemies; a group of Spaniards expelled from Chihuahua for openly aiding the enemies of the revolution; and white-haired General Don Luis Terrazas, who had once owned seventeen million acres, three-quarters of the state of Chihuahua.

"They got a right to fight, I suppose," said the Hearst man, "so long as they don't bother anybody's property. But when they start taking away property that belongs to a man—"

"But look here," Reed remonstrated, "didn't the Terrazas and Creel outfits steal this land from the peons?"

"Steal!" said the man, offended. "Hell, no! They got a deed for everything they own."

"You see," he went on, "the American people don't understand the Mexican character. Why, we'd have had intervention long ago, except that the people of the East and Middle West have a false idea of allowing the Mexicans a democratic government. We down here along the border know the Mexicans better than that."

Reed began to discover some things about "the Mexican character." What one was told depended, he found out, on whether one was a potential investor or a journalist who might write something about intervention. Investors were told that Mexicans were gentle, patient, good workers, and honest; journalists that they were treacherous, untruthful, lazy, and cruel. Journalists learned that Mexicans could never become skilled workmen; investors that they were easy to train. Journalists were warned that Mexicans were given to strikes and violence; investors heard tales of their docility. The bravery of the Mexicans was described to the investors; the journalists were informed that they were cowards, any six of whom could be beaten by a single American.

El Paso was even more crowded than it had been two months before with reporters, detectives, and secret agents. Reed, returning from his weeks at the front, was a little contemptuous of the reporters who sat around hotel lobbies and, over their liquor, wrote colorful accounts of what was happening five hundred miles away. The detectives amused him, with their secretive airs and their confidential tales. The Wall Street agents he hated.

It was with some relief that he slipped away across the border and into the desert. He needed to be among the peons again, to listen to their songs and stories and discuss with them their hopes. He was gone for three or four days, returning full of enthusiasm once more. He brought with him half a dozen ballads, to add to those he had already collected in Durango. There were love-songs, pathetic, humorous, tender. And there were the innumerable verses that told of Villa's greatness and Huerta's villainy. This was the Mexico he loved.

He did not love the First Chief of the revolution, Venustiano Carranza. Before he met him, he contrasted the feudal aristocrat, sitting idle in Nogales, with the peon who was re-making Chihuahua and completing his plans for the march on Mexico City. Villa might be a savage, but he was a fighter, and he gave the peons something besides promises. To the campaign that had won practically the whole of northern Mexico for the Constitutionalists, Carranza, so far as Reed could see, had contributed nothing but congratulations.

Carranza became so completely inactive that, Reed wrote with some irony, rumors grew of his death or disappearance. The *World* sent Reed to Nogales to find out what had happened. He arrived at midnight in the big straggling town that combines Arizona's Nogales and Mexico's. He crossed the international boundary, undisturbed by the lounging Mexican sentries at the customs-house, and went to the hotel at which the cabinet-members were staying. The proprietor kicked on various doors, until he discovered the collector of customs, who waked up the secretary of the navy, who routed out the secretary of the treasury, who discovered the secretary of hacienda, who produced the secretary for foreign relations, Isidro Fabela. Señor Fabela assured Reed that Carranza would see him but would only answer questions that had been submitted in writting. When, the next morning, he saw the questions that Reed had prepared, he shook his head, but agreed to submit them, and to bring such answers as were vouchsafed within twenty-four hours. In the meantime Reed would be permitted to shake hands with the chief but not to interview him.

For an hour or more Reed and another reporter waited in the patio of the municipal palace. Self-important Mexicans rushed about with portfolios and bundles of paper. When a door opened, they could hear the roar of typewriters. General Obregon talked loudly to a woman colonel about his plans for the march on Guadalajara. American concession-seekers and munition-salesmen shifted from one foot to another, hats in their hands. Sentries guarded the entrance to Carranza's office, and only Fabela and those he took with him entered.

Finally Fabela beckoned the two journalists, and they walked into the room. The blinds were closed, and the room was dark. There was an unmade bed, a breakfast tray, a bucket of ice with three or four bottles of wine. Carranza, a gigantic, khaki-clad figure, sat in a big chair. "There was something strange in the way he sat there, with his hands on the arms of the chair, as if he had been placed in it and told not to move. He did not seem to be thinking, nor to have been working . . . You got the impression of a vast, inert body—a statue." When he rose, he towered to a tremendous height. Reed felt, though he could not say why, that the man was unwell. Even in the half-light that came through shaded windows, he wore smoked glasses, and there seemed something unnatural about his ruddy complexion. His mouth suggested indecisiveness to Reed, who noticed his habit of gnawing his beard and clenching his fists.

When they had shaken hands and Fabela was ready for the reporters to withdraw, Reed said, "The *World* is a friend of the Constitutionalists, and is against intervention." Carranza stood there, a huge mask of a man, and his face remained vacant, but he stopped smiling and suddenly launched into a harangue on the Benton case. It was England's affair, he said and the United States should keep out of it. Fabela tried to stop him, but he hastened on, his voice higher and louder. "England, the bully of the world," he screamed, "finds herself unable to deal with us unless she humiliates herself by sending a representative to the Constitutionalists; so she tried to use the United States as a cat's paw. More shame to the United States that she allowed herself to join with these infamous Powers. I tell you that, if the United States intervenes in Mexico upon this petty excuse, intervention will not accomplish what it thinks, but will provoke a war which, besides its own consequences, will deepen a profound hatred between the United States and the whole of Latin America, a hatred which will endanger the entire political future of the United States!"

He stopped talking, "as if something inside had cut off his speech." Fabela hurried them from the room. Reed, in full agreement with Carranza's words on intervention, could only interpret them in the light of his impression of the man: "I tried to think that here was the voice of aroused Mexico thundering at her enemies; but it seemed like nothing so much as a slightly senile old man, tired and irritated."

The next day Reed received the answers to his questions, written in five different hands. He paid little attention to them. He felt sure that Carranza and his associates were petty bureaucrats, with no thought for the peons, no plan for fundamental reform, aimless if not corrupt. Before he left Nogales, he had a last glimpse of the First Chief. As he lounged in the patio, talking with some soldiers, the door of the office opened, and Carranza stood there, "arms hanging loosely by his sides, his fine old head thrown back, as he stared blindly over our heads across the wall to the flaming clouds in the west." He stood there for a long time, his hands clasped behind his back and his fingers working violently. "Then he turned, and pacing between the two guards, went back to the little dark room."

IT WAS a relief to be back in Chihuahua with Villa. The city was full of correspondents now, for the march on Torreon was about to begin. Reed became friendly with Johnny Roberts, a first-rate reporter and a man who knew Mexico. They went together to El Cosmopolita, the fashionable gambling hall, and played poker with the resourceful and invincible chief of police.

When the troops began to leave for Torreon, Roberts, Reed, and other reporters secured a box car, had a carpenter fit it with bunks, an ice-box, and a stove, and started off with two barrels of beer and a Chinese cook. Villa attached the car to one of the long trains that carried his supplies and the soldiers and their women and children. As the train started off into the desert, Reed whooped like an Indian. The soldiers displayed their exuberance by shooting at the insulators on the telegraph lines.

They made camp at Yermo in the midst of miles and miles of sandy desert, with jagged, tawny mountains in the west. Along the single track lay ten enormous trains, and about them nine thousand men were camped. A great cloud of dust rose, seven miles long and a mile high. From around the campfires the interminable stanzas of "La Cucaracha" went on and on.

On Thursday Villa arrived, having stopped at the wedding of a friend. "I danced too much," he said. "All worn out. But what a dance! And what beautiful girls!" That night there was a heavy wind, a deluge of rain, and bitter cold. But the next morning the sun was out, and the trains moved on. Reed went to see Villa, in his famous red caboose, and asked for a horse, which was refused. He also asked about the presidency, and Villa, again protesting his loyalty to Carranza, threatened to expel from Mexico the next reporter who questioned him on that subject.

The troops left their crowded cars at Bermejillo and Mapimi, on the outskirts of Torreon. On his way towards the Constitutionalists' lines Monday morning, Reed met wounded soldiers, and could hear the crash of exploding shrapnel, the whistle of shells, the nervous rattle of machine-gun fire, and the continuous chatter of rifles. As he reached the ridge on which the cannons were being placed, he saw the smokestacks of Gomez, suburb of Torreon and Villa's first objective. Villa himself rode up to inspect the placing of the guns, and, seeing Reed, asked him how he liked the fighting. "Fine," Reed answered. "Good," said Villa. "You're going to see plenty."

He did. That night Villa led a party of soldiers, carrying bombs and cigars from which to light the fuses, to the walls of the Gomez Palacio. The next day he took the Palacio, and hurtled on into Torreon. An epidemic of cholera had killed hundreds of Federal soldiers, and the streets were full of corpses. In blasting heat, with little sleep and often not enough food, Reed followed the course of the battle. He drank water that the Federals had poisoned, and spent a night of misery.

Thrown back into the Gomez Palacio by a surprise attack, Villa lost Torreon and was threatened by complete defeat. With ghastly loss of life, his troops held the Palacio, and began to press forward again into the barricaded streets of Torreon. When the reporters, after a week of almost complete censorship, were permitted to use the telegraph wires from Gomez, Reed devoted most of his dispatch to an account of the cost of the victory and the heroism of the men. And still the fighting continued, as the Federals, whose lines of communication had been captured and who could not retreat, were driven back from building to building and from one impromptu fortress to another.

In the end John Reed was bored with slaughter. The censorship was resumed, and reporters were forbidden to leave until after Torreon had been taken. Saturday he and a photographer bribed a section-hand to let them use a gasoline car on the railroad to Bermejillo, where they caught a hospital train that was going to Chihuahua. They lay on the roof of the caboose, sometimes sleeping as the train made its slow way. The wounded moaned and cried, and those who died were pushed out of the cars by the side of the track. On Monday he reached El Paso, and sent to the *World* an account of the battle. It was not until Thursday, however, that Villa completed the conquest of Torreon. The next day he was in Juarez, and Reed telegraphed to the *World* his account of his plans for the campaign on Monterey and Mexico City.

Reed had no desire to see more killing. The memories of the battle of Torreon he cherished were those of chance conversations with soldiers, and his meeting with his old friends of Urbina's troop. There was one incident that he recalled with particular pleasure. He had bought a horse and ridden to a mountain outpost, where he had discovered just such a band as La Tropa. The men were not disciplined professional soldiers, but peons who had taken arms for liberty. They insisted on his having lunch with them, and the colonel, eager to engage in the exchange of ideas, apologized politely when a skirmish with Federal troops interrupted their talk. It was the presence of such men in Villa's army that made the capture of Torreon important.

In El Paso, Reed discovered that he had a reputation as a war-correspondent. The first of the articles on La Tropa had appeared in the April *Metropolitan*, heralded by large advertisements in the daily press: "John Reed in Mexico. Word pictures of war by an American Kipling. Hot from the front has come John Reed's first story of Mexico. . . . It's literature. What Stephen Crane and Richard Harding Davis did for the Spanish-American War in 1898, John Reed, twenty-six years old, has done for Mexico." Even the chill intellect of Walter Lippmann was moved to enthusiasm. "It's kind of embarrassing," he wrote Reed, "to tell a fellow you know that he's a genius, but you're in a wild country now. I can't begin to tell you how good the articles are. . . . You have perfect eyes, and your power of telling leaves nothing to be desired. . . . If all history had been reported as you are doing this, Lord! I say that with Jack Reed reporting begins. Incidentally, of course, the stories are literature."

Reed knew as well as any one else that he had never done better writing, never done writing one half as good. He had, as Lippmann said, perfect eyes. After three minutes in a room, he could describe its contents. And Mexico held his eyes as no country had ever done. He had always been occupied, ever since Copey in English 12 lectured him about "high visibility," with finding the right words, the true images, to render what he saw. In Mexico the images seemed to come with the perception. At night, as he scribbled in his notebook, the scenes of the day stood sharply before him, and he described them in phrases that scarcely needed to be modified when his articles were composed. He did not hesitate to re-arrange incidents to suit whatever pattern he desired, but he was rigorously faithful to the visual impression of each event. He was indifferent to the accuracy of the historian, but he had the integrity of a poet.

Insurgent Mexico, made out of his articles for the *Metropolitan* and the *Masses*, is a book for the eye. But John Reed was not merely recording surfaces. The book has its own kind of insight. He made little effort to understand the history of the country and its revolutions, and his researches into economics were impressionistic. Steffens could have told him more about Federal and Constitutionalist policies than he could have learned if his four months' stay had been prolonged for four years. But he knew something that Steffens did not, and something that, in his mind, was more important than all Steffens' knowledge; he knew the people of Mexico. "He did not judge," Lippmann wrote in a cooler mood; "he identified himself with the struggle, and gradually what he saw mingled with what he hoped. Whenever his sympathies marched with the facts, Reed was superb."

Lippmann's distinction between sympathies and facts would have meant little to John Reed. What he hoped grew out of what he saw, and therefore he found no reason for keeping them separate. Everything that he was responded to the heroic struggle of long oppressed peoples for a decent life. "Liberty," said a barefooted peon in Urbina's army, "is when I can do as I want." Reed could think of no better definition. What they wanted, he discovered, was romance rather than comfort, glamor rather than wealth. There was no condescension in his calling them "delightfully irresponsible"; responsibility seemed to him far less important than the ability to live in the moment that was present. They should have freedom because they were brave enough to fight for it and wise enough to use it.

In identifying himself with the wild fighting men of Villa's army, Reed did more than discover a cause to believe in. He learned that fear could be conquered: "I discovered that bullets are not very terrifying, that the fear of death is not such a great thing." And the fact that these men accepted him, wanted him with them, made sacrifices for him, gave him back the confidence he had lost after his flight to Italy and the collapse of the Paterson strike. "I found myself again," he recorded, and added, as a simple corollary, "I wrote better than I had ever written."

VIII

Between Wars

MABEL DODGE came down to El Paso to meet him. He must have felt a little better about their relationship. He was no longer the promising poet who had caught the fancy of a rich, intelligent, aggressive woman; he was a man who had been accepted by Villa and his fighters and been hailed as the ablest of war-correspondents.

In New York his friends were eager to listen to his stories, which were sometimes accurate and always colorful. Copey praised the Mexican articles. Colonel Harvey told a friend that they were the best war-reporting he had ever read. Reed polished up for the *Metropolitan* his account of the battle of Torreon and his interview with Carranza, and worked at briefer sketches for the *Masses*.

During his absence there had been savage warfare in which the police had broken up meeting after meeting of the unemployed. The I.W.W. and the anarchists had entered the fight for free speech, and scores of skulls had been cracked. Both radicals and police were preparing for a battle on the Saturday after Reed's return. Lincoln Steffens, who had seen the violence of the preceding weekend, went to Colonel Arthur Woods, just about to be appointed commissioner of police, and told him it was the forces of law and order that made riots. Impressed, Woods called off the police. Reed was sent by the *World*—as a young man who had been jailed a year ago for activities on behalf of the I.W.W.—to report the meeting. Steffens was right: there was no violence.

Mexico was still foremost in Reed's mind. On April 21, 1914,

American marines took Vera Cruz. Though Reed believed that Wilson's purpose was to hasten the downfall of Huerta, he feared lest the interventionists seize the opportunity to arouse public sentiment for the conquest of all Mexico. The *World*, which had opposed intervention, joined the clamor for a march on Mexico City. Reed sought an interview with Joseph Pulitzer and urged him to take an unambiguous stand for Mexican democracy. The next day an editorial appeared. "There will be no permanent peace in Mexico," it said, "until the peon is on the land that belongs to the peon, and he is protected in his ownership." It praised President Wilson's refusal to recognize Huerta, defended him from the criticism of "men who profit by the reign of tyranny and privilege and corruption," and pledged its support to the Constitutionalist struggle to emancipate the Mexican people.

Reed had his own say in a statement printed by the New York *Times* on April 27, just as the threat of war was gravest. The headlines told of martial law at Vera Cruz, the shooting of treacherous Mexicans, the tearing down of an American flag at Monterey, the rescue of an American consul. Reed's statement, which was reprinted in pamphlet form by the American Association for International Conciliation, tried to break through the misunderstandings that were creating a popular sentiment for war. It won the praise of many people, and in its June issue the *Metropolitan* printed it, slightly changed, as a signed editorial, with a note remarking on the attention that had been paid the author's comments and observations, "even in the highest circles."

The article summed up the lessons of four months in Mexico. Reed began by denying that the revolution was being made by the middle class. It was a revolt of the peons—eighty percent of the population—who were fighting for land. He described the Diaz regime, the passing of the laws that permitted the small minority of Spanish aristocrats to seize the land that the peons had worked for generations, the sale of natural resources to foreign capital, the restriction of education, the supplying of forced labor to British and American corporations, the shooting of all who protested. "It is common to speak of the Orozco revolution," he wrote, "the Zapata revolution, and the Carranza revolution. As a matter of fact, there is and has been only one revolution in Mexico. It is a fight primarily for land." The peons would follow any man, from Madero to Villa, who would promise reform, and they would turn against him if the reforms were not made. In three years of revolution they had learned much, and their struggle would not cease until they had what they wanted.

Slowly progress was being made. "We Americans, if we enter Mexico, are going to check all this. The first American soldier across the Rio Grande means the end of the Mexican revolution. ... The Government of the United States has already expressed itself as opposed to the confiscation of private property; and the land question in Mexico cannot be settled in any other way." And if we did set up a government of our making in Mexico City, and then kept our promise to withdraw, we should simply leave things worse than they were before: "the great estates securely re-established, the foreign interests stronger than ever, because we supported them, and the Mexican revolution to be fought all over again in the indefinite future."

He tried to be calm and rational, but he could not conceal the bitterness against the interventionists that love of Mexico, added to hatred of capitalist greed, had bred. "We Americans," he said, "honestly believe that we will benefit the Mexicans by forcing our institutions upon them. We do not realize that the Latin temperament is different from our own—and that their ideal of liberty is broader than ours. We want to debauch the Mexican people and turn them into little brown copies of American business men and laborers, as we are doing to the Cubans and the Filipinos." And thinking of his friends in Magistral and Chihuahua and Juarez and Valle Allegre, he wrote: "The American soldiers will have nothing serious to anticipate in the opposition of the Mexican army. It is the peons and their women, fighting in the streets and at the doors of their houses, that they will have to murder. It is the patient, generous, ignorant race that has struggled for liberty and self-consciousness for four hundred years—unorganized and inadequately armed—that they will have to shoot down."

He told friends that, if the United States invaded Mexico, he would join his comrades of La Tropa and fight with them against the invaders. And he meant it. He could conceive of no worse blow to liberty than the infliction upon Mexico of what he called in the *Masses* "our grand democratic institutions—trust government, unemployment, and wage slavery."

EXACTLY the same emotions moved Reed to defense of the Mexican revolution as had brought him to support of the Paterson strike, and in both struggles the enemy was the same, big business. Beyond that, he made no attempt to go. But while he was writing and speaking against intervention, another battle between capital and labor had ended in bloody slaughter. On April 20, militiamen and mine-guards had marched upon the colony of strikers in Ludlow, Colorado, and set fire to the tents, burning to death several women and children.

"When there is war," said the *Metropolitan*, "John Reed is the writer to describe it." The *Metropolitan* had begun to reconsider its radicalism. "The kind of Socialism we are preaching," said an editorial, aims to "create a feeling and a desire on the part of the prosperous to share that property with the poor and needy." "Apparently the attempt to capitalize Socialism itself has failed," Max Eastman commented, "and it remains only to see whether any money can still be squeezed out of its name." But the magazine was liberal enough to give John Reed a chance to write a piece of labor-reporting that was as solid and as revealing as his war-correspondence had been colorful and romantic.

Reed arrived at Trinidad ten days after the massacre. The town seemed quiet enough; stores and moving picture houses were open; miners, dressed in their Sunday best, talked good-naturedly on the street. Then three militiamen came along. Everyone stopped, and the militiamen walked down the street between two lines of hate. "The strikers spoke no word; they never even hissed. They just looked, stiffening like hunting dogs." Only when the militiamen got on the train and left did the town return to life.

At the Trades Assembly Hall children were singing a song:

There's a strike in Colorado for to set the miners free
From the tyrants and the money-kings and all the powers that be.

Along the wall a dozen women crouched with black shawls over their heads. Some had lost their husbands, others their children. They had all lost whatever goods they possessed. One of them, whose husband had been killed in the Tabasco mine before the strike, had taken refuge in the cellar of her tent, and militiamen had come and robbed her of her little savings. Another had seen her husband shot as he tried to get their children to safety. All the women crowded around, each telling her story of horror in her own language.

The next day Reed went out to Ludlow. "Stoves, pots and pans still half full of food that had been cooking that terrible morning, baby-carriages, piles of half-burned clothes, children's toys all riddled with bullets, the scorched mouths of the tent cellars . . . this was all that remained of the entire worldly possessions of 1,200 people." He went down into "the death hole," the cellar from which the charred bodies of thirteen women and children had been taken.

He began to reconstruct the story. Here was southern Colorado, dominated by three coal companies, the largest of them controlled by John D. Rockefeller, Jr. Most of the towns were incorporated, with the superintendent of the mine as mayor. The company owned all the houses and the only store. The county sheriffs, elected by the companies, made mine-guards deputies. The miners were immigrants, many of them imported to break the strike of 1903. A miner had to buy his own tools for cash; he was charged rent in advance; he had to pay a poll tax, though there was no tax on company property; he had to pay preacher's, school, and blacksmithing fees; prices at the company store were from twenty-five to one hundred percent higher than outside the camp. The operators talked about miners making five dollars a day, but the average gross wage was $2.12, and the average working year was 191 days. More people were killed in the mines of Colorado than in those of any other state in the Union, and yet only once in five years had a coroner's verdict placed the blame for an accident on the company.

Into southern Colorado came the United Mine Workers. Despite the system of espionage and the ruthless terror, and despite all differences of language, organization grew. When the union asked the operators to discuss the enforcement of existing laws, the answer was the importation from neighboring states of gunmen, soldiers of fortune, and ex-policemen. These men were sworn in as deputies and armed with rifles, revolvers, and machine guns. The strike began in September, and the miners, driven from company houses, set up tent colonies at a dozen places, the largest at Ludlow.

The guards frequently shot at strikers, several of whom were killed, and the miners began to collect what arms they could. When the governor called out the militia, the miners, believing the soldiers would protect them from the deputized thugs, rejoiced. And at first soldiers and strikers fraternized. But the commanding officer ordered the fraternization to cease, and made plans for the cooperation of the militia and the mine-guards. The operators began to complain because the governor was not ending the strike, and he modified his order against bringing in strike-breakers. Thousands of men were brought from the East under false pretenses and then were forbidden to leave until they had worked off their transportation and board. Hundreds of them escaped and joined the tent colonies. Mother Jones was arrested, and militia cavalry rode down the parade of women organized in protest.

A Congressional committee came to Colorado to investigate; afterwards miners who had testified against the company were beaten with rawhide whips and wounded with bayonets. At the investigation in Washington, John D. Rockefeller, Jr., stated: "We would rather that the unfortunate conditions continue, and that we should lose all the millions invested, than that the American workmen should be deprived of their right, under the Constitution, to work for whom they please. That is the great principle at stake." "If I had failed in my duty," he added, "I would resign, but my conscience entirely acquits me."

The strikers did not waver, and spirits at Ludlow were buoyant. On April 19, the militia and the deputies surrounded the camp. Militiamen later told Reed that they were ordered to destroy the tent colony and every living thing in it. Early on the morning of the twentieth, three bombs gave the signal, and the attack began. Four hundred gunmen swarmed down on the colony, and the machine guns, mounted on the hillside, were turned full on the tents. Finally, when the firing had gone on for hours, the militiamen and guards advanced on the colony and set fire to the tents.

The outrage enflamed the workers of Colorado and the country against the coal companies. An army of miners, together with clerks and schoolteachers and even bankers, seized guns and started for Ludlow. Labor unions and citizens' leagues voted money to be sent the strikers for rifles and ammunition. Open warfare began. The militia, in an insane frenzy, shot chickens, horses, cattle, cats. They destroyed the automobile of a passing stranger. General Chase, the commanding officer, refused to allow a Red Cross delegation to enter Trinidad. The bodies of two women and eleven children had been discovered in the ruins of the tent colony, and it was thought that many more had been killed. Skirmishes continued between strikers and militia, with deaths on both sides, until, on the day of Reed's arrival, Federal troops began their four months' occupation.

Reed, enflamed by what he had seen, hastened to Denver, where he witnessed Governor Ammons' cowardly evasions and realized his abject subservience to the coal companies. Although the captain of one of the militia companies testified that ninety percent of his men were mine-guards, Ammons stated, "The Colorado National Guard is composed almost exclusively of young professional and business men, some of them sons of the best families of this state." Reed, after meeting some of the best families, families of the coal operators, was prepared to believe that their sons could have equaled the viciousness of the hired thugs. Lieutenant-Governor Fitzgerald said that, even if the strikers' claims regarding the actions of the militia were true, that could not justify the attacks on innocent mine-guards and harmless scabs and the destruction of mine property. "They have no justification," he cried, "for murdering men whose only offense is that they are seeking to earn a living without a permit from the United Mine Workers of America. It is terrible to contemplate, this merciless slaughter, and it must end." The officials of the state thus shamelessly echoed the words of Rockefeller and his associates. J. C. Osgood, president of the Colorado Fuel and

Iron Company and chairman of the board of directors of the
Victor American Fuel Company, after saying that a fire had
been started in the tent colony "in some manner which has not
yet been investigated or explained," attributed all the violence to
the "ignorant foreigners," who had "practically been made anarchists by the labor organizers and agitators sent among them
by the officers of the United Mine Workers." Most of the newspapers in the East were eager to accept the Rockefeller version
of what had happened. The New York *Sun* said editorially:
"Unfortunately, a generation of truckling to the violent striker
had bred in labor ranks a belief that the harrying of rival workers
and the spoiling of plants was the strikers' accorded rights. The
words meant as a warning were taken up by the labor leaders as
a challenge. Rifles and ammunition were distributed among the
strikers. Inevitable bloodshed followed. The events in Colorado
should lead to a re-awakening of consciousness of justice and
individual rights."

Reed spoke at meetings for strikers' relief, and worked with
George Creel and Judge Lindsey to win national support for
the strike. Upton Sinclair had already gone on to New York
City and had been arrested for picketing the office of John D.
Rockefeller, Jr. Reed learned, as Sinclair had already discovered,
that the Denver newspapers in the employ of the operators
would hasten to invent scandal about anyone who opposed them.
In this instance they sought to injure two enemies at once by
coupling Reed's name with that of a young widow who had
been sending aid to the strikers.

Stopping on his way home at Hull House, in Chicago, where
Jane Addams invited newspapermen to lunch to hear him talk
about the strike, Reed returned to New York to write his article. For perhaps the first time in his life, he was resolved to prepare a documented case. In Mexico his eyes had given him everything he needed, but now he went to documents and reports.
Emotionally aroused, he realized that Ludlow was a clear and
terrifying example of what the I.W.W. meant by the class struggle. This was what he must show, beyond any possibility of misunderstanding, in his article. If, for the sake of their profits,
employers would put into motion machinery that ruthlessly extin-

guished the lives of whole familes, there was but one conceivable conclusion: justice could be won for the workers only if they would fight back, using the deadly weapons that the employers did not hesitate to use against them. The cynical hypocrisy of Rockefeller and his associates confirmed the impression that the ruins of the tent colony had given Reed: there was no word for this but war.

Ludlow re-enforced the lesson Paterson had taught—the lesson Italy had partly obscured. Never again could anything conceal from Reed the great cleavage in society between the producers and the exploiters. The class war was a reality, and his sympathy for the workers was secure. The importance of that sympathy in the determination of his conduct would vary with the rise and fall of other interests and with the character of the events into which his headlong impetuosity precipitated him. He had no intention of limiting himself to labor organization or even to radical journalism, but he knew on which side, whenever fighting was necessary, he would fight.

MABEL DODGE was in Provincetown, and he joined her there. She lived in a respectable, well-appointed house, with her son and her servants, and Reed lived in a small camp near the ocean. They were frequently together, and for a time it seemed that the difficulties of the preceding autumn had vanished.

During the day Reed worked hard on his book and the articles that he was writing. Fred Boyd, who was serving as his secretary and assistant, would take down from dictation the first draft, and, as he transcribed it, would make suggestions for amplification, especially with regard to economics. Reed appreciated Boyd's wide experience in the labor movement and his knowledge of economic theory, but there was often difficulty in unifying the two types of material. While the final revision was going on, Reed would walk up and down the room, growing warmer and warmer as problem followed problem. His coat would come off, his tie, his shirt, and sometimes his trousers and his underwear.

When the manuscript of *Insurgent Mexico* was ready for the

publisher, Reed dedicated it to Copey: "To listen to you is to learn how to see the hidden beauty of the visible world; to be your friend is to try to be intellectually honest."

Reed was still thinking a great deal about Mexico, and wondering how to thwart the plans of the interventionists. He conceived the idea of interviewing President Wilson, both with the intention of telling Wilson his own opinions about Mexico and with the hope of persuading the President to express his views in such a manner as to aid the revolution and restrain the American foes of Mexican democracy. Steffens was skeptical, perhaps of the character of the information Reed would give Wilson, certainly of the possibility of conducting a publishable interview, but Reed went ahead.

He arrived in Washington in the middle of June and called on Secretary of State Bryan, to whom he had letters. As he stepped up to the door, he heard the maid singing hymns in the kitchen as she washed the dishes. She showed him into the parlor, and called, "Mr. Secretary! Mr. Secretary! Here's somebody to see you!" A voice called out, "I'll be right down." Reed looked around. "The parlor," he recorded, "was a remarkable room. Two enormous Oriental vases flanked the mantel-piece, at whose center sat a large bronze bust of William Jennings Bryan. There were other busts of him scattered about—of wood, marble, granite, cast-iron, and silver-gilt metal. Incongruous rugs lay upon the carpet, and several tall oil-paintings caught the eye. The furniture was hair-cloth, of the best period. And I retain an impression of lace window-curtains. Bead curtains separated the parlor from the dining-room, and through these the maid presently passed, still singing."

Mr. Bryan appeared, "wearing that famous cutaway of his, those famous half-glasses of his on the wide statesman's black ribbon, the well-known clerical white bow tie, and that familiar and appalling smile." After they had talked for a while, Mr. Bryan speaking "in the way a statesman should—slowly, impressively, and with massive seriousness," and Reed eagerly hastening on with his impressions of Villa, the Secretary unburdened himself. "Mr. Reed," he said, with a troubled expression, "I must confess to you that there is one thing that I cannot understand about the Mexicans. Do you know, when one faction captures a soldier of another faction, they stand him up against the wall and shoot him down!"

But Mr. Bryan was in favor of any policy that would preserve peace, and he undertook to make an appointment for Reed with the President. Precisely at the assigned moment, he was led into the executive offices. Mr. Wilson, dressed in white flannels, sat at his desk alone in the middle of the great round chamber. Remembering the noisy energy of Theodore Roosevelt, Reed was chiefly impressed with the calmness of the office. The President shook hands in a friendly, unaffected way, and Reed felt at ease. He noticed the quiet, tired eyes, the lack of gestures, the even, gentle voice, and the mobile, revealing lips.

Reminding Reed that he was not to be quoted, Wilson spoke frankly. His policy towards Mexico was the traditional policy of the early days of the Republic, a policy of friendliness to all strivings of the oppressed and of opposition to all tyranny. The refusal to recognize the Huerta regime was not based on Huerta's assassination of Madero but on the fact that it was not a government by the people. Wilson strongly opposed interference in Mexican affairs. The occupation of Vera Cruz did not constitute interference; its aim was merely to check the series of provocations by which Huerta, in a desperate attempt to unite the Mexican people in his support, sought to force intervention. The only weapon the government had used against Huerta was non-recognition. The policy of non-interference would also apply if the Constitutionalists should confiscate the great estates to provide land for the peons. The President would prefer to see the landowners compensated, but he would make no demand that this be done. So far as his powers permitted, he would prevent the exploitation of the Mexican people either by Mexican tyrants or by foreign capitalists, but he would in no way curb the will of the people themselves.

Reed, though he had learned to be wary of liberals, was impressed. He was a little shocked that problems seemed so simple to Wilson, that he seemed so confident in the ability of democracy to cure the evils of capitalism, but he left the executive chamber convinced that Wilson was sincere in his fight against "the small predatory minorities which balk the people's struggle for intelligence and life." What chiefly made him tolerant of Wilson, however, was that the President, so far as Mexico was concerned, was on the right side.

Reed reported the interview in the way that he hoped would do the most good. "I appreciate your desire to help," the President wrote, "and your whole spirit in this matter." But he would not be quoted. His secretary explained: "The President opened his mind to you completely, with the understanding that you were not to quote him. If you were to recast the article so as to leave out all quotes and all intimations of directly echoing what the President said, and confine yourself to your own impressions received from the interview, I think it would be possible to authorize its publication." Reed did his best, but when he had made the article safe, from the President's point of view, it was so void of news-value that the editors of the *Metropolitan* would not print it.

Steffens had proven at least partly right, and Reed was disappointed. But there was swimming at Provincetown and there were talks with the people who came there, his friends and Mabel Dodge's and the artists and writers and radicals who were spending the summer on Cape Cod. The appearance of the Ludlow article brought high praise and the satisfaction of a letter from Carl Hovey, reporting that a bookstore in Denver had cancelled its standing order for fifty *Metropolitans* as a protest against "the vile unwarranted sensational lies" and "untruthful filth" of his article. Lazily he made his plans. He wanted to visit Joe Adams, who was at Saranac with tuberculosis. He wanted to interest some one in a collection of Mexican ballads and a translation of the miracle play he had seen. His mind was full of ideas for poems and plays and short stories and novels. Hovey and he devised plans for *Metropolitan* articles. But all that could wait; there was plenty of time.

IX

THIS IS NOT OUR WAR

CARL HOVEY kept his eyes on Europe, and by the end of
July he wired Reed, asking him to be ready to go to
France as the *Metropolitan's* war-correspondent. Mabel
Dodge was indignant at the interruption of the Provincetown
idyll, but, almost before she could explain the unimportance of
wars, Reed was on his way to Portland, for the first visit he had
paid his mother in two years. He found that his fame had
reached the city, and persons who once had made fun of him
were now eagerly proposing teas, luncheons, and dinners. He
took pleasure enough in the recognition of his success, but the
affairs themselves bored him, and he was glad to escape from the
stuffy atmosphere of polite parlors to an I.W.W. hall in which
Emma Goldman was speaking. There he met a young artist, Carl
Walters, and his wife. It was surprising to find an artist in Portland, and especially a good one, and Reed, learning that no one
was paying any attention to Walters' work, wrote an article
about it for the local paper. He would like to have seen more of
Carl and Helen Walters, but his mother was eager to have all of
his time. And after all, it was only a few days before, proud and
worried, she saw him start back across the continent on the fast-
est, most expensive train available.

There was an Englishman on the train—a clean-cut young
man, with nice color, a neat mustache, clothes that fitted exqui-
sitely, and shoes much too large. When tea was served, the cattle-
kings and wheat-barons and their wives watched him eagerly
as a guide to proper procedure. Reed was fascinated by the absolute correctness of everything the man did, and could not resist

the temptation to make the strange creature talk. He was going back to fight, not because he liked the French or hated the Germans, but because he came from an army family; there were no underlying causes of the war; there could be no revolution in England because British laborers were very well-paid "for persons of their class." "He was a splendid sight," Reed recorded, "as he stepped along the platform, the pink of young English manhood, the quintessence of that famous English ruling class that has made itself the greatest empire the world has ever seen— without the least idea what it was doing. He went to glory or the grave, fearless, handsome, unemotional, one hundred and sixty pounds of bone and muscle and gentle blood, with the inside of his head exactly like an Early Victorian drawing-room, all knick-knacks, hair-cloth furniture, and drawn blinds."

Armed with a letter Secretary Bryan had given him "to the diplomatic and consular officers of the United States in Europe," Reed prepared to sail. New York seemed to him unchanged by the war. Aside from the extra editions of the papers, which contained unprecedentedly large headlines, scanty accounts of the conflict, and long editorials describing the advantages that would accrue to the United States from the war, the city was still John Reed's playground. But he had a sense that all this was soon to be changed.

For John Reed knew what was happening. "The real war," he wrote in the *Masses*, "of which this sudden outburst of death and destruction is only an incident, began long ago. It has been raging for tens of years, but its battles have been so little advertised that they have been hardly noted. It is a clash of traders." The German Empire began, he pointed out, as a trade agreement, and not merely the German army but the whole imperial system had been tolerated by the progressive burghers of the country because they believed that commercial advantage would depend on armed force. The French and English traders, having seized the most desirable colonies while Germany was disorganized, talked hypocritically about peace and the *status quo*. France blocked German trade expansion in northern Africa; England checked her advance in Asia Minor. It was no wonder that the business men of Germany supported the Kaiser in his belligerent gestures.

His talk about blood and iron was nauseating, but Reed found it less sickening than "the raw hypocrisy of his armed foes, who shout for a peace which their greed has rendered impossible."

And he regarded as even more disgusting "the editorial chorus in America which pretends to believe—would have us believe—that the White and Spotless Knight of Modern Democracy is marching against the Unspeakably Vile Monster of Medieval Militarism." "What has democracy to do," he asked, "in alliance with Nicholas the Tsar? Is it Liberalism which is marching from the Petersburg of Father Gapon, from the Odessa of pogroms?" "We must not be duped," he insisted, "by this editorial buncome about Liberalism going forth to Holy War against Tyranny. This is not Our War."

On the evening of August 14, Reed had dinner with Fred Boyd and Edward Hunt on the roof of the Astor Hotel. All three of them were sailing that night, on three different ships. Reed, in accordance with plans he had formulated with Whigham and Hovey, was going to Italy, to report that country's entrance into the war on the side of Germany and Austria. Hunt, representing the *American Magazine*, was going to Holland, to see the Dutch open the dikes when the Germans began their expected invasion. And Boyd was returning to England to take part in the revolution that, he was altogether certain, would break out within a few months.

On board Reed's ship there were two Italian nobles, an Italian capitalist who owned a silk mill in Paterson and had helped break the strike, several German barons, an Austrian count, and officers of all nationalities. They habitually referred to the people in the steerage as "vermin" and "animals." From the spaciousness and cleanliness of the first-class deck, they leaned their pongee and silken breasts on the rail and looked down upon the seething life beneath them. When a sailor turned a stream of water on an old man who had fallen asleep, the old man cursed, and the other steerage passengers muttered sullenly, but the persons in pongee and silk were amused, all except the Paterson manufacturer, who had felt the strength of the "vermin," and who shouted, "The beasts! They ought to be shot or starved to death."

Next to the suffering of the workers in the steerage, workers going home to be shot for the sake of the kind of men who laughed from the first-class deck at their misfortunes, what chiefly impressed Reed was the friendliness of the different nationalities. Two Germans, an Italian, and a Frenchman, all on their way to join their respective armies, played bridge together daily. The Germans and Italians read French novels. One German had spent most of his life in Paris; another was a student at Oxford. The young Italian marquis had been educated at the Sorbonne and had worked on a London newspaper. The wife of one of the Frenchmen came from Berlin. "Amusements, education, the intellectual strength of every man on board, came, at least in part, from the very sources they were going, blindly, to destroy. It was all so confused—so unutterably silly."

It was so silly as to be incredible. Even the sight of British battleships and torpedo-boats off Gibraltar could not make the war seem real. The arrival on board of a British force suggested a kind of elaborate, humorless joke. The officers were so extremely British, so satisfied with their ignorance of German and Italian, so clearly the kind of men who knew cricket and football scores and took a cold tub every morning, that Reed could scarcely realize the seriousness of what was happening for the German passengers. Fifty of them were taken off the ship to be interned. The one man who signed a promise not to fight, though he had weak lungs and had long been exempt from military service, was scorned by the others. It was more than silly; it was insane.

As the ship steamed into the harbor of Naples, the singing of the men and women in the steerage was sweet and healthy, but Italy itself was as mad as the rest of Europe. The pacifists had hoped to take advantage of the division of sentiment between the party of the Entente, largely made up of industrialists and financiers, and the party of the Triple Alliance, the clericals and the members of the nobility. But the business men, having checked the friends of Germany and Austria, had no intention of letting themselves be held back from war by the intellectuals and the workers. Their great problem was the unemployed, on whom the radicals chiefly relied, and so a movement was started to recruit an honorary volunteer regiment for Tripoli. One hundred and fifty thousand laborers, unable to get either work or relief, joined. The trained regiments were brought back and sent to the Austrian border, and the most dangerous elements of the Italian population were marooned in the Sahara desert.

It became apparent that nothing worth reporting was likely to happen soon in Italy, and Reed went on to Geneva, which glittered like Monte Carlo at the height of the season. Germans, English, and French dined, danced, and gambled together. There were gay revues from Paris and famous orchestras and brilliant evening clothes. Again Reed felt that war was "a remote, an incredible thing." By general consent, it was seldom mentioned. Somebody might say across the table, "Do you suppose that the Germans will get to Paris?" But then one looked across the sun-lit lake towards the mountains, with the little villages at their foot, and found something else to talk about.

Reed took what was said to be the last train to Paris. At Cernadon they pulled into the station beside ten third-class carriages, which rocked with singing and cheering. The doors and windows were decorated with green vines and tree-branches, through which he could see the young faces and waving arms of the class of 1914—"bound for the military centers to undergo a training that would stamp out all their impulses and ideas, and turn them into infinitesimal parts of an obedient machine to hurl against the youth of Germany, who had been treated the same way." The veterans whom he later saw did not cheer or sing; they had "the curious, detached professional air of men going to work in a silk mill in the morning." "Beasts, they wisely spent their spare time eating, drinking, and sleeping, and for the rest obeyed their officers. That was what the class of 1914 would become." With the ten third-class carriages joined to their train, they passed through crowded stations, where women cheered and wept and waved their handkerchiefs. At Bourg there was a glimpse of several cars of wounded men, and the sight of bandages and the smell of iodoform dispelled what was left of the sense of war's unreality.

The beautiful September morning on which Reed reached Paris carried him back—only three years, after all—to the morning when he had returned from Spain and had settled down in the city. It was just such a day, the kind of day on which Parisians came back from the country, and the city roused with gay expectancy for a new season. But this Paris was dead. There were no omnibuses, no trucks, no street-cars. Shutters were pulled over store-windows. No one sat before the cafés on the Grands Boulevards. Not a person could be seen on the Rue de la Paix. Above silent streets the five flags of the allied nations drooped somberly from every window. The flags were everywhere, ghastly, irrelevant. It was as if the city had decked itself out for some vast rejoicing, and then had sickened. At night the theatres were closed, and the streets were dark and empty. Only the great white beams of the searchlights could be seen crossing the sky, and the one sound that broke the stillness of the night was the marching of troops along the cobblestones.

Reed looked for the courage that he expected from the French, and the stoicism that so many correspondents had attributed to them. What he found was ignorance and apathy. The rich left the city, offering their mansions to the Red Cross in the hope that they would be saved from destruction. Shopkeepers boarded up their stores and announced that they had joined the army. Later he saw the rich come back to their mansions and the merchants to their shops. He found the leaders of the Confédération Générale du Travail cooperating with the government, and the Socialists and syndicalists supporting the war, while the capitalist press called for the suppression of civil rights, under the pretense of wartime necessity, and advocated the ending of the reforms that labor had won.

The war no longer seemed silly; but it was more confusing than ever, and infinitely depressing. It was difficult for Reed, as he saw the docility of the soldiers, to hold to his belief that revolutionary change would come out of the war. Moreover, although he had seen nothing of the front, what he witnessed in Paris was enough to convince him of the tremendous mechanized brutality of the struggle. There was no romance in it. To the personal depression of a sensitive young man with a deep feeling for humanity's sufferings was added the disappointment of the war-correspondent. Even if he had not been cooped up in Paris and half-sick with indigestion, this was not a war he could write about as he had written of Villa's battles in Mexico.

HE SAT about with the other correspondents, all of them barred from the front, discussing the likelihood of a siege, the causes of the war, and the badness of the meals. Occasionally a German airplane flew over the city, and citizens would hurry to the roof-tops to shoot at it. Official statements spoke only of the success of the army's tactical retreat. As stragglers came into the city, the conviction grew that the Germans were within a few miles of Paris. Robert Dunn, a correspondent as restless and as defiant of fear as Reed himself, suggested that they rent an automobile, secure a pass on the pretense that they were going to Nice for their health, and try to work their way to the front.

The pass carried them through the defenses of the city, frantic with preparations for a siege, and they soon turned north and east. After a time, they began to meet refugees, some pushing on towards Paris, others waiting by the roadside, their enormous farm-wagons piled high with bedding, furniture, and all the little treasures they had been able to snatch. Finally they came to a village that had been demolished the day before by the Germans. They stopped among the smouldering ruins, and soon a crowd of peasant women gathered about the car and, with tears and pitiful ejaculations, told of the burning and pillaging of the town.

They went on, reached Rozoy, and stopped for lunch. Two English correspondents came in, accompanied by two officers. The reporters had been arrested for being within the military zone, and they warned Reed and Dunn that they, too, would be caught. The officers paid no attention to what was none of their business, and the two Americans bade farewell to the two Englishmen, and went on. They tried by several roads to reach the front, but, though they were not arrested, they were in-variably sent back. Finally they reached Crécy, where they de-cided to spend the night.

That night Reed fell into conversation with the guard of an ammunition dump. The soldiers greeted him with kindly, gentle curiosity, and gave him rum. The Germans were no worse than others, a man told him. "Lord help us," he said, "the Germans as a rule are good enough chaps. It's a silly business, this killing of men." Another spoke up: "I'm not for war on any count. But us Socialists, we're taking the field to destroy militarism— that's what we're doing. And when we come back again after the war, and Kitchener says to the House of Commons, 'What will we do for these brave soldiers to show our gratitude for saving the Empire?' we're going to say, 'You can jest give us the Empire.' "

The next morning Dunn and Reed, deciding they could not reach the front without official permission, went to British field headquarters at Coulommiers. The provost marshal ordered them to prepare a written statement, and, as they worked on it, the two English correspondents appeared, gloomier than ever. The marshal told them they were not under arrest, but ordered them confined to their rooms. The correspondent of the London *Times* predicted that they would be given two years in prison, but the next morning they found that their sentence was much more lenient. They were turned over to the French gendarmerie, and sent by slow stages to Tours. There they were made to take an oath not to venture within the military zone again. Reed asked what would happen if he refused to sign, and the official drew his hand across his throat.

The experience, though they had not reached the front, had at least had its exciting moments, and Reed found the inactivity of Paris less tolerable than before. He thought of going back to Italy, and thence to Austria and Germany, but at the last moment he decided to join Fred Boyd in England. Boyd, he discovered when he reached London, was completely disillusioned. Men Boyd had known as ardent pacifists were making recruiting speeches, and labor leaders who had pledged themselves to the international revolution were talking about the necessity of exterminating the Huns. He was deep in despair; his own sacrifices and those of thousands of other radicals seemed to have accomplished less than nothing. Reed had seen enough to fear that his friend was right, and they made a gloomy pair.

With Boyd's aid, Reed planned to do an article on England. Having left a Paris only recently freed from the threat of siege, his first impression was that London was quite unaffected by the war. "The great gray town," he wrote, "still pours its roaring streams along the Strand and Oxford Street and Piccadilly; endless lines of omnibuses and taxicabs and carriages pass; in the morning the clerks go down to the city in their carefully-brushed silk hats and thread-bare frock coats,—and the amazing London bobbie embodies in his uplifted hand the dignity and precedent of the Empire. At night the theatres and restaurants are going full blast, thronged with an apparently inexhaustible supply of nice young men in faultless evening dress, and beautiful women; along Leicester Square and Piccadilly press the same thousands and thousands of girls, and the hundreds of slim young men with painted lips, which yearly grow to be more characteristic of London streets. The same ghastly ragged men rise up out of the gutter to open your carriage door; the same bums slouch along the benches in Hyde Park."

But there was a difference. For one thing there were the posters everywhere: "Your King and Country Need You! Enlist for the Duration of War. England Needs a Million." They were even on private cars, and once he saw a huge luxurious motor, two liveried men on the front seat, a silk-hatted broker in the tonneau, and on the back "Lord Kitchener Wants More Men."

Then there were the soldiers, the officers in the Piccadilly crowd, the territorials drilling in Hyde Park, and—of special interest—the volunteers. Lord Kitchener's appeal had, at the end of September, brought forth six hundred thousand men. "It is magnificent," Reed wrote, "and infinitely depressing. This patriotism—what a humanly fine, stupid instinct gives birth to it, the sacrifice for an ideal, the self-immolation for something greater than self. Generation after generation surging up to the guns to be shot to death for an ideal so extremely vague that they never know what they are fighting for. Ask one of these recruits what England is to him, and you will see that it is nothing but a name and a feeling. One of the most widespread accusations hurled at the Mexican revolutionists by virtuous Americans was that they didn't know what they were fighting for, and the

English know even less what they are fighting for than the Mexicans."

He had had many lessons in the power of patriotism, and he was not blind to the nobility to be found in even the vaguest idealism, but he was also conscious, as he walked about London, that other forces had helped to give Kitchener his volunteers. The Women's Patriotic League claimed one hundred thousand members, each of whom refused to receive any man not in uniform whose age and condition would permit him to serve in the army. Committees of society women stood in front of the National Gallery handing white feathers to civilians who passed by. Popular actresses in music halls singled out men in the audience and asked them why they did not enlist. Moreover, the paralysis of business at the outbreak of the war had thrown thousands of men out of work, and neither jobs nor relief would be given these men if they were of the age for service. Some firms discharged all men eligible for the army and filled their places with older ones. Others promised to help their employees' families if they would enlist and otherwise to discharge them. "It was really conscription," Reed realized, "conscription hiding under a pleasanter name, as has always been England's way—conscription ready to appear in its true colors the minute recruiting fell off."

Fundamentally, it seemed to him, the masses of people were not interested in the war. They were not much concerned about the invasion of Belgium, and the German peril, so terrifyingly portrayed by the press, still seemed to them remote. They were beginning to be disturbed by British losses, and two months of propaganda had had an effect, but in the factory towns of the north and west, where business in munitions and army equipment had brought prosperity, the people were more interested in football scores and moving-pictures than in the war.

It was the aristocracy, Reed came to believe, that wanted the war and was forcing it upon the rest of the country. "We in America," he wrote, "have long believed that the British upper classes were doomed, that their vitality was gone; and our final proof was the bridling of the House of Lords and the triumph of Liberalism. And now, like a waking lion, the British aristocracy crushes our teeming ant-hill with a blow of its paw, and shows us again, contemptuously, a servile England split into classes, where every man knows his place. Here stands erect what we thought was dead—the stupid, sterile, gorgeous Imperial idea."

For Reed, Lord Kitchener embodied that idea: "Kitchener of Khartoum is absolute ruler of England—Bloody Kitchener, the most complete expression of an imperial policy which has consisted in blowing men from the mouths of cannon in order to civilize them. There is something revolting about Kitchener, the cold, the merciless, the efficient—the very Prussian ideal of a military man." It was Kitchener who was making all England into a war-machine as efficient as the Kaiser's. He controlled the telephone, the telegraph, the mails. He had cowed the press. The English knew only what he wanted them to know. He had sacrificed Belgium for the sake of England, and, to save England, his will had held the French army firm. Through him the aristocracy ruled the country. The public school boy—"that peculiar, inhuman breed of aristocrat, as pestilential as the Prussian Junker" —was in the saddle.

The war was giving conservative England its opportunity. It was a fashionable war, with benefit concerts and receptions, at which social distinctions were carefully observed. It was true that the upper classes not only supported the war with social influence and forced their tenants and employees to enlist; they also sent their sons. But their sons went, in this great battle for democracy, as leaders. A rich American who had lived in England for twenty-five years wrote down for Reed the names of the leading families in his part of the country. Then he looked up the local regiment in the army list; almost every officer bore one of those names.

The aristocracy was fighting for survival, and it was ready to crush opposition with utter ruthlessness. But, Reed saw to his disappointment, there was no opposition worth crushing. He had expected much from the intelligent, politically-conscious working class of England, but the workers there seemed as docile as those in France. The Socialists, after a few mass meetings at the outset, had subsided. The intellectuals, with one or two honorable but impotent exceptions, were helping to create the myth of the German beast. Only a handful of Liberal and Laborite politicians had dared oppose the war, and they had been crushed.

The aristocrats wanted position, power, and prestige. The business men wanted, quite simply, the crushing of German trade. These two groups, a little minority of men who knew what they were after, overcame the inertia of the great majority. The business men were determined that, wherever Germany had secured a commercial foothold by superior manufacture and better salesmanship, English goods must be established. German property in England was confiscated, and German patents were revoked. A campaign was begun to induce the public to buy only goods made in England, and stores that had German stocks scratched off the German labels and substituted their own. The British fleet virtually blockaded Italy, Holland, Norway, and Sweden, to prevent goods from reaching Germany, and did not hesitate to ruin Swedish industry in the process or starve the Dutch people.

Reed had called it a traders' war, and it did not take much study of England's policy to prove how right he had been. For fifteen years England had been seeking to isolate Germany, just as Russia, her ally, had worked for the dismemberment of the Austro-Hungarian Empire, Germany's only support. "On my map," Reed wrote, "there is a small collection of islands off the northern coast of France, isolated from the Continent by a channel, and together a trifle larger than the State of Ohio. From there stretch the wires that control a tenth of the earth's surface. England's guns squat in the mouth of the Mediterranean; Egypt and Malta are hers; she grips the Red Sea, sucks the blood from all India, menaces half a billion human beings from Hong Kong, owns all Australia, half North America, and half of Africa. The fleets of the world salute her ensign on every commanding headland, and her long gray battleships steam unopposed from sea to sea. England's word is said in every council, conference, treaty. She is the great intriguer, sitting like a spider in the web of nations and disposing of them to her benefit. And it was England's will that Germany should be destroyed."

He would have been a poor Socialist if any of this had surprised him, but he could not help being shocked by the blatant hypocrisy of the Empire. The press was trying to popularize Russia, talking about the gentle Cossacks, the end of pogroms, and the growth of civil liberty, though members of Parliament spoke openly about the war with Russia to follow the extermination of Germany. Much was made of England's championship of treaty obligations and her befriending of smaller nations, though England's bloody record was spread on every history book. The very England that had butchered the people of India, China, and the Soudan, that had driven the natives of Tasmania into a sea-girt corner of the island and slaughtered them like rabbits, shrieked about German atrocities, and the England that had taken the Elgin Marbles and filled its museums with stolen property from Egypt and Greece, called upon the world to witness the iniquity of German looting.

He had no illusions about the superiority of Germany to England, but he hated and feared the monstrous hypocrisy of imperial policy. He saw clearly the danger of the British campaign of lies and distortions, which was doubly a menace because of British control of the sources of news. The article that he wrote in England—an article that the *Metropolitan* never printed—was a warning to America. "Do not be deceived," he cried, "by talk about democracy and liberty. This is not a crusade against militarism but a scramble for spoils. It is not our war."

And, despite the ignominious capitulation of the Socialists, he found signs that the people of the Empire might yet see through the vast deception. Riots in India, revolts in South Africa, and Sinn Fein demonstrations in Ireland hinted that the widely advertised loyalty of the colonies might be less strong than the press pretended to believe. Even in England the war was generally unpopular, and there was some bitterness. "It may be," he wrote, "that when the cold days come and the toll of wounded lengthens and the continual slackening of trade grips England with poverty labor in England will see its great opportunity, and that when this war is done there will be no more Empire."

At least one could hope so, though there was little enough evidence.

REED brought Boyd back to Paris with him. They had to spend the night in Calais, and, being restless, bribed a gendarme to tell them where there was a bistro that kept open after the nine o'clock wartime curfew. There were three submarine sailors in the place, two soldiers, and three large and unusually coarse women. Reed bought them all champagne, and they began to discuss the war. Boyd asked the soldiers and sailors why they were fighting. "Because France was invaded," a sailor said. "But the Germans say Germany was invaded," said Boyd. "That may be true," said the sailor; "perhaps we were both invaded."

With Boyd and Andrew Dasburg, Reed started on a walking tour through the valley of the Marne, to see the battlefield. There was another encounter with the military authorities, this time through no fault of Reed's own, and he was warned that he would be expelled from France if he was reported again. But he did have an opportunity to see the appalling destruction, and, after his disillusionment, the sight created an unfamiliar mood in him. He felt for the moment that wars and the struggle for peace were of no importance. The traces of the battle were already being obliterated. Peasants whose homes had been destroyed were working in the shell-torn fields. "The plowing and the sowing of the harvests, the swinging seasons—cold winters, and the stirring of the blood of the world in March—love and death and the need of food and clothing, will be the only reality of their life. As it has been from time immemorial, in spite of wave after wave of Hun and Visigoth and the devastation of forgotten wars. The fields shall heal themselves of their scars; but more patient than they, the people of the little village will do their will with the life force."

Such semi-mystical moods were rare. For the most part, he was the analytical observer, too analytical for the editors of the *Metropolitan*, who wanted colorful stories of heroic troops. It was surprising how much Reed understood, how much was clear to him, the impressionistic reporter, that was obscure to professional students of history and diplomatic affairs. His Socialism did not deceive him into finding evidences of revolution where they did not exist, but it did inoculate him against the sleek phrases of the liberal apologists for war.

It was his awareness of the true issues and his consequent inability to identify himself with either set of combatants that made it so difficult for him to write. He knew that the editors of the *Metropolitan* had reason for dissatisfaction with his work. They had not sent him to Europe to write general analyses: he was, except for the essential accuracy of his insight, unequipped for that kind of writing, and the other kind, impressionistic reporting, he could do—or, at least, he had done—better than anyone else. But the truth was that he saw nothing but dull, mechanical routine. There was no drama, no glory in the whole business.

Steffens tried to help him. "The things you see and hear in Paris and London," he wrote, "would probably hold me spellbound with interest if you should sit down and tell them to me. We are getting what you wanted to give: a grasp of the war as a whole. This is the best point of view of the war as a whole. New York gets the most news from the most places, and all the comments, for we have perspective, too, which you have not and cannot have. I think you should tell us what you see and hear, just as you did in Mexico. Your views on Mexico were not nearly so good as your descriptions and narrations. You're not wise, Jack; not yet. But you certainly can see and you certainly can write."

It was good advice, but not good enough. Steffens did not understand the depression that filled Reed at the spectacle of these mechanical armies, machine-like men tending their death-dealing machines. Reed had to come to terms with this horror, and his attempt to understand it rationally was the bravest, soundest way. What matter if he said things that Steffens had always known? It was more important for him to understand the war than to maintain his reputation as a correspondent. Steffens was right in telling him to use his eyes as he had in Mexico. What he did not realize was that the expression of what Reed saw with Villa's army had been guided by a deep emotion, whereas now, in Europe, with no emotion to unify his impressions, there could be no substitute for understanding. He was too honest to accept other men's patterns, especially those patterns that condoned and even glorified the war by selecting colorful incidents for romantic treatment. He would not be false to his own eyes; he saw too much not to know that what was most important lay deep below the surface and could not be seen.

Reed was depressed enough at moments, but even the facing of complex problems could not exhaust his energy or check his romantic nature. Mabel Dodge had come to Paris soon after his arrival there, and for a time they had got on very well. But suddenly there was a major explosion. Reed began to visit a couple he had known in the Village, and he became convinced that the woman was badly treated by her husband. One day he called and found her seriously ill. Her husband, she said, had gone away for a few days, though he knew she was sick. Reed's chivalrous spirit made him constitute himself her nurse. He took the most patient care of her, with the great gentleness of which he was capable, and, by the time she had recovered, was convinced that he was in love with her. They planned to elope, and, when she had her divorce, to be married.

Mabel Dodge sailed for New York. She called together her friends and Reed's and held a council of war. She said that she had freed Reed completely. She hoped that he would always be her friend, for she felt that she understood him, but she would in no way interfere with his plans. On the other hand, it was clear to her that the woman with whom he was at the moment infatuated was not suited to him. Even more apparent was the fact that he was not suited to her and that she would be less happy with him than with her husband. Mrs. Dodge called upon the friends to consider the matter and, if they agreed with her, to use their influence to prevent disaster.

Most of them were perfectly aware how little influence they had. Reed went his own way, but Mrs. Dodge was proved at least partly right, for it was not long before the affair bored him. By the time he reached Berlin, he was inclined to regard the whole episode as comic. Robert Dunn was there, and for his benefit Reed described his emotions when the girl's husband was threatening to shoot him at the same time that Mabel Dodge was trying to commit suicide.

And then, in Berlin, he found a girl staying at his hotel whom he had known in New York, had, in fact, met at Mabel Dodge's. She had had an unhappy love affair, and Reed was a good deal shaken by his narrow escape from matrimony and his rupture with Mrs. Dodge. The affair was romantic enough, but it was pleasant rather than intense, and there was little danger of tragedy or even ill will at the end. It made the weeks in Berlin considerably brighter.

Berlin needed sweetening for Reed. Although the German authorities had promised him that he would be allowed to visit the trenches, it took a long time for arrangements to be made. Meanwhile there was, aside from private diversions, little to do except stand around the hotel bars and drink with the other correspondents. There were concerts, which Reed enjoyed, but at one of them an actor recited a poem of hate against the Allies, and all the pleasure in Haydn and Mozart vanished. Everywhere were evidences of the efficiency of the German war-machine, and he was weary of war-machines. The blunt aggressiveness of the German leaders was only slightly less irritating than the hypocrisy of British statesmen, and the brutality of some German officers to their men was intolerable. Many of the reporters, he discovered, were privately sympathetic to Germany, though they were already shaping their dispatches to match the pro-Ally sentiments of the editorial columns of their papers. For himself, he could discover no basis for preference.

It was heartening, after all he had seen of the vacillation of Socialist leaders in France and Great Britain, to talk with Karl Liebknecht. The Socialist deputy, leader of the handful who had dared to oppose war appropriations, seemed diffident, almost shy. He played with a paper cutter as he talked, his dark, round face pallid in the light of a green-shaded desk lamp. His mouth, under the bristling mustache, was calm, and his brown eyes were gentle. Reed asked him if he stood by his attitude of opposition to the war. "What else," said Liebknecht, "can a Socialist do?"

At last came permission to go to Lille and then to the trenches.

Senator Beveridge, Robert Dunn, and Ernest Poole were in the group. They rode through German France, where, under the surveillance of German soldiers, French peasants were working in the fields. "Don't imagine," he wrote, "that German soldiers are a cruel, arrogant race. They have done admirable things. I am sure that some of these little northern French towns were never so clean, so intelligently organized. Everywhere they have re-opened schools and churches; they have re-established local institutions and local charities; they have scoured whole towns, lighted every house with electricity, placed up-to-date hospitals, served by the finest doctors in the world, at the free disposal of the humblest citizen." But the people were a conquered people, filled with bitterness and hatred, with their sons in the French army and all their hopes centered in a French victory.

At Lille the entire party stayed in the best hotel—at the expense, they assumed, of the German government. Actually, they afterwards learned, the bill was paid by the city. Soldiers, officers, and guests of the army were lodged in private houses and hotels, whose owners were permitted to charge a stated amount. The account was paid by a signed order, and the landlord collected his money from the city treasury. Direct war contributions amounted to two million francs a month. The Germans had confiscated food, leather, rubber, cloth, and copper. The population lived on bitter black bread, made half of bad flour and half of potatoes. Twelve hostages, including the mayor's son, were kept under guard.

And yet Reed found the German soldiers—and most of the officers, for that matter—friendly, decent people. The soldiers were jovial and childlike, with little animosity against the French. Reed could easily believe the story of the Christmas truce, when the men on both sides, in defiance of orders, ceased firing. But, unfortunately, it was just as easy to believe that when the truce was over, the firing was resumed. It was precisely as it had been in the French and British armies—no hatred for the enemy, no sense of anything to be gained by the war, no ability to give a reason for fighting—just cheerful efficiency in the business of killing.

Reed wanted to see actual fighting: perhaps it would help to explain the mystery; at least he could say that he had seen war at first-hand. The entire party was led to one of the quieter sectors. They could see both the French and German trenches and could hear the constant sound of firing. There was not a human being in sight, though within three hundred yards a thousand Germans were eating, drinking, sleeping, and shooting, and, two hundred yards beyond them a thousand Frenchmen were doing the same things. When they were back at the automobiles, their guide asked them if they were satisfied. Dunn promptly said he was not, and Reed joined him. One of the officers telephoned the general in command of the Second Bavarian Army Corps, and they were given permission to enter the trenches in a more active sector that night.

They had lunch with the general at his headquarters at Comines. Thousands of soldiers, having spent their three days in the trenches, were resting in the great barracks, a converted factory, in the city. As the correspondents left, they met column after column of heavily laden motor and horse trucks and long lines of slouching, mud-soaked soldiers. They came to Houthem, where recruits were given their final training within range of the French cannons. The road on which they passed was sporadically shelled, and by the time they came to the battery they were to inspect, the explosions seemed unpleasantly close. The captain of the battery was cordial and re-assuring. He exhibited his biggest gun, and gave the word to his men. There was a flat roar; flame and gray haze belched forth; and the whistling scream of the roaring shell rose and dwindled. In the dugout a soldier, with a telephone receiver strapped to his ears and an open novel in his lap, reported to the captain that French cannon were being moved into place to shell the battery. Outside, the captain pointed to a French plane hovering high above them in the attempt to find their position, and they saw two German monoplanes rise and drive the scout away.

Some of the correspondents thought they had seen enough, and their guide's account of the dangers of going into the trench convinced them that they had better return to Lille. Reed was inclined to agree with them, but Dunn insisted that at least they reconnoiter. After supper at field headquarters, the two of them left for the front.

They trudged on in the rain, talking with Lieutenant Riegel in fragmentary French and German. The French batteries were silent, but the German guns roared steadily. Reed visualized the great switchboard singing and humming in the kitchen of brigade headquarters and the quivering miles of telephone wire that led from where muddy men with night-glasses watched the French lines under the blinding glare of rockets. Smoothly the great machine functioned, calm questions and answers, deliberate judgments, the word passing from trench to gun, from gun to trench, from Houthem to Comines, to Lille, to Brussels, perhaps to Berlin.

They passed a field kitchen, and the two men tending it cried "Grüss Gott" like the simple Bavarian peasants they were. In the darkness they stumbled against men moving along in the rain, relieved artillery. On one stretch of the road rifle bullets spat in the mud, and just after they had passed there was a burst of machine-gun fire. They walked thirty feet apart. "We lose about twenty men a night here," Lieutenant Riegel commented.

In the stone-vaulted wine-cellar of a ruined chateau the major in command of the trench played the chateau's grand piano, which had miraculously survived the German artillery attack on the handful of English who had held the place a month or two before. He had been on a concert tour in America, and talked with them eagerly about the country, as he gave them beer.

The approach-trench, flooded when a shot hit the bank of the Ypres canal, was impassable, and they walked, again spread out, through an open beet-field. Bullets came close enough to splash them with mud, but they reached the approach-trench beyond the break and scrambled into it. Struggling on, staggering, falling, thrusting their arms to the shoulder in the wet slime of the sides, they came at last to the trench that stretched the entire length of the German lines.

The lieutenant gave them Munchener and then took them outside. Men stood shoulder to shoulder, shielded by thin plates of steel, each pierced with the loophole through which the rifle lay. Sodden with the drenching rain, their bodies crushing into the oozy mud, they stood thigh deep in thick brown water, and spent eight hours out of every twenty-four in shooting. The officer ordered a man to send up rockets, and in their light Reed could see the opposing trench, a black gash pricked with rifle-flame. Only a little way off lay the huddled, blue-coated bodies of the French who had been slain in an attempted advance of the week before. They were slowly sinking into the mud.

Suddenly the French guns began, far down the line. The firing swept along and began directly opposite them. Diabolical whistlings laced the sky, and shrapnel crackled overhead. The German howitzers went into action, and Reed could see the flames leap as their shells struck. The ground shook. Dunn and Reed staggered into the lieutenant's dugout. "You're safer in the trench," he explained. "But it doesn't last long," he continued, and just then the noise chopped suddenly off, and the rifle-fire sounded like crickets in a pasture.

They played poker with the officers in the dugout, and listened, over the telephone wire, as the major in the chateau wine-cellar played Chopin waltzes. As they came out of the dugout, before daybreak, the lieutenant called a soldier and took his rifle. "Would you like to have a shot?" he asked. Tense after their night in the trenches, they laughed feverishly, and both of them fired in the general direction of France. They left the trench with the men going off duty. The firing had dwindled away, and they felt almost safe. Many of the soldiers were bent over with rheumatism, and a few had to be carried on stretchers. They were silent with the silence of desperately weary men. Suddenly there was a scream, and, in the light of the lieutenant's pocket-lamp, they saw a man seized, bound, and gagged. His eyes were wide and staring, and his shoulders twitched convulsively. He was quite mad. And then, as they were nearly back to the chateau, they heard a humming deep chorus of hushed voices. It was the thousand men from Comines, washed, dried, fed, and rested, marching in for their three days in the trenches.

Neither Dunn nor Reed said much; they had, as Reed recorded, a good deal to think about. Reed had seen at last the actual conduct of the war. The experience gave him the material for the one first-rate article that grew out of his five months in western Europe. He had entered sympathetically into the emotions of the fighting men in the trenches. He took no such pleasure in the experience as he had in sharing the lot of La Tropa, but at least he had seen something that could be honestly recorded without comment or interpretation. This was war, the full brutal, mechanical force of it. He had felt the horror of death and the horror of military life. The fighting not merely lacked glamor; it was starkly terrible. But Reed could have accepted the horror if he had not sensed so fully the futility. He wanted to say to the soldiers of both sides, "This is not your war."

X

MANHATTAN REVISITED

JOHN REED sailed for New York in January, 1915, depressed
and bewildered by what he had seen. Steffens, he was ready
to believe, might be right in saying that people in the
United States understood the war better than people in Europe.
Two days after he landed, he knew that Steffens was wrong.
The idea that in New York one could see all sides of the struggle was, Reed soon realized, ridiculous. New York was getting
almost all of its news through London, and any one who had
been in England could recognize the subtle distortions of the
British propagandists. The completeness with which the people
of the North Atlantic states accepted the Allied interpretation
of the war stunned Reed. His own protests, especially with regard to the atrocity stories, were brushed aside as pro-German
prejudice or irresponsible nonsense. The American people were
reading the adroitly colored dispatches of such war-correspondents as Philip Gibbs and H. W. Nevinson and the lofty phrases
of Wells, Kipling, Galsworthy, and Bennett. They saw through
England's eyes, and nothing Reed could say made any impression.

As yet, only the most bellicose clamored for actual participation, but Reed was conscious that influential sections of the
population, especially in the Northeast, were making dangerous
assumptions. He foresaw, moreover, that Allied orders for war
supplies would increase, would offset the damage to American
business that the blockade had wrought, and would create for
American finance and industry a material stake in Allied victory.
The drift was towards war, and he could see no adequate resist-

ance. His Socialist friends understood the economic causes of the conflict, but many of them were chiefly interested in explaining away the collapse of Socialism in the belligerent countries. As for the pacifists, though he agreed with their desire to keep America neutral at all costs, he was a little doubtful about their methods. Their emphasis on the physical horrors of warfare seemed to him dangerously close to hysteria, and he objected to their making the opposition to war a moral issue.

That there was a strong sentiment against war he did not doubt, but no one seemed to know how it could be effectively canalized. Before he had gone to France, he had heard Walter Lippmann discussing plans for the *New Republic*, and he had hoped that the new weekly might provide the right kind of leadership. He returned to find that it had been launched. The money was provided by Mrs. Willard Straight, and Lippmann was associated in the editorship with Herbert Croly, Walter Weyl, Philip Littell, and Francis Hackett. Reed was familiar, of course, with Lippmann's *Preface to Politics*, which had appeared in 1913, and he knew Croly's *Promise of American Life* at least by reputation. He did not fully understand how Lippmann's Socialism could be reconciled with Croly's desire "to unite the Hamiltonian principle of national political responsibility and efficiency with a frank democratic purpose." Croly's Federalism, Weyl's Jeffersonianism, and Lippmann's Socialism seemed a strange combination, and yet Reed could see how much the three men had in common. For one thing, they were all realists and rationalists; that is, they emphasized the necessity of accepting the *status quo* as their point of departure; and they had complete confidence in the power of the intellect—more specifically, their intellects—to solve the problems of the social order. Reed had an uncomfortable feeling that realism such as theirs was closely akin to opportunism, and he had a strong sense of the fallibility of human reason, but he was a good deal awed by the erudition, poise, and aggressiveness of the *New Republic's* editors.

He was interested in the *New Republic* not merely as a phenomenon of American life but as a medium for the expression of ideas that many of his friends had long urged upon him. Not

only was Lippmann one of the principal editors; Bob Hallowell
was treasurer, and Lee Simonson and Alfred Kuttner were frequent contributors. He studied with particular care the editorials
on the war, and it seemed to him that they were singularly successful in adding to what he felt to be the universal confusion.
They were so superior to ordinary considerations of human suffering and material interests that he could find only a tenuous
relation between their assumptions and reality. It seemed reasonable enough to say, "The newer ideal of peace, whether in
domestic or foreign policy, has to be actively and intentionally
promoted," or, "A nation does not commit the great sin when it
fights. It commits the great sin when it fights for a bad cause or
when it is afraid to fight for a good cause," or "Nations do not
avoid war by preparing for war, but neither do they avoid war
by being unprepared for war." And yet Reed had the sense that
all of this elaborate logic could so easily provide a justification
for America's entry into the war. The slogan, "This is not our
war," might be less subtle, even in a sense less true, but it was
a good deal less dangerous.

He was equally puzzled by the *New Republic's* attitude towards the labor problem. There was a whole series of editorials
that maintained with great erudition what Reed knew to be
true, namely, that the Socialist Party of America had ceased to
be a revolutionary party. When this was said in the *Masses*, he
could heartily applaud, but the way in which the *New Republic*
said it left him bewildered and irritated. There was such an air
of condescension: "Its errors are less of the heart than of the
head, and its enthusiasm, its self-sacrifice, and its occasional
spurts of courage more than compensate for its obstinacy in misrepresentation and for a certain mendacity born of fanaticism.
The Socialist Party offers an opportunity to hundreds of little
groups all over the country to educate themselves in public
meeting if not in public affairs." Why Croly and Lippmann
should feel so superior to the Socialists, weak as the party was,
Reed could not see. When he looked for some positive statement of the *New Republic's* remedy for the inefficiency, injustice, and cruelty of American industrialism, he could find nothing but vague talk about industrial democracy. There is always

violence in a strike, the editors would observe; it is never possible to decide who is at fault; the only solution is to eliminate the causes of strife by setting up machinery for the peaceful solution of difficulties. John Reed, who was not a profound student of economics but who had, after all, been in jail in Paterson and seen the ruins of the Ludlow tent colony, would wonder precisely what sort of machinery would serve the purpose. "We do not expect," the editors reasonably assured him, "to jump straight from the present absolutism into a cooperative democracy. Industry will have to pass through the intermediate steps, through limited monarchy, through representative government, before self-government is possible."

It did not lessen Reed's bewilderment and irritation to find, in one of the first issues of the *New Republic,* an article by Walter Lippmann called "Legendary John Reed." Reed had satirized Lippmann in *A Day in Bohemia,* and the article was an appropriate enough response, defining the difference between them from Lippmann's point of view as the poem had defined it from Reed's. Lippmann said a number of complimentary things, and there was no doubt that the intention of the piece was friendly. But there was an undertone of condescension that Reed resented. Lippmann, the precocious author of *Preface to Politics* and *Drift and Mastery,* made a good deal of the playboy in Reed: "I can't think of a form of disaster which John Reed hasn't tried and enjoyed. He has half-spilled himself into commercialism, had his head turned by flattery, tried to act like a cynical war-correspondent, posed as a figure out of Ibsen." It was true, but Reed could not be blamed for feeling it was not the whole truth. And he was a little annoyed by the way Lippmann, evidently thinking of himself as the true revolutionary, poked fun at Reed as a pseudo-revolutionary: "For a few weeks Reed tried to take the *Masses* view of life. He assumed that all capitalists were fat, bald, and unctuous, that Victor Berger and the Socialist Party and Samuel Gompers and the trade unions are a fraud on labor. He made an effort to believe that the working class is not composed of miners, plumbers, and working men generally, but is a fine, statuesque giant who stands on a high hill facing the sun. He wrote stories about the night court

and plays about ladies in kimonos. He talked with intelligent
tolerance about dynamite, and thought he saw an intimate connection between the cubists and the I.W.W. He even read a
few pages of Bergson." Reed did not deny that Lippmann knew
ten times as much about Marx as he did, but he could not be
blamed for wondering why a couple of erudite books and a few
weeks as secretary to Socialist Mayor Lunn of Schenectady entitled Walter Lippmann to set himself up as a model revolutionary. He had called Lippmann "our all-unchallenged chief,"
and he meant it, but the article sounded as if Lippmann thought
of himself as a stern father and Reed as a spoiled child: "At times
when he seemed to be rushing himself and others into trouble,
when his ideas were especially befuddled, I have tried to argue
with him. But all laborious elucidation he greets with pained
boredom." Lippmann, as well as Reed, was considerably under
thirty.

REED was too busy to dwell long on the Lippmann incident. His
experiences on the western front had given him material for two
short stories, one of which he sent to the *Metropolitan*, the other
to the *Masses*. The *Metropolitan* story, "The Barber of Lille,"
had been suggested by his observations of the oppressed and
deeply bitter citizenry of German France. Out of a casual conversation with a barber, he fashioned a melodramatic tale of the
murder of a German officer. The wife, half in love with the
German, hysterically spurs her husband on to the deed, telling
him the murder will be the signal for the people of Lille to rise.
It would be pure melodrama if the barber's old father were not
given the last words: "Do you think the city will rise? Don't
you know that the grocer, and the tobacconist, and the cafetier,
and the baker are living off the Germans? Don't you know that
the town is sold? Can't you understand that the Germans buy
and pay money?"

As so often, the *Masses* got the better work. "Daughter of
the Revolution" grew out of one of the lonely nights in Paris, a
night spent in a café with two or three girls of the streets. It
was one of these girls—he called her Marcelle—who was the
daughter of the revolution. Her grandfather had been shot in the

Commune; her father and brother had led strikes and been beaten by the police. She was half-proud, half-ashamed of her revolutionary heritage. She, too, had wanted liberty, but liberty to enjoy at once the good things life offered. So she became a prostitute. "It was not vice that had twisted her," Reed commented, "but the intolerable degradation of the human spirit by the masters of the earth, the terrible punishment of those who thirst for liberty." In Reed's eyes, she, too, though she did not know it and either thought of herself as a sinner and a renegade or thought of her father and brother as narrow fools, was a revolutionary.

He was interested not only in short stories but also in plays. The Washington Square Players were presenting "Moondown" on their second bill, together with Andreyev's 'Love of One's Neighbor," Phillip Moeller's "Two Blind Beggars and One Less Blind," and Brock Pemberton's "My Lady's Honor." The success of the little play encouraged him to take out and revise *Enter Dibble*. He had probably begun this three-act play as early as 1913, but he had never been satisfied with it, and had from time to time tried to revise it. When he finished this further revision in February, 1915, H. J. Whigham of the *Metropolitan* sent the play to Granville Barker. Barker said it was extremely alive but derivative and technically weak. Later Reed tried other producers, but the play was never staged.

Barker was right in calling *Enter Dibble* derivative: it derived straight from Bernard Shaw. Reed had tried to write an intellectual farce, the story of an upper-class revolutionary and superman who disrupts a bourgeois family. Dibble takes a job as a ditch-digger in Fairfield, Ohio. He falls in love with Phoebe Willett, whose family is alternately shocked at his being a day-laborer and delighted at his being a Philadelphia Dibble. He tells her father, "I am the super-ditch-digger. I shall be the greatest ditch-digger the world has ever seen. I am the artist of ditch-diggers—because I understand the philosophy of my job. I shall make ditch-digging a great and honorable calling. I tell you, all the work men do is honorable, if they will only believe in it." When Mr. Willett informs Dibble that he cannot support Phoebe on a day-laborer's wages, Dibble says that that is quite true, that no ditch-digger can support a wife on the wages Mr. Willett pays. He has therefore organized a union and is about to demand a twenty percent raise and an eight-hour day. To Phoebe he expounds his dream of a new world: "Men and women together, equal, wise, and beautiful; neither owning each other nor being owned—not bound, not dominating, each doing his own work in the world. Struggling, fighting, creating beauty, filling the world with laughter." "I saw I must leave my friends and my home," he tells her, "and go out and find my job—and master it, and love it, and help others to find their work. Nothing else will ever make them happy." She is moved by his eloquence and tells him that they were made for each other, but when he says that science has exploded such sentimental notions, she is offended and breaks the engagement. He leaves, saying that he will not come back but that she can find him in his ditch if she wants him. Her family crowds in to congratulate her on getting rid of him, and she delivers the curtain-speech: "Don't you see? I know what life is now. Do you think I can ever be satisfied with anything less—?"

The play was, as Barker said, alive, in spite of its debt to Shaw and its immaturity and weak construction. The revolutionary comedy of ideas, as Steffens could have told him, was not the best possible form for John Reed to attempt, but the artificiality of the medium and its uncongeniality could not completely conceal the vitality of the man. Reed's whole indictment of the bourgeoisie centered in their stifling of life. He wanted freedom and beauty—but not merely for himself. His own generous passions escaped into the play. The dialogue was mostly feeble in its groping after Shavian wit, but it had moments of fire. Reed was always saying the same thing, even in the mawkishness of "Moondown": life can be infinitely rich, infinitely precious, and the enemies of life will have to be destroyed.

"Reed has no detachment," Lippmann had written, "and is proud of it, I think. By temperament he is not a professional writer or reporter. He is a person who enjoys himself. Revolution, literature, poetry, they are only things which hold him at times, incidents merely of his living." It was true. What Lippmann did not understand was how resolutely Reed held on to his belief in the possibilities of life, the significance of living, and how surely this belief was growing into a social philosophy. Living itself was all-important, and nothing could be tolerated, within oneself or in society, that stood in the way. The apparently reckless things Reed did were not the product of meaningless whims; they were the expression of deep impulses. If he risked his life with La Tropa or in the German trenches, it was because he knew the limitations of the terms on which life was worth living; he had to test his own courage before he would dare to oppose war. Even the silly pranks he engaged in were not wholly pointless; if he had happened to be a French poet, instead of an American, he would have thought of them as significant gestures. They were protests against stupidity, narrowness, sterility; they were manifestations, deeds proclaiming the glory of freedom.

THIS is not to say, of course, that Reed scorned bread and butter, and, at the moment, that meant working for the *Metropolitan*. The magazine was still engaged in its strategic retreat. It boasted of the fact that, though it had endorsed Socialism, it was "almost the only periodical in America that during the last two years of business depression, and in spite of the war, has constantly increased its advertising revenue." This, H. J. Whigham editorially stated, was a tribute to "the progressive character of the national advertiser" and "an evidence of the trend of the times." It was also, he added, an indication of the broadening of Socialism. "Two and a half years ago the Socialist Party was still dominated in part by men of the Haywood type. The class war was the essence of the political faith and direct action was freely advocated against political methods. . . . Today the Socialist Party has tacitly removed the class war as a test of faith. . . . The Socialist Party of America has finally and definitely cut loose from the advocates of brute force, and has thereby taken its place as a great civilizing and constructive body. . . . Socialism is not only a great and growing force against war between nations, but, what is even more important, it is becoming the main bulwark against war between class and class." It was true that Hillquit was still contributing a monthly article to the

Metropolitan, but his articles were chiefly devoted to exonerat-
ing the Socialist Parties of Europe for their capitulation to militarism and to demonstrating that the war, because the Socialists
had predicted it, was really a triumph for Socialism. Lippmann
was also writing each month, offering constructive plans for a
controlled imperialism and what he called democracy in industry. But even the radicalism of such practical men as Hillquit
and Lippmann seemed to Mr. Whigham to need a counter-
balance, and with the issue of February, 1915, Theodore Roosevelt became a regular contributor.

Roosevelt thundered away against President Wilson. He listed
the Americans killed in Mexico, and attacked those who opposed intervention: "The rape of women, the murder of men,
and the cruel treatment of little children leave their tepid souls
unstirred. Insult to the American flag, nameless infamies on
American women, cause them not one single pulse of emotion."
"To defend Villa," he cried, "as representing freedom and justice and democracy in the sense that the words are used in
speaking of civilized nations is literally like defending an old-
time Apache chief on the same grounds. The sincerity of such a
defense can escape question only if the defender is admitted to
be entirely ignorant of all concerning which he speaks."

He clamored for preparedness, calling for a regular army of
at least two hundred thousand men, so that the United States
could take over at a moment's notice the duty of policing Mexico. He called for universal military training: "Such a training
would be of immense benefit to all our young men in civil life.
It would much increase their efficiency in industry. It would not
in the least tend to 'militarism,' but it would tend to make us efficient to defend ourselves in time of need." He raged against
"those feeble but noisy folk, the peace-at-any-price people, the
professional pacifists," and called them mollycoddles.

Roosevelt, his father's idol, became, for John Reed, the epit-
ome of all that he hated in the New York he had discovered
on his return from the western front. Since they frequently met
in the *Metropolitan* office, it was inevitable that they should
quarrel. Reed took particular satisfaction in praising Villa in
Roosevelt's presence. "Villa is a murderer and a bigamist,"

Roosevelt said. Reed assumed his most superior manner. "Well, I believe in bigamy," he said. Roosevelt thrust out his hand: "I am glad, John Reed, to find that you believe in something. It is very necessary for a young man to believe in something."

But sometimes their meetings did not end good-humoredly. On one occasion Roosevelt was telling a group how he had ordered a soldier to be shot in the Spanish-American War. Reed broke in: "Why, Colonel, I always knew you were a murderer." And they went at it, each shouting at the other, their voices growing shriller and shriller, until Whigham and Hovey managed to separate them.

Roosevelt's appointment to the staff of the *Metropolitan* was an even clearer indication than Whigham's editorials of what was happening, but Reed realized that no other magazine that offered a comparable salary would be more congenial or give him more freedom. His one assignment during his two months in New York was an article on Billy Sunday, an assignment that he accepted with relish. He carefully prepared the way by having Sam McCoy, who was working on a Philadelphia newspaper, gather data for him, and then he and George Bellows, who was to illustrate the article, set off for Sunday's headquarters.

The evangelist would not see them until the next day, but Reed knew how to use the time, and began a canvass of the members of the committee that had invited Sunday to Philadelphia. He asked one of the ministers if Sunday had converted any business men. The minister cited a particular manufacturer. "When the manufacturer became a Christian, did he raise wages?" Reed asked. "You don't understand," he was told; "raising wages is a question of economics, not of religion."

Reed found that the twelve industrialists, twelve bankers, and four corporation lawyers on the citizens' committee entirely agreed. He went to see Alba B. Johnson, president of the Baldwin Locomotive Works, where there were low wages, many accidents, an open shop, and a record of savage strike-breaking. "I had long decided," Mr. Johnson told him, "that what the country needed was a moral awakening. People's minds are obsessed by material things. Billy Sunday makes people look to the salvation of their own souls, and when a man is looking after his own soul's good, he forgets his selfish desire to become rich. Instead of agitating for a raise in wages, he turns and helps some poorer brother who's down and out."

When they went again to the Sundays' headquarters, Ma Sunday refused to let them see her husband. She was a little puzzled by their questions about the social value of Sunday's preaching, and quoted, "The poor ye have always with you." They did manage to talk with Sunday for a few minutes, but his wife soon drove them away. Reed found him pleasant and apparently sincere. At the tabernacle he was impressed by the dramatic technique; it was a good show, and he liked good shows. He wrote a restrained, good-tempered article that demonstrated beyond any question Sunday's usefulness to capitalism. "We went away unconverted," he ended, "but Philadelphia was saved."

The *Metropolitan* wanted Reed to go back to France, but he had been barred from that country. On February 27, Robert Dunn had published in the New York *Post* an account of their night in the German trenches. As they emerged from the dugout, Lieutenant Riegel, he said, took a Mauser from one of the soldiers. "The next moment it was in Reed's hands, and with the muzzle pointing through the eyehole atop the bank, he was getting a bead on the low, jagged crest of mud across the short and hellish space. Be it on our heads, we did it, both fired twice, turn and turn about, wicked, full-fledged franc-tireurs. . . . That Reed should have done so, with his scorn of force and soldiering, is sufficient, if sophistical, excuse for me."

There had been tremendous protest—far greater, certainly, than would have arisen if the guns had been pointed in the other direction. President Hibben of Princeton wrote: "I wish to express my feeling of indignation and of protest against this cold-blooded and inhuman proceeding." Some of the papers published editorials. Richard Harding Davis denounced Reed and had to be reminded of certain exploits of his own. More important, the French government formally banned both Reed and Dunn from France.

Boardman Robinson, an artist who had been for some years on the staff of the *Tribune* and had occasionally contributed to the *Masses*, was supposed to accompany Reed to France, and it was suggested that they go together to see Ambassador Jusserand in Washington. Jusserand was friendly, and hinted that a letter from Roosevelt might move the French government. They hurried back to New York, and explained what had happened. Roosevelt dictated his letter in their presence. It ended, "If I were Marshal Joffre and Reed fell into my hands, I should have him court-martialed and shot."

Since there was no chance of going to the western front, it was decided that they should go to the Balkans and Russia. They were inoculated for typhoid and cholera, and passage was booked for March 20. In the meantime, Reed had a series of lecture engagements. On March 5, he spoke at Tremont Temple in Boston. The audience was pro-Ally and was frankly incredulous when he denied the atrocity stories and indignant when he maintained that England was as guilty as Germany. The next night he attended a *Lampoon* dinner in Cambridge, and found most of the undergraduates as settled in their prejudices as his Boston listeners had been. What he had feared was happening. Steffens might talk of the opportunities in America. for an impartial analysis of the issues of war, but Reed could see only that six months of British propaganda had had its effect.

There was a good deal to make him unhappy. Boyd, who had returned to this country and had been jailed in Paterson, was completely pessimistic. The surrender of European Socialists had convinced him that Socialism was impossible. He had renounced his affiliation with the I.W.W., and had sought a pardon on the ground that he no longer held the views for the expression of which he had been arrested. Reed was one of many who signed a petition for Boyd's release, and no one could have rejoiced more when he was freed. He had no thought of blaming Boyd, for he was deeply shaken himself.

But he could not drop the fight to keep America out of the war. He wrote for the *Masses* an article called "The Worst Thing in Europe." It was not a very carefully considered article, but there was tremendous passion in it. Reed began by describing the docility of the men in the French and Germany army, and attributed it to the fact that they had been disciplined by military training. The equal docility of the English soldier he blamed on the British caste system: men who know their place become obedient soldiers. "I hate soldiers," he wrote. "I hate to see a man with a bayonet fixed on his rifle, who can order me off the street. I hate to belong to an organization that is proud of obeying a caste of superior beings, that is proud of killing free ideas, so that it may more efficiently kill human beings in cold blood. They will tell you that a conscript army is democratic, because everybody has to serve; but they won't tell you that military service plants in your body the germ of blind obedience, of blind irresponsibility, that it produces one class of commanders in your state and your industries, and accustoms you to do what they tell you even in time of peace." "They are talking now," he concluded, "about building up an immense standing army. . . . I, for one, refuse to join."

XI

Eastern Front

ONCE more John Reed sailed for Italy, once more expecting to see that country enter the war, but this time on the side of the Allies. Mabel Dodge came to see him off, and from the boat he wrote her the letter that ended two years of intermittent intimacy. A friend, at his request, destroyed all the letters Mrs. Dodge had written him. They saw little of each other thereafter, but she remained convinced that she was the only person who understood John Reed.

From Italy he wrote his mother. "I have come to hate Europe," he said. "After this trip I want to stay in America about a year, and not return to Europe until I take you and Harry over here, after the war." But he was looking forward to the new adventure: "Of course it will be different, and better, in the East. The Caucasus is something like Mexico, they say, and I'm sure I'll like the people. It will be great to get on a horse and ride over mountain passes where Genghis Khan invaded Europe." And it was fun to be a noted war-correspondent: "I find that I am a celebrated figure already, as all the people on the boat have read my 'works.' Am treated with amusing marked deference by all."

Italy was disappointingly calm, but there were rumors of the imminent capture of Constantinople, and Reed and Robinson went on to Salonika. Their ship left from Brindisi and nosed up the Greek coast beyond Piraeus. In Salonika, where men talked twenty languages, they spoke with British agents, Armenian merchants, and Greek boot-blacks from America. Sitting at a table in the Place de la Liberté, they watched Greek, French,

English, Russian, and Serbian officers, Greek priests, Musselman hadjis, Jewish rabbis, porters, fishermen, and beggars. In the Street of the Silversmiths, bearded old men squatted on high benches and pounded lumps of raw silver. The markets were what Reed had dreamed of when he tramped New York's East Side: in the little booths, gold, blue, and silver fish lay on green leaves, among baskets of eggs and piles of vegetables, and the voices of the bargainers rose above the cackling of hens and the squealing of pigs.

All day long refugees poured into the city. Everywhere Reed and Robinson met the pitiful processions of men, women, and children, with bloody feet, limping beside broken-down wagons. The fighting in Turkey and the rumors of war in Bulgaria, Roumania, and Greece filled the city with all the different peoples of the Near East. One night Reed and Robinson found their way into a little café, where they were welcomed by seven refugees, Greeks, French, Italians, all of them carpenters, and all engaged in celebrating the strange co-incidence that had brought seven carpenters together in a Salonika inn. The two Americans celebrated with them, singing "John Brown's Body" to match the songs of Turkey and Arabia, Italy and Greece.

But the news from Constantinople promised no excitement, and they turned towards Serbia, "the country of the typhus—abdominal typhus, recurrent fever, and the mysterious and violent spotted fever, which kills fifty percent of its victims." The epidemic was ending: "Now there were only a hundred thousand sick in all Serbia, and only a thousand deaths a day." But an American from the Standard Oil office, who came to see them off, asked solicitously, "Do you want the remains shipped home, or shall we have you buried up there?"

They crawled slowly up between barren hills along the yellow torrent of the Vardar, while a lieutenant in the British Medical Mission described the plague as it had been at its height. The gorge of the Vardar broadened out into a wide valley rimmed with stony hills, beyond which lay high mountains. In the valley, crossed by irrigation ditches, every foot was under cultivation, and on the bare slopes of the hills bearded peasants watched sheep and goats. They came to a typhus cemetery beside the railroad, with thousands and thousands of crosses, and at last they arrived at Nish, war-capital of Serbia.

Nish was a city of mud, appalling stench, sickness, and death. Everywhere there were soldiers, in filthy tatters, their feet bound with rags, some staggering on crutches, many still blue and shaking from the typhus. Austrian prisoners worked as servants or manual laborers or loitered desolately about the streets. In the typhus hospital, so crowded that cots touched each other, men writhed under dirty blankets, or lay apathetically awaiting death. Reed and Robinson passed through fetid ward after fetid ward, until their stomachs could stand no more.

As they left Nish to go to the front, they heard again and again the story of the Serbian victory of December; how the Austrians had twice invaded the country and twice been hurled back, and how, as they came the third time, with twice as many men as the Serbs, they had steadily advanced beyond Belgrade, and then, suddenly, had been repulsed and slaughtered, until the Serbian general could proudly announce, "There remain no Austrian soldiers on Serbian soil except prisoners." Reed admired the courage of the Serbian people and their savage independence, and he could almost make himself believe they were as romantic as the followers of Villa, but, after all that he had seen, their nationalism, so arrogant in its claims, so pervasive in its influence, seemed to him both objectionable and absurd.

Belgrade, which the Serbs had tried to make into a modern European city, showed the effect of the constant bombardment. The university was in ruins; a shell had exploded within the walls of the military college; the interior of the royal palace had been gutted; the two top-floors of a five-story office-building had been blown off; everywhere there were private houses without a single pane of glass. The city was still within the range of the Austrian guns, and there had been a bombardment within the past few days. From the hills behind the town, French English, Russian, and Serbian batteries fired sporadically over the heads of the inhabitants.

They went up the Save by boat, under fire from an Austrian cannon, and then pushed on towards the front by wagon. In every village they heard stories of Austrian atrocities, and saw

reports, affidavits, photographs. At Lechnitza a hundred women and children were chained together and their heads struck
off. At Prnjavor Reed saw the ruins of a house; into that house
the inhabitants of the village had been crowded, those for whom
there was no room being tied on the outside, and the building
had been burned. Five undefended towns were razed to the
ground, and forty-two villages were sacked and most of their
inhabitants massacred.

On the top of Goutchevo mountain Reed saw what he regarded as the most ghastly spectacle of the war. There was an
open space, where, scarcely twenty yards apart, were the Austrian and Serbian trenches. Along the trenches were occasional
deep pits, the results of successful undermining and dynamiting.
Between the trenches were little mounds, from which protruded
pieces of uniform, skulls with draggled hair, white bones with
rotting hands at the end, bloody bones sticking from boots.
For six miles along the top of Goutchevo the dead were piled.
Reed and Robinson walked on the dead, and sometimes their
feet sank through into pits of rotting flesh and crunching bones,
and sometimes little holes opened and showed swarms of gray
maggots.

At Obrenovatz they tried to forget the valley of the dead
in the jovial company of the colonel and his staff. Over the
cognac, Reed expressed a desire to talk with a Serbian Socialist,
and they took him to see the captain of one of the batteries.
This man, who had been a lawyer in private life, and a leader
of the Socialist Party, had difficulty in recalling what, as a Socialist, he had believed. "You have no idea," he said, "how strange
it is to be talking like this again!" Finally he said, "I have forgotten my arguments, and I have lost my faith. For four years
now I have been fighting in the Serbian army. At first I hated
it, wanted to stop, was oppressed by the unreasonableness of it
all. Now it is my job, my life. I spend all day thinking of those
guns; I lie awake at night worrying about the battery. These
things and my food, my bed, the weather—that is life to me.
When I go home on leave to visit my wife and children, their
existence seems so tame, so removed from realities. I get bored
very soon, and am relieved when the time comes to return

to my friends here, my work—my guns. That is the horrible thing." Reed could agree; it was more horrible than even Goutchevo mountain.

ON THEIR return to Belgrade, Reed was suddenly attacked by an acute pain in his back. It became so intense that it seemed as if he could not continue to ride his horse. When at last, after much suffering, he reached the city, he went to the outstanding doctor, who dismissed his trouble as a venereal disease. A British army surgeon, informing Reed that the doctor was likely to make that diagnosis of any ailment, hazarded the guess that the left kidney was infected. He advised Reed to wait until he returned to America, and then have an operation.

After a fortnight the attacks became less frequent and less severe, though they bothered him sporadically throughout the remainder of his stay on the eastern front. Resting in Belgrade, Reed and Robinson had a chance to become better acquainted with both the Serbs and their allies. Serbian officers told them frankly that the government had known of the plan for the assassination of the Archduke Ferdinand at Sarejevo, and there were many references to Russian complicity. A British colonel explained that England had maneuvered to make Germany invade Belgium and would have sent its own army through Belgium if the maneuver had failed. In the face of the growing evidence of international greed and intrigue, Reed's phrase, "this traders' war," seemed the expression of innocent blindness; and yet he knew that, in America, the myth of Allied purity and German depravity daily gained new adherents.

Of course he could still be gay, and there were festive dinners as well as serious discussions. As he felt stronger, he spent much of his time in wandering about the battered city, seeking out secluded cafés and picturesque resorts. On one expedition he met a girl who interested him, not a woman of the streets, but an educated European. They spent the night in a deserted house with the sound of cannonading in their ears. Love among the ruins, Reed thought; romance.

By the end of May it seemed clear that Serbia was going to provide as little action as they had seen in Italy or Salonika,

and they began to think of Russia. The Russian army had retreated more than two hundred miles; they would go and report the retreat. The Russian ambassador at Bucharest told them
they would have to go to Petrograd for passes, but they had
learned from returning correspondents that no passes were being issued. The American legation gave Reed a list of American
citizens in Bucovina and Galicia, and, since the list did not seem
quite long enough, Reed added, for his own amusement, the
names of Sonya Levien of the *Metropolitan* staff, Fannie Hurst,
and Walter Lippmann. The claim that they were investigating
the situation of these Americans would, they hoped, satisfy any
suspicious officials. They went to Dorohoi, the northern ter-
minus of the Roumanian railway, and the chief of police took
them across the border to Novo Sielitza. They had got into
Russia by the back door.

Captain Madji, commandant of Novo Sielitza, welcomed them
with Gargantuan hospitality, and introduced them to his extraordinary household. About ten o'clock at night Captain Madji's
wife began to get dinner. To sharpen the appetite, there were
plates of sardines, smoked and raw herrings, tunny, caviar, sau-
sage, shirred eggs, and pickles, served with seven different kinds
of liquor. Afterwards came great platters of corn-meal polenta,
and then chunks of pork and potatoes. It was midnight when the
seven liquors were served again, and they settled down to drink
tea. Half a dozen officers told stories of the retreat, and Madji
protested when, at one o'clock, Reed and Robinson spoke of
going to their quarters.

They stayed in a Jewish home. There were Jews everywhere
in Novo Sielitza, bowed, thin men in rusty derbies and greasy
long coats, with desperate eyes, cringing from police, soldiers,
and priests. Reed remembered the proclamation the Tsar had
issued soon after the beginning of the war, informing the Jews
that all discrimination against them was to cease, that the highest rank of the army, the government, and the nobility would
be open to them. He asked a lieutenant in the Cossack regiment
if the decree had been enforced. The lieutenant laughed and
said, "Of course not. All Jews are traitors."

From Novo Sielitza they went to Zalezschick, where certain

of the persons were supposed to live whose names had been given them by the Bucharest legation. Captain Madji secured a horse, wagon, and driver for them, and persuaded General Bai-kov to give them a pass. All day long they drove beside the river Pruta, behind the Russian batteries. Zalezschick, they learned, had been captured by the Russians, taken from them by the Hungarians, and then recaptured. Each time the Jews had been persecuted and many of them massacred. The Amer-icans on Reed's list who actually had lived in Zalezschick had apparently been among the victims of either the bombardments or the pogroms. Both the debris in the streets and the expres-sion of terror and despair on the faces of most of the people bore witness to the horrors the city had seen.

The colonel in charge of Zalezschick received Reed and Robinson pleasantly, and they spent the evening discussing poli-tics, in fragmentary German, with him and his staff. He would not permit them to go to the front, but he arranged for them to see the general at Tarnapol. They slept that night on the train, and woke stiff and cramped from the benches of the third-class car. An officer who knew French began to talk with them, tell-ing them that all Russia was supporting the war. The peasants, for example, were in favor of it because they realized they could get rid of poverty and oppression if they beat the Germans. "If the peasants are going to beat anyone," Robinson said to Reed, "why don't they begin at home?"

At Tarnapol they discovered that their presence in Russia was so astounding that the staff officer who interviewed them could scarcely convince himself that they were really there. General Lichinsky was friendly, but insisted that they go to Lemberg to see the governor-general of Galicia. They were arrested four times in the course of the day, but each time the staff released them. General Lichinsky had them cared for while they were in the city, and sent them fare-free to Lemberg.

At Lemberg Prince Troubetskoi, promising to do all he could for them, introduced them to the governor-general's first ad-jutant, who was very encouraging. They asked Troubetskoi if they could visit Przsemysl. "I'm so sorry," he said regretfully, "but the Austrians entered Przsemysl this morning." Finally they learned that the governor-general would do nothing for them; they could either go to Petrograd or try to get the permission of General Ivanov at Cholm to visit the front. Loath to leave the neighborhood without a glimpse of the fighting, they chose to go to Cholm.

It took them two days to get there, traveling third-class or on hospital trains, sleeping on wooden benches, eating badly or not at all, and waiting for hours in obscure railway stations. One of the stops was at Rovno, and it was there that Reed learned what the Pale was like. They were arrested several times, but always released. On the last stretch they found a Russian officer who spoke English and who told them tales of Russian inefficiency. The regiment in which he served had arrived in Poland after three nights with almost no sleep and two days with almost no food. The general had immediately ordered them into action, and they were in the trenches for four days. They were so exhausted that they could not resist the German attack, and out of eight thousand men only two thousand came back, and twelve hundred of them went to the hospital. "But the amusing thing about it," he concluded, "was that all the time we were being butchered out there, there were six fresh regiments being held in reserve two miles away! What on earth do you suppose the general was thinking of?"

As they found their way to what was called the English Hotel, though no one spoke English there, they were so confident of winning General Ivanov's permission to go to the front that they argued about the kind of battle they wanted to see. Robinson hankered for an infantry charge; Reed stuck out for a ride with raiding Cossacks. But the next morning a staff officer very politely told them that he would have to telegraph the Grand Duke. It was only a matter of a few hours, he assured them, and they went back to their room. A little later an officer arrived, and asked them for their papers. It was a mere formality, he insisted; the Grand Duke had not been heard from, but without doubt he would soon reply, and they could proceed to the front. They were not under arrest, the officer told them, but he left three guards outside their door.

Protests were of no avail, but at last an officer explained the

situation. They had violated a strict regulation by coming to
Cholm. The officers who had let them proceed, step by step,
would be punished, but that did not excuse them. The Grand
Duke had ordered them to be held under guard. They were in
an attic room, hot and uncomfortable. The food was bad.
They had no opportunity to exercise, and nothing to read. They
could not leave the room except to go to the toilet, and then a
Cossack accompanied them. The Cossacks were friendly, and
there were usually half a dozen of them in the room, talking
with the aid of the French-Russian dictionary, marvelling at
Robinson's drawings, arguing among themselves—with only mild
academic interest—as to whether the captives were German spies
or not. There was only one who was at all obnoxious; when
Reed threw him downstairs, the others were delighted.

Fourteen days they spent in that hot attic room, with nothing
to do but engage in difficult conversation with the Cossacks or
watch the life of the Jewish section from their window. Reed
wrote poems, planned a novel, played double-dummy bridge
with Robinson, and fretted. They wrote telegrams to the British and American ambassadors and to Hovey, but the officials
did not dispatch them. Finally a telegram was delivered to the
American ambassador, who replied that he had learned from
the Department of Foreign Affairs that they were to be sent to
Petrograd. They waited two more days, and then, when Reed
was fully convinced that he was going to go crazy, a colonel
appeared and freed them.

The colonel gave them the impression that they could either
return to Bucharest or go on to Petrograd, where they might be
able to get passes for the front. Believing their detention to
have been due to a misunderstanding, and still eager to see the
battle, they proceeded to Petrograd. Although they had been
assured that they were free, they observed that their compartment was guarded, and at each station an inspector made sure
that they had not disappeared.

There was a general in their compartment, and he very carefully closed all the windows. Reed, who always insisted on having plenty of fresh air, walked up and down with his hands in

his pocket, thinking. He lay down in the upper berth—it was Robinson's turn to have the lower—and waited for the general to go to sleep. When he thought it was safe, he reached out and quietly opened the window. The general arose swiftly and shut it. Reed immediately opened it. They wrangled furiously, neither understanding the other, until the guard came in. He announced that it was a law that windows must be shut if any one objected to having them open. Reed tried to persuade the general, through a series of translators, that his health would be benefited by fresh air, but the most he would concede was the opening of the door.

As soon as he reached Petrograd, Reed hastened to find the ambassador, George T. Marye. Mr. Marye was having lunch at the Astoria Hotel, a precise, shrunken little man with glasses and a white mustache. Reed went over and told him who he was. "Mr. Reed," he said in a dry, quavering voice, "I am very glad to see you in Petrograd. You have given this office a great deal of anxiety—a great deal. Now, Mr. Reed, I do not want to insist on your misdemeanors, but my best advice is for you to leave Russia by the shortest route."

"Leave Russia!" Reed said in amazement. "What for?"

"Why," Marye answered testily, "it should be perfectly evident why. The dispatches which I have received from the foreign office concerning you are very alarming—very alarming indeed. When you were arrested, the military authorities asked me if you were known to the embassy; if not, they would hand you over to a military court-martial for severe punishment."

Reed demanded to know what charges had been made against him, and Marye led him to his office. When Reed lit a cigarette, the ambassador said, "No one smokes here." He refused to permit Reed to examine the papers himself, reading the notes aloud. The foreign office maintained that Reed and Robinson had entered Russia on false passports, had disobeyed a military regulation, and had been carrying letters to revolutionaries in Russia. Reed pointed out that there was nothing the matter with his passport, and that the alleged letters to revolutionaries were merely the authorization that the Bucharest legation had given him to investigate the condition of certain American citizens.

Marye remained skeptical. He understood, he said, that Reed was to be expelled by way of Stockholm, and when Reed said he had heard nothing to that effect, the ambassador advised him to leave in any case and leave immediately. Reed asked him why.

The ambassador leaned over with a frightened look. "There is a story going around, Mr. Reed, that you fired on the French from the German trenches."

"I have heard it," Reed said. "Do the authorities charge me with that?"

"They do not, Mr. Reed, but I am afraid they will find out."

"All right," Reed said; "if they are holding that against me, let them come out with it. I am not afraid to face that story."

Marye shook his head mournfully. "You are in a country," he said, "where, once suspicion is fastened on you, you might as well be guilty. Suspicion is fastened on you now, Mr. Reed. If that story should ever get out, it would be very damaging to me!"

The next morning Reed went again to the embassy and talked with the first secretary, who began by implying that Reed and Robinson were liars, and ended by advising them to remain quietly in their hotel.

"But the ambassador," Reed pointed out, "advised me to leave the country at once."

"Don't attempt to leave by any means," Mr. Wilson insisted. "It will be very serious if you do."

Reed was becoming thoroughly indignant, but he controlled himself, and asked if the embassy would receive the baggage which he had ordered sent from Bucharest. "I doubt it very much," Wilson said. "We are not in the shipping business. I am not sure that we can do anything for you."

Robinson in the meantime had been to the British embassy. Although he had taken out his first citizenship papers in the United States, where he had lived for eighteen years, and had applied for his second papers, he was still, having been born in Canada, technically a British subject. One of the secretaries assured him that he could not be expelled, and offered to intercede for Reed as well.

Reed continued to meet Marye in the lobby of the Astoria Hotel, and each time he would step up to him and ask, so that every one could hear, "Well, what are you going to do for an American citizen?" Finally he went to the office and insisted on seeing Marye, who shook his head dolefully, and said there was nothing he could do. "This will make a fine story in the magazine," Reed said, and, stepping to the telephone, called Robinson and formally requested him to place Reed's case as well as his own in the hands of the British embassy.

Sir George Buchanan personally went to see Sazonov, Minister of Foreign Affairs, and returned confident that the matter was settled. But there was still delay, and Reed was impatient. "I have a fine story which I want to publish," he wrote Hovey, "on an American ambassador whose coldness and negligence and cowardice in the affairs of American citizens in Russia is a byword here."

He was depressed at what seemed to be the failure of their trip. They had seen no active fighting, and, now that they were penned up in Petrograd, Italy had gone into the war, the Serbs were fighting again, and the Dardanelles campaign had entered a new phase. The stay in Petrograd was expensive as well as futile. They had moved from the Astoria to a cheaper hotel, but, because they could not get their baggage, they had had to buy new outfits.

The incompetence of the Russian government was infuriating. One cause of the trouble was the fact that Granville Fortescue, who had *Metropolitan* credentials, had gone direct to Berlin from the Russian front, and soon after his departure a battery had been wiped out. Since Fortescue was violently pro-British, the suspicions of the Russians were absurd, but that made it no easier for Reed and Robinson. Fundamentally, however, the situation resulted from the fact that a variety of officials had blundered in permitting them to go as far as Cholm, and the whole attempt of the government was to cover up these blunders.

Everywhere they went they were followed by spies. There were four types of secret police, and they were watched by representatives of all four. They could look out their window at any time of day or night, and see half a dozen of them standing around. Plaguing detectives became their favorite amusement. Once they threw a group into a mild panic by pointedly studying them through what appeared to be binoculars but were beer bottles. Another time they took a cab and ordered the driver to go fast, swing suddenly round a corner, and stop. As the detectives in their cab swung round the corner after them, Reed and Robinson rose, raised their hats, and bowed. They spent the rest of the afternoon following the detectives.

Ten days passed, and they decided, out of boredom, to try to escape. They bribed the Petrograd police to stamp their passports with an official permit, left the hotel suddenly, changed cabs several times, and took the train for Kiev and Bucharest. At Vilna the next morning a police officer courteously woke them up. "A thousand pardons," he said, "but I am ordered by telegraph to ask you to leave the train here and return to Petrograd—and to depart immediately from Russia by way of Vladivostok."

As soon as they were back in their hotel, two officers of the secret police came and took them to the chief. He read them the order received from the Grand Duke: "Mr. Boardman Robinson, British subject, and Mr. John Reed, American citizen, are herewith commanded to leave Petrograd for Vladivostok within twenty-four hours of the receipt of this; in case of noncompliance they are to be delivered to a military court-martial and severely punished."

Their interpreter discovered that no train left for Vladivostok within the specified time. Reed went again to Marye and explained what had happened, adding that he had no money. "I don't know what we can do for you, Mr. Reed," the ambassador said. "I am not sure whether the Department has authorized us to advance you any money. As for the difficulty about the train, we will see . . ."

"And if the Department has not authorized you to advance

me any money," Reed asked, "or if you cannot arrange for a stay of a few hours until the train goes, what am I to do?"

"I am sure I don't know, Mr. Reed," Marye answered.

While Reed was vainly arguing with Marye, Robinson went to Buchanan, who saw Sazonov and protested so forcefully that not only was the order canceled but the secret police were withdrawn. On the nineteenth of July, after writing Marye a letter that gave him much satisfaction, Reed, with Robinson, took the train for Bucharest.

THEIR papers had all been taken from them at Vilna, and were still held by the Russian government, but they were searched at the Roumanian border. Reed, for some reason, was given a more rigorous examination than Robinson. He was practically undressed, and the seams of his wallet were cut open. One section, however, in which he had a few notes on pogroms, was left untouched. The notes were unimportant, but Reed was delighted at having beaten the Russian police.

As soon as they were established in the Bucharest hotel, they set to work to make up for the loss of notes and sketches by immediately setting down their impressions. Casting up the balance sheet of his Russian experiences, Reed found much to like. He liked the broad-gauge railways, with the wide, tall cars and long, comfortable berths. They belonged to the amazing countryside through which the trains passed: leagues and leagues of ancient forest; thatched towns hours apart; fields, golden-heavy with wheat, stretching as far as the eye could see. The spirit of the people matched the country. "Russian ideals are the most exhilarating," Reed wrote, "Russian thought the freest, Russian art the most exuberant; Russian food and drink are to me the best, and Russians themselves are, perhaps, the most interesting human beings that exist." The Russian sense of space and time pleased him: "In America we are the possessors of a great empire—but we live as if this were a crowded island like England, where our civilization came from. Our streets are narrow and our cities congested . . . Russia is also a great empire; but there the people live as if they knew it were one." And he liked the freedom of the Russians from the conventions and traditions of the western world: "Every one acts just as he feels like acting, and says just what he wants to. There are no particular times for getting up or going to bed or eating dinner, and there is no conventional way of murdering a man, or of making love."

He disliked the constant sense of being spied upon, though the antics of the secret police often amused him. He was staggered by the revelations of graft, so freely talked about by the people he met: seventeen million bushels of wheat that had disappeared; a battleship paid for but never built; a fort that existed only on paper. Foreigners described the elaborate processes of bribery that were a part of every business transaction. Exposures led to the execution of some officials and the exiling of others, but the graft went on. And he was horrified by the treatment of the Jews, the shameless violation of the Tsar's pledges, the frank clamor for further persecution and more terrible oppression.

He observed that the middle class was ardently supporting the war. Through their hold upon the court and the aristocracy, the Germans had made Russia almost a commercial colony, and Russian business men were eager to throw off the double burden of German exploitation and imperial corruption. For the moment the workers, and even, in a vague way, the peasants were supporting them. But there had been many strikes in the early months of the war, and, though they had been cruelly suppressed, there was still talk of further uprisings. The revolutionaries were active, in the face of terror, and even a casual visitor caught a glimpse of what they were doing to prepare the people for the overthrow of the Tsar. It was a mysterious country, and Reed felt unwilling to prophesy, but he crossed the border with a strong conviction that violent change could not long be postponed in Russia.

He wrote down his impressions in his room in the Athenée Palace Hotel, while Robinson worked in the adjoining room at his sketches. At intervals they would examine each other's work. Often Robinson would say, "But it didn't happen this way; it happened that way." Reed would explode. Crying, "What the hell difference does it make?" he would seize one of Robinson's sketches. "She didn't have a bundle as big as that," he would

say; or, "He didn't have a full beard." Robinson would explain
that he wasn't interested in photographic accuracy; he was trying to give the right impression. "Exactly," Reed would shout
in triumph; "that is just what I am trying to do."

He did not hesitate to alter or even to invent. He might tell
as if it had happened to him something that he had learned at
second-hand. His deviations from factual accuracy were not, as
they might have been with another man, the result of failures
of his powers of observations, for his eyes and his memory were
almost perfect. His alterations and inventions were the deliberate result of a determination to give the reader precisely the impression he had received. If, in describing his visit to the hospital at Lille, he had said that a soldier threw his iron cross on
the floor, whereas actually the man had laid it on his bed, it
was because he detected in the soldier's manner a suggestion
of contempt that could only be conveyed to the reader in the
terms of a more violent gesture. So, as he worked on his stories
of Russia, he strove for the fidelity of the artist rather than the
accuracy of the statistician, and Robinson could testify that the
essential veracity of his stories was extraordinary.

For several days they worked in the baking heat, leaving
their rooms only after the sun had set. Reed learned that Bucharest meant literally "City of Joy," and that its residents were
fond of calling it the Paris of the Balkans. It was a "made" city,
less than thirty years old, a city of imitations. The inhabitants
boasted of their descent from the old Roman legions, making
much of their ties with the other Romance peoples and their
superiority to their Balkan neighbors. Living in the city was
more expensive than living in New York, and it was given its
tone by the fashionable rich, driving in handsome carriages,
flirting on the boulevards, visiting galleries filled with imitations
of French art, attending revues modeled after those of Paris,
Berlin, or Vienna. They were the land-owners, a few thousand
out of a population of nearly eight million, seven-eighths of
whom were working peasants, paid twenty cents or less a day
in a country with a cost of living that was high by American
standards. And over the heads of the peasants and the land-

owners and even the king, the financial interests of Germany and the Allies fought for the allegiance of Roumania.

It was in Bucharest that Reed met Frank, an American who worked for a subsidiary of Standard Oil. Frank was going to England to enlist. "England is fighting for the rights of small nations," he said, "and I don't see how anybody can keep out of it that's got any guts."

Reed, having finished his articles, left for Constantinople—alone because Boardman Robinson had a British passport. At the railroad station he saw Frank saying good-bye to a shabby, undernourished, weeping Roumanian girl. On the train Frank explained that he had lived with the girl for nine months. Everyone in the oil-fields, he said, took a girl to cook, wash, look after the house, and live with him. The girls weren't paid, of course; they had food and a place to stay and, if they were good, their clothes. In five years or so it would be advisable for him to marry and settle down. He'd look around at home in America, pick a pretty girl with no scandal about her and a social pull, and marry her. Reed was indignant and said so: "If I lived with a girl, whether we were married or not, I'd make her my equal, financially and every other way. And as for your plans for marriage, how can you marry any one you don't love?" "Hell," said Frank, "if you're going to get sentimental—"

They separated at Sofia, both considerably relieved. Reed, after talking with a few acquaintances, sent Robinson a post-card, predicting that Bulgaria would enter the war on the side of the Central Powers, and took the train for Constantinople. There were men of all nations on the train, and he noticed how naturally the French and English mingled with the Germans and Austrians, how easily the old habit of international intimacy re-asserted itself. But in the morning the English, French, and Russians had disappeared, for the train had entered the Turkish Empire and was driving south across flat, bare, sun-baked plains. Late in the afternoon, troop trains appeared, filled with Arabs, and at midnight Reed was in Constantinople.

He awoke the next morning to hear an immense lazy roar, the sound of shuffling slippers, the bellow of peddlers, the barking of dogs, the droning of schoolboys. From the balcony he

could see the tangle of wooden houses, the Golden Horn with
a few yachts and cruisers and swarms of little boats, and Stamboul's seven hills and innumerable mosques. Before he set out
with his guide, the porter informed him that the police had been
making inquiries, but Reed was used to the police. Daoud Bey,
a wealthy young Turk to whom he had a letter of introduction,
led him through the European section and the crowded square
to the bridge across the Bosphorus. The drawbridge was up,
and Daoud Bey hired a boat to take them to Stamboul. On the
other side they pressed through the crowd of peddlers, pilgrims,
merchants, porters, and soldiers. Daoud Bey showed him the
bazaars, and in one of the booths, with the air strong with scent
of drugs, perfumes, herbs, and love philters, they had coffee and
cigarettes. They wandered through intricate winding streets,
across the quiet courtyards of the great mosques, in and out of
bazaars. They dined in a garden in Pera, watching the German
and Austrian officers, civilian officials, merchants, and American
sailors as they strolled by. At night they returned to Stamboul
and saw an open-air vaudeville show. It was almost impossible
to remember that, just out of hearing, were the guns of Gallip-
oli, but that night, on his way back to his hotel, Reed caught
a glimpse of ambulances bringing the wounded from a Red
Crescent ship to the hospital.

He had hoped to be allowed to go to the front, but after
waiting day after day at the war department, the department of
foreign affairs, the press bureau, and the police department,
after being told on one day to get an identification card from
the American embassy and on the next to present a photograph,
after being sent from bureau to consulate and from consulate
to bureau, and after finally learning that the documents he had
so arduously collected had been mislaid, he gave up the attempt,
and contented himself with interviewing Achmet Effendi, a
prince of the imperial blood, seventh in line for the Sultanate.
In an abandoned English villa, after much preliminary exchange
of courtesies, Reed met a dumpy, bloated little man in a gray
cutaway suit, who asked him questions about New York and
told him nothing.

Once more Reed had been disappointed. After two weeks'

delay, Enver Pasha told him that he could not go to the front, and he was unofficially notified that he had better leave Turkey. At the Bulgarian frontier he was halted and told to return to Constantinople because his passport was not properly made out. Instead, Reed, waiting until the train was leaving the station, jumped aboard. He spent the night in toilets, on tops of cars, in the tender, and on the rods. Several times the train was halted and searched, but he managed to slip off and hide, thanks to the darkness, and to catch the train as it resumed its journey. The train crew, given a little money, helped him. In the morning he slipped into a toilet with his bag and changed his clothes. At Sofia, emerging in a linen suit and panama hat, he passed without difficulty through the police cordon. He immediately went to police headquarters and told the whole story, to the chief's amusement.

In Sofia Reed and Robinson met again. They had hoped to get out to the British fleet, and Reed had even had some idea of disguising himself as a melon-seller, but once more their plans were blocked. They were not sorry, however, that they had come to Sofia, for they soon realized that Reed's post-card prophecy was about to be fulfilled. Reed liked the Bulgarians, friendly, honest people, and he liked Sofia, so different in its simple practicality from the pretentiousness of Bucharest. There seemed to be no rich people, and the peasants, farming their land communally, appeared prosperous and contented. And because he liked Bulgaria and the Bulgarians, he hated to see the country drawn, against the expressed will of the people, into the war. Seven out of the thirteen political parties, representing a majority of the population, registered their disapproval of an alliance with Germany and demanded the calling of parliament, but the king, his ministers, and the military authorities delayed until they were ready to decree mobilization and suppress opposition. Both the Allies and the Central Powers had offered territory and loans, but the Germans had offered more.

Well-informed correspondents warned Reed and Robinson that they had better leave Sofia. They went to Nish in Serbia, where every one doubted their statement that Bulgaria was on the verge of mobilization and war, but two days later the de-

cree was issued. They had expected a warm welcome in Serbia,
but Reed's account of their observations of five months before
had already appeared, and the sensitive Serbs detected a note
of mockery. Reed, informed that he would probably be expelled
when hostilities commenced, was in any case weary of the Balkans. He and Robinson went to Salonika, where there were no
more rumors than usual, and they took ship for Italy and home.

In his ironic preface to the collection of his *Metropolitan*
articles, *The War in Eastern Europe*, Reed recorded the disappointments of the expedition. Having planned to spend three
months, they were gone nearly seven. They missed Italy's entrance into the war, and they saw no fighting in the Dardanelles.
They arrived in Serbia just after one Austrian drive, and left
just before another. Having expected to see a great Russian
advance, they were in Russia at the time of, but were not permitted to see, a great Russian retreat. But, though Reed liked the
personal excitement of active warfare and knew that his reputation as a war-correspondent depended on his reporting of
battles, their experience had not been unenlightening. "It was
our luck everywhere," he wrote, "to arrive during a compara-
tive lull in the hostilities. And for that very reason, perhaps,
we were better able to observe the more normal life of the
eastern nations, under the steady strain of long-drawn-out warfare. In the excitement of sudden invasion, desperate resistance,
capture and destruction of cities, men seem to lose their dis-
tinctive personal or racial flavor, and become alike in the mad
democracy of battle. As we saw them, they had settled down
to war as a business, had begun to adjust themselves to this new
way of life and to talk and think of other things."

"War as a business!" It was that, above all else, that Reed
could not tolerate. It was bad enough for men to kill each other,
but that murder should become a habit made one despair for
civilization. John Reed liked people. He enjoyed meeting the
men and women of all nations and all classes. He thought well,
by and large, of the human race. And war, despite individual
instances of courage or generosity, systematically crushed the
finer human qualities. For the sake of the profits of a few—and

that view of the war was not a dogma from a book but a simple fact verified again and again—millions of men were not merely sacrificing their own lives and taking the lives of others but surrendering everything that gave life value. He came back from the eastern front, as he had come back from the western, saying, "This is not our war."

XII

Breathing Spell

INANCIALLY it had been a profitable trip, for the *Metro-politan* had paid generously, and that was just as well. His mother and brother, in order to hold on to the debt-burdened property Mr. Reed had left, needed several hundred dollars at once, and this Reed cheerfully gave them. First and last, a good share of the thousands of dollars he earned during the years of prosperity went to Portland. He did not begrudge it, not only because he was naturally generous, but also because he did not forget the sacrifices his parents had made for him.

He planned to visit Portland, but first he had his articles to finish. While he was staying in New York, he delivered two lectures, one at the Harvard Club and one before the inmates of Sing Sing prison. The audience at the Harvard Club was skeptical of his stories, the tales of innumerable arrests, the flight from Constantinople, the sights of the battlefields. As he sensed the hostility of his listeners, he became arrogant, deliberately exaggerating the stories in order to shock these smug stay-at-homes. And afterwards, realizing that he had not been believed, had not even been taken seriously, had not convinced any one of the truth about the war, he was unhappy.

It was different at Sing Sing. C. J. Reed had known Thomas Mott Osborne well, and John Reed had followed with warm approval Osborne's attempts at prison reform. He had dinner with Osborne and Spencer Miller, who were fascinated by his accounts of his adventures. When he stood before the prisoners in the crowded chapel, he began, with complete naturalness, "Hello, fellows," and instantly there was applause. He talked a little about his own experiences in American and European jails, and then went on to speak of the labor movement and the peace movement as phases of the struggle for freedom. He spoke exactly as if he were talking to a group of workers in a labor union hall, and there was no doubt that he felt more at home than he had at the Harvard Club. The men listened eagerly, not particularly caring, perhaps, whether his stories were true or false, but relishing the boldness and humor of the speaker, and catching rather more of what he was trying to say than his fellow-alumni had caught. When he finished, the applause exceeded anything that Osborne and Miller could recall.

A few days later he left for Portland. "I have been here one day," he wrote a friend on December 5, 1915. "It is awful beyond words. Mother is so kind, so loving, so absolutely helpless from my point of view. I don't feel as if I could talk to a single person here. It seems to me very wrong to have to undergo another long period of suspended animation after the seven months' one I've just been through. I wish I were home! I wish I could see you all again!"

Within a fortnight the friend received another letter: "I think I've found Her at last. She's wild, brave, and straight—and graceful and lovely to look at. In this spiritual vacuum, this unfertilized soil, she has grown (how, I can't imagine) into an artist. She is coming to New York to get a job—with me, I hope. I think she's the first person I ever loved without reservation."

Her name was Louise Bryant Trullinger. She had been brought up by her grandfather, the younger son of an Anglo-Irish lord, and had gone to the University of Nevada and the University of Oregon. After her graduation, she found that she had no more funds and took a position as teacher on an island in Puget Sound. Unable to bear the isolation, she went to Seattle and worked for a short time in a canning factory. Subsequently, having gone to Portland, she did fashion drawings for a newspaper, and then began to write feature stories. It was at this time that she met and married Dr. Paul Trullinger.

Having had a glimpse of Reed during his visit to Portland in 1914, she had followed his work with admiring enthusiasm. When she learned from Carl and Helen Walters that he was coming to Portland in December, 1915, she was eager to meet him, and they arranged to have Reed and her for dinner. But Reed met her by accident that day, and went to her home to see some of her writing, and when the two of them arrived for dinner, the Walterses knew they were in love. They were delighted, for they liked Louise as much as they did Jack. She was beautiful, courageous, and talented. She was also unhappy, and John Reed became not merely a lover but a bold knight rescuing a fair maiden.

He returned to New York, and in a little while she followed, joining him in his apartment on Washington Square. He took her to see all his friends, boasted of her beauty and talent, and taught her to know and love New York as he did. They went on long walks to parts of the city that had aroused or excited him, and attended plays and concerts and operas. At the *Masses* ball, he was proud of the attention she attracted. When he had to be away, they wrote each other long letters every day.

Despite this new pre-occupation, and despite the fact that he was working very hard, for the demand for his writing was strong, he found time for lecturing. At the Labor Forum he not only denounced Theodore Roosevelt and the other advocates of preparedness but urged the workers to refuse to fight, and said, in the course of the question period, that a civil war would be necessary to take the government of the United States away from the plutocracy and restore it to the people. At Columbia, speaking before the Social Study Club, he told the students that they need not expect the war to disgust men with fighting; on the contrary, it would foster the habit of killing.

Because he recognized the strength of the martial spirit, he found the emotional pacifism of many of his friends unrealistic and ineffectual, and at the Intercollegiate Socialist Society he ventured the suggestion, to the horror of the pacifists, that the workers should arm. "A drilled nation," he said, "in the power of the capitalist class is dangerous, but a drilled nation in the hands of the workers would be interesting. For instance, if the men employed in the munitions factories should take it into their heads to train a little now and then, if they should familiarize themselves with guns, isn't there just a chance that their demands for better conditions would be listened to with somewhat more attention and respect?" He was beginning to feel that the great question was not whether force should be used but who should use it.

One of his briefest and most effective speeches was at a mass meeting called to protest Emma Goldman's arrest for advocating birth control. A dozen speakers addressed the meeting, each taking more time than had been assigned him. The audience, eager to hear Miss Goldman, who had been placed last on the program, grew restless. When Reed was called upon, he said, "I too am tired. I too want to hear Emma Goldman." And he sat down.

Suddenly the Mexican issue re-emerged. On January 10, nineteen employees of an American mining company were shot in Mexico. Immediately the interventionists were clamoring at Washington. "California and Texas were part of Mexico once," William Randolph Hearst wrote. "What has been done in California and Texas by the United States can be done all the way down to the southern bank of the Panama Canal and beyond. And if this country really wanted to do what would be for the best interests of civilization, . . . the pacifying, prosperity-giving influence of the United States would be extended south to include both sides of the great canal."

Reed gave an interview to Robert Mountsier, which was published in many papers throughout the country. He did not dwell on the moral issues but described the cost of intervention. "Every Mexican," he said, "of whatever faction, will take up arms against the hated gringo. Even the women and children will join in the fighting." He spoke of the courage of the Mexicans, their resourcefulness in guerrilla warfare, the possibilities of tropical disease, and the certainty of death for thousands of American soldiers.

Two months later came the attack of Villa's men on Columbus, New Mexico, with the death of nine civilians and eight American troopers. While Pershing prepared to pursue Villa, Reed gave another interview, and wrote a syndicated article. Once more he spoke of the dangers of intervention, and this time he paid tribute as well to Villa's personal qualities. He had

been convinced, to his regret, that Villa was not the social ideal-
ist he had assumed, but he still admired him. "I don't care if he
is only a bandit," he told John Kenneth Turner, after reading
Turner's analysis of Villa's course of self-aggrandizement; "I
like him just the same." He thought a little of going to Mexico
to report Pershing's expedition from Villa's side.

While he watched events in Mexico, he found New York
as exciting as ever. He went to Sing Sing for the electrocution
of a man named Hans Schmidt. After spending the night with
Spencer Miller, at 5.45 he saw Schmidt placed in the electric
chair. For some reason he could not analyze, the sight of the
death of this man at the indifferent hands of legal authority
affected him more than the battlefields and war-hospitals of
Europe. He went straight to the nearest bar, and, he told his
friends, drank a quart of whiskey without feeling it. Perhaps he
exaggerated the amount, for, though he sometimes gave the contrary impression, he was never a heavy drinker.

The same eagerness for experience sent him, with George Bellows, to see Jess Willard fight Frank Moran. He had hoped that
he might make a story of it, but the most it inspired him to write
was a sardonic commentary on the commercialization of boxing.
He made fun of the newspaper ballyhoo, Willard's statements,
Moran's statements, the prices charged for admission, the socially élite in the expensive seats, the people who were impressed
by the socially élite, the preliminaries, the semi-finals, the Harmonious Blacksmith who sang "Wake up, America," the camera-
men, the introduction of past celebrities, and the fight itself.
He was equally irritated by the greed of the promoters and the
stupidity of the spectators, and he was sorry he went.

Collier's sent him to Florida to interview William Jennings
Bryan. "The bloated silly people on this ridiculous private rich
man's train," he wrote Louise Bryant on the way, "throw pen-
nies and dimes and quarters to be scrambled for by the Negroes
whenever we stop at a station. Lord, how the white folks scream
with laughter to see the coons fight each other, gouge each other's
eyes, get bleeding lips, scrambling over the money. Why don't
you suggest to Floyd Dell that some one draw a cartoon about
it for the *Masses?* All the whites in this section look mean and

cruel and vain. Have you ever seen Jim Crow cars, colored waiting rooms in stations, etc.? I have seen them before, so they don't shock me so much as they did. Just make me feel sick. I hate the South."

Reed joined Bryan at Palatka, and the Great Commoner, remembering their previous meeting, welcomed him cordially and gave him a ticket to his lecture that night. The next morning they went together up the St. John River, with Bryan addressing the natives at each landing. In his private conversation, as in his public addresses, the former Secretary of State employed pompous platitudes, and Reed took pleasure in drawing him out. He was opposed to war, but, asked what he would do if his country were fighting for an unjust cause, he said that he could not answer hypothetical questions. He denounced trusts but praised capitalism: "Competition," he said, "is absolutely necessary to commercial life, just as the air we breathe is necessary to physical life."

He spoke eloquently about religion, and Reed led him from religion to morality and from morality, by way of censorship, to art. When Reed said that he personally opposed censorship of any kind, Bryan declared in amazement, "Well, I never met any one before who didn't believe that decency should be preserved." Reed went on to maintain that the human body was beautiful, and Bryan crushingly retorted, "I suppose you would advocate people's going naked on the street." When Reed said cheerfully, "Why not?" Bryan frowned and announced, "We won't discuss that subject any more."

In writing his account of the interview, Reed did not hesitate to emphasize Bryan's fatuousness, but at the same time he paid tribute to his humanitarianism. "After all," he wrote, "whatever is said, Bryan has always been on the side of democracy. Remember that he was talking popular government twenty years ago and getting called 'anarchist' for it; remember that he advocated such things as the income tax, the popular election of senators, railroad regulation, low tariff, the destruction of private monopoly, and the initiative and referendum when such things were considered the dreams of an idiot; and remember that he is not yet done." In recalling Bryan's service to reform,

Reed was making clear that, though he had little respect for the man, his criticisms were not to be identified with those of the reactionaries and war-mongers, who were trying in their ridicule of Bryan to discredit every effort to regulate private industry or preserve peace.

When Reed submitted his record of the interview, Bryan deleted most of the discussion of censorship on the ground that art was a field in which he had no expert knowledge. Otherwise he accepted Reed's report as correct. In returning the notes, he wrote, "If you will pardon my personal interest in you, I will enclose an order on my publishers for *The Prince of Peace*. I feel that in maturer years you will give more consideration to the faith in which you were reared, and which is a source of strength as well as a consolation to so many millions."

It was not difficult for Reed to secure magazine assignments such as the interview with Bryan, despite his reputation as a radical. In the spring of 1916, though the retreat from the new freedom was under way, a touch of radicalism was still something of an asset to a competent journalist. He was given an inkling of how wealth could be secured when a prominent industrialist with an eye on the presidency approached him and asked him to become his publicity manager. The industrialist had calculated the value of Reed's following among the liberals and radicals as well as his skill as a journalist, and he was willing to pay for both. It was an excellent chance to sell out, and many of Reed's Dutch Treat friends would have told him he was a fool to refuse.

The problem of integrity, however, was easy; Reed did not have to think twice before rejecting the steel magnate's offer. But the whole problem of his future as a writer was complicated. Robert Rogers told him that, good as his journalism was, it only expressed a small part of his nature. It was time, Rogers said, for a novel or a long poem. Reed knew Rogers was right, and he was constantly making notes and outlines for a novel, but he never got beyond the drafting of plans or the writing of a few tentative pages. There seemed to him to be something final about a novel, and he was not ready for finality. Not only was the world changing too rapidly; he felt that, if he began a novel, he would be a different person when he finished it. If he marked time by continuing with articles and doing occasional stories that were deliberate pot-boilers, it was because he felt that he was not ready for the pouring of his whole nature into some sustained effort.

He noticed to his surprise that he was writing much less poetry than he once had. Indeed, he had written almost nothing in recent months except two rather fine love poems, "Pygmalion" and "Love at Sea," and the somber "Fog." In dignified unrhymed verse, rich and musical, he translated the old legend of Pygmalion and Galatea into a delicate, nostalgic symbol of the quest for the ideal lover and its frustration—

> He wrenched the shining rock from the meadow's breast,
> And out of it shaped the lovely, almost-breathing
> Form of his dream of his love of the world's women,
> Slim and white was she, whimsical, full of caprice;
> Bright sharp in sunlight, languid in shadow of cloud,
> Pale in the dawn, and flushed at the end of day.

The poem ended:

> Rock is she still, and her heart is the hill's heart,
> Full of all things beside him—full of wind and bees
> And the long falling miles and miles of air.
> Despair and gnawing are on him, and he knows her
> Unattainable who is born of wind and hill—
> Far-bright as a plunging full-sailed ship that seems
> Hull-down to be set immutable in sea.

In the second poem he spoke of love's defiance of an indifferent world, using the image of the sea on which he was being carried from his beloved:

> This cool green fluid death shall toss us living
> Higher than high heaven and deeper than sighs—
> But O the abrupt, stiff, sloping, resistless foam
> Shall not forbid our taking and our giving!

. . . .

I cried upon God last night, and God was not where I cried;
He was slipping and balancing on the thoughtless shifting planes
    of sea.
Careless and cruel, he will unchain the appalling sea-gray engines—
But the speech of my body to your body will not be denied.

Simpler than either of the love poems was "Fog." Melancholy
was rare with John Reed. Even though he was often ill in the
spring of 1916, the thought of death seldom came to him. But in
some strange moment, there was sufficient lull in his fiery vitality
to give him a sense of what dying might be like. And he seized
upon it, curious about that as about all experiences.

> Death comes like this, I know—
> Snow-soft and gently cold;
> Impalpable battalions of thin mist,
> Light-quenching and sound-smothering and slow.

> Slack as a wind-spilled sail
> The spent world flaps in space—
> Day's but a grayer night, and the old sun
> Up the blind sky goes heavily and pale.

> Out of all circumstance
> I drift or seem to drift
> In a vague vapor-world that clings and veils
> Great trees arow like kneeling elephants.

With all his tasks and all his interests clear in his mind, with his
passion for Louise strong in his consciousness, he permitted himself to imagine the cessation of activity:

> Now Love and all the warm
> Pageant of livingness
> Trouble my quiet like forgotten dreams
> Of ancient thunder on the hills of storm.

And he ended in calm unfaith:

How loud, how terribly
Aflame are lights and sounds!
And yet beyond the fog I know there are
But lonely bells across gray wastes of sea.

It was finer work than almost anything he had written before.
He had not lost his creative ability, but he had lost his fecundity.
The impulses out of which his poetry grew were genuine
enough, but they seemed, now, to constitute only a small part of
his nature. He had been trained to the use of conventional forms
for the treatment of what were conventionally regarded as the
appropriate themes for poetry. He was ready to admit that
poetry should not be limited to these themes, and he admired the
work of Sandburg, Masters, and Lindsay, which expressed far
more of the world in which he lived than his own poems did.
But he knew that, hampered though he was by the older forms
he had mastered, it would do him no good to imitate the experi-
mentalists. He had to have his own form. And it was his way,
not to put everything else to one side and strive to create the
new form, but to submerge himself in the life roundabout and
wait for the new form to develop within him. In the meantime
he wrote poetry when it was ready to be written, but that was
seldom.

Throughout the spring of 1916, the idea persisted that it was
not in the novel, not in poetry, that he could find expression, but
in the drama. Writing *Enter Dibble* had been fun, but he was
ready to admit that the future of the theatre did not lie with
such plays. What kept recurring to him was the possibility of
building upon his experience with the Paterson pageant. He
wanted to create a theatre of the working class. Plans to give
plays for the workers, though he was interested in these, were
not enough. Hiram Moderwell, Leroy Scott, and others had conceived a theatre that would produce, at reasonable prices, plays
that workers would want or ought to want to see. Reed had a
bolder scheme: labor groups would dramatize the principal
events in their lives, just as the Paterson workers had dramatized
their strike. The idea grew: the best dramatizations from all over
the country would be presented once a year, on May Day, in

New York. Reed's friends caught his enthusiasm, and money for initial expenses was quickly raised, but he became absorbed in other things, and, since no one else would carry on the task of organization, the plan collapsed.

In facing the whole problem of what he should write, he never neglected the *Masses*, which published two of his earlier sketches, "The Capitalist" and "Broadway Night," his poem "Love at Sea," two brief articles on Mexico, and a major piece of journalism, his exposure of the munitions manufacturers and their propaganda for war. The *Masses* had been passing through one of its periodical crises, this time a battle between the writers and the artists. Max Eastman maintained that it was a struggle between Socialism and Bohemianism, but the artists could see in it nothing but an attempt to curb Eastman's single-handed domination of the magazine. Stuart Davis and H. J. Glintenkamp began the attack, but they allowed John Sloan, who was better known than they, to become their spokesman. Sloan proposed that the magazine be managed by three boards of editors meeting separately: the writers, to decide on the prose and poetry; the artists, to decide on the pictures; and the make-up editors, to decide how to fit into the paper what the others had chosen. Eastman, reminding them that it was he who raised the funds, threatened to resign. The meeting was deadlocked, and decision was postponed. At the next meeting, the rebels had a majority, but they agreed to wait a day to permit those who were not present to vote. On April 6, Floyd Dell and Art Young voted four proxies, including Reed's, all in favor of Eastman, who thereby won.

Reed's failure to attend the decisive meeting suggests indifference. He, too, found Eastman dictatorial, but he was able to take care of himself, and he recognized that Eastman was more interested than most of the editors in the serious discussion of economic questions. Reed was beginning to feel that the time for so much insistence on sprightliness and variety was passing. He wanted the *Masses*, without losing any of its gay effrontery, to be capable of striking heavy blows that the enemy would feel. He had no objection to colorful sketches, satirical comments, love poems, or anything else that was alive, courageous, and honest, but he saw that there was serious business at hand, and he believed it should be handled seriously.

Nothing disturbed him more in the spring of 1916 than the growth of the preparedness movement. He had watched with anger and alarm the founding of the National Security League, Wood's and Roosevelt's attempts at creating a private army, the opening of the business men's camp at Plattsburg, and the spread of military training in the colleges. The news that Samuel Gompers had joined Howard Coffin, Ralph Easley, and Hudson Maxim in working out details of industrial mobilization infuriated him. The preparedness parade, with its Wall Street sections, its thousands of bloodthirsty society women, and its blatant banners, made him pound on the furniture and shout with disgust. This was something that had to be written about, and he wrote about it in the *Masses*.

"At the Throat of the Republic," though it began with some colorful vituperation of the militarists, especially Theodore Roosevelt, was for the most part straightforward exposition, handling facts with vicious precision. Reed showed that the National Security League was dominated by Hudson Maxim, president of the Maxim Munitions Corporation, and that among its directors were representatives of United States Steel and Westinghouse Electric. He showed that the Navy League had as directors and officers J. P. Morgan, Edward Stotesbury of the Morgan interests and the Baldwin Locomotive Works, Robert Bacon and Henry Frick of United States Steel, George R. Sheldon of Bethlehem Steel, and W. A. Clark, the copper-king. He pointed out that the *Metropolitan*, in which Roosevelt advocated preparedness, was owned by Harry Payne Whitney, a Morgan man and a founder of the Navy League. He traced the various interlocking directorates of the Morgan and Rockefeller interests, and showed that they dominated both the preparedness societies and the newly formed American International Corporation, organized for the exploitation of backward countries. He touched briefly on the conditions in the industries owned by these gentlemen in America, and then he quoted Elihu Root: "The principles of American liberty stand in need of a renewed devotion on the part of the American people. We have forgotten that in our vast material prosperity. We have grown so rich, we have lived in ease and comfort and peace so long, that we have forgotten to what we owe these agreeable instances of life." Reed commented: "The workingman has not forgotten. He knows to whom he owes 'these agreeable instances of life.' He will do well to realize that his enemy is not Germany, nor Japan; his enemy is that two percent of the people of the United States who own sixty percent of the national wealth, that band of unscrupulous 'patriots' who have already robbed him of all he has, and are now planning to make a soldier out of him to defend their loot. We advocate that the workingman prepare himself against that enemy. That is our preparedness."

REED wanted to write novels and poems, wanted to found a workers' theatre, wanted to write for the *Masses*, wanted to fight against war, wanted to get the most out of New York City for himself and for Louise Bryant. But there were two problems that he could not forget: money and health. Money meant primarily work for the *Metropolitan* and incidentally articles and stories for other paying magazines. It was an unpleasant problem, but not a difficult one to solve: the magazines wanted what he wrote, and it took a relatively small part of his energy to earn enough for his own needs and for the assistance of his mother. Health had become a more serious matter. His kidney periodically bothered him, and his doctor was talking about an operation. In any case, the doctor said, he must have a rest. Remembering the weeks at Provincetown in the summer of 1914, he suggested to Louise Bryant that they go there.

They arrived at the end of May, and early in June he had to leave to attend the Republican, Democratic, and Progressive conventions for the *Metropolitan*. On the boat from Fall River to New York, he met William Allan Neilson, whose course in Chaucer he had enjoyed. They stayed up talking until two, and Reed, finding a sympathetic listener, voiced hotly his disgust with the warring nations, denying that one side was preferable to the other, either in aims or methods. Dr. Neilson thought he had gained in strength and self-reliance, but was still the impetuous, undiscriminating youth he had been at Harvard. Reed, he felt, was a man who needed a cause to believe in, and was un-happy because he could not find one.

In New York the doctors told Reed that he was better, and he set out for Chicago, encouraged, but, as he wrote her, lone-some for Louise Bryant. He saw Hughes nominated and wit-nessed the collapse of the Progressive convention. Then he went to Detroit for an interview with Henry Ford, with whom he spent part of two days. After observing the re-nomination of Wilson at St. Louis, he returned to Detroit, apparently to per-suade Ford to finance a newspaper devoted to the cause of peace. The attempt failed, though for a little while Reed was swept off his feet by a great ambition and a great hope.

In the division of the fruits of the trip, the *Masses* once more got the better of the *Metropolitan*. "The National Circus," which appeared in the *Metropolitan* for September, with car-toons by Art Young, was a perfunctory piece of reporting that conveyed little to the reader except the author's boredom and his sense of the futility of the whole performance. But for the *Masses* Reed told the story of Roosevelt's betrayal of the Pro-gressives. He began by stating the case against Roosevelt, and he stated it with some venom: "We were not fooled by the Col-onel's brand of patriotism. Neither were the munitions makers and the money trust; the Colonel was working for their benefit, so they backed him." For the Colonel he had only contempt, but, remembering his father, he sympathized with the Progres-sives. They were not intelligent radicals, he knew; they were "common, ordinary, unenlightened people, the backwoods ideal-ists." But they were loyal to their ideals, and they had an almost religious faith in Teddy. When he refused the nomination, they wandered around as if dazed, and more than one of them wept. Although, like other Socialists, Reed had predicted this would happen, and had laughed at these men for their devotion to a person, and to such a person as Theodore Roosevelt, he was moved to admiration and sorrow.

But on the whole, Reed's visit to Ford was more significant to him than anything that happened at the conventions. He liked Ford, the audacity with which he talked of millions of cars, the common sense with which he disposed of complicated problems,

the streak of romanticism that had resulted in the Peace Ship.
The efficient organization of production in the Ford plants over-
whelmed Reed's imagination. He had a vision of all this power
in the hands of the workers, and he convinced himself that the
vision was shared by Henry Ford. Clutching at the fact that
other industrialists and financiers criticized Ford, he made himself believe that here was a genuine revolutionary. The paternal-
ism in Ford's treatment of his employees irritated him, but he
argued that it was only a phase in the creation of an industrial
democracy. Ford was so powerful and seemed so benevolent,
and the working class was so docile, that, for a brief period,
Reed was ready to put his faith in a Utopia created by kindly
capitalists.

His enthusiasm did not long survive the failure of his attempt
to interest Ford in a newspaper, but that was less because he
made a conscious effort to analyze Ford's role in the capitalist
system than because he had other things to think about. In particular, he had to make up his mind about Mexico. There was
talk of enlarging the punitive expedition, and John Wheeler of
the Wheeler Syndicate wrote him, "It seems to me that this war
will be a vehicle on which you would ride to a position in the
literature of the country that would be above everybody else as
a war-correspondent." Carl Hovey told him, "You have the
chance to be the one correspondent in this war." F. V. Ranck of
the New York *American* wired: "Feel that you would be particularly effective. Wish you would decide to go. Don't believe you
will be able to keep out of it once things really begin to break.
Can't you give us definite answer?" But Reed steadily refused.
He was tempted, of course, but there was the question of his
health, the question of leaving Louise Bryant, and especially the
question of the kind of reporting that would be demanded of
him. He strongly suspected that he would be required to glorify
the American soldier in Mexico, and that he could not do.

None of the newspaper executives could understand why he
refused to go to either Europe or Mexico. His reputation was at
its height. The *Metropolitan Bulletin*, a little paper sent to advertisers, published an article called "Insurgent Reed," describing his
independence and courage, and calling him the best descriptive

writer in the world. The publication of *The War in Eastern Europe*, though the book had a small sale, brought excellent reviews, not only in the liberal and radical weeklies but also in the daily press. Most of the reviewers, including John Dos Passos, who reviewed it for the *Harvard Monthly*, spoke of the picturesqueness of the book, its unpretentiousness, and its humor. A few, notably Floyd Dell in the *Masses*, saw in it more than colorful reporting; they found an understanding of human beings that had significance for the student of international affairs. All agreed that John Reed was as able a war-correspondent as could be found in America.

And John Reed, instead of going off to see General Pershing catch Pancho Villa, stayed in Provincetown. Hippolyte Havel, anarchist and poet, arrived and insisted on doing the cooking. Mary Heaton Vorse was living not far away. George Cram Cook and Susan Glaspell, Hutchins Hapgood and Neith Boyce, William and Marguerite Zorach, Eugene O'Neill, Dion Nordfeldt, David Carb, Robert Rogers, Marsden Hartley were there. It was an extraordinarily pleasant life for John Reed and Louise Bryant, and they felt that any one would be insane who left Provincetown to go and report a war. Even the war in Europe seemed at times less important than the horror of the natives at nude bathing or the feud that developed when Reed, piqued at being called a parlor Socialist, described Hippolyte Havel as a kitchen anarchist.

The Cooks and some of their friends, had, the summer before, produced two groups of one-act plays, and they were eager to attempt further experiments. Reed's persistent interest in the theatre flared into enthusiasm. Soon he was devoting as much time to the Provincetown Players as he was to his own writing. They took a shed at the end of a fishing wharf, cleaned it out, and built a stage. Two days before the date of the first performance the theatre caught fire, and for a time its complete destruction seemed certain, but the building was saved, though the walls were charred and a new curtain had to be purchased. The first bill consisted of Neith Boyce's "Winter Nights," "Suppressed Desires," by Cook and Glaspell, which had been given the preceding summer, and Reed's "Freedom." The theatre was filled, and Cook immediately started securing subscriptions for a summer season.

"Freedom," which had been rejected by the Washington Square Players, was a good-humored satire of romanticism. It is a story of four prisoners, Poet, Romancer, Smith, and Trusty. After years of plotting and working, the Poet and the Romancer are at last ready to escape. At first they persuade the Trusty to join them, but, deciding that he has a place in prison and would have none outside, he chooses to stay. Then the Poet remembers that he has won his reputation as a prison-poet, and says, "For God's sake, how can I write about freedom when I'm free?" Romancer and Smith persist, but when Romancer discovers that the room has no bars and is on the ground floor, he declares that no man of honor would escape under such conditions. Smith says, "Well, the difference between you sapheads and me is that I want to get out and you just think you do. You're playing a little game where the rules are more important than who wins. I'm willing to grant that you have it on me as far as honor, and patriotism, and reputation go, but all I want is freedom." The others make so much noise in denouncing him as a coward and a traitor that the guards come. Romancer, Poet, and Trusty unite in attacking Smith for attempting to escape and say that they tried to stop him. Smith has the last line: "There's not a word of truth in it! I was trying to break into a padded cell so I could be free!"

Except in so far as it served to mark the distinction between Reed's own kind of romanticism and the romantic poses of the pseudo-revolutionaries, the play was unimportant, though possibly it had as much significance as the others on the same bill. The only major dramatic talent, of course, that emerged that summer at Provincetown was Eugene O'Neill's. "Bound East for Cardiff" was produced on the second bill, with Reed in the cast, and a little later Louise Bryant appeared in "Thirst." From the time he left Princeton, which he had entered in the fall that Reed came to Harvard, O'Neill had led a life that Reed envied. He had been a sailor, a prospector, a salesman in South America, an actor, and a reporter. He was more cynical than Reed, and would sneer at the workers for failing to revolt, whereas Reed would cheer them on, but they could join in common abuse of the existing order. And Reed, despite O'Neill's cynicism, found him curiously shy, and, in a way, innocent. In the simple matter of protecting his own interests, O'Neill seemed quite incompetent, and Reed, who, for all his romanticism, knew how to deal with editors and managers, was eager to look out for him.

Reed acted in several plays in the course of the summer, including "The Game," a morality play written by Louise Bryant and staged by the Zorachs, who provided an abstract setting and introduced a stylized type of acting. He also wrote a one-act play, "The Eternal Quadrangle" in which he and Louise Bryant and George Cram Cook took the leading parts. It was another Shavian farce, a burlesque of the "triangle" plays of Broadway with incidental comments on love and the institution of marriage. It was written in haste, to fit the needs of the Players, and Reed did not seek either to publish it or to have it produced a second time.

The conviction grew in Reed that the Provincetown Players had importance for the theatre, and he was insistent, in the face of skepticism, that the experiment should be continued in New York. On September 5, a meeting was called, with Rogers in the chair, and Reed, Cook, and a few other enthusiasts won a majority of the members to their side. The next day a constitution was presented and adopted, and plans were made for the first performances in the city.

Reed and Louise Bryant lingered on in Provincetown until the end of September. He was now negotiating with the editors of the *Metropolitan* with regard to a trip to China. Eager to have Reed in any land where there would be colorful scenes for him to describe, Whigham and Hovey approved the suggestion. But there was the question of his health. He was feeling stronger after his summer by the ocean, but he realized that the infection of his kidney was not cured. While he tried to make up his mind about an operation, he stayed in Provincetown and wrote.

For the most part, the work of the summer went into potboilers. His creative energies were absorbed by the Provincetown Players, and for the rest he sought only to make money.

His own needs, the demands of his family, doctors' bills, and the prospect of an expensive operation made him keep close watch on his income. He wrote a short serial for *Collier's* called "Dynamite," a purely melodramatic story of financiers, crooks, anarchists, a brave hero, a beautiful heroine, and a sweet romance. "And they all lived happily ever after," he concluded the story, lest any one should fail to realize that his tongue was in his cheek.

For the *Metropolitan* he revised "The Last Clinch," a story about a southern gentleman in New York that he had first written three years earlier, and laboriously created a humorous tale, "The Buccaneer's Grandson," in the heavily facetious manner he had attempted during his first year in New York. "The Buccaneer's Grandson" introduced Grampus Bill, making much of his misuse of the English language, his tendency to exaggeration, and his trick, modeled after Mr. Dooley's, of sententiousness. Carl Hovey liked the character and urged Reed to try another story, but "The Weaker Sect," in which Bill turned from privateering to caring for seals in a circus, did not appeal to Mr. Hovey, and no other magazine would take it. Later Reed tried to write a third Grampus Bill story, "The Wages of Neutrality," but he never finished it.

Facetiousness or melodrama, those seemed to be the alternatives, and Reed was not very adroit at achieving commercially useful products of either type. "The Edge of Asia," a story of an innocent American in Russia who falls in love with a notorious courtesan and is saved from destruction by a wily diplomat, was as melodramatic as "Dynamite," but it failed to find a purchaser. "Noblesse Oblige," a revision of an early story of an old gambler in France, also fell short of publication. Deeply worried by the failure of all this work to boil the pot, Reed returned to New York, hoping that he would be well enough to go to China without an operation. Although he had looked forward to life in the United States, when he came back from the eastern front, and had hoped that he would be able to remain here until the war was over, the trip to China came to seem the only possibility for continued work with the *Metropolitan*.

He was able to secure one assignment in New York that pleased him. The *Tribune* sent him down to Bayonne to report the strike in the Standard Oil plants, and he did an article for the *Metropolitan* as well. He described the strike as akin to those in the Colorado coal fields, the Michigan copper mines, and the Youngstown steel works—a desperate, unorganized revolt of oppressed workers. His gift for sharp portrayal returned now that he had a congenial theme, and he depicted the conditions of the immigrants, the Rockefeller domination of the city, the victimization of the workers by the tradesmen, the law, and the church, the progress of the strike, and the use of violence by the police and the company's thugs. It was the last article Reed wrote for the *Metropolitan*, and he showed once more that, when his sympathies were aroused, he had no superiors in journalism. The fact that his sympathies were always excited by the sufferings of workers meant that he was better as a labor-reporter than as a war-correspondent, but capitalist journalism had little place for labor-reporters like Reed, and the time was coming when there would be no place at all.

As the presidential election drew near, Reed came to feel that the only thing that mattered was to keep the United States out of the war, and that the only hope of doing so was to re-elect Woodrow Wilson. In the summer he had joined Albert Jay Nock, Lincoln Steffens, Boardman Robinson, and others in addressing a letter to Hughes, questioning him about his views on Mexico, neutrality, trusts, and the income tax. Now, together with Henrietta Rodman, Franklin Giddings, Carlton Hayes, and John Dewey, he signed an appeal to Socialists, asking them to vote for Wilson. "Every protest vote is a luxury dearly bought," the statement read. "Its price is the risk of losing much social justice already gained and blocking much immediate progress." He became a member of the group of writers that George Creel organized to support Wilson, a group that included Steffens, Fred Howe, Zona Gale, Hutchins Hapgood, George Cram Cook, and Susan Glaspell. In a widely syndicated article, one of a series by members of the group, he wrote: "I am for Wilson because, in the most difficult situation any American president since Lincoln has had to face, he has dared to stand for the rights of weak nations in refusing to invade Mexico; he has unflinchingly advocated the settlement of international disputes by peaceful means;

he has opposed the doctrines of militarism and has warned the American people against sinister influences at work to plunge them into war; and in this dark day for liberalism in the United States, he has declared himself a liberal and proved it by the nomination of Louis D. Brandeis and John H. Clarke to the supreme court, by forcing the enactment of the Clayton bill, the child labor bill, and the workmen's compensation act, and by the labor planks in the St. Louis platform."

Reed went on to attack the Republicans, especially Roosevelt, "the arch-disciple of Professor Bernhardi, believer in war for its own sake, the leader of the munitions makers' party, and a traitor to the people." One may suppose that Reed supported Wilson chiefly in order to oppose the Republicans. Indeed, later, when he was a little ashamed of the position he had taken, he said, "I supported Wilson simply because Wall Street was against him." It was ironical, of course, that, at the moment when Wilson was swiftly moving towards war, Reed should support him as a peace-maker, but he was only one of the millions who were deceived and betrayed. The fact that Benson, the Socialist candidate, deserted his party six months later to support the war, may have made Reed feel less guilty for having aided Wilson.

THE Provincetown Players presented their first bill in New York, and Reed acted in "The Game," but before their second bill, which included "Freedom," was ready, he was making arrangements to enter Johns Hopkins hospital. He strongly suspected that an operation would be necessary, and he knew that there was at least a chance of its being fatal. Therefore, before he left, he and Louise, who was now divorced from Dr. Trullinger, went to Poughkeepsie and were married. They entered the city hall, and the clerk, sitting in his shirt sleeves, called in two witnesses from an adjoining office. When the appointed words had been mumbled, he handed the bride the marriage certificate. "Here, lady," he said, "hang on to this; you may need it some day."

Reed entered Johns Hopkins on November 12, and for more than a week was given daily examinations, often extremely painful. The rest of the time he worked on "The Wages of Neutrality" and tried to revise "Noblesse Oblige." A classmate, Eric Parson, who had the room next to his, discovered that Reed was trying to earn money to pay for his operation, and offered a loan, which he refused. He had to be doing something, he explained, and he might as well be writing stories to pay his bills. Several of the doctors were also Harvard acquaintances, and one of them, Carl Binger, had at one time been a close friend.

Reed and Louise Bryant wrote to each other daily, he describing the progress of the examinations and his writing, she describing the life in the Village and especially the activities of the Players. Other friends wrote often. "I'm awfully touched," he wrote Louise Bryant, "by everybody's affection in New York." When it was finally decided to operate, Louise Bryant went down to Baltimore, accompanied by Walter Lippmann. She remained until after the operation had taken place. Dr. Young removed the left kidney on November 22.

The hospital records called Reed's recovery uneventful. For him, after the first few days, it was boring business lying in bed, with nothing to do between the painful dressings. After two weeks the wound had to be re-opened, but four days later he was sitting up, and he was discharged on December 13. During the last two weeks or ten days, he resumed his work on his stories, but he also found time to begin a series of poems. Three of them, grouped together as "Hospital Notes," were written in free verse and showed more clearly the imagistic influence than anything he had previously written. The best was "Coming out of Ether":

> Swish-swish—flash by the spokes of the Wheel of Pain;
> Dizzily runs the whining rim.
> Way down in the cool dark is slow-evolving sleep,
> But I hang heavily writhing in hot chains
> High in the crimson stillness of my body,
> And the swish-swish of the spokes of the Wheel of Pain.

He also wrote a pair of poems in blank verse called "Two Rooms." One described the patient in Number 60:

The nurse was excited. "Who d'you think's in 60?
Bertram C. Pick, you know, the Ice Trust man.
My, you just ought to see his overcoat—
Real sable. And the Mayor sent some orchids.
One of the girls went in to see if he wanted anything,
And he just opened his eyes and swore at her.
His night nurse is a friend of mine; Belle Stevens
Her name is; she says he's as democratic
As if he didn't have ten million dollars."

"Bright's," my doctor told me, looking serious.
"Too much drink, strong cigars—er—no exercise,
The cares and responsibilities of a great corporation.
A big man, splendid advertising for the hospital—
Not much hope—too bad—a loss to the country."
There were two world-known specialists in attendance—
One cabled for across three thousand sea-miles—
The house-physician and two jealous internes.
They gave out hourly bulletins to the papers,
And three reporters camped out in the waiting room
      .   .   .   .

Toward the end, as he twisted gasping on his bed
In that quiet room, with his special nurses and orderlies
And all that science can do, to ease his body,
And orchids to ease his soul, and telegrams and cables
From kings, presidents, parliaments, stock-exchanges—
I wondered if his burning kidney reminded him
Of that hot summer, when the fevered slums
Spewed out dead babies, and he made his pile.

In 53 there was a brick-layer, incurably ill, in agony, the bane
of nurses and orderlies. The doctor said:

> "A most interesting case.
> An acute cystitis, long neglected,
> Infected bladder, ureters, kidneys—in fact
> The entire superpubic—you wouldn't understand.
> Possibly a year's rest in a warm climate
> Might have cleared up all the symptoms.
> Yes, now there's nothing to be done
> But morphine injections to dull the pain.

How long? O, consciousness will probably
Persist six weeks–and by that time the sedative
Will be powerless; and then two weeks' coma.
It is extraordinarily virulent. I've never seen
Such rapid progress. Kill him? ha, ha.
Well, no, really. It's our duty, you know
To preserve life as long as possible–and besides
The last stages are particularly interesting."

The nurse said, "Those kind of patients are a bother," and the orderly asked him what the hell he thought he was. And when he died they were relieved–

But all I could think of was death in 53
Without love, or battle, or any glorious suddenness.

Reed may have planned a series of poetic studies, for he inscribed at the head of "Two Rooms" these lines from *Leaves of Grass:*

And I will make a song for the ears of the President, full of weapons
    and menacing points,
And behind the weapons countless dissatisfied faces.

Reed had not turned to Whitman before, nor had he ever seriously tried to see what poetry could be made of the common experiences of common men. The poems were not brilliantly successful, but there were true images in them, images that grew out of Reed's own way of seeing and feeling, and the poems seemed to belong, as even "Pygmalion" and "Love at Sea" had not, to the rest of Reed's experiences. The month at Johns Hopkins might have marked the commencement of poetic maturity, but the hospital poems were to remain isolated experiments. Three days after his discharge, he was at the *Masses* ball. The old life was beginning again, at a new tempo.

XIII

ALMOST THIRTY

THE *Metropolitan* for January, 1917, announced Reed's proposed trip to China: "He will hold up the mirror to this
mysterious and romantic country, and we shall see its teeming millions and the big forces at work there. Imagine Reed in
this rich 'copy' empire—the man of whom Rudyard Kipling said,
'His articles in the *Metropolitan* made me see Mexico.'" Reed
and Louise Bryant, securing their passports and a stock of letters
of introduction, made all their plans.

On January 22, 1917, Wilson delivered his famous speech advocating peace without victory. The next day Bethlehem Steel
announced a two hundred percent stock dividend. A week later,
Count Bernstoff informed the United States government that
Germany was about to engage in virtually unrestricted submarine warfare, and on February 3 the President announced the
severing of diplomatic relations. That week Hovey wrote Reed
that under the circumstances it seemed unwise to spend money
on articles about China. "Whigham and I," he said, "think that
we had best put off consideration of your trip to China until we
can see more clearly ahead. Meanwhile, is there anything in connection with the new situation you can suggest that we could do
in place of it?"

There was nothing. The abandoning of the trip to China meant
the end not only of one of Jack Reed's romantic dreams but also
of a very substantial reality, his profitable employment by the
Metropolitan. Roosevelt's policies had come more and more to
dominate the magazine; Socialism was forgotten, and only preparation for war mattered. Whigham and Hovey had been. all

things considered, uncommonly liberal, but they were responsible for a business enterprise with a heavy investment and growing profits, and there were limits to their tolerance. Art Young had been called from Washington and asked to talk over with them his monthly letter, and he knew that the end was near. Reed had been perfectly outspoken. He had said to Whigham, "You and I call ourselves friends, but we are not really friends because we don't believe in the same things, and the time will come when we won't speak to each other. You are going to see great things happen in this country pretty soon. It may kill me and it may kill you and all your friends, but it's going to be great." After that, Whigham and Hovey realized that, for all his talents, John Reed was a liability to the *Metropolitan* unless a way could be found for him to utilize those talents in a corner of the world that presented no issues on which *Metropolitan* advertisers felt deeply. When they decided that they could not send him to romantic and remote China, they knew that he was no longer useful to the magazine.

There was a brief interval before the actual break, but nothing that Reed wrote appeared in the *Metropolitan*. He did an article on Samuel Gompers, a discreet article, careful neither to discredit organized labor nor to offend the A.F. of L., but at the same time intended to expose the inadequacies of Gompers' leadership. It was a painstaking piece of work, with a documented account of Gompers' life and the growth of the Federation. In the sections that described Gompers' speech to striking garment workers and his conversation with Reed, it had some of the restrained irony that made the Billy Sunday article so effective. But on the whole it was weak because Reed could only hint at his real criticisms of the reformist bureaucrat. Hovey and Whigham were right: John Reed was no longer a *Metropolitan* asset.

He began a search for other employment. There were offers, lucrative ones, but he was made to realize that they were conditional on a promise to conform. Rejecting them, he went ahead with his own plans. A young anarchist, Konrad Bercovici, had done a series of sketches that Reed liked, and he wrote an introduction for them when they appeared in a book called *The Crimes of Charity*. He not only praised the vividness of the sketches; he endorsed Bercovici's bitter attack on organized charity. "Every person of intelligence and humanity," he wrote, "who has seen the workings of organized charity knows what a deadening and life-sapping thing it is, how unnecessarily cruel, how uncomprehending. Yet it must not be criticized, investigated, or attacked. Like patriotism, charity is respectable—like the tariff, the open shop, Wall Street, and Trinity Church. White slavery recruits itself from charity, industry grows bloated with it, landlords live off it; and it supports an army of officers, investigators, clerks, and collectors, whom it systematically debauches . . . Its object is to get efficient results—and that means, in practice, to just keep alive vast numbers of servile, broken-spirited people."

Reed pointed out, more sharply than Bercovici had done, that the crimes of charity were ultimately to be laid at the door of capitalism. He had begun to make an effort to understand Marxist theory, primarily because he wanted to understand why Socialism had failed to prevent the war. As he read the works of Marx and Engels and examined the records of the Socialist parties in the various belligerent countries, it seemed clear to him that the workers had been betrayed by their leaders. He commenced an article called "The Collapse of the Second International," in which he outlined the Marxist conception of the class struggle and analyzed the mistakes the Socialist functionaries had made. It was by no means an original piece of theory, and its somewhat romantic view of revolution showed the I.W.W. influence, but it was significant that Reed's sympathy for the oppressed had led him to the kind of theorizing for which he had once had contempt.

Reed was slowly realizing that a decision had been forced upon him. For four years he had taken the side of the workers in their struggle against exploitation, and he had become known as a radical; but radicalism had been only one of many interests. Now, in the months when the United States prepared for entrance into the war, he understood that, if he was to be a radical at all, revolutionary change must be, if not his only interest, at least the center of his life. He told a friend that henceforth he would write nothing that did not express his hatred of capitalism, nothing that did not aid the cause of revolution. He was still a poet, but a poet whose immediate task was something else than the writing of poetry.

With the feeling that the era of his life out of which his poetry had grown was ending, he collected his verse in a small volume called *Tamburlaine*, published by his friend Frederick C. Bursch. He included twenty-six poems, all but three of which had been written by the end of 1913. Even though he had written so little in the past three years, Reed had always been expecting that somehow he would return to the writing of poetry. Now, though he still thought of himself as a poet, he felt that a great deal would have to happen before poets could resume their normal functions.

THE pacifists had begun their frantic struggle to prevent the declaration of war, but Reed, though he took part in it, knew it came too late. Bernstoff had left, and the House had voted the largest naval appropriations bill in history. Though LaFollette had killed the armed ship bill in the Senate, Wilson had proceeded to arm merchantmen without Congressional authority. The pro-Ally partisanship that Reed had deplored was fast becoming hysteria. More and more clergymen joined Newell Dwight Hillis, S. Parkes Cadman, and Henry Van Dyke in preaching a holy crusade against the Huns. College presidents vied with one another in the coining of epithets for the Kaiser. And the liberals were hastening to get in line: the editors of the *New Republic* had decided that, in Floyd Dell's phrase, "a war patronized by the *New Republic* could not but turn out to be a better war than any one had hoped."

Reed kept on fighting. "I know what war means," he wrote in the *Masses* and the *Call*. "I have been with the armies of all belligerents except one, and I have seen men die, and go mad, and lie in hospitals suffering hell; but there is a worse thing than that. War means an ugly mob-madness, crucifying the truth-tellers, choking the artists, side-tracking reforms, revolutions, and the working of social forces. Already in America those citizens who oppose the entrance of their country into the European mêlée are called 'traitors,' and those who protest against the curtailing of our meager rights of free speech are spoken of as 'dangerous lunatics.' "

"Whose war is this?" he asked, and answered, "Not mine. I know that hundreds of thousands of American workingmen employed by our great financial 'patriots' are not paid a living wage. I have seen poor men sent to jail for long terms without trial, and even without any charge. Peaceful strikers, and their wives and children, have been shot to death, burned to death, by private detectives and militiamen. The rich have steadily become richer, and the cost of living higher, and the workers proportionally poorer. These toilers don't want war—not even civil war. But the speculators, the employers, the plutocracy—they want it, just as they did in Germany and England; and with lies and sophistries they will whip up our blood until we are savage and then we'll fight and die for them."

Reed, like most radicals, took some consolation in the overthrow of the Tsar, but he was not deceived into believing that a significant transfer of power had taken place. He described it as a revolution created by intellectuals, business men, and army officers, for the purpose of better organizing Russian capitalism and more efficiently carrying on the war. For this reason it had the approval of the commercial interests of the Allied countries. He saw a possibility that it might open the way for a genuine revolution by the workers and peasants, but he scoffed at the idea that any particular importance could be attached to the abdication of the Tsar and the consequent change in the form of government.

For the moment, Russia was less important than the last desperate fight against participation in the war. Now that it had become certain that President Wilson would call for a declaration of war, the pacifists could scarcely believe that what they had dreaded was at hand. Thousands of them poured into Washington as Congress opened, most of them frightened and confused, but still hoping. Reed joined them. LaFollette gave him a pass to the Senate and John M. Nelson, who also was to vote against the war resolution, a pass to the House.

But on the evening of April 2, when Wilson was addressing the joint session of Congress, Reed was not present. He was at a meeting held under the auspices of the People's Council, a meeting to which thousands of pacifists and radicals had come from all over the East. The more liberal members of the committee had asked him to speak, but he feared that, as a radical, he would be denied the chance. Grace Potter, who had helped with the Paterson pageant and had been his strongest supporter in his project for a workers' theatre, offered a suggestion. With his approval, she assigned loyal friends to places throughout the hall and gave them their instructions.

When, as the hour grew late and Reed had not yet been called on, he gave her a signal, she rose and waved her handkerchief. Instantly there were cries from all over the hall, "We want Jack Reed!" David Starr Jordan, who was presiding, rose and said, "We will come to Mr. Reed in due time." Another speaker was introduced, and went on and on with meaningless phrases. Grace Potter again waved her handkerchief, and again the cries came for Jack Reed. "Mr. Reed will speak if there is time," Dr. Jordan announced.

As the clamor continued, a man entered the back of the hall and walked rapidly to the platform. Every one was silent. The man reached the platform, and they all, knowing well what they were to hear, gasped as he briefly told them that the President had called for war. Dr. Jordan rose, saying in effect, "We were for peace, but we will follow our country." There were cries of "Jack Reed," cries that were repeated throughout the audience. "There is no time," Jordan said. The cries grew more and more insistent. Reed rose, stepped forward, raised his hand, and said, "This is not my war, and I will not support it. This is not my war, and I will have nothing to do with it." One man had refused to equivocate, and courage sprang up again in hundreds of hearts.

Outside on the street, Reed bought an extra and read the eloquent phrases of the President's message: "We must put excited feeling away . . . We will not choose the path of submission and suffer the most sacred rights of our nation and our people to be ignored or violated. The wrongs against which we now array ourselves are not common wrongs: they cut to the very root of human life. . . . Our object . . . is to vindicate the principles of peace and justice in the life of the world . . . We have no quarrel with the German people . . . A steadfast concert for peace can never be maintained except by a partnership of democratic nations . . . Only free peoples can hold their purpose and their honor steady to a common end and prefer the interests of mankind to any narrow interest of their own . . . We are now about to accept gauge of battle with this natural foe to liberty and shall, if necessary, spend the whole force of the nation to check and nullify its pretensions and its power . . . If there be disloyalty it will be dealt with with a firm hand of stern repression . . . The day has come when America is privileged to spend her blood and her might for the principles that gave her birth and happiness and the peace she has treasured. God helping her, she can do no other."

Wilson's high moral tone sickened Reed, and he fought to break through the fog of hypocrisy. He remained in Washington in order to testify at the House judiciary committee hearings on the espionage bill. He advanced, necessarily, the usual liberal arguments, re-enforced by his own observations in the belligerent countries. At the hearing on the conscription bill, however, which took place two days later, he definitely committed himself. After describing conscription as undemocratic, he set forth the case for persons like himself who, without religious scruples against war in general, opposed this particular war. "I am not a peace-at-any-price man," he said, "or a thorough pacifist, but I would not serve in this war. You can shoot me if you want and try to draft me to fight—and I know that there are ten thousand other people—"

Representative Greene of Vermont interrupted: "I do not think we need to hear this gentleman any further," and Representative Kahn of California added, "That kind of a man is found in every country, but we should be thankful that the country does not depend on them." But the chairman insisted that Reed should be heard, and he went on, reporting observations in England, France, and Bulgaria. When he paused, Kahn ominously asked him for his address.

Representative Shallenberger inquired why he would not fight, and Reed said that his experiences on five fronts and in the

capitals of most of the warring nations had convinced him that
it was a commercial conflict.

"I think," said the chairman, "Mr. Shallenberger wanted you
to state your personal reasons."

"I was trying to state them."

"It is not your personal objection to fighting?" Shallenberger
asked.

"No," said Reed, "I have no personal objection to fighting. I
just think that the war is unjust on both sides, that Europe is
mad, and that we should keep out of it."

What Reed did was less, perhaps, than many others were
doing, but such consistency had, nonetheless, become a rare virtue. And as the anti-war forces dwindled away, he found it difficult to keep from discouragement. It was easy enough to be
personally brave, but it was difficult to find any basis for hope.
The action of the emergency national convention of the Socialist Party in adopting a resolution against war helped a little to
restore his faith in the party, but he was disgusted by the prompt
desertion of such men as J. G. Phelps Stokes, Allan Benson, John
Spargo, William English Walling, and Harry Slobodin.

Of course his more respectable associates had already begun
to shun him. He met a group of Harvard acquaintances in Washington, and they were obviously uncertain whether to speak to
him or not. Finally, with marked embarrassment, they shook his
hand and went on with their talk about the war. "If I had the job
of popularizing this war," one of them said, "I would begin
by sending three or four thousand American soldiers to certain
death. That would wake the country up." It reminded Reed of
the day, a few weeks earlier, when he had overheard a young
Plattsburger discussing in the Harvard Club the sinking of an
American ship. "I must confess," the Plattsburger had drawled,
"that my ardor was somewhat dampened when I read that one
of the victims was a Negro."

Harry Reed had already volunteered. "I have done this," he
wrote his brother, "because I consider it my duty, not because I
want to be a soldier or fight. I wish you could see a little more
clearly just what the situation is in this country and how useless
it is to try to buck what can't be changed." Mrs. Reed wrote, "It

gives me a shock to have your father's son say that he cares nothing for his country and his flag. I do not want you to fight,
heaven knows, for us, but I do not want you to fight against us,
by word and pen, and I can't helping saying that if you do, now
that war is declared, I shall feel deeply ashamed. I think you will
find that most of your friends and sympathizers are of foreign
birth; very few are real Americans, comparatively."

John Reed could have endured all that if the workers had seen
clearly how they were being sent to death for the profits of the
men who all their lives had robbed them. The docility of most
of the workers was distressing enough, but the violent patriotism
of a good many brought him close to despair. He began a bit of
passionate doggerel, never published, not even completed, probably soon forgotten, but significant of a mood that recurred
again and again through the spring and summer of 1917:

Without that ye lifted a hand, without that ye uttered a cry,
While ye stood there stupidly wondering, as the ox stands to die,
All ye had won in a thousand years the Masters took again,
And drove your sons to be butchered and butcher the German men.

When they flaunted a painted cloth, red as the thongs of their
    whips,
White as your women's faces, blue as your children's lips,
Then ye must kneel and uncover, or walk stern ways alone,
So ye kissed the flag of the Masters, for ye had no flag of your own.

When they blatted a foolish jingle, set to a banal air
Then must ye stand and uncover, as if God walked there,
So under the eye of the Masters ye joined the chorusing
Though your throats ached with the lawless songs ye knew not
    how to sing.

When they took in their lying mouths the name of your dear desire,
And Liberty over your bloody backs hissed like a scourging fire,
Chained to the cannon-foundry. . . .

But he did not stop fighting. The Socialist *Call* printed his
open letter to the members of Congress, attacking conscription
in essentially the same words he had used before the committee

on military affairs. He signed the call for an American Conference for Democracy and Terms of Peace. And he wrote more and more for the *Masses:* an article in praise of LaFollette's fight against the armed ship bill, a discussion of the progress of the Russian revolution, an attack on Charles Edward Russell. In a note called "Flattering Germany," he wrote, "If it is continually flung in our faces that any man who speaks for freedom and justice is therefore pro-German, perhaps we'll come to believe it after a while." And in "The Great Illusion" he said, "It is the power of money that rules all countries, and has for many years. It is a cold economic force that fanned the fires which burst out in this war. The issue is clear, with these forces there is no alliance, for peace or war. Against them and their projects is the only place for liberals."

WHEN the inevitable break came with the *Metropolitan*, Reed looked about for work. It was out of the question to think of free-lancing, for one by one the magazines had been closed to him. At last Dr. Rumely, the editor of the New York *Mail*, hired him as feature writer, and on May 26 Reed began doing a daily signed story. The *Mail* was financed by money from the German government, but it is doubtful if Dr. Rumely knew this, and certainly Reed did not. All he knew was that the paper was not convinced of the total righteousness of Great Britain and was willing to resist some of the more absurd forms of war hysteria. He liked some of his associates, including Dr. Rumely, Ed Clapp, the chief editorial writer, and Sigmund Spaeth, who was covering music and tennis. The pay was a good deal less than Reed had been used to, but at least he was not obliged to write what he did not believe, and occasionally he could even say what he thought.

Early in June, Emma Goldman and Alexander Berkman held a meeting against conscription at Hunt's Point Palace in the Bronx. Reed attended, ostensibly as a reporter, but actually to try to protect the speakers. He had been informed that two hundred soldiers and sailors were going to break up the meeting, and earlier in the day he went to the secretary of the commissioner of police and to the deputy commissioner and asked for police protection. The former said there would be no protection unless trouble started; the latter promised to do what he could. When the meeting opened, the soldiers began to throw electric light globes, and a captain of police, whom Reed approached, refused to stop them. Reed resumed his place in the press box just as a young friend of his began to speak. Looking at the back of the hall, he saw a mob of soldiers running towards the platform. He leaped onto the stage, seized the speaker by the arm, and, holding off the soldiers, led him away. Outside, soldiers and workers were fighting, and the police were using dazzling spotlights to break up the crowd. Reed guided his friend through the tumult, got him into a car, and drove him through the park into safety.

As a result of their participation in the meeting, Emma Goldman and Alexander Berkman were arrested and charged with having obstructed the draft. At a conference, attended by Frank Harris, Max Eastman, John Reed, and others, they said that they proposed to ignore the prosecution and not attempt to defend themselves. Harris approved, but Reed urged them to fight every step of the way, and they finally agreed. He testified as a character witness for Emma Goldman, and stated that he had never heard Berkman advise men not to register.

He went to another anti-conscription meeting with Waldo Frank. When the police charged, the crowd drew back. Reed was angry. "If people would only find out that clubs don't hurt so much!" he said to Frank. That was what primarily disturbed him, the timidity of the masses, their failure to see how little they had to lose, how much to gain. He was willing to fight, but he could have fought more cheerfully if he could have seen some sign of cooperation from the men who should have been at his side.

Underneath the courage that his friends found so heartening in those days, underneath the gayety that made him a good companion, Reed was more depressed than he had ever been in his life. Since the bright September day, almost three years earlier, when he had entered wartime Paris, it had seemed to him that a decent, fruitful life could be lived only at odd moments and by the manifestation of the highest courage. Now, with hysteria triumphant in America, such a life was completely impossible. All one could do was to hang on and endure, and be ready for the opportunity, if it ever came, to build a new world on the ruins of the old.

To add to his distress, he and Louise Bryant had had their first serious quarrel of the eighteen months they had lived together. Whatever the cause, they had separated, and she had sailed, early in June, for France. He wrote her almost daily, insisting on his love, pleading with her to join him in the attempt to find a sound basis for their life together. "In this last awful business," he told her, "you were humanly right and I was wrong. I have always loved you ever since I first met you, and I guess I always will. That is more than I've ever felt for any one else." Later he wrote: "I realize how disappointed and cruelly disillusioned you have been. You thought you were getting a hero—and you only got a vicious little person who is fast losing any spark he may have had." And just before she returned, he assured her, "I am all to blame. I think I'm cured now—anyway I know that there is nothing I would do to hurt you, meaning to."

Through all his letters ran a frank admission of unhappiness that he would have made to no one else. "I'm awfully lonely and sort of depressed all the time," he wrote her late in June. "There is nothing much for me in this newspaper work I'm afraid. I don't feel like doing much of anything. Sometimes I feel energetic and interested; other times it doesn't seem worth while." A week later he said, "It gets more and more depressing here." The next day he wrote, "I am awfully tired a good deal of the time, lonely, and without much ambition or much incentive. I feel pretty dull and old. I don't know why all this is." Sometimes he tried to defend himself: "No one I love," he explained, "has ever been able to let me express myself fully, freely, and trust that expression. You've got to recognize that I am defective (if that is it) or at any rate different, and you must accept a difference in my feelings and thoughts." But his usual mood was one of self-condemnation: "I have discovered, with a shock, how far I have fallen from the ardent young poet who wrote about Mexico." He added, "Please God, I intend to get back to poetry and sweetness, some way."

The *Mail* divided his time between New York and Washington. From New York he wrote Louise Bryant of seeing Dreiser and Djuna Barnes at the Brevoort, of having dinner with Floyd Dell, of his room on Fourteenth Street, of Emma Goldman's trial, of meeting Harry Kemp and Bobby Rogers, of unhappy weekends at Croton. His letters from Washington described it as "the most exciting city in the world" and one of the most horrible. His respectable friends still hoped he would surrender. George Creel offered him a job in the censorship department, which he promptly refused, and Arthur Brisbane spoke of a position on the Washington *Times*. Steffens came back from Russia to tell President Wilson that Kerensky, despite his good intentions, was unable to prosecute the war. He talked to Reed about the break with Louise Bryant. "I said," Reed wrote her, "that I'd been a fool and a cad, and he just told me most people were at some time, in some way." That was consoling, but Reed felt, nevertheless, that he and Steffens no longer understood each other.

Despite his conviction that he was not suited for regular reporting, he did more than adequate work for the *Mail*. Part of the paper's policy was to work for an equitable taxation program, and much that Reed wrote was propaganda for an excess profits tax. It was perhaps not a distinguished service to the cause of justice, but at least the articles were honest, and occasionally he had a chance to express a forthright opinion. "No group or class of Americans," he wrote in the first article of the series, "should be permitted to have a vested interest in war, nor should they be permitted at the expense of the people to amass enormous sums of money out of the slaughter of mankind." Other articles described the vast profits of the rich and the living conditions of the majority of the workers. From Washington he pointed out that the motto of the Senate was, "Make the poor and the future pay for the war." He interviewed business men, a dozen Senators, a score of Representatives, even the President himself. The minor details of the job irked him, and once he made the mistake of listing as a committee-member a Congressman who had been dead six months, but he was able to work up considerable enthusiasm for the campaign, merely because it permitted him to attack, however indirectly, the forces that had made the war.

Reed was often successful in making the *Mail* serve his purposes. He did a story on the conscientious objectors, interviewed Jim Larkin on the Irish situation, described the dangers of venereal disease in the army, and went on board a Russian warship that was being managed by a committee of sailors. His dispatches from Washington described the lobbying profiteers, the madmen with inventions, and the idealists intoxicated with power. He wrote about the unsanitary conditions of one of the army cantonments. And he devoted two sardonic articles to a society benefit for the blind held in Macdougal Alley. "It was New York's last real laugh," he wrote, after describing the social splendor that had transformed the alley. "Within a few months now the casualty lists will be appearing, and in the rotogravure sections of the Sunday papers there will be pages of young, high-bred faces with the caption 'The Roll of Honor.' . . . Those pages and pages of young faces, you understand, will be pictures of officers—not of the countless private soldiers whose obscure and voiceless people will have nothing to comfort them but the common grief. . . . Our streets will slowly fill with pale figures in uniform, leaning on Red Cross nurses; with men who have arms off, hands off, faces shot away, men hobbling on crutches, pieces of men. Then New York will not laugh any more. Europe has stopped laughing long ago . . . Yet last night I was struck with one thing. That these rich and ever comfortable people are the only people in New York who can still laugh—even now, before battle, before loss, in time of peace. The poor who moved restlessly up and down on the fringe of the spectacle could no longer laugh, even though most of them were once Italians . . . Life was too exhausting, too harsh. I think that the most terrible calamities will never change the expression of these people . . . If I were Weir Mitchell or somebody like that I should paint a picture of flaunting wealth and extravagance, with the submerged and groaning masses of mankind, driven to desperation, thrusting their bloody fists up through the concrete floor of Macdougal Alley. But alas, I cannot. There is no bloody fist. It is Belshazzar's feast without the writing on the wall."

Of course he could not always do as he pleased. The *Mail* wanted human interest stories, and he supplied them—the electrocution of Dr. Waite, a whole series on the life of Benny Leonard, an account of a murder trial. Most of these assignments he disliked. He wrote Louise Bryant from Baltimore, "I've got to interview a damned actress about her damned marriage to a damned prizefighter." But Reed had a way of finding some satisfaction even in Dr. Rumely's eagerness for romantic color. He revived his old habit of tramping around the East Side, and wrote about it as "the city of dreadful night." He talked with an evicted woman, helped a man find a midwife, played craps with a group of sweat-drenched men, and wandered about among the restless sleepers in Tompkins Square. At an Italian theatre he grew excited about the acting of Mimi Aguglia, "the Sicilian Duse." He toured the dives of Hoboken. He talked with a deserter from the Roumanian army and with exiles who were planning to return to Russia. A murder trial gave him a chance to comment on the economic basis of crime; a visit to a subway excavation beneath Times Square made it possible to suggest once more the contrast between rich and poor; a plan to make sunken gardens in Central Park served as the occasion for satirical remarks about "fat ladies with jewels." He even went to Saratoga for the races, and stopped off at Lily Dale to spend three mirthful days at the spiritualists' convention.

If he had been in a different mood, he would have enjoyed much of his work for the *Mail*, and as it was, he contrived to find some pleasure and to write some excellent pieces. But at the same time he was constantly harassed by the sense that he was compromising with his principles. At one moment he could see that he was accomplishing a little towards the re-establishment of sanity by his articles in the *Mail*, but at the next he felt, as he wrote Louise Bryant, that perhaps he "ought to raise hell and go to jail." Even his trips to the East Side lost their savor when he caught sight of men in uniform.

As usual he turned to the *Masses* for frank expression. In "The Myth of American Frankness" he wrote, "We are a rich, fat, lazy, soft people, we Americans. This charactization of us was invented by that prize exaggerator, Theodore Roosevelt, when he was press-agenting preparedness, and wanted to explain why the nations of the world would all invade the United States." Wilson, he went on, had now borrowed the slogan, "as usual adopting Teddy's idea three years late." After giving figures to show that the rich had grown richer during the war and the poor poorer, Reed said, "We agree with Messrs. Root, Vanderlip, and Wood that the fat should be sweated, that the lazy should be forced to work. We even go so far as to venture an opinion that if those who could afford it should be forced to pay for this war, there would soon be peace. Meanwhile it is perfectly useless, we suppose, to remind these gentlemen that there is a limit to human endurance, even among a people as long suffering as Americans." He quoted "our anarchist contemporary," the *Wall Street Journal*, "We are now at war, and militant pacifists are earnestly reminded that there is no shortage of hemp or lampposts," and informed the gentlemen of Wall Street that, if they were not careful, they might find themselves on the wrong end of the rope.

In briefer notes in the same issue, that for July, he commented on Gompers' support of the war, listed some of the grosser attacks on freedom of speech, and ridiculed the plan of the so-called "first fifty" to help the war by reducing luncheons to three or four courses and dinners to five or six. He quoted Thomas Jefferson's remark, "The tree of liberty must be refreshed from time to time with the blood of patriots and tyrants. It is the natural manure," and commented, "I submit that the tree of liberty being now very greatly in need of refreshments, there are a few 'patriots' about ripe for slaughter," going on to list the profits of the coal trusts, the railroads, the munitions makers, and the manufacturers of flags.

In the August issue, under the title "Militarism at Play," he began, "We always used to say that certain things would happen in this country if militarism came. Militarism has come. They are happening." He described the systematic disruption of a meeting of the American Conference on Democracy and Terms of Peace. Hundreds of secret service men, some of them trying to disguise themselves as delegates, had been aided by soldiers and sailors sent to the meeting by their commanding officers.

He also described the breaking up of Emma Goldman's anti-conscription meeting, the raid on Socialist headquarters in the twenty-sixth assembly district, and the invasion of a meeting at Arlington Hall. "Just wait, boys," he warned, "until the crowd finds that clubs and butts and even bayonets don't hurt so much, and that there are too many heads to crack." In the same issue there was an extract from the New York *Tribune*, a report of Dr. Frankwood E. Williams' statement regarding the frequency of mental disease in the army. Over it Reed wrote a headline, "Knit a Strait-Jacket for Your Soldier Boy," seven words that, in some strange way, were to seem more seditious to the district attorney than anything else he had written.

It was inevitable, of course, that the *Masses* should be barred from the mails, along with fourteen other periodicals. "In America," John Reed wrote in the September issue, "the month just passed has been the blackest month for freedom our generation has known. With a sort of hideous apathy the country has acquiesced in a regime of judicial tyranny, bureaucratic suppression, and industrial barbarism, which followed inevitably the first fine careless rapture of militarism." Describing the conviction of Emma Goldman and Alexander Berkman, the attack of soldiers and sailors upon a Socialist parade in Boston, the driving of Arizona strikers into the desert, and the railroading of Tom Mooney, he pointed out that "law is merely the instrument of the most powerful interests and there are no constitutional safeguards worthy the powder to blow them to hell." "Meanwhile," he observed, "organized labor lies down and takes it—nay, in San Francisco, connives at it. Gompers is so busy running the war that he has time for nothing except to appoint upon his committees labor's bitterest enemies. I suppose that as soon as Tom Mooney and his wife are executed, Gompers will invite District Attorney Fickert to serve upon the Committee of Labor."

THE two most ambitious articles that Reed wrote in the early months of the war appeared neither in the *Mail* nor in the *Masses*. One of them was never published; the other was printed in the *Seven Arts*. The first was an autobiographical essay called "Almost Thirty"; the second was "This Unpopular War," an essay that said what Reed most deeply felt about the war and especially American participation.

The *Seven Arts*, founded two years earlier by Waldo Frank, Van Wyck Brooks, and James Oppenheim, had sought to be, and with considerable success, the organ of the renaissance in American literature. Sherwood Anderson, Theodore Dreiser, Amy Lowell, Maxwell Bodenheim, John Dos Passos, Eugene O'Neill, Carl Sandburg, and Robert Frost were among its contributors. John Reed had submitted stories, but they had always been rejected. The *Seven Arts* was interested in originality, and Reed's stories, like his poems, owed much to the literary manners of an earlier generation.

It is significant that Reed's first—and only—contribution to the *Seven Arts* was a political essay. The renaissance, if the brief upsurge of new talent deserves to be called by that name, was, as we have already seen, closely related to a strong, though usually undirected, desire for a more decent civilization. There was a single impulse behind the manifold experiments in art and literature and all the vague aspirations for social change. Reed was slow in recognizing the need for literary experimentation, and slow, once he had seen the need, in creating the forms that he could use. On the other hand, he responded much more sharply and wholeheartedly than most of his fellow-writers to the inhumanity of capitalist society. In no sense a theoretician, he merely felt deeply what he saw and acted upon his feelings. Despite his happy-go-lucky ways and his insatiable eagerness for all kinds of experience, he was dragged along, step by step, by the strength and the soundness of his emotions. And the war had proven that he was right, that one could not simply go on writing poetry in so disorganized a world. The editors of the *Seven Arts* felt it, though their magazine had originally been almost purely literary, and they published Randolph Bourne's "The War and the Intellectuals" and John Reed's "This Unpopular War."

Reed found a satisfaction, his letters to Louise Bryant show, in writing the article that lifted for a time his persistent depression. It said little that he had not said before, but it impressively brought together the observations he had made and expressed

the emotions that had been roused in him in the trenches, behind the lines, and in the cities of the warring nations. Everywhere he had been convinced that the masses of people did not
want to fight; even in war-mad America he saw signs of an
opposition that dared not express itself. How the people had
been led to battle against their own common-sense judgments,
why they had let themselves be betrayed, he could not explain.
He only knew that, if they had been left to themselves, there
would have been no war, and that even at the moment, after
three years of adroit pressure from schools, churches, newspapers, the masses, if they could have their way, would end the
war.

Through all that Reed wrote on the war ran a feeling that it
marked an ending; a beginning, too, but certainly, for him and
for the world, an ending. That was why he sat down and tried
to write a brief autobiography. "I am twenty-nine years old,"
he wrote, "and I know that this is the end of a part of my life,
the end of youth. Sometimes it seems to me the end of the
world's youth, too; certainly the great war has done something
to us all. But it is also the beginning of a new phase of life; and
the world we live in is so full of swift change and color and
meaning that I can hardly keep from imagining the splendid and
terrible possibilities of the time to come."

He looked at himself and what he had done, the way he had
scattered himself in a hundred different directions in "the all-
sufficient joy of mere living." "I must find myself again," he
wrote. "Some men seem to get their direction early, to grow
naturally and with little change to the thing they are to be. I
have no idea what I shall be or do one month from now. Whenever I have tried to become some one thing, I have failed; it is
only by drifting with the wind that I have found myself, and
plunged joyously into a new role. I have discovered that I am
only happy when I am working hard at something I like. I never
stuck long at anything I didn't like, and now I couldn't if I
wanted to; on the other hand there are very few things I don't
get some fun out of, if only the novelty of the experience. I love
people, except the well-fed smug, and am interested in all the
new things and all the beautiful old things they do. I love beauty

and chance and change, but less now in the external world and more in my mind. I suppose I'll always be a romanticist."

He looked back on life in Portland, the splendor of the Greens, the joy of reading, the boredom of schools, the unhappiness of a shy, sickly boy among his robust and cruel fellows, and the glamorous figure of his fighting father. He recalled Morristown and self-discovery, Harvard and its defeats, still bitter in memory, and its triumphs, still pleasant to savor. He paid tribute to Copeland and Steffens. He wrote of the enchanted city and its romantic life, of Paterson and the excitement of the pageant, of Mexico and companionship in danger.

He said little of the three years immediately preceding the writing of the essay, but he summarized what at the moment he felt about the two struggles that had occupied most of his attention in those years, the war of the classes and the world war. "I have seen and reported many strikes," he wrote, "most of them desperate struggles for the bare necessities of life; and all I have witnessed only confirms my first idea of the class struggle and its inevitability. I wish with all my heart that the proletariat would rise and take their rights—I don't see how else they will get them. Political relief is so slow to come, and year by year the opportunities of peaceful protest and lawful action are curtailed. But I am not sure that the working class is capable of revolution, peaceful or otherwise; the workers are so divided and so bitterly hostile to each other, so badly led, so blind to their class interest. The war has been a terrible shatterer of faith in economic and political idealism. And yet I cannot give up the idea that out of democracy will be born the new world—richer, braver, freer, more beautiful. As for me, I don't know what I can do to help—I don't know yet. All I know is that my happiness is built on the misery of other people, that I eat because others go hungry, that I am clothed when other people go almost naked through the frozen cities in winter; and that fact poisons me, disturbs my serenity, makes me write propaganda when I would rather play." Of the war he could only say, "It is just a stoppage of the life and ferment of human evolution. I am waiting, waiting for it all to end, for life to resume, so I can find my work."

Once more John Reed faced an apparently hopeless barrier. It was the situation of the fall of 1913, intensified by the war. Now there was the question not only of what he wanted to do but also of what he could do. His position on the *Mail* was by no means secure. It was doubtful if another magazine or newspaper would employ him—without guarantees that he was unwilling to give. He might at any moment be imprisoned for what he had written. And yet he looked toward the future not merely with courage but with anticipation. Moments of gloom did not endure. He was ready for whatever might come.

XIV

Passage to Russia

IF Reed had no idea what he would be doing a month hence, he knew well enough what he would like to do. Within two months after the abdication of the Tsar, he had begun to change his opinion of the Russian revolution. "We make our apologies," he wrote in the *Masses*, "to the Russian proletariat for speaking of this as a 'bourgeois revolution.' It was only the 'front' we saw, the wished-for consummation of Kapitaltum. The real thing was the long-thwarted rise of the Russian masses, as now we see with increasing plainness; and the purpose of it is the establishment of a new human society upon the earth." Something new had appeared in Russia, the Soviet of Workers' and Soldiers' Deputies, and Reed felt with the certainty of a good journalist that here was the decisive factor in the country's future. He wanted to go to Russia.

Louise Bryant, returning from France with news of the kindling of revolt in half a dozen countries, was eager to go to Russia with him. Personal difficulties forgotten, they hastened, in the first fortnight of August, to find the means for the trip. A press syndicate was willing to make Louise Bryant its correspondent, but the whole newspaper world was afraid of Reed. He battered at editors in New York, Baltimore, and Washington, but without success. Eastman was eager to have him represent the *Masses*, but the *Masses* could not pay his expenses. Finally, friends of the magazine, notably Eugen Boissevain, raised the money. Less than a year before, Reed could have gone almost anywhere in the world for almost any paper in the country and been paid almost any sum he wanted to name; now he was going to Russia, to do the best reporting of his life, for the *Masses* and the *Call*, with the *Seven Arts* thrown in for kudos.

Before he could leave the country, the question of military service had to be settled. Although he had been told that the removal of his kidney was almost certainly sufficient cause for exemption from the draft, he had hesitated to take advantage of such an accident. Now, confident that he would be more useful in Russia than in Leavenworth, he appeared before the Croton draft board. He was apparently in good physical condition, and the examiner refused to exempt him until a telegram was received from General Crowder, ruling that nephrectomy was disqualifying.

Reed was exempted from military service on August 14. On the same day he and Louise Bryant applied for their passports, and three days later they sailed on the Danish steamer, *United States*. In applying for his passport, Reed stated that he wished to visit Sweden and Russia as a correspondent. The authorities, who had been instructed not to permit any one to attend the conference that the Socialists were trying to hold in Stockholm, immediately questioned his application, and it seemed likely that he would be delayed and perhaps prevented from going at all. Once more influential friends came to his aid, and, by taking an oath not to represent the Socialist Party at the conference, which he had neither intention nor right to do, he satisfied the State Department.

The ship was held for a week at Halifax while English authorities searched it for contraband and examined its passengers. "The world has grown used to British domination of the seas," Reed wrote, "and it is considered perfectly natural that we should sail first to Halifax, and stay there as long as London wishes, without any explanation." A party of marines came to search Reed's cabin. He had concealed his letters to Socialists in Stockholm under the carpet, but, to make perfectly sure, he gave the men whiskey and talked with them. Wishing him a good trip, they left without even the pretense of an examination.

During the long delay he became acquainted with his fellow-passengers. There were Scandinavians, Russians, and a handful of American college boys going over to be clerks in an American bank in Petrograd. There was a Hughes Republican, born in Venezuela of Dutch parents, who was by far the most patriotic American on board. One passenger had been in Petrograd all through the February revolution, but he had seen nothing except shouting crowds. Another was a Russian diplomat, who was returning to serve the new government, whatever it might be by the time he got back. Every one was suspicious of every one else, and rumor peopled the ships with German spies, delegates to the Stockholm conference, and Russian revolutionaries.

In the steerage there were Russian Jews from New York. They arrived in Halifax by train, and came on the boat, with trunks and bundles that held all they owned, looking like a picnic excursion from Henry Street. At night they gathered on the third-class deck and sang. One of them would wave his arms, and they would begin the old songs of the harvest and of labor, great, surging, hymnlike songs with up-sweeping, strong chords that lifted Reed's heart. "At once," he wrote, "they ceased to be Jews, to be persecuted, petty, and ugly—that grand music transformed them, made them grow and broaden, until they seemed great, gentle, bearded moujiks, standing side by side with those who overthrew an empire—and perhaps a world."

As the ship finally drew away from Halifax and British scrutiny, suspicion dwindled, and a kind of fellowship grew. Beyond the Newfoundland Banks, they left the steamer lanes and began to climb towards the Arctic Circle, sweeping north by east until at last, one blue morning, they caught sight of an Iceland glacier. By that time they were friends. The captain posted a notice: "As this ship belongs to a neutral nation, the passengers are requested, on receipt of war news, to avoid all public manifestations of political sympathies or antipathies." It was unnecessary: with the exception of the captain himself, who was strongly pro-Ally, and the ardent Dutch-American, every one was weary of the war.

It was pleasant to feel oneself even to so small an extent out of the war. The ship's band played all day. There was marvelous Danish food: great quantities of meat with rich sauces, raw fish and sausages, beautiful pastry, and all kinds of beer and wine. There were dances. People dressed for dinner, and not a single military uniform was visible. Late one night, Reed decided to give a party for the half-dozen women on board, and went the rounds of the staterooms, informing the occupants that only wives were desired.

Whenever discussion turned to the war, the longing for peace became apparent. The young college boys, pledged to return if they were drafted, frankly admitted their hope that they would not have to serve. Two drummers, bound for Russia with no knowledge of the people, customs, or language, boasted a little about what American troops would do to the Germans, but they confessed that they had voted for Wilson because he had kept us out of war.

The Russians in the steerage were for the most part political exiles, returning at the expense of the provisional government. Reed listened to their stories. This man had participated in the killing of the chief of police of Dvinsk, had been arrested, had been sentenced, had seen his companions die, and had escaped. This couple had been unjustly accused of belonging to a revolutionary society and sent, without trial, to northeastern Siberia, beyond Irkutsk, thirty-five days from the railroad, to be released by the revolution of 1905. There was a sailor who had been on the *Potemkin* when it revolted in the Black Sea. There were two delegates from foreign-speaking Socialist groups to the Stockholm conference. One man was viewed with awe because he was rumored to have a letter from Kerensky.

The most amusing passenger was the opportunist diplomat, a large, sleek, quiet man, who maliciously baited the two drummers. He told them first that it was necessary to be a Socialist to survive in Russia. It would be all right, he pointed out, to say one was a Socialist, even if one were not, but of course one would have to be able to give evidence; and they went scampering off to the steerage to take lessons from the exiles. When they returned, armed with revolutionary phrases, the Russian proved to them, with quotations from Marx, that the revolution could not possibly take place in Russia. To add to their confusion, he maintained that officers of the army, who had taken an oath to the Tsar, should defend him even if they were sympathetic to the revolution. "I will tell you the story of my wife's brother," he said, "he was a guard officer on duty at Tsarkoe Syelo when the revolution broke out. Now he was also a revolutionist, secretly; yet when the mob came to the palace to capture the Tsar, he confronted them with drawn sword, and would not let them pass. 'I am a revolutionist', he said, 'but also I have given my oath to serve and protect the Tsar. You must kill me to pass, and I will fight. Long live the revolution.' And so he died there, at his post, honorably."

By the time the salesmen recovered, their tormentor was challenging them to prove that the earth was round, and they were having difficulty in doing so. Their bewilderment grew when he told one of them, a Christian Scientist, that the Russians regarded Christian Science as the refuge of idiots, and the other that it was considered the only desirable form of religion. They insisted that Reed, who had been enjoying their discomfiture, go with them while they confronted the Russian with these conflicting stories. The Russian calmly told them that he was a man of ideas, arguing for the sake of the argument. "Then you are not an officer?" asked the Russian who was secretly sympathetic to the Tsar.

"Oh, no," said the diplomat.

"And what about your brother-in-law at Tsarkoe Syelo?" inquired one of the salesmen.

"I have no brother-in-law," he said. "In fact," he added, "I have no wife." He paused. "I believe in free love," he went on. "Would you gentlemen like to discuss this interesting subject?"

CHRISTIANIA, Reed found, was a brisk little city, new and rather ugly but pleasantly unpretentious. It reminded him of Sofia, both because it was so new and because the people seemed so friendly. Living expenses were high. A few speculators and shipbuilders had grown rich and could afford to pay the seventy-five dollars that, he discovered, was charged for a bottle of whiskey. But the peasants and fishermen were getting less than ever of the raw fish and black bread that was their usual fare. There was also a shortage of clothes, and Reed, noticing the frost in the air, wondered what the winter would bring.

The Reeds hurried on to Stockholm, a trip that before the

war had taken only six hours but now took eighteen. Many of
the returning Russian exiles from the ship were on the train, hoping that the Swedish government would allow them to remain
for the Stockholm conference. Once more Reed was impressed
with their spirit. They had risked their lives and suffered imprisonment and exile for the revolutionary cause. Now, permitted to return to their own country, they were harassed by
the officials of every nation they passed through, and no one
could tell what they might find when Russia was reached. Yet
the news that the conference had been postponed, which met
them on their arrival in Stockholm, troubled them more than
their own plight.

Reed went at once to see Camille Huysmans, secretary of the
International Socialist Bureau. He noticed the thin, drawn face,
the high forehead, the wispy mustache, and the quiet, watchful
eyes. Huysmans did not want to talk, but to listen, and he asked
some shrewd questions about the Socialist Party in America. He
did give Reed a statement: "The committee is sitting in perma-
nence. Yes, the conference is postponed—but it will be held—
now we know that. When we first came here most of us were
profoundly discouraged. We hadn't any encouragement from
any Socialist body in any belligerent country. We were laughed
at. But then the Germans came, and then Henderson from England, and Thomas from France, and the Russians. And now, to
the invitation to the second conference, issued by the Russian
Council of Workmen and Soldiers, the Socialist and labor groups
of the whole world have accepted. That is beyond our greatest
dreams. Now only the governments prevent the Socialist parties
from sending their appointed delegates here. At last things are
clearing. Now it is at last the people who want peace, and the
governments alone who want to continue the war."

Reed talked with other Socialist leaders: Panin, representative
of the Workers' and Soldiers' Soviet, Axelrod, representative of
the Russian Social Democrats, Van Kol, Dutch Social Democratic senator, and others. From Panin he learned the story of the
rise of the Soviets. The more he heard, the surer he was of the
importance of what was happening in Russia, and he rejoiced
that he was going to see it with his own eyes.

In the meantime he knocked about Stockholm. The city was crowded with people, many of them conspirators or spies. Not since he left El Paso had he seen so many secret agents. A young English journalist was said to be on a confidential mission for the French government. A German princess, supposedly caring for her health, was doing business in smuggled diamonds. Polish, Finnish, Ukrainian, and Czech nationalists were holding their private conferences. Whenever Reed and Louise Bryant left their room, spies, they believed, entered and ransacked their papers. Yet, with all this intrigue, the city was very gay. Operas and theatres and movie-houses were filled; crowds gathered in the restaurants and side-walk cafés; bands played and the uniforms of twenty nations could be seen on promenade.

The rich seemed very rich, but the workers had little share in Sweden's war-prosperity. Unlike Norway and Denmark, the country had refused to surrender its commerce to England, and had continued to trade with Germany. As a result there was a shortage of certain articles. Regulations, so easy for the rich to evade, were rigidly enforced upon the poor, and they could not get enough sugar or bread. Their discontent had found expression in a demonstration of thirty thousand workers a few months earlier and in the election of a menacing proportion of Socialists to the Riksdag.

On September 7, Reed happened to be going down a dark, twisted little alley behind the palace when he noticed a crowd of workmen—big, blond men, with their arms tattooed and their shirts open at the throat. One of them stopped, gesticulated at Reed, and went through a pantomime to signify that he was thirsty. As Reed grinned and produced a crown, some one noticed his red tie, and said, "Sozialista?" When he nodded, there was a babble of cries, and they produced their red membership books. Leading him down an even fouler alley, they took him up four flights of stairs to a dingy room with a little bar. Reed could not understand what they said, but he liked the revolutionary songs they sang as they drank the schnapps he paid for.

On the eighth he cabled to the *Call* the statement of the committee in charge of preparations for the Stockholm conference. Aimed directly at America, it explained that the United States was principally responsible for the refusal of the Allies to permit delegates to attend the conference. "We do not understand President Wilson's course of action," the statement read. "When, in the Senate in December, 1916, he addressed the peoples of the world, the Socialist and labor organizations of Europe supported him with all their strength. In all Wilson's public utterances, it has been made perfectly plain that the main obstacle to American peace with Germany is the German political autocracy, and that America's object in the war is to secure the democratization of the German government. The Stockholm conference is the best and, perhaps, the only opportunity for the representatives of the Entente peoples to make clear to the German masses the conditions upon which peace is possible. And yet President Wilson refuses to allow the delegates of American Socialist and labor groups to come to Stockholm. The people of the world are sick of war, whatever policy their governments see fit to publicly adopt. In the invitation to the Stockholm conference and its acceptance by democratic political and economic elements in all the belligerent countries is to be seen the first action of the international masses, growing conscious of their power, awakening to the colossal error of unending war, and determined that government shall be of, by, and for the social democracy."

Two days later Reed was on his way to Russia. News had come of the fall of Riga, and there was a rumor that the Russian frontier would be closed. Moreover, his task at Stockholm had been, so far as possible, accomplished.

As they whirled north, Reed was reminded of the Pacific Northwest by the interminable forests of dark green fir and pine trees, the range on range of wooded hills, and the swift plunging rivers. There were a few stony fields with barley shocks, a few wooden houses and barns, a few flat-faced blond giants and squat, bowed women in kerchiefs. Occasionally he could see the lonely huts and kilns of the charcoal burners. At every station there were hunters with guns and dogs. The sun was bright, but there was a tang in the air.

In a third-class carriage ahead rode the political exiles, making the last stage of their exhausting pilgrimage. In the car with Reed and Louise Bryant was an old Russian general, who had been with a technical mission in England. With him were an artillery captain and a cavalry lieutenant. A tall old man with a gray beard, frock coat, and wide-brimmed hat sat with his fat wife and child, his arms full of teddy bears and bundles of food, very emotional as he neared Russia. He was an old-fashioned anarchist, who had spent a busy exile of thirty-eight years founding radical libraries in London and Paris. There were also five or six happy-go-lucky Russian boys, just graduated from an English aviation training camp, and a ruddy beef-eater of a British general, with three adjutants and a servant to brush their boots.

At Haparanda the Swedish authorities searched the baggage for food, taking away the anarchist's many bundles. Everybody was huddled upon a little boat, which moved slowly across the Baltic to Finland. As their baggage was again examined, the Russian general cried out at the spectacle of a sentry smoking on duty. The soldiers had all torn off the brass buttons with the imperial coat of arms, and were wearing revolutionary insignia. The artillery captain approached the guards, asking that the general, whose name and rank he mentioned, should be examined first. He was roughly told that he must wait his turn.

Every one was discussing Kornilov's march on Petrograd. The most recent news was two days old. What had happened in those two days? The British were frankly hopeful. The exiles were alarmed. An American officer and the British consul warned the Reeds not to go on to Petrograd, hinting that the streets ran with blood. They were particularly disturbed at the thought of a woman's entering Russia, and the consul told Reed he must not think of permitting Louise Bryant to go. "But she wants to," Reed said.

Soon they were rushing across flat Finland, with its thrifty fields, wide-spaced, substantial wooden houses, neat little towns, and Protestant spires. It was very much, he thought, like the Middle West, except for the flat, slant-eyed faces of the people. At every station there were revolutionary proclamations on the walls. From the soldiers came new rumors of Kornilov: he had taken Petrograd; he had been repulsed. The hopes of those in the car rose and fell. Reed was amazed at the sharpness of the class lines: the bourgeois invariably hoped for counter-revolution. "Things have gone too far," they said; "business is ruined; we must have order."

The train roared on through the dark night and the beating rain, the engine belching showers of wood-fire sparks. There was plenty of food available at the stations, but it was expensive. Inspections were frequent, usually by soldiers with red arm-bands. The next day Reed noted that the temper of the crowds at the stations had changed. Peasants stared through the windows and muttered ominously. It was, he thought, like being an English traveler going from Boulogne to Paris in 1793, with the fierce hairy faces of the Jacobin militia thrust in at the coach window whenever there was a stop to change horses. No one in the car mentioned Kornilov's name, and the officers and merchants sat tense in their seats. At Viborg there was a story that a general who had tried to aid Kornilov had been drowned, with all his staff, in the canal. But still there was no authoritative news of the fate of Petrograd.

When at last Reed reached the city, he found, to his infinite relief, that Kornilov's counter-revolution had failed. His first concern was to piece together the story. The Cossack general, appointed supreme commander-in-chief by Kerensky, had planned, under the pretext of preserving the provisional government from attack from the left, to seize power. Having carefully plotted his moves, he demanded that power be placed in his hands. The leadership of the provisional government was as indecisive as usual, but the radicals, and especially the Bolsheviks, formed the Committee for Struggle with Counter-revolution. The workers and soldiers, determined not to surrender the gains that had been made, supported the committee, and Kornilov's army almost withered away. Not only was the revolution safe; it was stronger than it had been before.

Reed and Louise Bryant, taking a small apartment, began to orientate themselves. There were Americans, of course, in the city, but they were not particularly interested in the diplomats and business men. They did find, however, two young sympathizers, Albert Rhys Williams, a Socialist, who had arrived in June, and Bessie Beatty, a journalist. Then there was Alexander Gumberg, a Russian from New York, who was acting as translator for Colonel Raymond Robins of the Red Cross. And there were a number of Americans who were cooperating with the revolutionary forces, including Bill and Anna Shatoff and Gumberg's brother, Zorin. With the aid of these, and with the smattering of Russian he had picked up eighteen months before, Reed had little difficulty in finding out what was going on.

One of the first things he did was to attend a meeting of shop committee delegates, where he listened to discussions of plans for the transfer of control to the workers. He was delighted; this was what he had long hoped to see. Soon afterward he was present when the Bolsheviks won a majority in the Petrograd Soviet, and he did not miss the significance of that event. Tremendously excited by all that he saw, full of high spirits, playing pranks, talking with every one who would talk with him, he felt himself swept ahead on the full tide of history. "The old town has changed!" he wrote Boardman Robinson. "Joy where there was gloom, and gloom where there was joy. We are in the middle of things, and believe me it's thrilling. There is so much dramatic to write that I don't know where to begin. For color and terror and grandeur this makes Mexico look pale."

A week after his arrival he could see the situation clear. "This revolution," he wrote, "has now settled down to the class struggle pure and simple, as predicted by the Marxians. The so-called 'bourgeois liberals,' Redzianske, Lvov, Milyukov, et al., have definitely aligned themselves with the capitalist elements. The intellectuals and romantic revolutionaries, except Gorky, are shocked at what revolution really is, and either gone over to the Cadets or quit. The old-timers—most of them—like Kropotkin, Breshkovskaya, even Alladdin—are entirely out of sympathy with the present movement; their real concern was with a political revolution, and the political revolution has happened, and Russia is a republic, I believe, for ever—but what is going on now is an economic revolution, which they don't understand nor care for. Through the tempest of events tumbling over one another which is beating upon Russia, the Bolsheviki star steadily rises. The Workers' and Soldiers' Soviet, which has gained immense power since the Kornilov business, is the real government of Russia again, and the Bolshevik power in the soviet is growing fast."

JOHN REED was using his eyes. They were still the eyes of a poet, but they were also the eyes of a partisan. "Already I have thousands of comrades here," he wrote a friend. He was not reporting battles like those of the World War, to whose outcome he was quite indifferent. It was not even the same as in Mexico, where merely his sympathies were on the side of Villa's men. He had not been adopted by the Russian revolutionists; he belonged with them, for they were fighting his battles. The distrust of the working class that had so long plagued him disappeared. The gloom that the war had fostered vanished before the great hope that steadily grew in his mind. The old questions as to what he could and should do simply never occurred to him. He found himself, not only emotionally, as had happened in Mexico, but also intellectually, for now the revolutionary ideas he had absorbed came to life. He was gayer than he had been for many months, but he was also more serious than he had ever been before.

He made no secret of his partisanship, and some of his fellow-countrymen became alarmed. On September 30, a mass meeting was held in the Cirque Moderne on behalf of Alexander Berkman, with Bill Shatoff as the principal speaker. The meeting sent greetings to Berkman, Goldman, and "all those who in 'free' America fight for the social revolution." The American ambassador, David R. Francis, received from a secret agent a report that Reed had told the Bolsheviks that Berkman was likely to be executed. The agent also stated that Reed had had the Associated Press barred from the Democratic Congress on the ground that it was capitalistic. Francis was particularly dismayed because Reed, when he made a formal call at the embassy, had brought a letter of introduction from Dudley Field Malone, who, as Collector of the Port of New York, was an official of the Wilson administration. Francis' agents stole Reed's wallet, in which they found a letter from Morris Hillquit to Camille

Huysmans, and one from Huysmans to the Scandinavian Socialist Committee.

From that time on, Reed was watched by secret service men.
One of the agents contrived to talk with him, and noted down
each of his heterodox remarks. Reed said that he was a Socialist,
said that workmen could manage factories themselves, said that
if workmen were paid in proportion to their labor they would
get all the profits, said that the Bolsheviks were the only party
in Russia with a program. He even, the agent noted, mentioned
"the Marx theory." To make a thorough job of it, Reed, who
very possibly knew a spy when he saw one, added that the Bolsheviks, when they took power, would expel all ambassadors.
On receiving the agent's report, Francis hastened to cable Washington for instructions.

Reed went his own way, his notebook in his pocket. He went
to every important meeting, interviewed every influential leader
he could reach, talked with scores of people in whatever mixture
of Russian, English, French, and German would serve his purpose. He took elaborate notes on the conditions of industry, the
army, and the church. He saw Tolstoy's *Death of Ivan the Terrible*, heard Chaliapin sing, watched Karsavina dance, visited the
art galleries. He had tea with wealthy merchants and talked with
the poor in their bread-lines.

On the tenth of October, he and Albert Rhys Williams and
Boris Reinstein, a leader of the Socialist Labor Party in the
United States, went to the northern front. In their compartment
was an Orthodox priest, a volunteer chaplain on his way to the
trenches, who explained in detail the position of the Orthodox
Church, and the relation between religion and revolution, while
Reed carefully took notes. Then there was a captain who spoke
French. "Tseretelli, Dan, Lieber, Gotz, and Chkheidze are the
Girondins of our time," he said. "They will share the fate of the
Gidronde. I am with them."

They slept all night in the cold car, and woke, stiff and numb,
to look out on bright autumn foliage, yellow wheat stubble, and
miles of the pale blue-green of cabbages. Soldiers became more
common at the station, and they passed troop trains. At Venden
they left the train and inquired for staff headquarters. "You don't

want the staff," some one explained; "the Iskosol is in charge of things here." So they went to the Iskosol, the central executive committee of the soldiers' deputies. There were three or four young officers and soldiers in the room, and one of them was reading aloud, with sardonic comments from his companions, the names of the members of the new cabinet. Near the window sat Voitinsky, a Kerensky supporter, author of a famous book and now a civilian commissar in charge of building up the military machine.

One of the officers told them the story of the founding of the Iskosol, during the March revolution, and explained its functions. Listening to him, Reed began to understand the terrible eagerness for self-government and self-expression that had taken innumerable organizational forms along a thousand miles of front. In the twelfth army there was an intricate system of committees, half political and half military, culminating in the Little Soviet of Soldiers' Deputies, composed of one delegate from each regiment, and the Big Soviet, with five from a regiment. It was the Big Soviet that, every three months, elected the Iskosol, which served as a commissariat department, ordering oil from Baku, wheat from the Volga, lumber from Archangel, and munitions from Petrograd, and also maintained the morale of the army and actually, in time of stress, took command of its military actions.

Thanks to the Iskosol, the Americans were provided with a room for the night, and, the next morning, with an automobile, to take them to the lines. Reed, being active, was happy, and sang and joked as they drove in the rain, bumping along the pitted, muddy road to Riga. They passed trucks and groups of soldiers and little knots of peasant women. Soon they came to the fertile country of the Estland barons, powerful German land-owners, the most reactionary in Russia. There were elaborate chateaux and once prosperous farmhouses, now roofless and looted. Cabbages were rotting in the fields. As they entered a little village that was under fire, shells tore apart houses only a block or two from them, and Reed cheerfully commented on the bad aim of the Germans. Creeping behind a cedar hedge, they came at last to a Russian battery. There was much talk about the betrayal of Riga, many questions about the events in Petrograd. The soldiers, without enough food or clothing, helpless in the face of the German attack, talked about going home.

They came back at night, passing by the fires of the refugees' camps, weaving their way through a miserable procession of homeless men and women, barefooted soldiers, wounded men, patrols, and reliefs. Early the next morning an ambulance took them to the headquarters of a Lettish brigade, where the soldiers' committee was to investigate a complaint regarding the inefficiency of sixteen officers. The colonel was a frank Tsarist, who said that the army had been spoiled because the soldiers had been permitted to think. He and his staff were good-natured and hospitable, but they expressed only contempt for the soldiers' committees. The committee in charge of the investigation was composed of five privates and one non-commissioned officer. One of them, Reed noticed, was reading Lenin's *Imperialism*. It was the soviet, he realized, that was actually doing the work of the officers, providing supplies, assigning quarters, locating troops, and administering justice.

On Sunday there was a double mass-meeting in Venden, Russian in one corner and Lettish in the other, with some fifteen thousand troops in attendance. Though the rumble of artillery was never silent and German airplanes repeatedly passed overhead, the theme of the meeting was peace. When the airplanes came too close, both meetings moved from the square to the grounds of a medieval castle of the Teutonic Knights. Here, for five hours, speaker followed speaker, most of them crying, "All power to the Soviets, land for the peasants, an immediate democratic peace." And when the band came, playing "The Marseillaise," the thousands, Letts and Russians, joined in thunderous, exalted song.

The train back to Petrograd was crowded. On the roof soldiers stamped their feet and sang shrill songs in the freezing night air. Inside the compartment a group of nurses and young officers made love. A captain coughed and spat blood. All through the night the accordion on the roof wheezed, and feet stamped rhythmically. Reed, in the half-light, crouched over his notebook, filling out the details of the trip.

In Petrograd every one was a little more tense. Reed went to see Stepan Georgevitch Lianozov, known as the Russian Rockefeller because of his vast interests in oil. He groaned about the increases in wages and the shop-committees' interference with his business. Conditions would be bad, he said, until the workers came to their senses. Trade unions were all right in their place, and he had voluntarily introduced arbitration boards in his plants, but the workers must be shown where the power lay. "Revolution is a sickness," he said. "Sooner or later the foreign powers must intervene here—as one would intervene to cure a sick child." The Bolsheviks, he thought, were cowards, and could easily be disposed of by a show of force. He expected the restoration of the monarchy.

The class lines were being drawn more and more sharply. Reed went out to Sestroretzk, a little way from Petrograd. What had once been a wealthy summer resort had become, during the war, a munitions center. The military officials had been driven out of the factories at the time of the March revolution, and shop-committees had been established. These committees had reduced hours, increased wages, lowered costs, and raised production. They had finished two buildings that government graft had delayed since 1914, and had built a hospital for the workers. They had arranged for the transportation of food, maintained discipline in the factories, and reorganized the town.

On October 21, he went to another munitions plant, the Obukhovsky Zavod, where a Bolshevik meeting was being held. Ten thousand black-clothed men and women crowded into an unfinished building. Petrovsky, who had been in America, was on the shop-committee there, and had played an important part in the administration of the factory. He spoke, slight, slow-voiced, implacable: "Now is the time for deeds, not words. The economic situation is bad, but we must get used to it. They are trying to starve us and freeze us. They are trying to provoke us. But let them know that they can go too far—that if they dare to lay their hands upon the organizations of the proletariat we will sweep them away like scum from the face of the earth!" Lunacharsky also spoke, and Reed and Williams brought greetings from America.

On the way home, as the ponderous steam tram shuddered through the black mud of the Viborg district, a soldier who had been at the meeting came up to them. Wringing his hands, he told about the front, about the unnecessary retreats and the futile advances. "Why," he cried, "did American workers allow America to enter the war and prolong it? Why won't they rise and help us stop it? My God, it is awful that we revolutionary Russians must die, that our revolution must be crushed in blood, because our brothers, for whom we are fighting, will not raise a hand!"

The reactionaries seemed determined to provoke popular anger. On the twenty-third Reed had a talk, in the press gallery of the Council of the Republic, with Burtsev, editor of *Common Cause*. "Mark my words, young man," he said. "What Russia needs is a Strong Man. We should get our minds off revolution now and concentrate on the Germans." His paper advocated a dictatorship of Kornilov, Kerensky, and Kaledin. Three or four papers were clamoring for the extermination of the revolutionary democracy.

In the Council of the Republic Kerensky sat with his eyes closed or with his gray face in his hands. Every day the gulf between the two sides of the chamber deepened. The Bolsheviks had withdrawn from the Council, but the Menshevik Internationalists and the Left Socialist Revolutionaries were driven by the arrogance of the Cadets to adopt what was practically the Bolshevik position. Martov, so sick that he could scarcely stand and so hoarse that his voice could only be heard near the platform, shook his finger toward the right benches. "You call us defeatists," he said, "but the real defeatists are those who wait for a more propitious moment to conclude peace, insist upon postponing peace until later, until nothing is left of the Russian army, until Russia becomes the subject of bargaining between the different imperialist groups. You are trying to impose upon the people a policy dictated by the interests of the bourgeoisie." Kerensky, making a vain effort for unity, became hysterical, burst into tears, and ran from the chamber.

Gorky's paper, *New Life*, pointed out the menace of the Cossacks. Kaledin had refused to resign after the Kornilov affair, and the government had been forced to overlook his insubordination. Russia was breaking up: nationalist movements grew bolder in the Ukraine, Finland, Poland, and White Russia. At Helsingfors the Finnish Senate declined to lend money to the provisional government, and at Kiev the bourgeois Rada hinted at a separate peace with Germany. Kerensky was helpless. Hundreds of thousands of soldiers were deserting; peasants were burning manor-houses and seizing land; great strikes paralyzed Moscow, Odessa, and the coal-fields of the Don. The government, torn between the two factions, could do nothing.

Attention focused on the approaching Congress of Soviets, opposed not only by the government but also by the moderate Socialists. Bolshevik orators, touring the barracks and factories, explained the purposes of the Congress. Reed heard them everywhere, always demanding peace and all power to the Soviets, always giving direction to the vast, vague passion of revolt. Two new Bolshevik papers appeared, making four in all. At Smolny Institute, once a famous convent-school for daughters of the nobility, the committees of the Petrograd Soviet were in constant session. The corridors were filled with hurrying soldiers and workmen, many of them laden with newspapers and pamphlets. Reed stood in line with a thousand others in the old refectory, and got cabbage soup, hunks of meat, and a slab of black bread. Outside the office of the credentials committee for the Congress, he watched the soldiers, workers, and peasants as they filed in and out—the men, he knew, who would shape the future of Russia.

Petrograd, in those last days of October, was a strange city. In the factories, committee-rooms were stacked with rifles, and the Red Guard drilled outside. Meetings were held every night in the barracks. Crowds fought for newspapers. Hold-ups became common. Bread-lines grew. Gambling clubs were open all night, and prostitutes in jewels and furs crowded the cafés. Smolny was buzzing. In the rain and the cold the city waited.

On the twenty-ninth of October Reed sent a short article to Boardman Robinson for publication in the *Call*. "I have so far learned one lesson," he wrote, "and that is that the working class and the employing class have nothing in common." Summarizing the various parties and issues, he wrote, "It is possible that the proletariat will finally lose its temper and rise; it is possible that the generals will come with fire and sword." He described Kerensky's physical condition, and commented, "Life is hideously swift for compromisers here." Nothing seemed so significant as the growth in power of the Bolsheviks. "It looks," he concluded, "like a showdown soon."

XV

THE WORLD SHAKES

JOHN REED in Petrograd on the eve of the revolution, was a
good reporter, going everywhere, seeing every one. No one
could have made the rounds more faithfully or followed
leads more diligently. His reporter's legs took his poet's eyes into
every corner of the city, and those eyes missed nothing. Moreover, he felt the significance of events, in their relation both to
Petrograd's present and his own past. The rightness of what he
had become was being tested: if the revolution succeeded, he
would know his intuition had been sound and his doubts super-
fluous; the present would lead by a plain path into the future.
If it failed—

As if for the precise purpose of rounding out his education,
Kerensky at last consented to give him an interview. How many
hours he had waited, with generals and commissars, outside the
minister-president's office! Always there had been excuses, but
on the morning of October 20, as Reed and Louise Bryant sat in
the Tsar's billiard-room and looked at the rosewood panels inlaid
with brass, a naval adjutant came and led them to the private
library. Kerensky walked towards them, his face an unhealthy
color, his hair bristling, his hands nervous. Reed had watched
him in the Democratic Congress and the Council of the Republic, seen the man's strange magnetism work miracles, seen him
mount from eloquence to hysteria and collapse in weeping.
Even now he felt something of his charm and surrendered to the
impression he gave of passionate sincerity.

Reed, permitted to ask only a few questions, had planned them
carefully. "What do you consider your job here?" was his first.

Kerensky parried with a smile: "Just to free Russia," he said. "What do you think will be the solution of the present struggle between the extreme radicals and the extreme revolutionaries?" It was the crucial question; Kerensky refused to answer it. "What have you to say to the democratic masses of the United States?" There was a smile and a shrug, and an easy answer pattered out: "Let them understand the Russian democracy and help to fight reaction—everywhere in the world. Let them understand the soul of Russia, the real spirit of the revolution." Finally Reed asked, "What lesson do you draw from the Russian revolution for the revolutionary democratic elements of the world?" But Kerensky was not to be caught. "Do you think the revolution is over?" he asked. "It would be very short-sighted for me to draw any lesson. The revolution is not over—it is just beginning! Let the masses of the Russian people teach their own lesson. Draw the lesson yourself, comrade—you can see it before your eyes."

Reed could. He knew, if Kerensky did not, that the provisional government could not endure. And he went straight from the Winter Palace to Smolny, where the future was taking shape. Here, in the session of the Petrograd Soviet, the Central Executive Committee of the All-Russian Soviets, the Tsay-ee-kah, was making its last stand for compromise and moderation. And the members were being heckled and hooted down by the representatives of the workers, soldiers, and peasants. These were the forces that would destroy the provisional government: this peasant who said Kerensky was protecting the land-owners, this machinist who charged the Putilov factory superintendents with provocation and sabotage, this soldier who began, "Comrades! I bring you greetings from the places where men are digging their graves and call them trenches." Against this passion of revolt the eloquence and evasiveness of Kerensky and the caution of the Tsay-ee-kah could not stand.

The session of the Petrograd Soviet went on and on through the night. A tall, gaunt young soldier rose to speak, and was greeted with roaring applause. It was Tchudnovsky, who had been reported killed in the July fighting. The officers, he said, were betraying the soldiers, and he threatened violence if the

Constituent Assembly was postponed. He was followed by an officer, a Menshevik, whose call for the prosecution of the war was greeted by hoots. "Let us for a moment forget the class struggle—" he said, and a voice cried, "Don't you wish we would!"

As Reed attended the various meetings, he tried to learn the plans of the Bolsheviks. The city was full of rumors, and it was not always easy for him to determine the truth. Some one told him that, at a meeting of the Central Committee of the Bolshevik Party on October 23, only Lenin and Trotsky, among the intellectuals, had advocated insurrection. The decision was against an uprising, his informant said, until a workman arose and demanded action in the name of the proletariat. It was a story that appealed to Reed's sense of the romantic, and he wrote it down, though as a matter of record ten out of the twelve members of the committee had voted for the seizure of power.

As far as Lenin's position was concerned, it was explained in his "Letter to Comrades," the first installment of which appeared in *Rabotchi Put* the morning of the first of November. Reed was enough impressed to take time to record in his notebook the arguments with which Lenin dismissed the objections of Kamenev and Zinoviev to a Bolshevik uprising. He relished the powerful irony: "Let us forget all that was being and has been demonstrated by the Bolsheviks a hundred times, all that the half year's history of our revolution has proven, namely, that there is no way out, that there is no objective way out and can be none outside of either a dictatorship of the Kornilovists or a dictatorship of the proletariat. Let us forget this, let us renounce all this and wait! Wait for what? Wait for a miracle: for the tempestuous and catastrophic course of events from May 3 until September 11 to be succeeded (due to the prolongation of the war and the spread of famine) by a peaceful, quiet, smooth, legal convocation of the Constituent Assembly and by a fulfilment of its most lawful decisions. Here you have 'Marxist' tactics! Wait, ye hungry! Kerensky has promised to convoke the Constituent Assembly."

For a day or two there was a pause, as Petrograd braced itself. On November 3, Zalkind told Reed that there was to be an important Bolshevik party conference, in which Lenin would participate. Reed, alive with curiosity and anticipation, hastened to Smolny, to wait in the corridor outside the conference room. As Lenin left, his face was calm and his low words to his companions had a ring of hard certainty in them. Reed watched him, wondering if he was equal to the tasks that history had thrust upon him. When he saw Volodarsky, whom he knew, Reed plunged into a series of questions, and from the cautious answers he gathered that Lenin had called for action within three or four days.

In the confusion of the period of preparation, the whole city was open to an audacious reporter. The Bolsheviks, so far as they troubled about the matter at all, accepted Reed as a friend, and he had free access to Smolny. His credentials, his nationality, and his appearance satisfied the officials of the provisional government. Thus he could watch both sides as they made ready for battle. He knew that loyal regiments were being brought into Petrograd and that the junker artillery had been placed in the Winter Palace. He was not surprised when Petrograd, Kronstadt, and Finland were declared in a state of siege.

When he left his room on the fifth, it was cold and the streets were muddy. After watching the crowds, he went to Smolny. In room 10, on the top floor, where the Military Revolutionary Committee was in continuous session, Lazimir, the boyish chairman, told him that Peter-Paul Fortress had come over to the committee. Reed watched the people coming and going: Podvoisky, thin, bearded, wrapped up in plans for insurrection; Antonov, unshaven, his collar filthy, drunk with loss of sleep; Krilenko, always smiling, violent in gesture and speech; Dibenko, a giant with a placid face. "These," he recorded, "were the men of the hour—and of other hours to come."

On the way downstairs, he noticed Seratov, assigning arms to the factories. In the Petrograd Soviet Trotsky was speaking, and there was great applause when he announced that the Left Social Revolutionaries had agreed to send representatives to the Military Revolutionary Committee. As Reed left Smolny at three in the morning, he met Bill Shatoff. "We're off!" Shatoff shouted. "Kerensky sent the junkers to close down our papers, but our troops went down and smashed the government seal, and now we're sending detachments to seize the bourgeois newspaper offices." He clapped Reed on the shoulder and ran into the building.

As a boy in Portland, John Reed had read history and dreamed of taking part in some event that the future would call epoch-making. At Harvard he had longed for adventure. During six years of journalism he had imagined the perfect story. Now, conscious as he was of the social importance of what was happening, and of its significance for all his hopes of a better world, he was jubilantly aware of his own good fortune. And when Bill Shatoff shouted, "We're off!" John Reed looked speechless at Louise Bryant, his eyes sparkling, a grin slowly spreading the corners of his mouth. The revolution had begun, and he was there to report it.

The next morning, after having sent a dispatch to the *Masses*, Reed went to the Marinsky Palace to hear the end of Kerensky's passionate and incoherent speech. Once more he took the crowded trolley to Smolny, where the Petrograd Soviet was still in session. All through the afternoon and until after midnight, he listened to the debate, knowing, even when he could not understand the speeches, that more and more of the soldiers and workers were demanding the seizure of the government. It was nearly four in the morning when, in an outer hall, he saw Zorin with a rifle slung over his shoulder. There were regiments, Zorin said, on the march to capture the telephone exchange, the telegraph agency, and the state bank.

It was late when Reed got up. He and Louise Bryant went to Albert Rhys Williams' room, where they tried to make out from the papers what had happened the night before. As the three of them went out on the streets, they noticed the numbers of soldiers in front of the telephone exchange. At the door of the Marinsky Palace there was a great mass of soldiers and sailors, and a cordon had been thrown across the square. A barricade of boxes, barrels, and furniture blocked one street, and others were being built. Soldiers and sailors were thronging into the square from as far as they could see. Reed heard a sailor telling of the end of the Council of the Russian Republic: "We walked in there and filled all the doors with comrades. I went up to the counter-revolutionist Kornilovitz, who sat in the president's chair. 'No more council,' I says. 'Run along home now!'"

The trio went to the Winter Palace. The guards looked at them with surprise, but were impressed by their credentials. Reed led the way to Kerensky's office, and they spoke to the young officer who was nervously walking up and down outside. "Alexander Feodorovitch is extremely occupied just now," he said in French. "In fact, he is not here." They turned away, and wandered through the ornate corridors until they came to the front of the palace. A guard told them they could not enter, but he left them alone, and they opened a great door and walked into the midst of the junker companies. Reed pitied these boys, students from the officers' training school, who seemed as bewildered at the revolution as they were at the presence of three Americans.

It was five-thirty when they left the Winter Palace. In some sections the trolley-cars had stopped running, and a few streets were dark, but the theatres were all open, and many store windows were bright. Up the Nevsky the whole city seemed to be out promenading. Noisy discussions went on at every corner. Richly dressed men and women shook their fists at grinning soldiers. Armored cars drove through the streets, their sirens shrieking.

Outside Smolny automobiles and motorcycles came and went, and Red Guards sat around a blazing bonfire. The extraordinary session of the Petrograd Soviet, having proclaimed the victory of the proletariat, had ended, and many of the leaders came hurrying out, with harassed, anxious faces and with bulging portfolios under their arms. Reed managed to detain Kamenev, who read him in French the resolution the soviet had adopted. "There is much to do," he said. "Horribly much. It is just beginning."

The great hall in which the All-Russian Congress of Soviets was about to open was crowded. Reed sat beside Petrovsky, who was exhausted from three nights' sleepless work on the Military Revolutionary Committee. Gotz, Dan, Lieber, and the other representatives of the old Central Executive Committee were on

the platform, white-faced, hollow-eyed, and indignant. Dan announced the Congress open, and the new presidium, fourteen out
of its twenty-five members Bolsheviks, took charge. While the
leaders of the moderates launched their attack on the conduct
of the Bolsheviks, the majority of the workers, peasants, and
soldiers in the congress thundered their approval of the seizure
of power. Realizing their defeat, some fifty Mensheviks and
Socialist Revolutionaries marched out of the congress, hooted,
threatened, and cursed.

Reed, Louise Bryant, and Williams, who had by now been
joined by Bessie Beatty and Alexander Gumberg, left the hall.
The Military Revolutionary Committee gave them passes, and
a motor-truck carried them into the city. As they rode, they
helped throw into the street leaflets announcing the end of the
provisional government and the victory of the Soviets. At the
corner of the Ekaterina Canal, a cordon of armed sailors was
drawn across the Nevsky, stopping a procession of three or four
hundred people, many of them well-dressed. Reed recognized
among them some of the Menshevik and Socialist Revolutionary
delegates who had withdrawn from the congress. He questioned
a reporter he knew, who said cheerfully, "They're going to die
in the Winter Palace." But, after some oratory, they decided not
to make the gesture.

Reed and the other Americans took advantage of this diversion
to slip past the guards and start in the direction of the Winter
Palace. Just as they arrived, soldiers, sailors, and Red Guards
suddenly surged forward, and, without a shot being fired,
pressed into the palace. The junkers were disarmed and released.
Half a dozen members of the provisional government, discovered in secret rooms and passages, were arrested and taken to the
Peter-Paul Fortress.

Unhindered, the five of them wandered about the palace, even
reaching the gold and malachite chamber with crimson brocade
hangings where the ministers had been in session all the preceding night. On the table were scribbled sheets of paper, one of
which Reed took as a souvenir. And that was not all he took. As
the group left the palace, the guards who had been stationed at
the exits to prevent looting started to search them. Reed insisted

that he and his friends were above suspicion, and finally grew so convincingly indignant that the guards let them all pass. As soon as he was safely out in the street, he flung back his coat, and showed the others a jeweled sword. And when they turned on him, saying that he had risked their lives as well as his own, he chuckled and refused to believe they were in earnest.

They went to the City Duma, but the oratory of the anti-Bolsheviks did not interest them, and they left. Though it was after three when they came out into the cold, nervous night, Reed insisted that they must go back to Smolny, and, after a long search, found them a cab. As they entered the hall, as crowded as ever despite the secession of many delegates, Kamenev was reading to the audience, weary but still noisy, the names of the arrested ministers. A commissar from Tsarskoe Syelo announced that the garrison there was with the Soviets and would defend Petrograd. A Menshevik Internationalist proposed to elect a special committee to find a peaceful solution. Among cries of "There isn't any peaceful solution" and "Victory is the only solution," the motion was defeated, and the Menshevik Internationalists left the congress. A proclamation was issued to all the workers, peasants, and soldiers of Russia, promising peace, land for the peasants, and bread. At a few minutes after five Krilenko, staggering with fatigue, climbed to the tribune and read a telegram, announcing that the twelfth army had formed a Military Revolutionary Committee, which had taken charge of the northern front. Men shouted, wept, embraced each other. For the time being, Petrograd was safe.

REED marveled that, on the eighth, life in Petrograd could be so normal. Hundreds of thousands of people went about their work as usual. The street-cars were running, and stores, restaurants, and theatres were open. At the session of the City Duma and the meeting of the newly formed Committee for Salvation, Reed indignantly watched the open plotting of counter-revolution. Sleek journalists and business men talked about the filthy Bolsheviks and boasted of what would be done to them. And useful lies were already being circulated: a Constitutional Democrat, formerly secretary to Milyukov, told Louise Bryant and Reed that the capture of the Winter Palace had been led by officers in German uniforms, and that the women in the Death Battalion had all been raped.

Smolny was tenser than ever. In the dark corridors men ran back and forth. Leaders explained, argued, ordered—unshaven, filthy, with burning eyes. They did not know when they had last slept. Riazanov explained to Reed, in a kind of humorous panic, that he, Commissar of Commerce, knew nothing of business. Menzhinsky, Commissar of Finance, sat in the corner of the upstairs café, wrapped in a goat-skin cape, figuring on a dirty envelope. Four men came running out of the office of the Military Revolutionary Committee, commissars sent to the four corners of Russia to carry news, to argue, if necessary to fight with whatever weapons there might be.

The congress was to meet at one o'clock, but at seven the presidium had not appeared. Lenin, Reed heard, had spent the entire afternoon convincing the Bolshevik fraction that compromise would be fatal. At 8:40 the presidium entered the hall. Lenin was among them, a short stocky figure, with a big head set down on his shoulders, bald and bulging. His heavy chin was again bristling with the beard that was soon to become so familiar. His eyes were small, his nose short, his mouth wide and generous. His clothes were shabby and his trousers much too long for him. A strange man, Reed thought once more, a man who led by virtue of his intellect, undramatic, unpicturesque, but with the power of explaining profound ideas in simple terms, and with the greatest shrewdness and the greatest audacity.

After reports by Kamenev and speeches from the floor, Lenin rose, his hand gripping the edge of the reading stand, his little eyes traveling over the crowd as the ovation rolled on for minute after minute. When it ceased, he said, "We shall now proceed to construct the Socialist order." Again that overwhelming human roar. He read the proclamation to the peoples and governments of the belligerent nations: immediate negotiations for a just and democratic peace, no annexations or indemnities, the publication of the secret treaties, a three-months' armistice. "The revolution of November sixth and seventh," he said, "has opened the era of social revolution. The labor movement, in the name of peace and Socialism, shall fulfill its destiny."

After some hesitation, support for the resolution grew more and more enthusiastic, and, when Kamenev called for a show of hands, the vote was unanimous. They stood, Reed with the rest, singing "The Internationale." A grizzled old soldier sobbed. Alexandra Kollontai was winking back her tears. "The war is ended! The war is ended!" cried a young soldier near Reed. And then, after an awkward hush, some one began the funeral march, slow, moving, and yet triumphant: "You fell in the fatal fight." Reed thought of the martyrs of March, in their Brotherhood Grave on Mars Field, of the thousands and tens of thousands who had died in prison, in exile, in the Siberian mines. It had not come as they had expected it would come, but it had come, rough, strong, and real.

On Friday the ninth, Reed went to a meeting of armored-car troops at the Mikhailovsky Riding-School. To these troops, who could control the city for whichever side they supported, came representatives of revolution and counter-revolution. They hesitated, swayed this way and that. Then Krilenko spoke, telling them that Kerensky, Kaledin, and Kornilov were coming. "The government is in your hands," he cried. "You are the masters. Great Russia is yours. Will you give it back?" When the motion was put, there was a moment of doubt, and then hundreds of soldiers surged over to the left of the hall. And this, Reed knew, was happening in every barrack of the city, the district, the front, all Russia, happening in all the locals of every labor union, in every factory, in the battleships. Millions of men, listening anxiously, trying hard to understand, thinking intensely—and then deciding.

Again Reed went the rounds, Smolny, the Committee for Salvation, the Duma. The mayor announced that he would go to the Peter-Paul Fortress to investigate the conditions of the prisoners who had been arrested at the taking of the Winter Palace two nights before. A commission was appointed. Reed boldly followed, bluffing his way past the guards. He spoke to some of the prisoners, and he questioned the mayor as the commission left. "There is no truth in the reports," Schreider told him. "Except for the incidents which occurred as the ministers were being brought here, they have been treated with every consideration. As for the junkers, not one has received the slightest injury."

Reed went back to his rooms through dark streets, watching the lights in the buildings where counter-revolution was being plotted. The next morning counter-revolution moved towards action. An airplane flew low over the city, distributing a proclamation in which Kerensky threatened vengeance on all who did not submit, and it was rumored that he would be in the city, at the head of an army, within a few hours. Reed wanted to see Kerensky's forces, and he went, with Louise Bryant and Albert Rhys Williams, to Tsarskoe Syelo. Kerensky had not arrived, they found, and they returned to Petrograd.

They missed the capture of Tsarskoe Syelo, which came the next morning, but they saw the fighting in Petrograd. Reed, awakened by the sound of firing, hurried into his clothes, and went out into the streets. The life of the city still seemed to be going its normal way, but battles were in progress in half a dozen sections. The Military Hotel and the telegraph agency were captured by junkers and then re-taken. The telephone exchange, which the Bolsheviks had lost the night before, was being besieged by sailors. Reed spent the day in going from one front to another, his hopes falling with each junker victory and rising with every gain made by the Red Guard. When he returned to his room, he found that Louise Bryant had come closer to actual bullets than he: while she crouched in an archway in St. Isaac's square, junkers had fired on a street crowd from an armored car and killed seven.

They set out together on the twelfth, going first to Smolny. Reed was always fascinated by the Bolshevik organization. Kerensky was only a few miles away, and no one knew how the battle was going. The tasks of the various committees and the different officials seemed inhumanly difficult. The minister of finance had once been a clerk in a bank. The minister of commerce had been an historian. A common sailor, a military cadet, and a civilian were in charge of the army and navy. But nothing could discourage the Bolsheviks, and apparently no task was too much for them. Men fell on the floor, blind with fatigue, but the work went on.

While contradictory rumors came from Tsarskoe Syelo, Reed and Louise Bryant went to the Duma, to a secret meeting of the Committee for Salvation, and then back to Smolny. In the meeting of the soviet, Kamenev was speaking, denouncing the proposals for peace that the Mensheviks had made. "All they ask of us," he said, "are three little things: to surrender power, to make the soldiers continue the war, and to make the peasants forget about the land." Other speakers followed him, explaining, exhorting, arguing, soldiers and workmen, each standing up to speak his mind and his heart. Then, at three o'clock in the morning, the great news came: Kerensky had been decisively repulsed.

It had been a strange battle. From Petrograd and the surrounding country, soldiers, sailors, and armed workmen had rushed into the suburbs of the city. Commissars met them and assigned them positions. This was their battle, for their world, under leaders of their choosing. The vast anonymous horde swept over the Cossacks. The sailors fired until they ran out of cartridges, and then stormed. Untrained workmen rushed at the charging Cossacks, and tore them from their horses. Before the ragged troops of the proletariat, Kerensky's army broke and fled.

John Reed seemed as tireless as the Bolsheviks themselves. Night after night he had stayed late at Smolny, riding home with the soviet delegates in the trolleys that loyal carmen kept at their disposal. He had eaten when he could and where he could. Always tense, swept along by the shivering excitement of the revolution, he had traveled miles each day, gone from meeting to meeting, strained to understand the speakers or demanded a translation from any one he could press into service. In defiance of a dozen regulations, he had torn proclamations of all parties from the walls, and the piles of leaflets and newspapers mounted higher and higher in his room. He could scarcely believe that three months earlier he was complaining of the loss of his old energy.

And so, though he had left Smolny not much before dawn, he was back again on the snowy Tuesday morning after Kerensky's defeat, and at noon he persuaded the driver of an ambulance to take him to the front. First they had lunch at the driver's barracks, where, as Reed ate his cabbage soup, the score of soldiers questioned him about America, especially Tammany and the selling of votes. When the colonel asked if he could go to Tsarskoe Syelo, Baklanov, the chairman of the soldiers' committee, explained in a whisper to Reed that the officer had no authority except in action, when he was delegated by the committee to command. Not only the colonel but most of the others went with them, as they drove out along the highway, thronged with Red Guards going to or coming from the front.

So Reed came again to Tsarskoe Syelo, this time filled with the happy heroes of the proletarian army. In the office of the soviet, Dibenko was bending over a map, marking positions in red and blue with one hand, while the other swung an enormous blue-steel revolver. Casually he placed Baklanov in charge of the town, and Reed went with the new commandant to the Ekaterina Palace. When the colonel who was surrendering control explained that he had no keys to the money-chest, Reed, as a neutral, was assigned to smash it open. It was empty, and the colonel, protesting, was arrested.

In front of the palace there was a truck that was going to the front. Reed was given permission to go in it, and sat on the floor while bombs rolled back and forth and crashed against the sides. A Red Guard questioned him about Mooney and Berkman, and he tried to shout back above the roaring of the motor. At a crossroads two soldiers stopped the truck and insisted on examining the passes of each of its occupants. Reed's, they observed, was not like the others, and, despite the protests of the friendly Red Guard, they made him dismount. After some talk they led him to a wall, and suddenly he realized that they proposed to shoot him. Arguing for his life, he persuaded them to take him to a farmhouse, where there was a woman who could read. "A representative of the American Social Democracy," she read aloud. Puzzled, they led him in the half-dark along a muddy road to the regimental committee. When he came to the barracks, there was a rush of soldiers, and once more he thought he was going to be shot. But this time a member of the regimental committee appeared, read the pass, and welcomed Reed to the regiment. He had dinner with the officers, who were very pleasant but seemed much like officers anywhere in the world. The difference appeared when he saw them taking their orders from the chairman of the committee.

He returned to Tsarskoe in the regimental staff automobile. Just as he arrived, Dibenko left for the Cossack camp, where he was to bring about the surrender of the army and the final humiliation of Kerensky. Reed went back to Petrograd on the front seat of an auto truck, driven by a workman and filled with Red Guards. The truck had no lights, but it plunged furiously along a road filled with troops, columns of artillery, and supply wagons, wrenching to right and left, scraping wheels, hurtling on. On the horizon were the glittering lights of Petrograd. The driver threw an arm around Reed's shoulder. "We have done it," he cried, "we, the workers and soldiers; we have brought peace and killed poverty." And then, as they came into the city, he swept his arm grandly while the truck veered, and he shouted, "Our city! Ours! We saved it, the Red Guard!"

XVI

REVOLUTIONARY AND POET

HAVING gone through the Russian revolution, John Reed's first concern was to report it as accurately as possible. On the morning of November 13, the morning when the news reached Smolny of Kerensky's defeat, Lenin had given him a short statement to American Socialists. On the fifteenth Reed got permission to cable this message, together with an account of Kerensky's downfall, to the New York *Call.* After being held by the censor in this country, the dispatch was released on November 21 and published the next day under a seven-column banner.

At about the same time Reed sent the *Masses* by mail the first of a series of articles under the general title of "The Rising of the Proletariat," carrying the story of the revolution down to the eve of the All-Russian Congress of Soviets. With the article he wrote, "Have cabled many times for money and instructions, but no reply whatever. We are broke. I want to stay till January and return by way of China. Please telegraph my mother we are all right." A week or so later he sent the second part of "The Rising of the Proletariat," principally concerned with the background of the revolution, and promised other articles in a week or two.

Reed did not yet know, of course, that, with the November-December issue, the *Masses* had been suppressed, and its editors, himself included, indicted, and that neither the articles he had sent from Stockholm nor those he was sending from Petrograd could be published. It would be three months before the editors could manage to bring out the magazine under a new name, the

Liberator, and in the meanwhile his articles were accumulating in the office. The first part of "The Rising of the Proletariat" was to appear in the March *Liberator*, with some changes, as "Red Russia—The Triumph of the Bolsheviki." His article on his trip to the northern front before the seizure of power would be used in April and May, his articles on Kerensky in April, his article on Tsarskoe Syelo in July. But the *Liberator* could not catch up with him, and many of his articles remained unpublished until finally he used them as notes for his book.

Reed had become a different kind of reporter. In Mexico he had looked for color; in Russia he sought substance. He had filled his Mexican notebooks with poetic phrases, so that he might render with precision the look of the sky or the cast of a man's face. His Russian notebooks were devoted to figures and exact quotations. When he did not understand what a man said, he found some one to translate for him. If he could not grasp the significance of an argument or the purpose of a decree, he went to one of the Bolshevik leaders for an explanation. He had not lost his sharp awareness of appearances, and he created phrases as vivid as any he had written in Mexico, but he was not content with catching the surface of events.

The articles that he somehow found time to hammer out on his typewriter between visits to Smolny and explorations of the Petrograd streets, were shaped by his eagerness to understand and to interpret. He had learned much in the three years between his leaving Mexico and his sailing for Russia. The European war had taught him to look for forces that molded history, and he had at least a glimmering of the insight Marx could give. But he learned more in his first two months in Russia than all the years before had taught him. He shared in the Bolsheviks' understanding of what they were doing. This was not, so far as the leaders were concerned, a blind revolt, such as he had watched and welcomed in Mexico; the leaders knew precisely where they were going. For this event twenty years of Marxian study had prepared Lenin, and Reed could look through Lenin's eyes.

It was a Marxist-Leninist education, given in the form that Reed could best appreciate. Here were the events before his eyes, and here was the only possible interpretation of them. He did not become, did not want to become, a theorist, but he had to understand the significance of what he was witnessing. He learned that there could be no compromise betwen the bourgeoisie and the proletariat, that capitalism must be destroyed, and that the proletariat could and only the proletariat would destroy it. His faith in the working class had grown strong. He had seen the bourgeois liberals shrink from the consequences of their own theories. He had seen the intellectuals, turning in horror from the violence of the proletariat, support and participate in the violence of the bourgeoisie. And he had seen the masses of workers, soldiers, and peasants, in a situation of the utmost complexity and in spite of gross misleadership, stand firm, seeing clearly and fighting bravely.

It would not be far wrong to say that John Reed came to maturity during the ten days that shook the world. Of course as a writer his development had been precocious: conspicuous in college, he had been praised as a man of letters long before he was twenty-five and had been famous when he was twenty-seven. But until August, 1914, he had remained a playboy, not merely in his reckless exploits but in his whole impulsive way of thinking and feeling. The war had saddened him, robbed him of some of his boyish confidence in the future, bred doubt of himself and the world. Now the revolution, restoring hope and courage, gave his life a center. Whatever his career might be—and he had no intention of becoming a professional revolutionary—it would be set in a world that he understood and would have its due relation to goals that he knew were both desirable and attainable.

It was not a sudden conversion, a miraculous transformation of character; it was a simple ripening. To outward appearances John Reed was just what he had always been. He could still, to the delight and despair of his friends, be madly irresponsible. He was by no means purged of vanity. There would even be moments of doubt, of longing for old certainties instead of new convictions and old comforts in place of new hardships. But fundamentally John Reed had found himself. Every question that tortured him when he wrote "Almost Thirty" was answered. He had a purpose, and it could be fulfilled.

He knew that the revolution was not over: "It has just begun," he wrote the *Masses* on November 17. "For the first time in history the working class has seized the power of the state for its own purposes—and means to keep it. As far as any one can see, there is no force in Russia to challenge the Bolshevik power. And yet, as I write this, in the flush of their success, the new-born revolution of the proletariat is ringed round with a vast fear and hatred. The proletarian revolution has no friends except the proletariat."

For a week after the defeat of Kerensky, Reed watched the struggles of the Bolsheviks to make their new government function. While the Council of People's Commissars hammered at the scaffolding of the Socialist order, strikes of government employees crippled every department of the government. Offices were locked and buildings unheated; funds were taken. And in the ranks of the Bolsheviks themselves there was opposition to Lenin's adamant refusal to compromise. The suppression of the bourgeois press led to the resignation of five commissars, and Kamenev, Zinoviev, and three other members resigned from the Central Committee of the Bolshevik Party. Instantly delegates poured in from factories and the front, denouncing the deserters. "There is not a shadow of hesitation in the masses of Petrograd, Moscow, and the rest of Russia," Lenin had said in attacking the resignations, and he was proved right.

From Moscow came stories of barbaric destruction, and on the twenty-first of November Reed and Louise Bryant decided to go to see for themselves. They were given passes, and went to the station to wait patiently for the train. When at last it came, hundreds of soldiers, carrying huge sacks of food, stormed the doors, smashed the windows, and crowded into the compartments. Discovering that Reed and Louise Bryant were American Socialists, they left them room. All through the night soldiers argued in the corridors, and those on the roof sang songs and kicked their heels to keep warm. The train was hours late, and it was not until noon the next day that a peasant-woman appeared with bread and a coffee-substitute. Whenever the train stopped at the station, there was a raid on the buffet. Once Reed caught a glimpse of Nogin and Rykov, seceding commissars who were returning to Moscow.

The station was deserted, and the man in charge, whom they went to see about tickets for their return, was anti-Bolshevik—overlooked in the turmoil of the city's capture. There was not a cab in sight, but they finally found a sleigh, whose driver agreed to carry them to the hotel for fifty times the usual fee. "It takes a good deal of courage to drive a sleigh nowadays," he explained. The snow-piled streets were quiet, but there were shell-holes and ruined buildings. One hotel after another was full, but at last the big Hotel National took them in, chiefly because the Military Revolutionary Committee had promised to protect foreigners and the manager thought he would be safer for their presence.

They went to the headquarters of the Moscow Soviet in the palace of the former governor-general. In one room fifty women were cutting and sewing streamers and banners for the funeral of the revolutionary dead. In the hall Reed met Melnichansky, whom he had known in Bayonne as George Melcher, a watchmaker. Melnichansky, who was secretary of the Moscow Metal-Workers' Union, told Reed about the bloody six-day battle. The City Duma had led the junkers and White Guards. It was the mayor who had advised the occupation of the Kremlin, arguing that the Military Revolutionary Committee would not dare to bombard the sacred building. The counter-revolution had been better organized than in Petrograd, and the soviets less disciplined. It had taken a long time to bring the masses into action, and the losses had been great.

In the evening the Moscow Bolsheviks met at the Nobles' Club to listen to Nogin and Rykov explain why they had left the Council of Commissars. The intellectuals were obviously with them, but the workers burst out in jeers and angry shouts. Bukharin, short, red-bearded, with the eyes of a fanatic, spoke against them, savage, logical, with a voice that plunged and struck. The workers applauded him and adopted the resolution to support the Council.

Early the next morning Reed went to Skobeliev Square, where, in the pale half-light the Central Executive Committee of the Moscow Soviets waited with red banners. A vast stirring roar grew throughout the city. Down the Tverskaya, Reed and Louise Bryant marched under the great flags. The stores were closed, and the chapels were locked and dark. Reed noticed that the people with him did not cross themselves as they passed the famous churches. In the crowded Red Square huge mounds of earth marked the trenches that volunteers had worked all night to dig. A band began "The Internationale" as gigantic banners unrolled from the top of the Kremlin to the ground, red with great letters in gold and white that said "Martyrs of the Beginning of World Social Revolution" and "Long Live the Brotherhood of Workers of the World."

From the far quarters of the city workers of the different factories came, bearing their dead in dull red coffins, crude boxes made of rough wood and daubed with crimson. The men, many of them weeping, carried the coffins high on their shoulders, while behind them walked the women, sobbing or with white, dead faces. Some of the coffins were open, the lids carried behind them; others were covered with gilded or silvered cloth, or had a soldier's hat nailed on top. There were many wreaths of hideous artificial flowers.

The procession slowly moved through the crowd, while a band played the revolutionary funeral march, and against the immense singing of the mass of people, standing uncovered, the paraders sang hoarsely, choked with sobs. Behind the factory-workers came companies of soldiers with their coffins, squadrons of cavalry riding at salute, and artillery batteries with their cannon wound with red and black. The marchers came to the edge of the great grave, and the bearers clambered up with their burden and went down into the pit. All day long the funeral procession passed, coming in by the Iberian Gate and leaving the square by way of the Nikolskaya, a river of red banners, bearing words of hope and brotherhood and stupendous prophecies. One by one five hundred coffins were laid in the pits, and at dusk, as fifty thousand people sang the funeral march, two hundred men began to shovel in the dirt.

The next day Reed and Louise Bryant inspected the Kremlin, for rumors of Bolshevik destruction had reached Petrograd and were traveling around the world. In his notebook he set down: "No interior damage to churches—except Resurrection, where 2 shell-holes in roof. Little Cathedral has porch hit by shell, frescos sprayed with brick-dust. Upper church hit by three shells, outside damaged. Ivan Veliki, one or two shells, negligible . . . Little Palace Church upper story smashed, some looting. Red monastery hit many times, window moldings (several) smashed and doors. Barricades of *ammunition cases!* Upper gate tower hit several times, ikon smashed . . . Tip lower tower knocked off. Spasskya tower hit by big shell square in the clock." So he went about, surprised to find how little damage had been done. Yet even so the cost had been considerable: "Angry priests," he wrote down. "Angry bourgeois-artists, etc. Angry poor pious folks, crossing themselves as they look toward Kremlin and muttering. Arguing angry groups on Red Square." And he trembled to think of the effect on Russia, where the story had gone forth that most of the Kremlin was in ruins.

Reed returned to Petrograd in time for the Peasants' Congress, which had been called by the Council of People's Commissars over the heads of the Executive Committee of the Peasants' Soviets. The land decree had roused the peasants, and the return to the farms of thousands of revolutionary-minded peasant-soldiers had sharpened the eagerness for change. Despite the protest of the executive committee, more than four hundred delegates went to Petrograd for the congress. The first sessions showed that the Left Socialist Revolutionaries controlled a majority of the delegates, whereas the Bolsheviks had less than a fifth. The old executive committee consented to open the congress, but subsequently withdrew in protest against the radicalism of the delegates. They were not radical enough, however, to accept Bolshevik leadership, and, when Lenin rose to speak on the third day of the congress, he was met with cries of abuse.

Day after day Reed went between Smolny and the Peasants' Congress in the Duma building. Snow had fallen, making the city seem light and wide. Smolny was a little calmer, despite the tenseness over the Peasants' Congress. Each of its more than a hundred rooms was functioning as the meeting-place of some committee or department. Problems were gradually being solved. Counter-revolutionary forces were dwindling away.

Everything depended on the Peasants' Congress. Gradually its temper changed, and now Lenin was listened to with attention when he explained that the question of land could not be settled apart from the other problems of the revolution. Simply and clearly he showed how the interests of the land-owners were linked with those of the industrialists. "No compromise with the bourgeoisie is possible," he said; "its power must be absolutely crushed." Meanwhile the Bolsheviks and the Left Socialist Revolutionaries were holding a series of conferences, and at last an agreement was reached. When, on November 29, the union of the Peasants' Soviets with the Workers' and Soldiers' Soviets was announced, the peasants poured forth from Alexander Hall, marching through the city to the music of "The Marseillaise." When they came to the great white room in Smolny, in which the Executive Committee of the All-Russian Congress of Soviets, together with the Petrograd Soviet and a thousand spectators, were waiting, a grand echoing roar greeted this new triumph of the revolution.

THERE was still more than enough for a good reporter to see. Reed went one Sunday to the trial of the Countess Panina, formerly Minister of Public Welfare, who had refused to turn over the funds of the department to her successor, Alexandra Kollontai. The trial was held in the music room of the Palace Nicolai Nicolaievitch, and two soldiers and a workman presided. A worker spoke in favor of the countess, telling how she had taught him to read. Another worker, declaring this mere sentimentality, said the question was whether she had taken the money or not. The countess, speaking in her own defense, explained that she felt no responsibility to the Council of People's Commissars and would make her accounting to the Constituent Assembly. In the end she was sentenced "to return the money and then be liberated to the public contempt."

Another case came before the revolutionary tribunal, that of a soldier who had stolen money from a newspaper stand. He charged that the woman who owned it was a capitalist who sold counter-revolutionary as well as revolutionary papers. She maintained that she was not a capitalist, for she stood in the cold for long hours to sell her papers and make a very little money, and, moreover, that she performed a valuable educational service. The president asked the crowd in the courtroom to decide, and they voted that the man should not be punished but should be compelled to give back the money he had taken. When he admitted that the money was gone, the court ruled that he must give her something, and finally, at the suggestion of the crowd, she took his rubbers.

But Reed was not satisfied to be merely a reporter. Immediately after the revolution a Bureau of International Revolutionary Propaganda, in charge of Boris Reinstein, was formed under the supervision of the Department of Foreign Affairs, with committees of Germans, Hungarians, Roumanians, and English-speaking men and women. With the assistance of the Department of War Prisoners and the Bureau of the Press, directed by Karl Radek, this group issued three papers: *Die Fackel*, afterwards called *Volkerfriede*, to the Germans; *Nemzetkesi Szocializta* to the Hungarians; and *Inaïnte* to the Roumanians. These papers were carried to the trenches, where, in devious ways, they were distributed. Millions of copies of *Die Fackel* were circulated, and eventually papers were published in half a dozen languages.

Reed worked on *Die Fackel*, and he and Albert Rhys Williams edited a weekly illustrated paper called *Die Russiche Revolution in Bildern*. The captions were of the simplest sort. A picture of the supreme revolutionary tribunal, for example, bore the legend: "This group of four workmen and three soldiers is now the highest court of justice in the Russian Republic. Most of them spent long years in prison because of revolutionary activity. Now these common workmen and soldiers are themselves the judges of all those who have oppressed the people." There were pictures of soldiers and sailors, of barricades in the street, and of the celebration of victory. A picture of a workman tearing down the imperial eagles from a building was captioned: "It is easy to overthrow autocracy. Autocracy rests on nothing but the blind obedience of soldiers." A picture of soldiers in a palace was inscribed: "Here in Russia for the first time you can see workmen-soldiers, whose sweat and labor built the palace, whose blood was shed defending it, enjoying a palace as their home."

Reed was in the best of spirits, and, as usual when he was happy, he was full of ideas, many of them fantastic. When some one told him about a band of prospectors who were going to find a great cache of gold in Siberia, he was determined to join the expedition. When comrades from the Ukraine described the strike of intellectuals, Reed told Williams that they must go at once to Kharkov and fill the vacant offices. Williams, he said, could be Commissar of Education, and, in view of his ecclesiastical training, could have supervision of churches and religious affairs as well. For himself, he would be Commissar of Art and Amusement.

"What will you do?" Williams asked.

"Oh, thousands of things," Reed answered. "First of all, put joy into the people. Get up great pageants. Cover the city with flags and banners. And once or maybe twice a month have a gorgeous all-night festival with fireworks, orchestras, plays in all the squares, and everybody participating." A day or two later he was laughing at the idea, but he still insisted that, terrible as conditions were, singing and dancing could do the revolution no harm.

Both of the young men were frequently asked to speak at public meetings, and there was one cold morning when they went to address a gathering of soldiers at the Cirque Moderne. As they came near the vast gray building, accompanied by Alexandra Kollontai, they saw a black mass of people around the doors. "Why don't they let them in?" Williams asked. "There are fifteen thousand inside already," Kollontai told him. Guided by her, they entered the hall, which was completely dark, for there was no coal in Petrograd to operate the power plant. Reed peered out from the platform, and it seemed to him that the place was empty, but when Williams began, "Comrades! I speak for the American Socialists," there was a deafening cry of "Long live the International!"

Reinstein was proud of his young assistants, but, after his years in the labor movement, their ignorance occasionally amused and distressed him. When he lamented their inexperience and their failure to study Marx, Reed would poke fun at the Socialist Labor Party. "How many members are there?" he would ask. "Three-and-a-half or four." And once, when Reinstein was introduced as "a leader of the powerful Socialist Labor Party in America," Reed burst into a guffaw.

In the Reeds' apartment American sympathizers frequently gathered. The apartment was bare and often cold, and sometimes, when food was scarce, Reed would start a fire on the tiled floor of the bathroom and heat up a can of soup for the guests to eat. The most common subject of discussion was the possibility of getting American aid for the Soviets. Colonel Robins, though completely opposed to Bolshevik principles, believed that the regime should be allowed to go its own way, and he saw no reason why trade relations should not be established with America. With this idea in mind, Reed interviewed both Bolshevik and Left Socialist Revolutionary leaders, and prepared a skeleton report, which he submitted to Robins. After pointing out that trade relations would have to be subject to the conditions of a country that was building Socialism, he listed some of the immediate needs of the Soviets, especially machinery, canned food, shoes, and clothes. A policy of real, material help, he argued, would build a strong friendship for America. He closed by saying, "We American Socialists are going to organize here shortly, and I think you could help America if you would cooperate with us."

It was still a period when it seemed that anything, so far as America was concerned, might happen. Although Ambassador Francis was having him shadowed, Reed went in and out of the embassy like any other American citizen. There were relatively few Americans in Petrograd, and, however strongly they disagreed, they went through the formalities of friendship. When, for instance, Colonel Robins gave a Christmas dinner, he invited Louise Bryant, Reed, and other Socialists, members of the diplomatic staff, and representatives of American business firms. So it happened that Reed found himself sitting beside a Tammany politician who had become a war profiteer, a man violently opposed to the revolution and quite incapable of understanding it.

In the clash between them Reed caught a glimpse of what he would have to face when he returned to America, and any hopes of American sympathy for the new order dwindled.

As soon as Reed heard of the *Masses* indictment, he resolved to return in time for the trial, but he received word that it had been postponed, and he decided to wait for the convening of the Constituent Assembly. One of the first promises of the provisional government had been the democratic election of a legislative body, but it was a promise Kerensky had been loath to fulfill. Delay had followed delay, but after the Bolshevik seizure of power, the liberals and moderate Socialists began to insist that the Constituent Assembly must be held. The Bolsheviks agreed, but from the first they pointed out that the election could not take into account the changes brought about by the seizure of power. The ballots, for example, lumped all Socialist Revolutionaries together, ignoring the fact that the party was now divided into three factions, of which only one supported the new regime. It was the Socialist Revolutionaries who, thanks to their strength among the peasants, had the largest number of delegates, but there was no way of telling whether, in electing these delegates, the peasants were voting for or against the Council of People's Commissars.

The Constituent Assembly met on January 18, 1918. The Tauride Palace, in which the session was held, was surrounded by Red Guards and revolutionary soldiers and sailors. Sverdlov appeared, just as the assembly was to begin, and read a declaration of Soviet principles. This the assembly refused to consider, and the Bolshevik delegates left. The session lasted throughout the night of the eighteenth, with constant and boisterous interruptions by the soldiers and sailors in the gallery. The assembly passed a land decree, approved with qualifications the armistice with Germany, and proclaimed Russia a democratic federative republic. As Chernov, early on the morning of the nineteenth, was reading the decree on land, the commandant of the palace, a sailor, stepped forward. Pointing to the empty seats of the Bolsheviks and the Left Socialist Revolutionaries, he said, "You fellows had better go home. The rest have gone. The guard is getting tired." Half an hour later the Constituent Assembly adjourned, never to meet again.

The next day the Central Executive Committee of the All-Russian Soviets proclaimed the dissolution of the Constituent Assembly. Reed, examining the committee's statement, was convinced that it marked the death of old-fashioned representative democracy. The fact that nowhere in Russia, not even among the peasants who had elected the Socialist Revolutionary majority, were strong objections raised proved to him that the Bolsheviks were right in regarding the soviets as the political form for the workers' state. The Constituent Assembly, because it could not keep abreast of the changes in popular sentiment, would have become, if it had been tolerated, a center of counter-revolution. Its convening had been necessary to demonstrate this fact to the masses of workers, soldiers, and peasants; that the demonstration had been conclusive acquiescence in its dissolution showed. The soviets, deeply rooted in the factories, the trenches, and the fields, were the expression of the people's will.

Louise Bryant left for the United States on January 20, but Reed remained for another fortnight. On the twenty-third, the third All-Russian Congress of Soviets was opened. In the first congress, which had met June 16, the moderate Socialists had been in the majority. The second congress, meeting November 7, had approved the Bolshevik seizure of power. The third congress met to consider the problems of preserving the revolution and putting its principles into action.

Reed, Reinstein, and Williams were invited to attend the congress, and they drew lots to determine which would be the spokesman. Williams was the one selected, but, after he had expressed the greetings of the American Socialists, Reed decided that he also wanted to speak. Reinstein introduced him in Russian, saying that he was returning to face trial, with the other editors of the *Masses*, under the espionage law. Reed, after the indignant cries that followed Reinstein's announcement, stood up, and there was loud applause. He spoke first of the satisfaction and courage he would draw, on his return to the kingdom of capitalism, from the victory of the proletariat in Russia. Then he paid tribute to the revolutionary martyrs, spoke of the significance of the soviets as a new form of government, and promised to devote himself, on reaching America, to telling the story of the revolution.

Perhaps one reason for Reed's eagerness to speak was the warning he had received from Edgar Sisson. Sisson, formerly editor of Hearst's *Cosmopolitan*, had come to Russia for George Creel's Committee of Public Information, and, while ostensibly devoting himself to distributing Wilson's speeches and otherwise legally propagandizing for the United States, had actually spent his time in spying on the Bolsheviks, with the aid of both the American and the British intelligence services and the numerous groups of counter-revolutionaries. Sisson had threatened Reed a few days earlier because he had done patrol duty in front of the Foreign Office, and had told him that he must not take any part in Bolshevik activities. He was in the audience at the Tauride Palace when Reed spoke, and he sputtered to his friends about madness and treason.

A few days later Sisson was given more cause for worry, for Reed's appointment as consul to New York was announced. He had asked that he might be made a courier, as Louise Bryant had been, so that his notes and papers would be safe, and Trotsky had thereupon proposed the consulship. Meeting Arno Dosch-Fleurot, a newspaper man, Reed expressed his joy in the indignation the appointment would arouse. There was some serious discussion, in the course of which Dosch-Fleurot predicted that Reed would be arrested. "Perhaps it's the best thing I can do to advance the cause," Reed said. Then, with a grin, he hitched up his trousers and said, "When I am consul I suppose I shall have to marry people. I hate the marriage ceremony. I shall simply say to them, 'Proletarians of the world, unite!'"

Washington indignantly informed the press that Reed would have no official standing. The *Call* applauded the appointment and ironically suggested that Theodore Roosevelt and Charles Edward Russell be appointed a welcoming committee. It also printed a tribute to Reed by Max Eastman. "John Reed's ap-

pointment as consul general in his own country by the Bolsheviki," Eastman wrote, "is the most beautiful and astute expression they have yet given to the international character of the class
struggle and the social revolution. In his own country, John
Reed has been proscribed by the respectables and indicted by
the courts as a traitor. He will present his credentials from the
sovereign proletariat of Russia to a bourgeois government that
has plans already on foot to put him in jail . . . John Reed was
born to fill a high place in revolutionary times. He is one of the
few universal men—the men who combine that arrant imagination and headstrong will of adventure which are the attributes
of poetic genius, with a diligent and real power to achieve and
understand. There is nothing that needs to be done, either in the
technical routine of a consul general's office or in the extraordinary and delicate duties of a revolutionary emissary that John
Reed is not abundantly equipped to do. . . . Starting off with
brilliant emotions, perceptions, and word combinations in his
mind, I have watched him add to these native gifts the habit of
verification and clear analytic understanding. And I know that
his history—the intimate history—of those great days at Petrograd will be a light in the world's literature."

Meanwhile the American officials in Petrograd were beginning to act. Ambassador Francis asked Colonel Robins to try to
persuade the soviet government to withdraw the appointment.
Sisson asked Gumberg to see what he could do, and Gumberg
did his best. Apparently it was brought to Lenin's attention that
Reed had at some time considered a proposal to edit an official
American propaganda newspaper in Russia, and this was interpreted to mean that he had been secretly bargaining with the
capitalists while claiming to be a supporter of the Soviets. However it came about, the appointment was canceled, and Reed was
greatly disappointed. Sisson had assured him that the Bolsheviks
were merely trying to exploit his reputation, and Reed had replied that, if his reputation would do the Bolsheviks any good,
he was satisfied. What he saw in the appointment was a recognition that pleased him and an opportunity for a dramatic gesture
of a kind that he enjoyed. If, however, his services were to be
of a different sort, he would still be able to serve.

REED left Russia early in February. The best Francis would do for him was to give him a letter authorizing passport control officers and censors to pass him without examining his papers until he reached the United States, where, the letter said, his possessions would be thoroughly scrutinized. Sisson took more drastic steps, and, as a result of his interference, Reed was detained in Christiania. He arrived there on February 19, expecting to sail on February 22, but the consul informed him that he had been instructed by the State Department not to visa his passport. He was not under arrest, but he could not proceed. Since the next boat from Christiania to New York did not sail until April, he rented a room and impatiently set to work on his history of the revolution.

On February 25 he received two cablegrams. One read, "Don't return, await instructions. Steffens Louise Reed." The other: "Trotsky making epochal blunder doubting Wilson literal sincerity. I am certain President will do whatever he asks other nations to do. If you can and will change Trotsky's and Lenin's attitudes you can render historical international service. Steffens."

Steffens was upset because Russia had, on February 19, offered to agree to the terms of peace proposed by Germany at Brest-Litovsk. The negotiations, which had begun on December 22, had revealed more and more clearly the German intention to seize as much as possible of the former Russian Empire. By the end of January the Bolshevik leaders were divided into three groups: Lenin, Stalin, Kamenev, and Zinoviev favored an immediate peace; Bukharin and others wanted the proclamation of a revolutionary war against Germany; Trotsky proposed a kind of passive resistance. Negotiations were broken off on February 10, and on February 18, the German army moved against Dvinsk and Reval. Lenin's view prevailed, and a dispatch was sent to Berlin.

Steffens, in common with many anti-war liberals and a certain number of radicals, believed that Russian capitulation would be a catastrophe. They felt that, since the rise of the Bolsheviks, the defeating of Germany was a revolutionary duty. Wilson's fourteen-point speech, which had actually been brought forth by Sisson's plea for plausible propaganda that would keep Russia in the war, seemed to hold out the hope for an agreement between the Soviet government and the Allies. Trotsky had hinted to Bruce Lockhart that, if the Allies would recognize the Soviets and aid them, he would prevent Russia from signing the separate peace. Lenin saw that it was impossible to expect the Russian armies to keep on fighting, realized that the Allies could not send any considerable assistance, and completely distrusted their intentions. He did not like the terms proposed by Germany, but he preferred them to war.

Reed had no doubt of the wisdom of Lenin's position. He cabled Steffens that, if a group of revolutionary leaders, including Eugene Debs and Bill Haywood, asked him to, he would go back to Petrograd and see what he could do; otherwise he would not. He knew that he was safe, and in any case it was too late. Although the Germans had replied to the Russian offer by imposing even more drastic terms, Lenin, on February 23, delivered his personal ultimatum to the Council of People's Commissars, and on March 3 the Brest-Litovsk treaty was signed.

With the exception of the cablegram she signed with Steffens, everything Louise Bryant wrote Reed was intercepted, and only one of his letters reached her. In this letter, written on March 27, he told of the arrival of Robert Minor, and the joy that he expressed at having some direct word from his wife and from his friends in America showed how trying his isolation had been. Even then he did not know when he would be allowed to return; indeed, he was ready to believe that he was permanently exiled. Of Steffens' plan he said, "From my viewpoint it looks absolutely ridiculous." His own situation he barely touched upon: "I am working very hard on my book . . . I am selling some articles on Russia to local papers and also doing stenography." He had appealed to the American Minister, saying that, since he was detained against his will, the government should pay his expenses, but he had no hope of success.

He had already written an introduction for the book he planned to do on the revolution. It was, as much as anything else, an interpretation to himself. "It is difficult," he wrote, "for the bourgeoisie—and especially so for the foreign bourgeoisie—

to understand the ideas that move the Russian masses. It is all very easy to say that they have no sense of patriotism, duty, honor, that they do not submit to discipline, or appreciate the privileges of democracy; that, in short, they are incapable of self-government. But in Russia all these attributes of the bourgeois democratic state have been replaced by a new ideology. There is patriotism—but it is allegiance to the international brotherhood of the working class; there is duty, and men die cheerfully for it—but it is duty to the revolutionary cause; there is honor, but it is a new kind of honor, based on the dignity of human life and happiness rather than on what a fantastic aristocracy of blood and wealth has decreed is fitting for 'gentlemen'; there is discipline—revolutionary discipline, as I hope to show in these pages; and the Russian masses are showing themselves not only capable of self-government but of inventing a whole new form of civilization."

But what he was most concerned with writing during his two months in Sweden was not his history of the revolution—that could and would have to wait. Most of his energy went into a poem, the longest he had ever written and the last, with the exception of a few hastily scribbled lyrics, he was to write. It was America that inspired the poem, his America, the America he loved as distinguished from the America he hated. At last he knew himself, knew where he stood and what he wanted, and the old tenderness came back. He had suppressed it when it seemed likely to betray him into the hands of the eagle-screaming patriots. Now that his position was clear, he could give voice to his emotions and, from his exile, sing the song of America.

He began:

> Across the sea my country, my America
> Girt with steel, hard-glittering with power,
> As a champion, with great voice trumpeting
> High words, "For Liberty . . . Democracy . . ."
>
> Deep within me something stirs, answers—
> (My country, my America!)
> As if alone in the high and empty night
> She called me—my lost one, my first lover
> I love no more, love no more, love no more . . .

And he went on to tell how he knew his America:

> By my free boyhood in the wide West,
> The powerful sweet river, fish-wheels, log-rafts,
> Ships from behind the sunset, Lascar-manned,
> Chinatown, throbbing with mysterious gongs,
> The blue thunderous Pacific, blaring sunsets,
> Black smoking forests on surf-beaten headlands,
> Lost beaches, camp-fires, wail of hunting cougars . . .
> By the rolling range, and the flat sunsmitten desert,
> Night with coyotes yapping, domed with burst of stars,
> The gray herd moving eastward, towering dust,
> Ropes whistling in slow coils, hats flapping, yells . . .
> By miles of yellow wheat rippling in the Chinook,
> Green-golden orange-groves and snow-peaks looming over . . .
> By raw audacious cities sprung from nothing,
> Brawling and bragging in their careless youth . . .
> I know thee, America!

Almost without thinking, he swung into the long, rolling rhythms of Walt Whitman as he sang the America that Whitman had loved:

Fishermen putting out from Astoria in the foggy dawn their double-
    bowed boats,
Lean cow-punchers jogging south from Burns, with faces burned
    leathery and silent
Stringy old prospectors trudging behind reluctant pack-horses across
    the Nevada alkali . . .

He went on with his saga:

> By my bright youth in golden eastern towns . . .
> Harvard . . . pain of growing, ecstasy of unfolding,
> Thrill of books, thrill of friendship, hero-worship,
> Intoxication of dancing, tempest of great music,
> Squandering delight, first consciousness of power . . .

When he came to New York, he forgot Whitman and spoke with the tones of his old love, Christopher Marlowe:

Manhattan, zoned with ships, the cruel,
Youngest of all the world's great towns,
Thy bodice bright with many a jewel,
Imperially crowned with crowns . . .

Who that hath known thee but shall burn
In exile till he come again
To do thy bitter will, O stern
Moon of the tides of men!

But he went back to Whitman to tell of the city, the deep excitement it always roused in him shining through, as it shone through in his essay, "Almost Thirty." He spoke of Fifth Avenue, "Peacock Street, street of banners"; of Broadway, "gashing the city like a lava-stream"; of Greenwich Village, "battle-ground of all adolescent Utopias." Like Whitman, he wanted the reader to know that he was part of all this:

In dim Roumanian wine-cellars I am not unwelcome,
Pulsing with hot rhythm of scornful gypsy fiddlers . . .
In Grand Street coffee-rooms, haunt of Yiddish philosophers,
Novelists reading aloud a new chapter, collecting a dime from each
    auditor,
Playwrights dramatizing the newspaper headlines, poets dumb to
    deaf America . . .
        . . . .
Dear and familiar and unforgettable is the city
As the face of my mother . . .
        . . . .
Have I omitted you, truck-quaking West Street, dingy Death
    Avenue,
Gracious old Church of the Sea and Land, Inwood, tip of Man-
    hattan,
The rag shops of Minetta Lane, and the yelping swirl of the Broad
    Street Curb,
Macdougal Alley, gilded squalor of fashionable artists,
Coenties Slip, old sea-remembering notch at the back of down-
    town?
Nay, across the world, three thousand miles away, without map or
    guide-book,

Ask me and I will describe them and their people,
In all weathers, drunk or sober, by sun and moon . . .
I have watched the summer day come up from the top of a pier of
　　the Williamsburg Bridge,
I have slept in a basket of squid at the Fulton Street Market,
Talked about God with the old cockney woman who sells hot-dogs
　　under the Elevated at South Ferry,
Listened to the tales of dago dips in the family parlor of the Hell-
　　hole,
And from the top gallery of the Metropolitan heard Didur sing
　　"Boris Godounov."

　　　　　.　.　.　.　.　.　.　.　.

Dear and familiar and ever-new to me is the city
As the body of my lover . . .

　　　　　.　.　.　.　.　.　.　.　.

All professions, races, temperaments, philosophies,
All history, all possibilities, all romance,
America . . . the world . . . !

Six months in revolutionary Russia—not predictably an experience to bring a poet to maturity. Yet. "America, 1918," begun
in Petrograd, most of it written in Christiania, finished in New
York, was as much a product of Reed's participation in the Bolshevik revolution as was *Ten Days That Shook the World*. It
was an affirmation of love of country, born out of recognition
that that country could be made worthy of love. Reed was
returning with not merely the hope but the expectation that the
United States would, in some not very distant time, follow Russia's example. It would become a nation that he could respect
and serve. He was no longer afraid of it, and the poem was the
expression of hope and love.

It was not the America of the future Reed sang but the
America he had actually known. Like Whitman, he hailed the
future in the present. The poetry of revolutionary struggle was
yet to be written—and, as it happened, not by him. But he had
conquered at last the confusions and reticences and false traditions that had circumscribed him. This was poetry in which the
whole John Reed, and not some romantic fragment of him,
lived and spoke.

XVII

America, 1918

On April 28, 1918, exactly five years after his arrest in Paterson, John Reed reached what the *Times*, with military secretiveness, called in its dispatch "an Atlantic port." The port was, of course, New York. Being under indictment in the *Masses* case, he was met by federal agents, who held him on board for more than eight hours, while they searched his baggage and clothes. His papers were seized, but he was finally liberated after Morris Hillquit had promised that he would be at the Federal Building the next morning. Louise Bryant had waited for him from the time the boat docked, early in the morning, and together they went in a cab to the Brevoort. The next day he appeared before Judge Rufus E. Foster, with Dudley Field Malone as his counsel, and bail was fixed at $2000.

It was a clear warning to John Reed that wartime America was no place for the writing of poetry; there were other things that had to be done first. A year of war had successfully infected the majority of the American people with hysteria. Day after day they had read in the papers that Germans were beasts who must be destroyed. Sunday after Sunday ministers of the gospel had preached the crusade. Moving pictures and plays portrayed the frightfulness of the enemy and the heroic idealism of the American soldier, and between the acts four-minute men converted sentiment into cash. Education almost ceased that children might listen to tales of Hun atrocities or participate in liberty loan, Red Cross, war saving stamp, or Y.M.C.A. campaigns.

It was no wonder that the slightest opposition to war roused the cruelest of passions. Many of Reed's friends had suffered. Conscientious objectors were beaten, set at exhausting labor, and underfed. Wobblies had been mobbed, tarred and feathered, lynched. Pacifist preachers had been driven from their parishes, some with whips and clubs. Persons of remotely German parentage were suspected of espionage and subjected to the machinations of amateur detectives as well as the jeers of self-righteous patriots. Workmen who refused to buy liberty bonds lost their jobs and found themselves blacklisted. Mild critics of the war had their houses splashed with yellow paint, and were forced by frenzied vigilantes to kiss the flag. Madness was not even chastened, as it had long since been in Europe, by the somber thought of death, for American casualties had only been sufficient to titillate popular passions. Insanity prevailed, and war-profits grew.

Reed had left Russia with every intention of arriving in time for the *Masses* trial, but Mr. Sisson and the State Department had interfered. The trial began on April 15, and the day before Reed reached New York the prisoners were freed by a hung jury. Eastman, Dell, Merrill Rogers, Art Young, Josephine Bell, Glintenkamp, and Reed, together with the Masses Publishing Company, had been charged with conspiring to promote insubordination and mutiny in the military and naval forces of the United States and to obstruct recruiting and enlistment to the injury of the service. The first part of the indictment was quashed by Judge Hand, but the second stood.

Reed could, of course, understand why the government would not permit criticism of its conduct. What amazed him was the tremendous effort that was made to preserve the fiction of legality. All the ingenuity of the prosecution, he discovered, had been devoted to an attempt to prove that the editors had quite literally conspired, had got together one day and said, "Go to, now, we will obstruct recruiting and enlistment to the injury of the service." The fantastic nature of the case was underscored by the fact that he personally had been indicted for the simple headline he had put over a clipping from the *Herald*, "Knit a Strait-Jacket for Your Soldier Boy." For ten days the legal battle had gone on; for two days the jurors had argued; and then, on April 27, the jury had been discharged and the first *Masses* trial ended.

As soon as he had an opportunity to look about him, what impressed Reed, next to the prevalence of hysteria, was the interest in Russia. In spite of the patriotic indignation that had been whipped up when the Brest-Litovsk treaty was signed, in spite of the legend that all radicals and Bolsheviki in particular were German spies, people wanted to know what had happened. His first statement, published in the *Call* on May 1, emphasized the fight of the Bolsheviks against German as well as Russian imperialism. He followed it with a statement in the *Liberator*, disposing of current myths about Bolshevik terrorism and briefly describing the aims of the Soviet regime. He ended with an account of what the revolution had taught him: "That in the last analysis the property-owning class is loyal only to its own property. That the property-owning class will never readily compromise with the working class. That the masses of the workers are not only capable of great dreams but have in them the power to make dreams come true."

But Reed soon found that written messages were not enough. People were demanding to hear him speak. As soon as his legal status was clarified—his papers were held but he was released, his appearance at the second *Masses* trial having been secured by bail—he began his long series of speeches. He spoke first at the meeting, held on May 9, to celebrate the end of the *Masses* trial. The next night, with Hillquit and Santeri Nuorteva, at the time representative of the Finnish People's Republic, he spoke at a mass meeting on behalf of free Finland. A week later, after a vain trip to Washington to try to secure his papers, he addressed the James Connolly Socialist Club. On the eighteenth, in Carnegie Hall, he defended the Bolshevik attitude towards the moderate Socialists. His meeting at the Star Casino on the twenty-third filled the aisles and the window-sills. On the twenty-sixth he was guest of honor at a dinner for the *Call*.

So it went, and it was not in New York alone that he was wanted. He spoke in Tremont Temple, Boston, with Harry Dana as chairman, and kept an organized group of reactionaries, mostly Harvard students, in check with his humor and his solid marshaling of facts. On June 1, he was scheduled to speak in Philadelphia, but, when he arrived, he learned that the permit had been revoked. He walked down to the hall and found five hundred persons outside the locked doors. Leading them to a quiet street, away from traffic, he began to speak. Immediately a police lieutenant rushed up and kicked away the box on which he was standing. Reed protested that he was breaking no law, and that, if he was, he should be arrested. Two policemen took him to the station-house in a car. Meanwhile a Finnish shipyard worker named Kogerman was hit by a zealous policeman. When he wanted to know why he had been hit, the policemen gave him a thorough beating and arrested him. Kogerman was accused of assaulting four policemen, urging the crowd to rescue Reed, and resisting arrest. Reed was charged with disobeying a municipal ordinance, inciting to riot, and inciting to seditious remarks. Bail was fixed at $1500, but, at the request of a man from the district attorney's office, was raised to $5000. The same amount was set for Kogerman, and Reed helped him to raise it. Trial was postponed till fall.

One June 4 Reed spoke in the Bronx, on June 6 in Newark, on June 7 in Brooklyn. There were more than two thousand people in his audience at the Bronx, and he took off his coat, rolled up his blue shirt-sleeves, and talked to them for two hours. He described the shop-committees and the sabotage of the managers, told how the soviets worked, and gave examples of Bolshevik propaganda in the German army. At Newark, just as he was about to begin his address, the crowd rose and sang "The Marseillaise." Reed cried "Long live the social revolution" in Russian.

On the twelfth he was in Detroit. Moose Hall was filled with people, many of them Russians. James Couzens, recently made police commissioner, sat near the platform with the representatives of the Department of Justice, and his officers were in every part of the hall. The meeting was subdued by such a display of force, but when Reed rose and began "Tovarischi," the applause thundered forth. All evening the hallfull of people kept him there, in their eagerness to know what had happened in Russia. As the audience filed out, the police seized a hundred and fifty men and women, chosen more or less at random, and held them all night in a room of the Municipal Building with no sleeping accommodations and no toilet.

Reed went home with Walter Nelson, who had presided at the meeting, and asked if he might stay a day or two. He was tired and spent most of the time in sleeping. Despite the great crowds at his meetings, he felt, he told Nelson, that the majority of Americans, especially the native-born, did not catch the significance of the revolution. It seemed to him that he must shake them out of their indifference, make them see that a new era of human history had begun. And, tired as he was, he hurried back to New York for another meeting, then to Worcester, and back to New York once more. Somehow the word must be carried to the American people.

IN THE midst of all this, he tried to make plans for the future. His first task was, he knew, to tell the story of the revolution, and he kept hammering away at the State Department so that he might get his notes and documents and start work on his book. But in the meantime, there was the question of earning a living. He was usually paid for his speeches, but the income was neither large nor dependable. Louise Bryant had syndicated her articles, and put them in a book, *Six Red Months in Russia*. The paying magazines, however, were closed to Reed. Oswald Villard was warned that the *Nation* would be suppressed if it printed anything of Reed's. *Collier's* took a story, put it in type, and then sent it back. Here was the finest reporter in the country, with the biggest story in the world, and during the whole of 1918 and 1919 he published nothing in a non-radical magazine except one brief article, "The Case for the Bolsheviki," in the *Independent*.

His fertile mind suggested many schemes, including a plan of doing movie scenarios. He had caught a glimpse of the propaganda possibilities of the films, and the idea occurred to him that, if he could get some sort of post, he might support himself and at the same time lay the foundation for work that could some day be done. He went so far as to make an appointment with Willard Mack, head of Goldwyn's scenario department, but the movies were not looking for radicals.

Another plan was suggested by Frank Harris, who was editing *Pearson's*. Harris, Reed, and Floyd Dell, Harris suggested, would found a new magazine, to be called *These States*. Reed was interested enough to draw up a prospectus. The magazine, to conform with Burleson's censorship, would have to be non-political, but it would be "the best expression of uncorrupted American artists." Harris finally withdrew his support, and Reed was forced to realize that such a magazine was as impossible in a nation at war as his scheme of propaganda movies.

Much of the time he felt distressingly lonely. Professor Copeland, whom he had seen on his trip to Boston, was friendly, but, as Reed said, "in a frame of mind that thinks no one is a he-man who hasn't gone into naval aviation." Realizing how Copey felt, and genuinely eager to spare him any trouble, Reed told him that they must stop corresponding.

In Washington he met Marlen Pew, who had once been business manager of the *Masses*, and was now directing publicity for the war department. Reed looked out of the window of Pew's office at marching soldiers and talked about the silly sheep in uniform. Pew assured him that life was what it was, and that it was absurd to ruin a career trying to change it.

Even Steffens had no hope. Reed wrote him about the newspaper blacklist against him, about the holding of his papers, about his arrest in Philadelphia. His mother was lamenting his smirching of the family name, and his brother was sailing for France. Intervention in Russia seemed certain. It was an unhappy letter, as Reed apologetically recognized, but Steffens had only cold comfort for him. "You do wrong," he wrote, "to buck this thing. In the first place, the war was inevitable; in the second place, the consequences of the war, its by-products, are normal and typical; in the third place, the public mind is sick. This last is what I learned in my experiences with it. I gave pain. I tried to speak, always, with consciousness that an audience was in trouble, psychologically, and I was just as tender as I could be. But sometimes I saw that what I said cut like a surgeon's knife into a sore place, and I was sorry. I must wait. You must wait. I know it's hard, but you can't carry conviction. You can't plant ideas. Only feelings exist. I think it is undemocratic to try to do much now. Write, but don't publish."

Such counsel bewildered Reed but could not stop him. On Independence Day he and Art Young were in Terre Haute to interview Eugene Debs. Debs had been arrested. A month before, a rumor had been circulated that he was leaving the Socialist Party. His answer was an eloquent, forthright statement in the *Call*, followed by a tour of the Middle West. Everywhere on the tour he had been threatened by police and vigilantes, and finally he had been arrested in Cleveland.

Going through the rich trim Indiana country, Reed had the feeling that this was the real America, and Debs seemed the perfect Middle-Westerner, shrewd, tender-hearted, eloquent, and indomitable. He was in bed when they got there, but he insisted on coming downstairs. He was gaunt and tall and seemed tired, but the warmth of his smile and the radiance of his whole person swept over them. He talked with charm such as Reed had never known, his face glowing, the words tumbling swiftly out of his mouth. He told about his trip, describing how he had outwitted the detectives watching him in Cleveland. People celebrating the holiday went by and stared, with malice and fear, at the house. "Let's go out on the porch and give them a good show," Debs proposed; so they sat on the porch, with their coats off, and laughed at the uneasiness of the passers-by.

It did Reed good to be there with Art Young and Gene Debs, these two men who miraculously combined courage with calmness and defiance with humor. What impressed Debs was that, in the face of such tremendous pressure from the patriots, opposition to war refused to die. "If this can't break them down," he said, "why then I know nothing can. Socialism's on the way. They can't stop it, no matter what they do." And as they went down the steps, he wrung their hands and clapped their shoulders, saying—and loud enough so that the neighbors could hear —"Now you tell all the boys everywhere who are making the fight, Gene Debs says he's with you, all the way, straight through, without a flicker!"

Two days later Reed spoke in Cleveland, where Debs had

been arrested. The city had been thoroughly terrorized by the American Protective League, made up of the younger, brighter capitalists. Spies were everywhere, and dictaphones were placed in the homes of suspected persons. Reed arrived in the city earlier than he had been expected, disconcerting police, Department of Justice operatives, and members of the Protective League. He gave his suitcase to a friend, who was pursued all over town and finally seized. The suitcase was broken open, though the detectives had no warrants, and Reed's papers removed. When he complained to Department of Justice officials, they restored his property and assured him it was all a mistake.

The armory was crowded and the meeting enthusiastic. After it was over, federal officers examined all the men, holding those who did not have their military registration cards with them. Meanwhile, a group of twenty detectives and Protective League business men surrounded Reed on the platform. They yapped and snarled, but the agent of the Department of Justice said that Reed could leave town, since he could be arrested later if the stenographic record showed that he had committed treason. The leaguers, deeply disappointed, saw him leave for his hotel, escorted by two policemen. "We got this place sewed up," one of the officers said. "We know everything that's going on about everybody in the place. You can't eat your dinner in a restaurant, you can't go to a theatre, you can't lay down to sleep, without we hear every word you utter."

Reed and Young went on to Chicago. Reed spoke at a big meeting in one of the theatres, and his classmate, Stuart Chase, who was working for the Federal Trade Commission, had him speak for the Fabian Club he had organized. But his chief purpose in Chicago was to report the I.W.W. trial. In the federal court-room, beneath pictures of the barons at Runnymede and Moses on Sinai, Judge Kenesaw Mountain Landis presided. "A wasted man with untidy white hair, an emaciated face in which two burning eyes are set like jewels, parchment skin split by a crack for a mouth; the face of Andrew Jackson three years dead." So Reed described him. "A fighter," he said, "and a sport, according to his lights, and as just as he knows how to be." And the prisoners: "One hundred and one *men*—lumber-jacks, harvest-hands, miners, editors; one hundred and one who believe that the wealth of the world belongs to him who creates it, and that the workers of the world shall take their own."

In the early morning the prisoners came over from Cook County Jail, where most of them had been rotting for three-quarters of a year, for bail had been set so high that only a few could be released. Reed knew some and came to know others —Haywood, Ralph Chaplin, Harrison George, George Andreytchine, Charley Ashleigh. They crowded together inside the rail of the court-room, some reading papers, one or two asleep, some sitting, some standing up. Reed felt that there could not be gathered together in America one hundred and one men more fit to stand for the social revolution. Somehow the scene seemed familiar to him, and suddenly the explanation came: it was like a meeting of the Central Executive Committee of the All-Russian Soviets in Petrograd. For a moment it seemed to him as if he were watching the Central Committee of American Soviets trying Kenesaw Mountain Landis for counter-revolution.

Reed knew their stories, stories of a long war, a war against an enemy that had limitless power, gave no quarter, and obeyed none of the rules of civilized warfare—"the class struggle, the age-old guerrilla fight of the workers against the masters, world-wide, endless, but destined to end!" Lawrence, Paterson, Mesaba Range, Everett—these were the battle-fields on which the one hundred and one had learned to fight. All Reed's old admiration for the I.W.W. came back. He thought of their singing and of Joe Hill, their beloved maker of songs. For seven months these men had been in jail, before the trial had begun. From the first day, the one issue had been the class struggle. Through the two months before Reed and Young came to Chicago, and for two months thereafter, strike-leaders, gunmen, rank-and-file workers, agitators, deputies, police, stool-pigeons, and secret service operatives filed through the court-room, building the story of the bloody war of the classes. Reed heard Frank Rogers tell of the Speculator mine fire and of the murder of Frank Little. He heard A. S. Embree describe the Arizona deportations. And he listened to an agricultural worker named Eggel: "Well, they grabbed us. And the deputy says, 'Are you a member of the

I.W.W.?' I says, 'Yes'; so he asked for my card, and I gave it to him, and he tore it up. He tore the other cards up that the fellow-members along with me had, so this fellow-member says, 'There is no use tearing the card up, we can get duplicates.' 'Well,' the deputy says, 'we can tear up the duplicates too.' And this fellow-worker says, he says, 'Yes, but you can't tear it out of my heart.' "

REED's articles on Debs and the I.W.W. trial appeared in the September *Liberator*, and on a back page of the issue was a letter:

Dear Max:

I'm going to have to resign as one of the contributing editors of the *Liberator*. I've thought about it for a long time, and I make this decision not without emotion, remembering our long work together on the *Masses*.

But I feel that I must take my name off the editorial page. The reason is, I cannot in these times bring myself to share editorial responsibility for a magazine which exists upon the sufferance of Mr. Burleson.

Of course, this does not mean that I want to stop contributing to the *Liberator*. And in the happy day when we can call a spade a spade without tying bunting on it, you will find me, as you have in the past,

Yours for the Profound Social Change,
John Reed.

And with it was Eastman's reply:

Dear Jack:

I haven't a word of protest—only a deep feeling of regret.

In your absence we all weighed the matter and decided it was our duty to the social revolution to keep this instrument we have created alive toward a time of great usefulness. You will help us with your writing and reporting, and that is all we ask.

Personally I envy you the power to cast loose when not only a good deal of the dramatic beauty, but also the glamor of abstract moral principle, is gone out of the venture, and it remains for us merely the most effective and therefore the right thing to do.

Yours as ever,
Max Eastman.

It was not a hasty decision on Reed's part; it was not, as Eastman implied, a grandiloquent gesture; it was not the result of a
personal quarrel, though both Max Eastman and his sister Crys-
tal, who was managing editor, felt that it was. Reed meant what
he said and no more. Perhaps the talk with Debs and the sight
of the I.W.W. prisoners had strengthened him. However that
may be, he had determined not to follow the path of compromise. That some compromises were necessary he did not doubt;
he had no craving for martyrdom. But he could not commit himself, as the *Liberator* was and had to be committed, to a deliberate
policy of concessions and evasions.

What Reed was looking forward to and what he knew he
must keep himself free for was the actual organization of the
revolutionary forces of America. From the first he had had this
in mind, and had discussed plans with the Bolshevik leaders.
Exactly what form the organization should take he did not
know; he was not, after all, a labor leader or a revolutionary
tactician; his relation to the movement had been merely that of
a close sympathizer. But he had not addressed some forty or
fifty meetings without discovering that there was a powerful
sentiment for revolution. If there were timid reformers in the
Socialist Party, there were also revolutionaries, and he wanted
to be ready to help them.

The time had not quite come for militant action, and while he
waited, he continued to devote himself to the interpretation of
Russia. Article followed article in the *Liberator*, and speech followed speech. In an article in the *Call*, he answered Herman
Bernstein, who had begun attacking Russia in the New York
Herald. On August 29, he spoke in Moline, Illinois, and on
Labor Day in Chicago. His trial in Philadelphia was postponed,
and his efforts to secure his papers from the government bore
no fruit. He and Louise Bryant took a small apartment on
Patchin Place, that they might have some foothold in the city,
and often enough Reed came home to report that he was being
followed by a detective.

To many of his acquaintances Reed seemed bitter and headstrong. So many friends were embarrassed when he spoke to
them at the Harvard Club or avoided him on the street or took

pains never to visit him that he became suspicious of almost every one. Always forthright and stubborn in the defense of his opinions, he became harsh and intolerant, for he saw everywhere the wreckage that what passed as tolerance had made of integrity. And people who were glad of an excuse for dissociating themselves from John Reed complained about his arrogance. The playboy, they said, had become conceited and humorless and dogmatic; they meant that he was dangerous.

But there were satisfactions in the kind of life Reed was living. There was the almost pathetic gratitude of the great throngs of European-born workers to whom he spoke, and there was his sense of solidarity with the handful of serious revolutionaries. Bill Haywood, after the conviction of the I.W.W. in Chicago, wrote him from Cook County Jail, speaking as one comrade to another: "The big game is over; we never won a hand. The other fellow had the cut, shuffle, and deal all the time. But we will do better when we get organized and can tie them on the industrial ground." Debs wrote: "I have read and been deeply moved by your fine article in the September *Liberator*. You write differently than any one else and your style is most appealing to me. There is a living something that breathes and throbs in all you say." Charles Erskine Scott Wood, out in Portland, praised the Debs and I.W.W. articles and approved the resignation from the staff of the *Liberator*. Almost every day such letters came, not so often as the letters, anonymous and signed, of abuse, but often enough to make Reed know that he was not alone.

On September 13, he spoke at Hunt's Point Palace, where, fifteen months before, he had witnessed the arrest of Emma Goldman and Alexander Berkman. Four thousand persons crowded into the hall, and three thousand were turned away. His theme was intervention. He charged that the British had inspired the recent attempt to assassinate Lenin, that the Czecho-Slovaks had broken faith with the Soviets, and that Wilson could have prevented the treaty of Brest-Litovsk. The next morning he was arrested and charged with making seditious utterances. Federal Attorney Barnes asked that bail be fixed at $10,000, but $5000 was finally set. What irritated Reed more than anything else

were the reports in most of the papers that he had promised
not to make any more speeches and the assertion in one of them
that he had broken down in Commissioner Hitchcock's office
and cried. "As a rule," he stated in the *Call* the next day, "I do
not take the trouble to deny the lies of the capitalist press, but
in this case I believe the stories are part of a deliberate scheme
to discredit Socialist speakers in the eyes of the rank and file.
In order not to burden my friends with heavier obligations on
my behalf, I promised that in case no bail was fixed I would not
make any public speeches until my hearing, which is fixed for
tomorrow morning. Since bail of $5000 was fixed, I, of course,
have made no promise not to speak. If people are to be imprisoned for protesting against intervention in Russia or for
defending the workers' republic in Russia, I shall be proud and
happy to go to jail."

The hearing finally took place on September 23, and Reed
was indicted for "wilfully, knowingly, and feloniously uttering
scurrilous and abusive language" about the Siberian expedition
of American troops. According to the records of the Federal
agents, he had said, "This intervention that I am talking to you
about is not allowed to be spoken about here in any other way
than the government wants it to be spoken about. But in every
other country in the world, in France and in Italy, the intervention is characterized very boldly as a direct adventure of
brigands."

REED was now under three indictments, the total bail amount-
ing to $12,000. The preliminaries of the second *Masses* trial
started on the day he was indicted for his Hunt's Point Palace
speech, and the trial itself began a week later. Reed had seen
enough of the temper of the American people to know that the
editors were in many ways fortunate: they all came from old
American stock; the judge was rather more lenient than most;
it had never been possible to whip up in New York City the
hysteria that dominated most smaller communities; and patriotic
emotion, despite all the artificial stimulants, was beginning to
slacken. Nevertheless, it was a fairly grim sort of humor that

inspired him to say to Young, as they entered the court-room, "Well, Art, got your grip packed for Atlanta?"

The drive was on for the fourth liberty loan, and as in the first trial there was a band in the City Hall Park that played the national anthem. Hillquit and Malone, the attorneys for the defense in April, were unable to serve, and Seymour Stedman came on from Chicago to take their place, assisted by Charles Recht and Walter Nelles. In the selection of the jury, class issues were sharply raised. Earl Barnes, the prosecuting attorney, insisted on questioning each talesman about his attitude towards Socialism, and, naturally enough, Stedman objected to most of the men Barnes approved. Reed was at first, in spite of himself, a little shaken; the court seemed a relentless machine that would grind and grind and grind. But the selection of the jury became a kind of game, rather boring in the end, and he amused himself by making notes on the talesmen. There was one man who announced that he didn't know what Socialism was but opposed it. There was a cotton manufacturer, grown wealthy in the war, who loudly protested his impartiality. There was a German who was determined to prove his patriotism. And there was one juror about whom Reed wrote simply, "Son of a bitch."

At first the emphasis was chiefly on the question of conspiracy, as it had been at the first trial, but gradually the issue sharpened, as the defendants took the stand and explained their position on the war. Reed was called to the stand on October 3, and Stedman began his examination. Gradually he led Reed to the point at which he could talk about his war experiences. "I began to be a war correspondent in 1913," he said, and up to the time I wrote that headline ("Knit a Strait-Jacket for Your Soldier Boy") I had been in action some fifty-five times." He spoke of Mexico—the siege of Torreon, the corpses piled high in the streets of Gomez, the death of his friends of La Tropa.

He grew pale and tense. He told of what he had seen at the Marne, in Serbia, in Galicia. He described the German trench in which he spent a night: "We were in this trench, up to our waists in running water; in the back of the trenches, where it was slightly drier, were dugouts, where the men lived four or

five days before they were taken back for rest. And the walls
of these dugouts were of soft mud; they moved slowly down as
the men lay down; and the only sounds were the snores of the
exhausted people sleeping, and then next were the screams of
rats. As we could look at the people as they lay there in the
light of a candle, you could see over their faces where insects
were crawling, vermin crawling. From this German trench, I
remember, lights were going up at one time; they were flashing
the lights, lighting up the other trenches; and we looked through
the port-hole, to the enemy trench, the French trench, eighty
yards away. It had been raining for two weeks, two solid weeks
of rain had come down, and in this mud midway between the
two trenches—"

"Keep your voice up, please," Stedman warned.

"Between these two trenches, in the mud, forty yards from
each trench, there lay a heap of bodies, all that was left of the
last French charge, and these bodies were slowly sinking in the
mud, had been left out there wounded to die. Nobody dared to
come out, although they were only forty yards from the French
trenches, and forty yards from the Germans. There had been no
cessation of fighting; the wounded had lain out there screaming
and dying in the mud, and they were sinking in the mud, and in
some cases there wasn't anything left of those bodies but an arm
or a leg sticking up out of the soft mud with the flesh rotten
on it."

"Now, I came back here," he went on, after telling of other
things he had seen, "I came back here, and what did I find?
What happened while I had gone to war? At the time I came
back, which was at the beginning of 1916, the society columns
were full about people getting up war benefits, giving war plays,
and the hotels and the houses of the upper West Side, upper
Fifth Avenue, were full of knitting parties, knitting socks for
soldiers. They were not knitting socks for soldiers because their
sons were in the trenches, as they knit socks for soldiers now;
they were knitting them for soldiers because it was the thing to
do. They had Caruso sing there in the afternoon while they
were knitting socks for soldiers, and the talk was all of frivolity
about the fact there was a war going on in Europe; England

and France were in it, it was fashionable to be in it, and we were not in it—why weren't we in it? It made me sort of sick."

"And that is why you wrote that?"

"That is why I wrote this thing. There was nothing—"

"Didn't you think," the judge interrupted, "it was time we got into it if you saw all that?"

Reed was dumbfounded. For nearly an hour he had told story after story of the horror of war, selecting deliberately the most gruesome incidents he had witnessed in Mexico and in Europe. "No," he stumbled, "I—I did not think—I do not see the analogy. I think it was a reason to keep out."

Judge Manton instructed Stedman to continue, and the next question concerned Reed's conception of war. "I was opposed to our going into the European war," Reed said. "One of the reasons, I was a student of history, and I still am, and I do not think at that time anybody disputed that the reasons for the European war were based on the commercialized interests, of certain groups of European interests. I think in the last half of the nineteenth century—"

Judge Manton broke in: "Now, we are not interested in that. We are interested in your state of mind."

"My state of mind is dependent on what I think about the war."

"You will not be permitted to argue it," Manton ruled, and he proceeded to take up the questioning himself. "Were you opposed to the war after our going into it?" he asked.

"Yes, sir."

"You have been opposed to it ever since?"

"Yes, sir."

"Therefore, of course, you are opposed to obtaining the necessary military forces."

It was the crucial point, and Reed had been carefully instructed by the defense attorneys. He parried and quibbled, but at last he said, "No, I was not opposed."

Stedman resumed, questioning Reed on his activities in Russia. Once more the judge interfered. "Are you a Socialist?"

"I am now, sir."

"How long since?"

"Well, I have been working with the Socialist movement for a long time. I did not become a Socialist until last summer."

Stedman turned the witness over to Prosecuting-Attorney Barnes for cross-examination. Barnes first asked about intervention in Siberia, which Reed said he opposed. Then Barnes brought up the old story about Reed's shooting from a German trench. Reed, again under instructions, said that he had fired into the air. "Do you agree," Barnes asked, "with the views announced in the *Masses* with regard to the desirability of a proletarian revolution against the capitalists and the bourgeoisie?"

"Yes, sir; all Socialists do."

"All Socialists do?"

"Yes."

"And that, in your mind, is the only war that is worth fighting in?"

"Well, to tell you the truth, it is the only war that interests me."

The smiling avowal left Barnes with nothing more to say, and, after Stedman's redirect examination, which was chiefly concerned with his activities in the Bureau of International Propaganda, Reed was allowed to leave the stand. In some respects it had not been a brilliant performance; in others it had. In the testimony regarding his experience as a war-correspondent, he had introduced into the trial an argument that had no legal weight but did impress the jury. He had stated without equivocation his opposition to the war and his belief in Socialism and the class struggle. The one point on which he compromised was the question of intentional obstruction of the recruiting of military forces.

On the whole, the defendants were firmer than they had been in the spring. In the spring, as Reed wrote, Germany had been invading Russia; now the United States was the invader. The bitter persecution of all pacifists and radicals had sharpened the issue. "I think we all felt tranquil," he wrote, "and ready to go to prison if need be. At any rate, we were not going to dissemble what we believed." Even Eastman, in his eloquent summation of the defense, was far more outspoken than he had been in the spring, and made fewer concessions to the hysteria of the moment. Complete frankness would unquestionably have brought conviction, with a probable sentence of twenty years in prison. Reed had no love for compromise, and he did not compromise one whit more than was necessary, but he was more useful out of prison than in.

Both Eastman and Stedman carefully announced to the jurors what District Attorney Barnes would say, and in his closing address he, rather lamely, fulfilled their prophecies. After he had strained to achieve the maximum of patriotic eloquence, he spoke of a friend of his who had died in France. "Somewhere in France," Barnes cried, "he lies dead, and he died for you and me. He died for Max Eastman, he died for John Reed, he died for Merrill Rogers. His voice is but one of a thousand silent voices that demand that these men be punished."

Art Young, who had been quietly sleeping, woke and looked about him. He listened for a moment, and then leaned across the table. "Who's he talking about?" he asked. "Didn't he die for me too?"

The jury disagreed, eight for acquittal, four against. The second *Masses* trial was over, and the indictment was soon to be dismissed, one less for John Reed to face. He knew that it might have been very different if he had not been born in Portland, Oregon, and educated at Harvard. It was by no means an unqualified triumph for free speech; to no small extent it was a victory for the air of respectability. The next week, in the same court-room, he saw six Russian boys and girls given sentences of from fifteen to twenty years for distributing leaflets against intervention in Russia. If the *Masses* trial had inspired any illusions about fairness and freedom of speech, this was enough to dispel them. The enemy had no intention of surrendering.

XVIII

Spokesman of the Soviets

FROM the moment he landed at the Atlantic port until he sailed from it again, eighteen months later, John Reed did more than any other one person to make known the truth about the Russian revolution. Not only did his book prove to be much the best written by an American eye-witness, both the most vivid and the most intelligent; before and after the book appeared, his speeches and his articles answered the questions that Americans were asking. During 1918 he published in the *Liberator* articles on Kerensky, the Russian army, the Department for Foreign Affairs, intervention, propaganda in the German army, and the structure and operation of the Soviet government. These articles were reprinted in radical papers all over the United States and Canada, and workers found in them the truth that the capitalist press was determined to conceal. His appointment as an official representative of the Soviets had been canceled, but he was nonetheless the spokesman of the Bolsheviks in the United States.

In the fall of 1918 there was a new attack on the Bolsheviks, led by the Hearst-trained Mr. Sisson. With the imprimatur of George Creel and the approval of a committee of professors made somewhat less than sane by the war, Mr. Sisson issued his famous collection of forgeries, purporting to show that the Bolshevik leaders were in the pay and under the orders of Berlin. There were letters from the German general staff, correspondence between Bolshevik leaders, orders on banks, reports of telephone conversations, all revealing with not quite credible thoroughness and naivete, the direct connection between the

Germans and the Bolsheviks. Mr. Creel said that the documents were, on the face of them, genuine, and the historians solemnly agreed.

Although it had been known in Petrograd that Sisson was in the market for "documents" of this sort, Reed had scarcely believed he would dare to publish them. Since the article in which he exposed the forgeries was not ready in time for the November issue of the *Liberator*, the editors published it as a pamphlet. Many of the documents, he pointed out, had been discredited when they were used by the Kerensky government at the time of the July uprising. They had been hawked about by an unscrupulous editor named Semenov, and had been rejected by the French and British governments as insufficiently plausible. Robins of the Red Cross had told Sisson they were forgeries, and doubts of their authenticity were expressed by others, including Graham R. Taylor and Arthur Bullard, who in a cable to Creel minimized their importance, "even if genuine."

Apart from the history of their shady origin, there was, as Reed pointed out, plenty of internal evidence to discredit them. The first two documents, supposedly orders for the destruction of evidence of the German-Bolshevik plot, carefully told what the evidence was. Several letters referred to events that had not taken place at the time the letters were supposedly written. The authors often showed an amazing ignorance of details with which they should have been familiar, speaking of Volodarsky, for example, as a commissar, referring to Joffe as chairman of the Military Revolutionary Committee, placing Tarasov-Radionov in Tomsk at a time when he was living in Reed's hotel in Petrograd. Sisson's notes, moreover, were full of errors, and although, as Reed recognized, this did not discredit the documents, it threw doubt on Sisson's ability to judge their authenticity. That some of the documents might be genuine, Reed granted, but these were given a false significance by their juxtaposition with forgeries. The collection as a whole was a preposterous fabrication.

Reed had no time to make a detailed analysis, but he spoke out, as almost no one else did, and he spoke convincingly. He was always ready to speak out. When an article by M. L. Larkin appeared in the *Public*, attacking the Bolsheviks, Reed wrote to point out Larkin's errors. When Upton Sinclair wanted to have Gorky's attitude towards the Soviets explained, Reed wrote a letter, published in Sinclair's magazine, explaining the limitations of the intelligentsia. The magazine, called *Upton Sinclair's*, later published another exchange of letters between them. "The war to you seems simple," Reed wrote Sinclair, "the Russian revolution complicated. I must confess that it seems the other way round to me; not that the Russian revolution is entirely simple, however. I cannot see how any Socialist can doubt either the integrity of the great majority of the Soviet leaders, or the splendor of the Bolshevik dream, or even the possibility of its practical working-out. All intellectuals will criticize and be disappointed with the social revolution when it starts; and if it seems hasty, unprepared for, or based on irrealizable dreams, they will perhaps oppose it. But if the overwhelming masses of the people are going quite consciously somewhere, neither you nor I will stand off and refuse to participate. I know it is the facts I tell you that you do not believe; and I must be content to wait for history. But I know that I am right. I have not dreamed, but have studied and investigated as I never did before."

Lecturing went on night after night. And on November 7, the anniversary of the Bolshevik triumph, there was a series of meetings, in Hunt's Point Palace, the New Star Casino, Brooklyn Labor Lyceum, Brownsville Labor Lyceum. Reed, though he was coming down with influenza, made the rounds with the other speakers, Albert Rhys Williams, Scott Nearing, Eastman, and Nuorteva. Always there were cheers when he described the events of November 7, 1917, the flight of Kerensky, the All-Russian Congress, the capture of the Winter Palace. At the meetings a booklet was distributed, *One Year of Revolution*, and of course there was an article of Reed's included.

These were exciting days. Close on the anniversary of the Russian revolution came the false armistice, the uprising in Germany, the abdication of the Kaiser, and then the real cessation of hostilities. Reed was in bed with influenza, but he felt the elation of the moment. It seemed certain that the era of world revolution had begun.

Immediately militant Socialists throughout the United States began to organize their forces. In Chicago the Communist Propaganda League was founded. The Boston Socialist local began to issue the *Revolutionary Age,* with Louis Fraina and Eadmonn MacAlpine as editors and Scott Nearing, John Reed, N. I. Hourwich, Ludwig Lore, Sen Katayama, and G. Weinstein as contributing editors. It was at first a four-page tabloid issued three times a week, and later an eight-page semi-weekly. The paper described events in Russia and Germany, printed statements by Lenin and other Bolshevik leaders, fought for Mooney and the other class-war prisoners in the United States, and agitated for a militant policy for the Socialist Party. Reed wrote for almost every issue.

John Reed had no doubt that revolution was imminent. He told Roger Baldwin, who was being sent to jail as a conscientious objector, that he would be freed by the workers long before his sentence had ended. And yet he had no illusions about the actual state of mind of the American working class, which he called, "the most uneducated working class in the world." He felt that the Socialist Party was partly made up of petty bourgeois, and that nothing was farther from their normal desires than a revolution. "The Socialists have some power," he wrote. "They can swing a million votes. The official majority in the Socialist Party is more interested in 'swinging' those votes than in Socialism." But he was counting on history: "Nothing teaches the American working class except hard times and repression. Hard times are coming, repression is organized on a grand scale. In America for a long time there has been no free land, no opportunity for workers to become millionaires. The working class does not yet know this. But if Tom Mooney stays in jail, if wages go down, if Socialists are arrested and the red flag suppressed, there will be a revolutionary movement in this country in five years."

ALL through November and December Reed was active in the left wing, speaking at its meetings and writing for the *Revolu-*

tionary Age. But time for such activities was hard to find. The government had at last returned his Russian material and he was writing *Ten Days That Shook the World*. With an advance from Boni and Liveright to meet immediate needs, he settled down to day after day of solid writing. Finding that he was too often interrupted, both in the Croton house and in his little apartment on Patchin Place, he took a room in Paula Holladay's Greenwich Inn, way up in the attic, and told no one where he was.

Rapidly the book took shape. It was to be simply the story of the Bolshevik triumph. A second book, he planned, would describe Russia's foreign relations, the origins and functions of revolutionary organizations, the evolution of popular sentiment, and the structure of the Soviet State; it would be called *From Kornilov to Brest-Litovsk*. And there would be a third, *The Smoke of Insurrection*, to contain the impressionistic sketches he had written or planned to write. But this first book would take the reader day by day through the revolution. It was Arthur Garfield Hays who suggested the title.

The book was not a compilation of what he had written on the revolution. Even the beginning he had made in Christiania was discarded. He used his articles, of course, as notes, and often took over phrases and occasionally paragraphs that he liked. But the book grew, page by page, in three months of tense writing, into an organic expression of all that he had seen in Russia and all that he had learned since his return. For the backbone of the book he used his notebooks, the record of his own experiences. But this was not a story of personal adventure. It was documented as nothing Reed had written had been documented. He had complete files of the *Russian Daily News*, the *Journal de Russie, Entente*, and the *Bulletin de la Presse*. He had hundreds of Russian newspapers of all parties. He had his extraordinary collection of proclamations and decrees, which he had had translated. He was poet, journalist, and scholar.

It is no wonder that *Ten Days That Shook the World* is a great book. John Reed knew how to use his eyes: *Insurgent Mexico* had shown that. He knew all the tricks that a good newspaperman knows, and could think in terms of headlines as well as in terms of color and romance. And he had learned, slowly and resistingly, the value of accuracy and documentation, learned it at Ludlow and Bayonne and in the fight against war. He was perfectly trained for the task of reporting a revolution. But there was something more than that: he was a participant as well as an observer, and his book was a weapon as well as a report, all the more effective for its restraint and precision. In those three months that he spent bent over a typewriter, surrounded by his great piles of papers and pamphlets, he knew what he was doing: the world must be shaken again and again.

By the middle of January the book was on the press, and Reed was once more speaking four or five nights a week. The board of education in New York City had forbidden the use of a public school for a meeting against intervention in Russia, and Reed and Eastman spoke in protest. There was a meeting of Finns, hundreds of whom came and maintained a stolid silence in the face of Reed's hot enthusiasm. There was a meeting in Erie, Pennsylvania, at which a group calling themselves the Erie Soviet of Workers presented Reed with a written testimonial in appreciation of "the valuable and faithful services you have unflinchingly rendered the Russian Socialist Republic since your arrival in this country from Russia." In Boston, under the auspices of the Committee for a Democratic Peace, Reed spoke to three thousand people, saying, "No one who thinks it was wrong to go into Belgium can think it is right to go into Russia," and, "The Red Terror isn't confined to Russia; we have a little terror over here."

In Brooklyn a hundred policemen were assigned to one of his meetings. Having been told that he must not criticize the government, he began, "My family came to this country, both branches, in 1607; one of my ancestors was Patrick Henry, who signed the Declaration of Independence; another of my ancestors was a general under George Washington; and another was a colonel on the northern side in the Civil War. I have a brother, a major in the aviation corps, now in France. I am a voter and a citizen of the United States, and I claim the right to criticize it as much as I please. I criticize the form of it because I claim that it is not a democratic enough government for me. I consider the

Soviet government a more democratic government at the present time than our own government." He spoke of America's professed war aims. "Well, the war is finished, comrades, and where in hell is the democracy? Now in New York City free speech is suppressed; Socialists are not allowed to meet; the red flag is banned; periodicals are barred from the mails; all the evidences of Prussianism appear." The government had pretended that it was a war between two ideas, democracy and autocracy, but it had been merely a war between two sets of capitalists. "Now the war is ended," he said, "but a new war is beginning; and this time it is a war between two ideas."

In the *Revolutionary Age* Reed wrote on capitalist terror in Europe and America. "The workers of Bridgeport," he wrote, "the workers of Bethlehem, are now witnessing the discharge, not only of all active union men, but also of members of workers' committees instituted by the United States Government's War Labor Board . . . Out in Arizona the detectives and hangers-on of the copper mine owners who deported striking miners, who deliberately broke the law and spat on the Constitution, have been acquitted. . . . Does any American worker now doubt the innocence of Tom Mooney, or the filthy crookedness of the California court and district attorney which convicted him? . . . And Eugene Debs, sentenced to ten years, and Rose Pastor Stokes, and all the brave men and women who dared to tell the truth when it was dangerous, and now suffer in prison; is it difficult to guess why they were punished? . . . There is but one alternative to this: industrial unions, the Socialist Party, the general strike, and a labor democracy, in which those who do all the work shall have all the power."

The whole question of tactics was beginning to trouble him. Most Socialists, he wrote, seemed to try to give the impression that "Socialism is really Jeffersonian democracy, to intimate that all we want are reasonable reforms, labor legislation, and the full dinner pail." Their theory appeared to be, "First make a liberal, and then convert him to Socialism." "Fully a third of the Socialist votes are, in normal times, cast by middle-class persons who think that Karl Marx wrote a good anti-trust law." "I have no quarrel," he said, "with that kind of propaganda—except that it does not make Socialists." The comrades of the left wing "must find out from the American workers what they want most, and they must explain this in terms of the whole labor movement, and they must make the workers want more—make them want the whole revolution."

Reed did not cease writing for the *Liberator*. The March issue contained a warm tribute to Karl Liebknecht, murdered with Rosa Luxemburg in Berlin. Recalling his visit to Liebknecht in the winter of 1914-15, Reed wrote of his courage and faith. "When at last the revolution came, with the Kaiser Socialists half-timorously holding the wheel, the first thing done by the workers was to set Karl Liebknecht free from prison. He must have known, as he was drawn in his flower-filled carriage through the shouting streets, that his hour was near. He must have known—when he cried to the throng from the balcony of the Russian embassy, the red flag floating over him, 'The future belongs to the people!'—that for him there would be no future. . . . He was killed by the international capitalist class, it is true. What else could be expected? But remember! Those whose hands are red with Liebknecht's blood and the blood of the German workers are the German Majority Social Democrats—the Kaiser Socialists—Ebert, Scheidemann, and the rest—who put down the workers' insurrection with the help of the Kaiser soldiers, and paid for it with the lives of Liebknecht and Rosa Luxemburg."

In the same issue was Reed's last play, a fantasy called "The Peace That Passeth Understanding." The curtain rises upon Wilson, Lloyd George, Clemenceau, Orlando, and Makino. Orlando rebukes Wilson for having said in Turin, "The industrial workers will dictate the peace terms." "You must remember," Orlando says, "that Italian workers are not educated—we have no Samuel Gompers." When Wilson explains that such expressions are only to be interpreted in their Wilsonian sense, Clemenceau congratulates him on his finesse, especially in inventing that fine phrase, "League of Nations," to describe the old idea of the balance of power. This reminds Makino of an earlier American phrase, "the open door in China," and he adds his praises. Wilson says modestly, "A trifling achievement. Why in

America, my second campaign was won by the phrase, 'He kept us out of war.' "

After the Serbian, Belgian, Czecho-Slovakian, Roumanian, Armenian, Yugo-Slav, Polish, and Central and South American delegates have been disposed of, and the peace conference made safe from democracy, Wilson explains the fourteen points, one by one, to the satisfaction and delight of his companions. While Makino and Lloyd George roll dice for the Pacific colonies, Wilson prepares a statement describing the moral victory that his "earnestness and eloquence, supported by the unselfish motives of the United States government in entering the war" have won. But just as he is giving it to the press, news comes of revolution throughout the world, and the delegates, seeking a stable government under which to live, decide to go to Russia.

The playlet, which was repeatedly produced by the Washington Square Players, suggested what had happened to John Reed's sense of humor. Certainly he had not lost it, but it had sharpened into a sardonic sense of the vast hypocrisies and absurdities of capitalist civilization. He was, as a matter of fact, rather more likely than he had once been to find amusement in the annoyances of his own life as well as in the blatancies of a Palmerized America. When the Fifth Avenue Bank used the excuse of an overdrawn account to refuse to accept more deposits, and when the Harvard Club suspended him for an unpaid bill, he was irritated, but only for a little while. These were the petty tactics of bankrupt men, and he knew that he could afford to laugh at them.

Reed found time to write the little play, but he could not find time for poetry. He wished he could. One snowy night, when he was hurrying back, without coat or hat, to Patchin Place, he met Sherwood Anderson on the corner of Fifth Avenue and Ninth Street. For an hour they talked: did a poet do more by lying low and trying to get understanding, or whatever it was poets were after, or by giving himself to the fight? Reed didn't know; he wouldn't say the other way was wrong; but for himself, well, somebody had to do the fighting. And yet: "If I could be dead sure I had something on the ball as a poet . . ." he said. He knew of course that he had plenty on the ball. That was not the question. It was too bad, but poetry would have to wait.

THERE was another opportunity for Reed to strike a blow for Russia. On September 19, 1918, as a result of charges made by A. Mitchell Palmer, then custodian of alien property, a sub-committee of the Senate was appointed to investigate brewing and liquor interests and German propaganda, with Senator Lee S. Overman as chairman, and Senators King, Wolcott, Nelson, and Sterling as his associates. Sessions began on September 21, and for some weeks Mr. Palmer's charges were investigated. After the end of the war, however, German espionage became an old story, and the committee turned its attention to Bolshevism. Mr. Jacob M. Kennedy, secretary of the Montana Commercial and Labor League, helped to accomplish the transition when, on January 17, 1919, he announced that there was a connection between pro-Germanism and Bolshevism in Montana. On January 21, Thomas J. Tunney, a New York City inspector of police, appeared and confirmed Kennedy's insinuations about the relations between the two forms of anti-Americanism. Finally, when Archibald E. Stevenson was called, the committee had no difficulty in recognizing its duty.

Mr. Stevenson, who had been chairman of the committee on aliens of the Mayor's Committee of National Defense of New York, and subsequently a special agent for the Department of Justice and a member of the military intelligence division, was prepared to demonstrate that pro-Germans, pacifists, and Bolsheviks were one and the same. With the assistance of Major E. Lowry Humes, who had been assigned to the committee by the War Department, he thoroughly covered the various liberal, pacifist, and working-class organizations of the country. At last he came to the Russian revolution. "The interesting feature of the Bolsheviki movement," he said, "is that every one of these currents that we have spoken of is now cooperating with the Bolsheviki emissaries. We have several avowed agents of the Bolsheviki government here—avowed propagandists."

"In this country; operating here?" Senator Nelson cried in amazement.

"In this country; operating today," Stevenson insisted.

Nelson asked for names. "Two of them are American citizens," he was told. "One is John Reed, a graduate of Harvard University."

"You don't say?" Nelson ejaculated.

In describing Reed's appointment as consul, Stevenson mentioned his having brought official forms for marriage and divorce with him. "What are the forms and requirements for marriages and divorces under the Soviet government in Russia?" Major Humes asked.

"Simply a statement before the proper commissary that they want to be married, or that they want to be divorced."

"Do they have as many wives as they want?" the chairman asked.

"In rotation," Stevenson answered.

"Polygamy is recognized, is it?" Humes insisted.

Stevenson hedged. "I do not know about polygamy. I have not gone into the study of their social order quite as fully as that."

Nelson, always a little slow but enormously persistent, would not let the question drop. "That is," he said, "a man can marry and then get a divorce when he gets tired, and get another wife?"

"Precisely."

"And keep up the operation?"

"Yes."

"Do you know whether they teach free love?" Overman asked.

"They do," Stevenson assured him.

Though there were still a few witnesses to be heard on the subject of German propaganda, the committee was eager to get on to Bolshevism. On February 2, Louise Bryant and Albert Rhys Williams spoke on Russia in a meeting held in Washington. The newspaper publicity roused the Senate, which, on the motion of Senator Walsh of Montana, voted to extend the power of the Overman committee so that it could make a sweeping investigation of Bolshevism. Hatred of the Huns was no longer necessary, but hatred of the Bolsheviki had practical value in a nation whose industrial leaders were entering on a campaign for the open shop and pre-war hours and wages.

On February 11, the first witness appeared, William Chapin Huntington, who had served as commercial attaché of the Department of Commerce to the American embassy in Petrograd, and who testified to the chaos in Russia and the unpopularity of the Bolsheviks. He was followed by Professor Samuel N. Harper, of the University of Chicago, who, though anti-Bolshevik, insisted on academic qualifications and reticences, and disappointed the committee. The Reverend George A. Simons, however, who came to the hearing as "a one hundred percent American and a Christian clergyman," quoted the Jewish Protocols as authoritative, said the Bolsheviks "rape and ravish and despoil women at will," and attacked Reed and Williams by name.

For a week the committee examined a procession of witnesses, each of them hostile to the Soviet regime: Y.M.C.A. workers, business men, and refugees. R. B. Dennis, a teacher at Northwestern University, said, "I do not know Mr. Williams or Mr. Reed. I have read their stuff and John Williams' wife's book." Robert F. Leonard, who, like Mr. Dennis, had been with the Y.M.C.A., was persuaded to talk about Bolshevik morality. Senator Nelson observed, "That man, Maxim Gorky I believe his name is, whom they have taken into the fold, is about as immoral as they make them." A business man appearing anonymously during an executive session, described the demoralization of the workmen. Madame Breshkovskaya, who had come to the United States, attacked Lenin and Trotsky. Two employees of the National City Bank in Petrograd testified to the evil state of affairs, and Roger E. Simmons of the Department of Commerce read to the committee the famous "decree" regarding the nationalization of women.

By this time it was apparent that the committee had no desire to hear any one who was even mildly sympathetic to the Bolsheviks. Reed, Louise Bryant, Williams, and their friends wrote and telegraphed Senator Overman, and finally it was announced that they would be permitted to testify.

Louise Bryant came first, on the afternoon of February 20. The Senators began: "Do you believe in God?" "Do you believe in the sanctity of an oath?" "Are you a Christian?" "Do you believe in Christ?" "Do you believe in a punishment hereafter and a reward for duty?" Finally she explained, "It seems to me as if I were being tried for witchcraft!" "This is important," Senator King explained, "because a person who has no conception of God does not have any idea of the sanctity of an oath, and an oath would be meaningless."

When the oath had finally been taken, the questions chiefly concerned her activities in the woman suffrage campaign. "You said that you were at the National Women's Party headquarters?" Nelson asked.

"Yes, sir."

"Did you belong to the picket squad?"

"I do not know what that has to do with the truth about Russia, but I did. I believe in equality for women as well as men, even in my own country."

"Did you participate in the burning of the President's message?"

"Yes."

"You did not participate in the burning of the effigy?" Overman asked.

"I did; and I went on a hunger strike."

"What do you mean by that; you went to jail?"

"I went to jail and went on a hunger strike. If you go without food and become weak, the authorities let you out because they do not want you to die in jail."

Senator King took up the examination, asking her about her marriage to Trullinger and her divorce. Miss Bryant suggested that she was supposed to be telling about Russia. "We want to know something about the character of the person who testifies," King explained, "so that we can determine what credit to give to the testimony."

King went on to ask if she had taken an oath, when she got her passport, not to engage in political activities, and, on her admission that she had, he tried to force her to say that she had violated it. Failing in that, he turned to the subject of Reed's oath.

Nelson took a hand. "Was your husband employed by the Bolsheviki?"

"Yes, sir."

"Employed for what purpose?"

"He worked in the propaganda department, and I will show you the kind of papers. There has never been any secret about this kind of propaganda. For instance—"

Nelson interrupted: "We do not care about that."

"Do not care about it?"

"About those papers. We want the facts."

"Those are the facts. You must admit the facts. Here is a paper printed in German, prepared for sending into the German lines in order to make—"

Enraged, Nelson said, "Do not be so impertinent!" There were hisses and applause, and Senator Overman threatened to clear the room. Louise Bryant broke in: "You said, Senator Overman, that I am not on trial here. I am a free American citizen. I expect to be treated with the same courtesy as former witnesses, and I have not gotten it so far." Immediately there was applause, and Overman ordered every one, except the stenographer and the reporters, from the room. Reed rose from his place in the audience, and asked if he might stay. Permission was granted him.

The executive session was somewhat less belligerent, but its spirit was the same. The committee was obviously quite uninterested in anything Louise Bryant might have to say about Russia, seeking only to extract from her incriminating facts about Reed, Williams, Raymond Robins, Jerome Davis, and any one else who was known not to be bitterly critical of the Soviets. Major Humes finally took up the questioning, and, after raising the subject of the nationalization of women and then refusing to allow her to explain the origin of the "decrees," permitted her to tell a little of what she had seen.

When the committee re-convened the next morning, Humes was armed with a valuable discovery he had made during the night. Louise Bryant had said that she had credentials from the Philadelphia *Public Ledger*, whereas actually her credentials were from the Bell Syndicate. The truth was that when the *Ledger* bought her articles, they had asked her to make it appear that she had represented them in Russia. She had kept up the fiction, and the *Ledger* now repudiated her.

While Humes tried to make as much as possible of this, Louise Bryant suddenly shifted the attack. "I want to know," she said, "why, after my testimony yesterday, you sent a telegram to Mr. Williams, whom you accused of spreading Bolshevik propaganda, and said 'Disregard telegram of February 19. Subpœna withdrawn.' And if it is also true that you withdrew the subpœna to Colonel Robins because you were afraid that too much truth would come out here?"

It was Humes' turn to object: "I do not know that I am on the witness stand," he said with dignity, "or that it is a matter with which the witness is concerned." Having the advantage, Louise Bryant pressed on, protesting against her treatment the day before; she had been given an examination for heresy by Senator King, lectured on her morals by Senator Nelson, and heckled by every one. She went on to speak of the persons who had asked to testify and had not been called. Humes denied that Reed had asked to appear, and Reed spoke up from the audience, so that Overman had to suggest that the letter might have been mislaid. On the whole it was Louise Bryant's morning, and, though the committee and Major Humes did their best to discredit her testimony, she managed to tell her story of the revolution.

Reed was called at three-thirty that afternoon. Having seen the treatment his wife had been accorded, he was prepared. There he was, tall, strong, impressive, with a smile on his face and ruthlessness in his eyes. He swaggered a little, eying the senators with a kind of careless defiance. But he was deadly serious. If the committee proposed to browbeat him, they would find him too quick and too strong. If they wanted to play a game, he would beat them at it.

There was the usual wrangle about the oath, and then, with ostentatious cheerfulness, Reed answered Humes' questions about his newspaper career, the assurances he had made with regard to the Stockholm Conference, and his behavior in Petrograd. His description of conditions before, during, and after the revolution was so clear that the senators could find no chance for objections. He discussed factory management, the status of the press, the use of violence, the dissolution of the Constituent Assembly, the handling of food cards, the amount of crime, and the operation of the soviets. His work with the Bureau of International Propaganda he defended, as usual, on the ground that it had been directed against the Kaiser. And the defense was by no means specious, even from the point of view of the American government, for General Hoffman, Germany's military representative at Brest-Litovsk, had said, "Immediately after conquering those Bolsheviks, we were conquered by them. Our victorious army on the eastern front became rotten with Bolshevism."

Humes did his best to make Reed admit that he either did or did not advocate the overthrow of government by force. Reed insisted that he held merely to the opinion that, under certain circumstances, extra-constitutional methods of change might be necessary. Humes shifted his ground, bringing up the famous Dunn story of the shooting from the German trenches. "I do not know how many times this thing must be contradicted," Reed said, "but I am perfectly willing to keep on contradicting it."

Senator Wolcott brought the investigation back to Reed's views, and Humes asked, "Have you in any of your public speeches advocated a revolution in the United States similar to the revolution in Russia?"

"I have always advocated a revolution in the United States."

Humes was startled. "You are in favor of a revolution in the United States?"

"Revolution," Reed explained, "does not necessarily mean a revolution by force. By revolution I mean a profound social change. I do not know how it will be attained."

"Do you not in your speeches leave the impression with your audiences that you are talking about a revolution of force?"

"Possibly."

"Do you mean," Wolcott asked, "to leave that impression?"

"No. My point is that the will of the people will be done; the will of the great majority of the people will be done."

"That is a sound point," Wolcott admitted.

"That is my point, and if the will of the great majority is not done by law, it will be done some other way. That is all."

"Do you not know, Mr. Reed," Wolcott went on, "that the use of the word 'revolution' in the ordinary meaning carries the idea of force, arms, and conflict?"

"Well, as a matter of fact, unfortunately, all these profound social changes have been accompanied by force. There is not one that has not."

A moment later Wolcott said, "Your mental agility is, I confess, too much for me." It was true. When Humes raised a point about the land decrees, Wolcott again tried to argue with Reed. "Suppose you lived in one of those villages," he said, "and you had a couple of sons—and they were twins . . ." Reed politely bowed, "Thank you, sir," he said. The committee was glad to let him go. Before he left, he named a number of men he would like to have called: Frank Keddie, Raymond Robins, Major Allen Wardwell, who, he thought, "would be a peach," Major Thacher, and Jerome Davis.

A number of these people were summoned. Albert Rhys Williams fared reasonably well, perhaps because the committee had been a little chastened by their experience with Reed and Louise Bryant. Senator Nelson, however, could not resist the temptation to bully Bessie Beatty, and Overman had to apologize for him. Frank Keddie, a representative of the American Society of Friends, was heckled because of his pacifism. Colonel Robins met unconcealed hostility with dignity and courage. Ambassador Francis, in his testimony, satisfied the committee on every point and attacked Robins so unscrupulously that the committee had to hold a special session to permit Robins to reply.

When Oliver Sayler began by saying, "I want to insist in advance, Senator, that I am no Bolshevik," Nelson said, "You need not mind that. We will judge whether you are a Bolshevik by what you tell us." That was the attitude of the committee: anybody who did not vociferously damn the Soviets must be a Bolshevik and therefore was not to be believed. The testimony of Reed and the men he had recommended did not alter in the slightest the opinions of the committee, but at least he had the satisfaction of saying his say and of discomforting the men who had started out to heckle and confuse him.

What irritated him was that the newspapers could so easily turn his victory into a defeat. After having forced the committee to listen to the facts about Russia, he saw those facts twisted in the press. The papers could not ignore his testimony and him; so they distorted and belittled. Stanley Frost in the *Tribune* called him "a man to whom clever phrases are an intoxication and patient study utterly impossible," "a soldier of fortune," "a matinee idol." Like the other reporters, he seized on Reed's facetious statement that he might be able to get money from wealthy women to establish a bureau of information about Soviet Russia. "Good sport," he wrote. "Money from rich women, speeches urging force that he doesn't believe in, the distinction of wide disapproval, stir and excitement and revolution. Good sport and little risk—for Reed!"

Then there was a paper that carried an editorial entitled "One Man Who Needs the Rope." "John Reed," it said, "told the Senate committee investigating Bolshevism that he was a firm advocate of revolution in the United States. . . . If there is no law for handling a case of this kind one should be enacted speedily. If a man should be hanged for instigating another to murder one man, he should certainly be hanged for instigating men to kill thousands of men. If the law is defective, why wait until tomorrow to remedy its defects? A law should be passed at once against such utterances as those brazenly made by this man Reed, and then as soon as possible ten thousand hangings should follow."

But all this was nothing compared to the actual misrepresentation that kept his testimony from the public. "My one complaint against you and the other paid agents of the capitalist class," he wrote the New York *Times* in a letter it refused to publish, "is not that you oppose Bolshevism, but deliberately pervert and suppress the truth about it and about what is going on in Russia. It is all very well to state that Bolshevism means wholesale murder, socialization of women, robbery unrestrained, and then say that I stand for it. It is all very well to say that the Bolsheviki are anarchists (although anarchy in Russia and America is openly opposed to the strongly centralized proletarian state built up in Russia), and then call us, who defend Bolshevism, anarchists. This of course is a very convenient method of carrying on a sinister propaganda for the benefit of those ruthless interests who plunged the world into a war which cost more than seven million lives, and who are rich with blood-money. But it is not the truth—and you know it is not the truth."

He went on to comment on the way the committee had conducted its sessions and to illustrate the *Times'* treatment of the evidence. He alluded to the charge that he was growing rich on Moscow gold. "There is no money," he said, "in speaking to working-class audiences, or writing in working-class papers, which are the only audiences and papers open to any advocacy of the truth about Soviet Russia. All persons who work for an unselfish purpose for little or nothing are incomprehensible to persons who never work for nothing and can be hired to work for anything."

FROM Washington Reed went straight to Philadelphia, where his trial began on February 24. The charge of "incitement to seditious remarks" had been dropped, and both Kogerman and Reed were charged with riot and assault and battery. The more conservative Socialists of the city refused to have anything to do with the case, since Reed was a Bolshevik, and he had to secure his own lawyer. At first he tried to persuade Seymour Stedman to take the case, but Stedman believed a local lawyer would be more successful, and Charles Ervin, of the *Call*, recommended David Wallerstein. Most of Wallerstein's work had been for corporations, but he liked Reed, when Ervin introduced him, and the charge seemed to him absurd. He insisted on taking the case without pay. Henry J. Nelson defended Kogerman.

The judge, Raymond MacNeille, knew nothing about Socialism and boasted of the fact. The jurors and District Attorney Fox were equally ignorant. Fox made, of course, the most of his patriotic opportunities, and the newspapers clamored for a conviction. Reed believed that acquittal was impossible. Wallerstein, however, handled the case with great skill. He first succeeded in having the charge of assault and battery dismissed, and then had Reed testify. Reed told his story simply and well. In cross-examination Fox concentrated on Reed's motives in going to the hall after he had been informed that the permit had been canceled, trying to maintain, of course, that he had gone there with the deliberate intention of provoking a riot. When Wallerstein called a number of witnesses, Fox made much of the fact that most of them were foreigners, and the judge refused to sustain Wallerstein's objections. Wallerstein, in summing up, placed all his emphasis on the right of freedom of speech. "I am not a Socialist," he said, "but when the superintendent of police can say who shall or shall not speak, it is better that we stop talking about democracy." He maintained both that Reed had every right to test the police ruling and that no riot had taken place. Despite Fox's harangue and the judge's patriotic charge, the jury acquitted Reed on the first vote, and, after two hours' discussion, freed Kogerman as well.

This was a clearer victory for freedom of speech than the *Masses* case. Fox told Wallerstein that it was one of the most disastrous verdicts in the history of Philadelphia and insisted that the jurors were moved by fear of Bolshevik bombs. The liberal press, beginning to return to sanity, congratulated the court, Reed, and Wallerstein. Reed felt that Wallerstein deserved the credit. During the three or four days that Reed and Louise Bryant spent in Philadelphia, they stayed in Wallerstein's home, and Reed was filled with respect for this simple, unpretentious, honest liberal. The Wallersteins, on their side, were delighted with his brilliant talk, and listened to tale after tale of adventure in Mexico and Europe.

An ordeal that Reed had particularly dreaded had been transformed into a pleasant and gratifying episode. The *Masses* indictment had been dropped, and now, with acquittal in Philadelphia, and with the strong possibility that the Hunt's Point Palace case would be quashed because of the end of the war, he felt relatively free. And when, on the nineteenth of March, *Ten Days That Shook the World* finally appeared, he had a strong sense of achievement. Many of the reviews were, of course, unfavorable, but from all over the country came the only kind of praise that counted. Scores of Wobblies wrote him from Leavenworth and other penitentiaries, telling him that this was the real thing. Walt Whitman's friend, Horace Traubel, a revolutionary veteran, wrote him, "I have great respect for all you do —and better still, for all you are." A radical bookseller in Colorado packed a hundred copies from mining camp to mining camp, and sold them all. Wherever Reed spoke to radical groups, he found that *Ten Days* was regarded as a kind of handbook of revolution. What did he care if Charles Edward Russell damned it in the New York *Times?* Passed from hand to hand, and read till the pages fell apart, the book was what he had wanted it to be—a weapon. "You are correct," he said, in his letter to the *Times*, "when you call information about Russia Bolshevik propaganda, for the great majority of persons who learn the truth about Russia become convinced Bolsheviki." The statement may have been extravagant, but it would not be easy to compute the number of persons whose interest in Communism dates from the reading of *Ten Days That Shook the World*.

XIX

DISCIPLINE

REED's resignation from the *Liberator*, his work as contributing editor of the *Revolutionary Age*, and his close identification with the leaders of the left wing were natural stages in the transition from the task of giving information about Bolshevism in Russia to the task of organizing Bolshevism in America. It was an easy transition because Russia was the touchstone that divided the right from the left in the Socialist Party. In the winter of 1918–19, Bolshevism was the great topic of debate, not so much between Socialists and one-hundred-percent Americans as between Socialists and Socialists.

Joseph Shaplen was one of the few right-wing Socialists who had been in Russia during the revolution, and the *Revolutionary Age* invited him to debate with Reed. He refused, on the ground that the *Revolutionary Age* was fighting the Socialist Party; he would, he said, debate under the auspices of a Socialist local. It made little difference to Reed who sponsored the meeting, and on March 6, in the Manhattan Lyceum, the debate took place. Shaplen, of course, argued that the Bolshevik regime was undemocratic. Reed replied, "The Bolsheviki believe in democracy of the working class, and no democracy for anybody else," and proceeded to show the sensitiveness of the soviets to the will of the workers and peasants. He cited Marx's views on the dictatorship of the proletariat, which Shaplen and other right-wing Socialists had contrived to forget, and offered statistics on the productivity of industry under working-class control.

In the heat of the debate Reed forgot the rules of parliamentary procedure and used the last five minutes of his rebuttal to make personal charges against Shaplen. Shaplen, he alleged, had had Tsarist associations in Russia and had advocated American intervention. Shaplen, who could not answer Reed in the course of the debate, brought charges against him before the grievance committee of the New York local. In the meantime, the Philadelphia local, to which Shaplen belonged, was considering the charge that he was a counter-revolutionary.

How sharp the cleavage had become had been made apparent by the publication, in the *Revolutionary Age* for February 8, of the manifesto and program of the left wing, to which Reed had helped give literary form. The manifesto announced that the left wing did not intend to split the Socialist Party but to make it truly Socialist. Explaining the collapse of the Second International during the war on the ground that it had been corrupted by bourgeois reformers and self-seeking trade-unionists, it described the German Spartacists and the Russian Bolsheviks as the true followers of Marx. In the United States the end of the war had brought unemployment and a concerted capitalist effort to reduce the standard of living. The workers were answering the employers with militant strikes. In this surge of revolt lay the Socialist Party's opportunity, but the leaders were too concerned with their petty reforms to seize it. Whereas the syndicalists were blind to the possibilities of political action, the reform Socialists misused political methods. The left wing proposed a new policy, in both politics and industry, looking towards the overthrow of capitalism and the establishment of Socialism through a dictatorship of the proletariat.

The strategy of the left wing was based on the assumption that a revolutionary crisis was approaching in the United States. In Portland, Oregon, John Reed's birthplace, a Council of Workers, Soldiers, and Sailors had been formed, proclaiming the class struggle, the bankruptcy of capitalism, and the coming seizure of power. The *Soviet World* of Philadelphia, hailing the Portland Council, predicted that the next two years would see the birth of the Socialist Soviet Republic of the United States of America. Nothing seemed impossible when one looked at Europe. Although reaction had triumphed in Finland and Poland, and moderate Socialists had strangled the revolutions in Germany and Austria, proletarian forces were still strong. In Hungary, Bela Kun's brief rule was about to begin, and the workers of Italy were seizing factory after factory. As for the United States, even without exaggerating the militancy of the workers at that particular moment, one who had seen Russia in 1915 and again in 1917 knew that docility might change to revolt in a year or a few months or, under sufficient pressure, a few weeks. Reed, hopeful as he was, was not the most sanguine member of the left wing.

If the world revolution was beginning, sooner or later to reach this country, the policies of the officials of the Socialist Party were not merely stupid; they were a betrayal of the working class. Although the party had officially voted against war, many of its leaders, including the Socialist aldermen in New York City, had supported the government, endorsing liberty loan drives and other war measures. With the armistice, these officials had been chiefly concerned to preserve the party from the stigma of Bolshevism. To the members of the left wing, the whole policy of the Socialist Party leadership seemed to aim at suppression of the growing militancy.

The left-wing leaders could not reach the membership through the party press nor through the ordinary organizational methods. The party had a machine, and the conservatives controlled it. Therefore the members of the left wing formed special units. The creation of the Communist Propaganda League of Chicago, the founding of the *Revolutionary Age,* and the issuing of the manifesto and program were steps in this process. And on February 15, a left-wing section of the Socialist Party of Greater New York was officially organized at an all-day conference. Reed was appointed as the New York representative on the staff of the *Revolutionary Age* and was elected to the city committee of fifteen. Maximilian Cohen was elected executive secretary and Rose Pastor Stokes treasurer.

The manifesto and program of the left wing were endorsed by many of the Socialist locals and by the Lettish, Russian, Lithuanian, Polish, Ukrainian, South Slavic, Hungarian, and Esthonian Federations, foreign-language groups which included a large proportion of the members of the Socialist Party. The movement towards the left wing was accelerated by the news that the Communist Party of Russia had issued a call for a congress to form a new International, soon followed by information that the Third or Communist International had come into existence. The left wing immediately initiated a referendum for adherence to this International.

Members of the right wing were as determined as their opponents. To them it was absurd to believe that a revolutionary crisis was at hand and wicked to suggest that power should be violently seized. Although they were as emphatic as the militants in affirming their desire for the destruction of capitalism, they could conceive of no other weapons than education and the slow achievement of parliamentary power. This being true, they regarded the program of the left wing as futile and its tactics as suicidal.

The left wing began to call for a national emergency convention. It also entered candidates in the election of international delegates and members of the national executive committee, nominating Reed as an international delegate. He devoted more and more of his time to left-wing affairs, and meetings of the city committee were sometimes held in his home in Croton. To one meeting he brought Howard Scott, who, after expounding the unique importance of the engineer in the reconstruction of society, was distressed to find that the left-wing leaders clung to the old-fashioned opinion that the proletariat would have to make the revolution. At another meeting Reed unfolded a plan for rescuing Debs from jail, presenting it so vividly that, for an hour, the committee listened to every detail.

Despite the liveliness of his mind, which had room for the notions of a Howard Scott and for schemes of jail-delivery, his comrades on the committee found Reed a devoted, informed revolutionary. Never a Marxist scholar, he was perfectly clear, thanks to his experiences in Russia, on the fundamentals of scientific Socialism. And he had an extraordinary feeling for the working class. The kind of sympathy he had felt in Paterson and Ludlow had ripened into actual unity with the workers. He understood their point of view and the way their minds worked so completely that they never hesitated to accept him as one of themselves.

With his understanding of the Marxist conception of classes and the struggle between them, Reed naturally speculated on the forces that had made him a traitor to his own class. He knew that Marx had foreseen the adherence of a certain section of the intelligentsia to the proletarian cause, and he could see how, in statistical terms, that could come about, but he was interested in what had happened to him as an individual. It was clear that his rebelliousness, which went back into his early boyhood, had much to do with it, and for that he could be grateful to the example of his father and perhaps to certain repressive influences in his environment. His passion for experience had also played a part, never allowing him to accept an easy, blinding routine. But rebelliousness and the desire for a richer life were characteristic of most of the writers of Reed's generation. When he tried to decide why he, unlike most of the others, had taken the revolutionary path to the fulfillment of their common hopes, he could only see that he had been fortunate in his experiences. The East Side, Paterson, Mexico, Ludlow, and the war had taught him much, preparing him for the crowning good fortune of being in Russia during the revolution.

When Upton Sinclair called him "the playboy of the social revolution," Reed was hurt. That he had been a playboy he was not inclined to deny, but he was not playing with revolution. He made little pretense to leadership, and was satisfied to do whatever work was assigned to him. The fact that he had been through the Russian revolution and had written of it so well in *Ten Days That Shook the World* made him enormously useful to the left wing, and he took his responsibilities as public spokesman with great seriousness. But he was unwilling to be merely a front; he did his share of the drudgery.

Significantly, his greatest interest was in the actual technique of working-class control. In an article in the *Revolutionary Age* he pointed out that, despite the high efficiency of the American worker, control would be difficult because of the specialization of labor. He recommended the formation of shop-committees to study problems of production, manufacture, cost, and price.

In this way the worker would discover the inefficiency of capitalism, realize the extent to which he was being robbed, and at the same time learn how to control the industry in which he worked. "It is not only necessary," Reed wrote, "to plan the political downfall of the capitalist class, but also to get into the minds of the workers some conception of the industrial framework which will underlie the new Socialist political commonwealth."

If he had felt that he was unnecessary to the movement, his mail would have destroyed the notion. In the first three months of 1919 he received forty-four invitations to address meetings. There were a dozen letters from workers who were puzzled about this detail or that of the Socialist program. Russians asked him how to communicate with their families, and revolutionaries sought his help in getting into Russia. There was a Finnish boy, amazed because the Boston *Transcript* rejected his article on revolution, who wanted Reed to help him get it published. A Spanish Jew, writing in French, offered to do translations from a Greek revolutionary paper. Such letters came every morning, and almost every morning there were letters of abuse that testified as unmistakably to his effectiveness.

During February Reed was contemplating a lecture trip to the Pacific Coast. His mother, eager though she was to see him, urged him not to come to Portland, for "they are arresting Bolsheviks out here." Irritated by the suggestion that only in Portland were Bolsheviks arrested, Reed replied sharply. Usually their affection for each other conquered the hostility that each felt for the other's ideas, but this time disagreement flared into a quarrel. They were reconciled only when she learned that her brother-in-law, a general in the regular army, had been publicly attacking Reed.

Reed did not make the trip, for, after the Overman hearing and the Philadelphia trial, he was occupied with the work of the left wing. Louise Bryant, however, left for the West early in March, speaking in Detroit, Chicago, Minneapolis, and St. Louis, and then in Seattle, Portland, San Francisco, and other cities on the Coast. A fortnight later Reed went as far as Minneapolis, addressing meetings in Cleveland, Detroit, Toledo, and Chicago, but he was back in Croton within ten days, writing Louise that the crocuses were up.

One reason for remaining in the East was that he had, for the moment, profitable employment. Solon Fieldman, president of Press Forum, a newspaper service syndicate, asked Reed to take part in a debate on "Bolshevism—Promise or Peril?" Fieldman originally planned to secure Madame Breshkovskaya, or possibly Charles Edward Russell, as Reed's opponent, but in the end Henry L. Slobodin, a Socialist who had withdrawn from the party because of the St. Louis declaration against war, took the assignment. After a definition and an outline had been agreed upon, each debater was to submit a first argument on the first topic. This was to be delivered to the other debater, who, in his second argument could both answer his opponent and introduce new material. The third argument was to serve purely as a rebuttal. The topics proposed included internationalism, government, democracy, militarism, industry, agriculture, the family, social welfare, education, religion, culture, and scientific progress, each in its relation to Bolshevism.

Fieldman, who had had considerable success with smilar debates, proposed to pay fifteen cents a word. Reed, though a little skeptical about the practical possibilities of the scheme, hired Fred Boyd as research-assistant and set to work. Slobodin was a rhetorician—he defined Bolshevism as "the maniac's delirium, the fool's paradise, the apache's valhalla"—and Reed had no difficulty in meeting his arguments. But he wanted to use to the full his opportunity to reach what Fieldman confidently asserted would be a large number of readers, and, though Boyd was thoroughly trained in Marxism and Reed had mastered the history of Bolshevism in Russia, both of them spent many hours in the library, documenting and sharpening Reed's arguments.

Reed worked on the debate through most of March, submitting ten or twelve of the brief articles. They were accurate and logical, and he was justified in writing Louise Bryant, "The debate with Slobodin is going very well; up to date he has said absolutely nothing, and I have him licked to a frazzle." But by the end of the month Fieldman, discovering that newspapers were interested in only one side of that particular question, abandoned the plan. Reed, however, had been paid several hundred dollars, and had advanced a little further in the mastery of Marxism.

As much of his time as possible he spent in Croton. "How I hate to leave the country!" he wrote his wife, after describing "two hectic days in town, spent speaking at meetings, attending the executive committee of the left wing, and reading in the library for my debate." Louise Bryant, in the meantime, had seen his family and was relieved to find them friendly. His brother Harry was disillusioned because his good war-record did not get him a job and had taken to selling securities. Mrs. Reed was having financial difficulties, and some of the money Reed earned from his debate went to her.

On the fourth of April the indictment in the Hunt's Point Palace case was quashed, and Reed was for the moment a free man. Early in April he spoke at two meetings to welcome L. C. Martens, the representative of the Soviet government, and he went to Philadelphia for "Red Week." On April 19, the New York *Communist* appeared, the official organ of the city's left wing, with John Reed as editor, Eadmonn MacAlpine as associate editor, and Maximilian Cohen as business manager. The editorials set forth the position of the left wing, praised the *Revolutionary Age,* endorsed the proposal for a national left-wing conference, and called for a demonstration on behalf of Debs. The paper was barred from the Rand School and condemned by officials of the Socialist Party.

When the second issue appeared, a week later, the conservatives, not content with controlling the *Call,* founded a paper of their own, called the New York *Socialist.* Adopting the jeering tone of its rival, it surpassed the *Communist* in personal attack. "A crisis has arisen in the Socialist Party," it proclaimed. "An enemy has appeared within our ranks. At a time when unity of purpose and unity of action are prime necessities, this enemy has raised the black banner of anarchy among us. It is to meet this enemy that the *Socialist* is published." Reed was described as "a well-known journalist who is in the party about six months." Other left-wing leaders were condemned as anarchists, petty bourgeois, and criminals. Even the charge of Moscow gold was made.

Reed's new seriousness could not withstand the temptation that the *Socialist* offered. On May 17, the *Socialist* appeared and was sold as usual at the Rand School. Several thousand copies were distributed before it was discovered that this particular issue had been prepared, not by Berenberg, Waldman, and the regular staff, but by John Reed and Eadmonn MacAlpine. The leading article, printed under an exact replica of the *Socialist* heading, purported to be a speech delivered by Louis Waldman on April Fool's Day. "I do not wish to descend to personalities," Mr. Waldman was made to say. "This is not a matter of persons, but of principles. But let us call the roll of the so-called 'leaders' of the so-called 'left wing.'" After denunciations of Hourwich, Larkin, Reed, MacAlpine, Gitlow, and Rose Pastor Stokes, and a learned exposition of Marxism, he continued: "You have heard here tonight a great deal of talk about insurrection, mass action, and the like. Well, comrades, you know me. I have been on every barricade so far erected in this country, and I shall be the first man to mount whatever barricades may be thrown up in the future." He concluded with an attack on the left wing: "So evident is their intention to disrupt the party that it has been necessary to expel all left-wing branches and exclude the members from any vote on party affairs. If this is not disrupting the party, what is?"

The *Socialist* might be the fair butt of Reed's humor, but the situation was not humorous and Reed knew it. On the one hand, there was the increasingly brutal repression of all radical activities. On May Day uniformed soldiers and sailors roamed through the streets of New York, breaking up meetings and beating Socialists. A group of them attacked the *Call's* printing plant, injuring a number of employees, while police stood by and watched them. In Boston the police openly cooperated with the mob that raided a peaceful procession, firing upon women and children, and arresting more than one hundred of the marchers. In Cleveland, where more than twenty thousand workers marched, the police and the Loyal American League shot two men, severely injured at least a score, and arrested one hundred and fifty.

And on the other hand, the revolutionary movement was split into two warring camps. So sharp had the conflict become that on May 21 Morris Hillquit, under the guise of counseling a peaceful separation of the two factions, gave the signal for the expulsion of the left wing. His article in the *Call* was intelligent and adroit. He did not defend the Second International and he did not attack Russia. The failure of the European Socialist parties in the war he attributed to the opportunism of the labor movement. The great necessity, therefore, was the re-education of labor, and for this the moment was ripe. But the left wing, which he described as "a purely emotional reflex of the situation in Russia," stood in the way of this great program of propaganda. "I am opposed to it," he declared, "not because it is too radical, but because it is essentially reactionary; not because it would lead us too far, but because it would lead us nowhere." The preaching of reconciliation would be futile, for antagonism was too intense. Better for the comrades to separate: "The time for action is near. Let us clear the decks."

The national executive committee of the Socialist Party, meeting in Chicago in the last week of May, followed Hillquit's instructions by expelling the entire Socialist Party of the state of Michigan and suspending seven foreign-language federations with a membership of thirty thousand. In explaining the suspension of the language federations, Adolph Germer, national executive secretary, called attention to the remarkable growth of these organizations, which had doubled their membership. This he regarded as a dangerous symptom, since their almost unanimous support of the left wing indicated that they could not rise above "nativistic and nationalistic prejudices." The Michigan organization was expelled because of two resolutions it had adopted, one forbidding its members to support reform measures, the other requiring speakers to take a firm and presumably hostile attitude towards religion. Socialists in Michigan opposed to these two resolutions were urged to organize so that they could be represented at the national convention. A little later the Massachusetts and Ohio charters were revoked, because a majority in both organizations had voted to affiliate with the left wing; in both states the right-wing minority was recognized. By these measures the national executive committee reduced the membership of the Socialist Party to less than half of what it had been on May Day. The committee also ruled that the elections that had taken place were invalid. The left wing had elected all four international delegates—Reed receiving the largest number of votes—and twelve out of fifteen members of the national executive committee. The existing committee, which was supposed to retire June 30, announced that it would remain in office until the emergency convention, called for August 30.

The members of the left wing were indignant. Reed was not amused by the irony of a leadership that defended democracy by disregarding the will of the majority and that used Tammany tactics to maintain its power; he was angry. He believed that the rank and file of the Socialist Party were ready for a new revolutionary policy. The adoption of this policy he regarded as important, whether the revolution came in five or in twenty-five years. It was easy for Hillquit to say that the leaders of the left wing were thinking in terms of Russia, and it was true that many of them advocated policies that were entirely inappropriate to the American situation. But the fundamental concepts of Leninism that Reed adhered to had not been created in the stress of the Bolshevik uprising; they had been stated by Lenin as early as 1901 in *What Is to Be Done?* They derived, indeed, from what Marx had said in *The Civil War in France* in 1871 and *The Critique of the Gotha Program* in 1875. Their first statement had been made by Marx and Engels in the *Communist Manifesto* of 1848.

Reed had known for a long time that it was the breakdown of capitalism that created a revolutionary situation, but he had learned in Russia that only a proletariat that was led by a disciplined, clear-thinking, Marxist party could take advantage of the breakdown. The Bolshevik Party of Russia had not suddenly sprung out of the chaos of the spring of 1917; it had been shaped for twenty years by Lenin's Marxist insight, tested in the revolution of 1905, and prepared by a decade of action for its task. On the other hand, the kind of thinking that Hillquit, Germer,

Waldman, and the other officials were doing, and the policies they recommended, had proven a failure in every country of Europe. It was foolish to argue as to when the revolution would come; the important thing was to prepare for it; certainly it would never come if no one was ready.

IN THE first three months after publication, nine thousand copies of *Ten Days That Shook the World* were sold. The book had been surprisingly well reviewed in the Philadelphia *Public Ledger*, the Los Angeles *Times*, the New York *American*, the New York *Sun*, and the *Review of Reviews*. Several papers, following the lead of the New York *Times*, reviewed it with John Spargo's *Bolshevism*, using Spargo to offset Reed. Others, adopting the tactics that Spargo himself employed in the *Tribune*, praised it as reporting but damned its interpretation. Only a few reviews were completely hostile: the Chicago *Tribune's* reviewer took the occasion to pray for the sudden death of Lenin and Trotsky, and the Boston *Transcript's* asked why Liveright had stooped so low as to publish the volume.

With the May 15 issue of the New York *Communist*, Reed began a series of articles entitled, "Why Political Democracy Must Go." Like all of his theoretical writing, the series was not brilliant, but it was serious and thoughtful. The first article traced the rise of the labor movement, interpreting the policies of the A.F. of L. in terms of American economic conditions. The second, concerned with Socialism in America, was a brief historical survey, preparing the way for the discussion in the third and fourth of parliamentary Socialism and the failure of Congressmen London and Berger and Mayors Lunn and Van Lear. The last two articles described the capitalist nature of the state, both in terms of the origin of the nation and in terms of the contemporary situation.

Sketchy as the articles were, they showed Reed's appreciation of Marxism as a method of interpreting history and his understanding of the importance of re-examining the American past. He knew far too little about American history—one of the subjects that his preparatory school teachers had managed to make hopelessly dull—to construct a convincing analysis, but he had caught a glimpse of the interplay of social forces in the growth of the United States. And in the closing articles, as well as in another piece he wrote for the *Communist*, "The I.W.W. and Bolshevism," he showed how thoroughly he had learned the lesson of the Russian revolution. Repeating the arguments of Lenin's *State and Revolution*, he defended the dictatorship of the proletariat as the necessary instrument of the revolution—in Russia, the United States, or anywhere else.

On June 16 he went to Atlantic City for the convention of the American Federation of Labor. The convention had met on June 9, with the usual congratulatory telegram from the President of the United States and the usual attack on the Reds by Gompers. There was much debate on a motion for the recognition of Russia, and Wilfred Humphries attempted to get the floor to tell about the Soviet government. Failing in this, he arranged a separate meeting on Russia, and wired Reed, asking him to come and speak. Unfortunately, Humphries innocently hired a hall in a non-union hotel, and the officials, using this as an excuse, demanded a boycott of the meeting. There was a fair attendance, but with very few delegates. The next day the convention voted to urge the withdrawal of troops from Europe, especially Russia, but defeated the motion for recognition.

The few days at Atlantic City gave Reed the first rest he had had in many months, and—far more important to him than rest —a chance to swim. With Carl Sandburg, who was reporting the convention for the Chicago *Daily News*, Bill Gropper, and Louis Stark, he went swimming twice a day. There was also an opportunity for a satirical expression of the contempt he had long felt for the leadership of the federation. In an article for the *Liberator*, illustrated by Bill Gropper, he described Gompers, sitting in his "tall, carved, grand-ducal chair," as "the most grotesque figure that ever presided at any human gathering—squat, with the face of a conceited bull-frog, the sparse gray hair hanging from his bald head in wisps, as if it were glued on." After portraying the officials one by one, he summed them up: "They were expensively dressed, and their figures portly. Long absence from their trades had filled out the hollows of their cheeks, leaving heavy jowls, and the strong lines made by hard work coarsened and overlaid with self-indulgent fat. Sinister suggestions of graft, of murderous violence bought and paid for, of political trading, of strikes betrayed, union treasuries looted, hung about them." And with all the sharp vividness there was sound analysis. He called the article "The Convention of the Dead."

Reed returned to New York for the left-wing conference, which had been initiated by revolutionary groups in Boston and Cleveland. It began on June 21 with ninety-four delegates from twenty states in attendance. William Bross Lloyd, of Chicago, was chosen chairman, and Reed was elected to the committee on labor. The report of the committee, which was accepted by the conference, stated: "The purpose of the left-wing organization is to create a revolutionary working-class movement in America, which, through the action of the working masses themselves, will lead to workers' control of industry and the state, as the only means of expropriating capitalist property and abolishing classes in society. . . . With the legislatures, courts, police, and armies under control of the capitalists, the workers can only win the state power by extra-parliamentary action, which must have its basis in the industrial mass action of the workers." The report called for revolutionary industrial unionism, the organization of shop-committees and workers' councils, and the formation of a permanent labor committee with the power to issue a general propaganda periodical for the special purpose of reaching workers on their jobs. Reed was appointed to this committee and was given charge of the paper it proposed to publish.

Although there was no disagreement about revolutionary principles, the conference of the left wing was not harmonious. Certain delegates, especially those who represented the foreign-language federations, had despaired of winning over the Socialist Party, and proposed to issue at once a call for a convention to organize a Communist Party. Reed hotly opposed this, believing that it was still possible to depose the bureaucrats of the party and to re-organize it as a revolutionary instrument. The call for a separate convention would, he argued, antagonize those members who, without supporting the policies of the right wing, desired to preserve the unity of the party.

The proposal for the immediate organization of a new party was defeated by a vote of fifty-five to thirty-eight. Thirty-one delegates, representing the Slavic federations and the state of Michigan, withdrew from the conference. Reed and the other members of the majority went on with their plans for forging a revolutionary party. Before the conference adjourned on June 24, it elected a national council to conduct its affairs in the interval before the emergency convention of August 30. It also announced another left-wing conference, to meet in Chicago August 31, which would support the Socialist Party if the left wing had won control, and otherwise would organize a Communist Party. As a theoretical basis for the activities of the left wing, the council issued a long manifesto, analyzing the effects of the war, the collapse of the Second International, the development of Socialism in America, and the rise of the left wing, and discussing the problems of political and industrial action and the nature of proletarian dictatorship.

On July 7, the group that had withdrawn from the left-wing conference published in *Novy Mir* a call for a national convention to organize a Communist Party. It attacked the majority of the left wing as "centrists, struggling for a false unity." The majority, in reply, charged the minority with desertion. Fraina, writing in the *Revolutionary Age*, pointed out that the majority had always intended to organize a new party if it proved impossible to rescue the Socialist Party from the right wing, and jeered at the inconsistency of the alliance between the Slavic federations and what he called the Menshevik Michigan organization. The minority proceeded to issue a paper, which they called the *Communist*, the New York *Communist* having been combined with the *Revolutionary Age*. "Those who realize," this new *Communist* said, "that the capturing of the Socialist Party as such is but an empty victory will not hesitate to respond to our call and leave the right and center to sink together with their 'revolutionary' leaders."

So bitterness grew. Reed pawned his watch and he and Louise went to Truro on Cape Cod for a few weeks with their Portland friends, Carl and Helen Walters, who had recently come east. For a little while he seemed as carefree as he had ever been, spending long hours swimming and lying on the dunes. He did not spend much time with the people in Provincetown, but he walked over one evening to talk with Susan Glaspell and George Cram Cook. "I wish I could stay here," he said. "Maybe it will surprise you, but what I really want is to write poetry." They asked him why he didn't. "I've promised too many people," he said.

It was true: John Reed was committed. He could not turn back now; all he could do was to look ahead. He regretted nothing, knowing that he could not have done differently. Indeed, he had constantly enjoyed himself. But all this activity was extraneous to his main purpose. It was necessary, and he had to do his share, but he longed for a time when it would be possible not merely for him but for all poets to write poetry.

HE COULD not stay long in Truro; there was too much to be done in New York. After the combination of the New York *Communist* with the *Revolutionary Age*, he was at first, because of a misunderstanding, not a member of the staff, but Fraina soon made him a contributing editor with a salary. At the same time he made preparations for the first issue of the *Voice of Labor*, the journal of the labor committee of the left wing, and wrote for it a long article on shop committees in Russia.

At the end of July the unofficial executive committee, made up of the left-wing Socialists who had received the majority vote in the spring elections, met in Chicago. It announced that Reed, Fraina, Ruthenberg, and Wagenknecht had been elected international delegates and Kate Richards O'Hare international secretary. Germer, the official executive secretary, was requested to turn over national headquarters to this committee, and a motion was passed, stating, "We declare the office of national executive secretary vacant, inasmuch as the present incumbent violates his functions by refusing to tabulate the vote on referendums expressing the will of the membership, and refuses to recognize the regularly elected N.E.C." Alfred Wagenknecht was appointed temporary executive secretary. The committee also voted to reinstate the expelled and suspended organizations and to affiliate with the Communist International.

All this was, of course, merely a gesture, but a significant one insofar as it showed a determination to carry out to the end the attempt to capture the Socialist Party. Since several members of this unofficial national executive committee were also members of the national council of the left wing, which represented the majority group at the June conference, the council seemed to be further committed to the policy the conference adopted. But almost immediately after the new N.E.C. meeting, representatives of the council began negotiations with representatives of the Slavic federations, who made certain compromises. The result was a majority vote in the national council to support the call for a Communist Party convention. Although the council continued to urge left-wing members to attend the emergency convention of the Socialist Party, the fact that they were committed to a separate convention and the organization of a new party, regardless of the outcome of the Socialist convention, meant that their old position had been abandoned.

On August 23, the *Revolutionary Age* carried the joint call for a Communist Party convention, to be held in Chicago September 1. The same issue announced the resignation of Reed, Gitlow, and MacAlpine in protest against the action of the national council. The members of the council who signed the joint call, Ruthenberg, Fraina, Cohen, and the others, justified their action on the ground that it was the only way to preserve the unity of the left wing. To Reed, however, it seemed a fundamental abandonment of principle. Not only did he believe that the plan of working as long as possible within the Socialist Party was sound; he held that the national council had been committed to this program by all the preparations for the left-wing conference, by the conference itself, and by the steps that had been taken since the conference.

Certainly the joint call did not achieve the unity of the left wing. The Slavic federations, the officials of the expelled Michigan organization of the Socialist Party, and now the majority of the National Council of the Left Wing had agreed that a Communist Party must be formed. But the minority of the council was opposed to this decision, and in this respect the minority almost certainly represented a majority of the members of the

left wing, exclusive of those who belonged to the Slavic federations. Moreover, the left wing had had many sympathizers who
remained in the Socialist Party, and there were many other
members who might in time have been won for a Communist
program. The decision to form a Communist Party, without
waiting for whatever action might be taken by the national
emergency convention of the Socialist Party, confused and
offended a number of these sympathizers, and the animosity that
developed between the two factions of the left wing completed
their alienation.

That was the situation when, on August 30, the national
emergency convention, the first to be held since the St. Louis
meeting in 1917, opened in Chicago. Reed and some eighty members of the left wing arrived early at Machinists' Hall and held
a caucus, in which it was decided that they should simply invade
the convention without arguing about credentials. "The way to
get the hall," Reed said, "is to go and get it." They marched
upstairs and were met at the door by Julius Gerber, secretary
of the New York local, who had charge of seating arrangements.
An altercation followed, in which talk led to a brief flourish of
fists. One observer remarked that Gerber could have licked Reed
if Reed hadn't held him so far up in the air that he couldn't
reach down. Gerber was reported to have said that he made
Reed understand that swinging a sledge-hammer with the proletariat was as good training as playing football in college. In any
case, Reed and his left-wing followers entered the hall.

A few minutes later Adolph Germer, national executive secretary, arrived, accompanied by two policemen. After requesting
the left-wing delegates to leave, he turned to the officers and
asked them to clear the hall. Once Reed and his followers had
been ejected, Germer declared the convention open. There was
applause when he said, "We intend to follow the splendid
example set by our comrades in Russia," but silence met his
qualification, "I want it distinctly understood that we do not
intend to adopt the same methods." Much of his speech consisted in proving by references to the St. Louis platform that
the party was really revolutionary. The leaders of the left wing
he denounced as thieves and gangsters.

While Jack Reed, hatless and wearing a picturesque Norfolk jacket, led the expelled delegates to another room downstairs, the convention proceeded to elect a temporary chairman. Seymour Stedman was the candidate of the right wing and J. M. Coldwell of the left. The party, it should be remembered, had been reduced from 109,589 members to 39,750, and the expelled members were all supporters of the left wing. Every delegation, moreover, had been carefully scrutinized, and several had been unseated though they came from states that had not been expelled. Finally, the national executive committee had permitted the right wing in expelled states to elect the number of delegates to which the membership of January 1 would have entitled them, so that, for example, Michigan's 139 right-wing Socialists had seven delegates, the quota due 3500. And in spite of all this, Coldwell received thirty-seven votes to Stedman's eighty-eight.

Even after Coldwell had marched out thirty delegates, in protest against the refusal of the convention to make the examination of contested elections the first order of business, there remained considerable sentiment against the party bureaucracy. Again and again delegates protested against the use of police. "I just heard one of these policemen threaten to throw a comrade downstairs," a delegate stated, "and he said, 'You won't light on your feet either, you'll think you came down in an airplane.' I ask you if this is the way visiting Socialists are going to be treated by this convention." "What kind of Socialists are they?" a New York official asked. The Chicago machinists, in whose hall the convention was meeting, protested against the presence of police. Claessens, Hoan, and Berger defended Germer's action. "We in Milwaukee," Berger said, "would have done it a good deal better than Germer did, because we have our own police. If the police had not been here, we would not be here now. The two-fisted Reed and the other two-fisted left wingers would be here."

The remainder of the sessions were for the most part devoted to self-justification on the part of the officials. Judge Panken of New York denounced the left wing as "a bunch of anarchists," and other speakers followed his lead. Nevertheless, the convention refused to be satisfied by the national executive committee's explanation of its expulsions and suspensions and voted an investigation. It also voted to bring before the membership by referendum a minority as well as a majority report on international relations. The minority report called for affiliation with the Communist International, whereas the other proposed the formation of a new international, which the Communist Party of Russia should be invited to join. A national executive committee, composed with one exception of new members, was elected.

While the regular convention was proving how much militancy existed among the rank and file, the left-wing delegates, including both those who had been expelled and those who had left in protest, met, on the evening of the thirty-first, in another room of the same building. There was no machine here, and the session was often disorderly, but it was enthusiastic, spontaneous, alive. The gathering proclaimed itself the true national emergency convention of the Socialist Party, and elected Owens of Illinois as chairman. After sending greetings to Debs and the other class-war prisoners, the delegates discussed the question of left-wing unity. C. E. Ruthenberg, who was present despite the fact that he had signed the Communist call, urged the delegates not to organize a party until after the Communist Party convention had met. This raised the issue that was uppermost in many minds, the issue of submission to the Slavic federations. Jack Carney declared that, if the convention went over to the federations, he would go home and tell the workers of Duluth that there was no revolutionary party in existence. Reed proposed to amend Ruthenberg's suggestion by proclaiming this the party of Communism and inviting all other revolutionary groups to join it. With some changes, his motion was adopted.

The next morning, while Reed's group proceeded to the routine business of electing committees, the Communist Party opened its sessions. Just as Dennis E. Batt, one of the Michigan delegates, was about to proclaim the convention opened, police arrived, arrested Batt, and destroyed decorations and placards. Rose Pastor Stokes cried, "They are arresting our comrades—

three cheers for the revolution." "Shut up," the police-sergeant shouted; "it's always a woman that starts the trouble."

The Communist Party convention showed no desire to conciliate the other section of the left wing, and Reed and his associates felt there was nothing to do but form a separate party. On September 2 this was done. The delegates, meeting in the I.W.W. hall on Throop Street, proclaimed themselves the Communist Labor Party. John Reed was made chairman of the committee to draw up a program, and it was his report that precipitated the principal struggle of the convention. For this gathering, too, was divided. On the one hand, there were those who wanted to create a revolutionary party, based on the teachings of Marx and guided by the experience of Lenin and the Bolsheviks. On the other were persons who had left the Socialist Party chiefly as a protest against the high-handed conduct of its officials, and who were a little afraid of too concrete a commitment to revolution.

Reed's program called for the training of the working class for the seizure of power. Margaret Prevey was among those who objected. "We must use political power in order to get a hearing for the working class," she insisted. "I want to see a working-class judge to pass sentence upon the workers, a working-class jailor to open the doors of the prisons for the working class. I want to see the working class get control of the police and the United States army, so that they can be used on the side of the workers, instead of against them in their industrial battles."

Reed rose, gave a hitch to his pants, and answered her in his one burst of oratory. "When the Socialist mayor of Minneapolis," he told her, "wanted to use the police to protect the meeting of the workers, his policemen were superseded by a body of special deputies appointed by the governor of the state. When a radical governor of Illinois, Governor Altgeld, tried to use the state power to protect the workers in the Pullman strike in Chicago, Grover Cleveland sent the United States army into Illinois to protect capital. And if you had a Socialist president in the place of Grover Cleveland, the Supreme Court would come to the protection of capital. And if you had a Socialist Supreme Court, J. P. Morgan would organize a volunteer White Guard, and the interests of capital would still be protected. So it will always be. The struggle is between economic forces and cannot be settled on the political field."

Another of Reed's opponents was Louis Boudin, of New York, famed as a student of Marx. Boudin laughed at one of the phrases Reed had incorporated in the platform. Reed said nothing, but left the building, returning with a copy of the *Communist Manifesto*, in which he showed Boudin the precise words to which he had objected. Boudin was completely routed when Ben Gitlow rose, and accused him of using his knowledge of Marx to destroy the integrity of the platform. In its fundamentals, Reed's program was adopted. "Wonderful convention," he wired Louise Bryant that night; "everything going fine."

After that, after it had been decided that the Communist Labor Party was a revolutionary party, the sessions did go smoothly, so smoothly that they sometimes failed to hold Reed's interest. One afternoon he got hold of Sherwood Anderson, who was living in Chicago, and showed him some unpublished poems. Anderson liked them, and his saying so pleased Reed. After they had talked for a time in a toilet, in the convention building, Reed said, "Hell, Sherwood, they've got to the resolutions stage up there; let's go out in the park." They walked for half an hour, talking about poetry, until Reed said, "Well, well, that's enough of this. I guess I'd better get back in there and see what's doing."

The party accepted the principles of the Third International, proclaimed the dictatorship of the proletariat as its aim, and adopted a program of action. Although its manifesto differed in no fundamental way from that of the Communist Party, negotiations for the merger of the two groups were futile. The Slavic federations, even after the English-speaking delegates to the Communist convention had brought strong pressure, would agree to no compromise that threatened their power. After electing officers, with Wagenknecht as executive secretary and Reed as an international delegate, and after making a standing offer to discuss unity with the Communist Party, the convention of the Communist Labor Party adjourned.

Returning to New York, Reed, though troubled by the division of revolutionary forces, was elated. In the conventions he had felt the stirring of the revolutionary spirit in America, and he had no doubt that unity would soon be achieved. The convention of the Communist Labor Party, because it had been so loosely organized, had given him a constant sense of the upwelling of spontaneous zeal. At the same time, discipline, whose importance he had learned to recognize, had not been absent. It had given him satisfaction to be a part of all this, and not an unimportant part. He felt that things were moving, and he was glad.

REVOLUTIONARY'S RETURN

For two or three weeks Reed spent most of his time in the New York office of the Communist Labor Party. Although two months remained before the party was outlawed by the United States government, the operations of the city police, federal agents, vigilantes, and the Lusk committee forced Reed and his companions to work with as much secrecy as possible. Carlo Tresca, who was editing an Italian paper in a deserted building on Twelfth Street, invited them to share his hiding-place with him, and an issue of the *Voice of Labor* was brought out in this vacant loft. Every night there were meetings, held in the homes of sympathizers, at which Reed reported on the convention.

The conflict between the two Communist parties sent Reed to Russia late in September. Each party was convinced that it was truly Communist and that the other was the obstacle to unity of the revolutionary forces. Since both parties were eager to affiliate with the Communist International, and since the recognition of one by the International would discredit the other, both hastened to send emissaries to Moscow. Reed, as a regularly elected international delegate, was chosen to represent the Communist Labor Party.

All this was decided in the three weeks after his return from Chicago. They were busy weeks, spent in attending committee meetings, speaking to little groups of sympathizers, writing articles, publishing the *Voice of Labor*, and dodging the police. Don Marquis, riding on the top of a Fifth Avenue bus, caught sight of Reed on the street, and got off to speak to him. When Marquis asked him what he was doing, Reed laughed and said he was in hiding. "This is the dickens of a place to hide," Marquis said. "None better," Reed told him, "and besides, the redhunters never catch anybody."

George Falconer, the Denver Socialist who had sold *Ten Days That Shook the World* on a trip through the Rocky Mountains, found Reed in Croton one afternoon, in the cabin he used for writing. He brought him a message from Haywood, sick in Leavenworth. Reed showed him the great piles of Russian magazines and pamphlets and talked to him about Lenin, and they toasted Lenin and Bobby Burns in Scotch whiskey.

There were a hundred things Reed wanted to do. He wanted to write poetry. (In her listing of the year's awards Harriet Monroe had given honorable mention to "Proud New York," the fragment of "America, 1918" she had published in *Poetry*.) He wanted to write *From Kornilov to Brest-Litovsk*, his second book about the Russian revolution. He wanted to build the Communist Labor Party. But what he had to do, what the moment obviously demanded of him, was to return to Russia. He was not sorry that he would find out what the Bolsheviks had done in a year and a half, and he was as eager as any one else to win for the Communist Labor Party the recognition of the International, but he would not have chosen to return at just that time. The decision was taken out of his hands; he was doing his revolutionary duty.

There was no possibility, of course, of his going as a passenger or under his own name. He went as a stoker on a Scandinavian ship. A few friends accompanied him to the dock, and he was full of laughter at his rough clothes and the bundle slung over his shoulder. It was nine years since he had last worked his way across the Atlantic, on the cattleboat *Bostonian*. He was a different John Reed, and in body as well as mind, for he had never entirely recovered from the removal of his kidney, and irregular habits of eating, drinking, and sleeping had weakened him. It would be a different kind of voyage, too: no tents on deck, no special favors, no extra food; just the ordinary fare of an ordinary stoker. But he was as gay as if he were a college boy starting out for a summer's sport, not a police-hunted revolutionary, bound for a land of famine and civil war, which he could reach only by passing through the hostile armies that surrounded it.

It was a slow and arduous trip across the ocean, but Reed found that the hard work agreed with him. Jim Gormley was the name on his seaman's identification card, and his companions in the stokehold had no complaints about Jim's doing his share of the work. They knew that he was not altogether what he pretended to be, but that did not trouble them. They were not particularly surprised when, at Bergen, he went ashore and did not come back. It was not the first time such things had happened.

Reed reached Christiania in the middle of October, and immediately got in touch with left-wing Socialists in the city. He found that the police had become more vigilant in arresting men without proper credentials, and of course even Jim Gormley's papers were not in order since his desertion of the ship. As quickly as possible, he placed the documents he was carrying in safe keeping, and then devoted himself, before he took the next stage of his trip, to discovering the situation in Norway and the rest of Europe.

Before he left Christiania, he managed to send a letter to Louise Bryant by courier, a strange letter, full of personal endearments for her and of news for the leaders of the C.L.P. "From now on," he wrote, "it seems to me we must never be separated. . . . This is not altogether a joke trip, but more or less a grim business. . . . The Communist Party will get no sympathy here or anywhere in Scandinavia. I am the big cheese in these parts. . . . The *Voice of Labor* is greatly admired here. . . . I was never in better health and am doing well. . . . Write me very seldom. Inform mother I am well. Back before Christmas, I hope."

But the body of the letter described political conditions. The Russian situation he called heartrending. The report that Yudenitch had taken Petrograd, which he had heard on his arrival in Christiania, had been denied by the time he wrote, but the city had nearly fallen. Denikin, moreover, was within two hundred and fifty miles of Moscow. "In Hungary," he wrote, "thanks to the American Food Controller, who smashed the Hungarian

Soviet government, there is at present the most terrible white terror." In Germany, on the other hand, the Communists seemed to be gaining. In Norway and Sweden the left wing controlled the Socialist Party, but, he explained, "there can be no revolution in Scandinavia and other small countries until the great capitalist countries go, for these small countries have to import their food and could be starved at once."

On the night of October 22, Reed crossed the boundary into Norway on foot. In Christiania he had met Hungarians, Finns, Russians, and Letts who had performed prodigies of heroism in going to and from Russia. They told him of comrades who had been shot and others who had been arrested. But he reached Stockholm without mishap, and remained there for more than a week. Again he studied the revolutionary forces, and again he realized the peculiar complexity of the situation. Once more he managed to write Louise, mingling expressions of his affection and his sorrow at their separation with news of radical progress in Scandinavia and of developments in Russia. And as usual he made new friends, friends who would always remember him despite the briefness of their meeting.

On the first of November, comrades helped him to stow away on a ship bound for Finland. All through the hours of that Baltic crossing he lay huddled in a pile of greasy rags, without food or drink. When the ship was near Abo, he climbed, as he had been instructed, into a shaft that led from the engine-room to the deck, and for four hours he clung to the rails of the ladder. Gusts of hot air came from below, and as the steam condensed on the brass plate above his head, drops of water fell on him. Feet shuffled across the plate, and he could hear men talking and coughing. Once there was the gleam of flashlights below him—Finnish police looking for just such stowaways as he.

At last he heard somebody hiss sharply in the silence below. Stiff and dizzy he climbed down. A match was lighted, and he found his overcoat in the pile of rags. "Quick, Christ's sake, quick!" a voice said. A hand took his, and he mounted a ladder and a companion-way, and came out on the snowy deck. Two steam-cranes were dipping into the forward hold, and longshoremen were heaving at great packing-cases, said to be parts of tanks to be used in the attack on Petrograd.

Seeing soldiers and policemen on the dock, Reed remembered that this was Finland, land of the broken revolution, country of bourgeois terror. Two workmen were supposed to be on the dock to meet him. They would recognize him from a description that had been given them, and, when they saw him, they would walk away. He was to follow. He saw workmen, but there were half a dozen of them, and none seemed to be looking for him. His guide led him to the gangway, saw a policeman, and pulled him back. As they retreated, Reed felt the hand in his trembling. Hurrying through the ship, they came at last to the cargo-deck, where men were rigging the tackle of the great cranes. "Go," his companion whispered, and pushed Reed into the busy throng of men.

He walked across the gangplank, shoving past the customs officials as if he were one of the crew attending to his job. A policeman eyed him suspiciously, but he hurried on. Two men detached themselves from a group of loafers and walked away. Reed followed, pulling his coat collar about his black, oily face. In the little market-square he saw two young men in shining boots, long, dark gray coats with green facings, swords, and peaked caps. On his left arm each had a broad white band, with a monogram in a black circle—S.K., symbol of the Salvation Corps, the bourgeois militia which had provoked the red insurrection and then, with the help of the Germans, ruthlessly put it down, murdering twenty thousand workers after they had surrendered.

The men Reed was following walked steadily on, through wide, rough-cobbled streets, until at last they came to the outskirts of the town. They looked back over their shoulders, but made no sign. When they turned into a court-yard gate, he went after them into a dimly lighted little hall-way. Frightened and surprised, they stared at him. "Woodrow Wilson," he said, giving the appointed password. They looked at him in bewilderment, and one of them sharply asked a question in Finnish. "Woodrow Wilson," Reed said again, and gave the name of the boat he had come on. They shook their heads. One of them muttered to the other, who unlocked a door. In a moment they were inside, and Reed heard the key turn.

He was alone, without a passport, in a country whose language he did not know, and whose government was bitterly hostile to Russia, and he had failed to find his guides. There was nothing to do but go back to the dock, risking arrest, and look for the right men. This time he found them, frantic with anxiety, and they took him to the home of a Finnish writer, woman whose Bolshevik sympathies were not suspected. She fed him and put him in bed, and a day or two later helped him to reach Helsingfors.

In Helsingfors there was another comfortable home for him to stay in. He was impatient because he had been so long delayed, but he learned that it had been fortunate. Sudden police raids had captured the entire Communist organization in Viborg, and if he had been there, he would certainly have been jailed. Because of the disorganization of Viborg, there was nothing for him to do but remain for a fortnight in Helsingfors. He managed to write another letter to Louise, sending it by a messenger to be mailed in Stockholm. "I fret and fume," he wrote, "at my delay, and spend my time thinking of my honey and wanting her." He told of two Norwegian intellectuals who had praised her *Six Red Months in Russia*. "I have told everybody how my honey broke the Overman blockade," he said, "and shall tell at headquarters. Am very well and happy and still expect to be with you before Christmas. Don't try to come this way. It would be ghastly for you just now."

While Reed waited impatiently in Finland, his departure was discovered in New York. On November 8, led by the Lusk committee, seven hundred policemen raided seventy-one Communist Party and Communist Labor Party headquarters in New York City, seizing several tons of literature and arresting thirty-five men. Examination of C.L.P. records revealed that Reed was on his way to Moscow. This Lusk committee onslaught followed by one day A. Mitchell Palmer's raid on the Russian People's House, in which hundreds of Russian workmen were beaten with blackjacks. The series of raids, arrests, deportations, hysterical convictions, and long sentences that was to mark the

winter of 1919–20 had begun. It was not only in Finland that
there was a white terror.

AT LAST the time came when the comrades felt that it was safe
for Reed to move towards the Finnish-Russian front. Passed on
from sympathizer to sympathizer, he was guided safely through
the lines, and finally he reached the headquarters of the Red
Army. In the quarters of the agitation committee there were
several young men and a girl, who welcomed Reed. An officer,
who lay asleep across four chairs, woke up and greeted him. The
girl made coffee. Reed was tired, but it was so cold that he could
not sleep. The officer lay down again on the chairs, waking from
time to time as sentries arrived to make their reports. All through
the night there was the sound of firing not far off. Occasionally
one of the men spoke to Reed, but they all seemed busy with
their various duties. Reed gathered that they were engaged in
smuggling supplies from Finland. After the girl explained that
the coffee was all gone, he sat and shivered until morning.

Soon after sunrise he was driven in a sleigh to the railroad.
Along the road cavalry and artillery were marching towards the
front, and there were sentries every few hundred yards. For
miles camouflage experts had been at work, creating the appearance of a great forest, to protect the road. The station was
crowded, mostly with soldiers. Reed noticed that, where the
shrine used to be, there were revolutionary proclamations and
posters. When the train came, his companions bade him farewell, and he started on the last stage of his journey to Petrograd.

It was nearly two years since he had left it, and during those
years the country had been constantly at war. Scarcely had the
treaty of Brest-Litovsk been signed when a brigade of Czecho-
Slovak troops, moving from Kiev to Vladivostok, with the
intention of sailing for France, had involved themselves in hostilities against the Soviets and had become the center of counter-
revolutionary organization. Allied intervention had quickly followed, and Archangel and Murmansk had been captured in the
summer of 1918. After the signing of the armistice, the French
and British governments had been able to give more support to
the anti-Bolshevik forces, and in the spring of 1919 Kolchak

drove far into Soviet territory in Siberia, and Denikin pushed northward from the Black Sea. It was the concentration of the Red Army on these fronts that made impossible the sending of aid to the Soviet governments in Hungary and the Baltic countries, with the result that they were overthrown by bourgeois forces, supported by the Allies.

While Reed was on his way from America, a change had come. Archangel and Murmansk were abandoned in the early autumn, and Yudenitch's surprise attack on Petrograd was repulsed by an outpouring of the city's workers. Denikin's advance on Moscow was checked, and his defeat made possible the recapture of the Ukraine. With the collapse of Kolchak's army, Allied intervention in Siberia was almost at an end.

The Soviet government had been saved, but at a dreadful cost. Not only had Communism been defeated in the countries to the west; Russia itself was so weakened that the winter of 1919–20 would be the most terrible in its history. To all the inevitable difficulties of the organization of Socialism had been added the burden of civil war—the loss of life, the disorganization of the food supply, and the concentration of industry on war preparations. France and England, fearing disorders at home, had not dared to send sufficient troops to destroy the Soviets, but they did great damage, and their blockade, which continued, deprived Russia of the supplies that it needed for reconstruction.

From Petrograd Reed went on to Moscow, where he immediately presented the case for the Communist Labor Party to the executive committee of the International. He found the leaders changed. Lenin, especially, was more genial. He chuckled and gestured as he talked, and hitched up his chair until his knees touched Reed's. But his eyes were as terrible as ever, and Reed felt them boring through him. Trotsky and Kamenev both were plumper. Kamenev reminded Reed of a cocker spaniel and Karakhan of a heavy in the movies. They all listened carefully to what he had to say about America, particularly Lenin, who seemed to know exactly what was happening.

The executive committee offered him the privileges ordinarily extended to distinguished guests, a special apartment and better food, but he refused, taking a room in the working-class section of the city and preparing his own meals on a little iron stove. He was eager to return to America, but first there had to be an extended discussion of the party situation, and in the meantime he used his opportunity to see what the new Russia was like.

It was a cruel winter in Moscow. There was never quite enough food. The soldiers were given the best possible treatment, and the factory employees were organized to take care of themselves. Clerical workers, however, were often overlooked, and Reed pitied them. Because of the blockade, there were almost no medical supplies, and sanitary conditions were bad and epidemics common. Although the terror, which had been necessary to suppress counter-revolution, was relaxing, stories still came of the horrors of civil warfare.

Reed was constantly impressed by the heroism of the workers. The day after Christmas, he went to Serpukov to speak to delegates of all the factory shop-committees in that section. Men came from miles away, some walking twenty versts through the deep snow. In the great white hall that had once been the Nobles' Club they gathered, their faces gaunt and their clothes ragged, to listen to Reed talk about America. They asked him countless questions, about wages, bread, working conditions. "What do American workers think of us?" they asked, and "Why is America so slow to get Socialist ideas?" Reed stood there, the one dim kerosene light shining on his face, and talked. When he finished, a young worker jumped up and proposed a resolution: "Tell our brothers in America that for three years the Russian workers have been bleeding and dying for the revolution, and not our own revolution, but the world revolution. Tell our American comrades that we listen day and night for the sound of their footsteps coming to our aid. But tell them, too, that no matter how long it may take them, we shall hold firm. Never shall the Russian workers give up their revolution. We die for Socialism, which perhaps we shall never see." And as they sang "The Internationale," their desperate faces shone, though their voices were hoarse from weakness.

Reed was also amazed at the way in which, in the midst of civil war, in a winter in which Moscow went for weeks without light and men and women froze in their apartments, the foundations were being laid for the new social order. New medical centers were being built all over Russia, even in villages that had not had a doctor before. A great educational campaign had been begun to secure better sanitation. Free maternity hospitals had been established, free dispensaries, free centers of child-care. Schools were springing up everywhere, and the educational system was being remade.

He talked with Lunacharsky. The thin, delicate, nervous Commissar for Education told him not only of what was being done in the schools but also of the way in which literature and art were being created for the enjoyment of the people. Reed went to the Prolet-cult center in Moscow, where, in cold studios, painters were at work. "Sculpture, paintings, and engravings, very interesting," he wrote in his notebook. "Character all their own—proletarian." He talked with Demyan Byedny, a great smiling man in a yellow sweater, a poet who had a million readers, and with Pasternak, who condemned artists too lazy to master their craft. No one tried to tell Reed that there had been a renaissance in the arts, but he recognized the vigor of a new spirit.

Often Reed went to visit Lenin in his apartment in the Kremlin, and Lenin was glad to see him, not merely because he was interested in conditions in the United States but also because he liked the gay alertness of the young American. He commended Reed's decision to live in a working-class quarter, telling him it was the best way to learn Russian and to know Russia. He lectured him about his carelessness with regard to his health, showing a knowledge of physiology that amazed Reed. They talked on all sorts of topics, sometimes until dawn, and Reed felt the humanity as well as the greatness of the man.

It was at Lenin's suggestion that he prepared for the official organ of the Communist International a long article on the revolutionary situation in America. The first part described the A.F. of L.'s support of the war, the capitulation of many leading Socialists, the persecution of the I.W.W., the rise of patrioteering societies, unemployment at the end of the war, and the passing of laws to legalize the terrorization of the working class.

It ended, "Capitalism in America has entered the period of decay, and what will come in its place depends on the power of the workers. If the workers are not prepared to resist, the capitalists will set up a military dictatorship and reduce the proletariat to slavery." The second part, which analyzed the growing militancy of American labor, showed how carefully Reed had followed the strikes of the past two years. He described in intelligent detail the general strikes in Seattle and Winnipeg and the Boston police strike, discussed the Plumb plan, told what he had been able to learn about the steel strike, and commented on the policies of the A.F. of L. and the I.W.W. The concluding section of the article described the decline of the Socialist Party, which Reed dated from the resolution against direct action in 1912, the rise of the left wing, and, with familiar acrimoniousness, the split between the Communist Party and the Communist Labor Party.

Subsequently he wrote an article on the I.W.W., an article that combined his old admiration for its spirit and his new objections to its policies. After paying tribute to Joe Hill, Frank Little, and the other I.W.W. martyrs of the class struggle, he told the history of the organization and described the break with the Socialist Party. The leaders, he said, had proven themselves poor organizers but magnificent propagandists. The weaknesses of the I.W.W. he attributed, of course, to its anarcho-syndicalist principles, and he outlined and refuted the objections of its theorists to the Marxian doctrine of the dictatorship of the proletariat. But he had not forgotten Paterson and the Chicago trial. "If we could reach these men," he ended, "and make clear to them in their own language the position of the Communists, their innate common sense would show them we are right. And we must do that, for the I.W.W. is the vanguard of the American proletariat, which must lead the assault against capitalism in America."

The writing of these articles was one of Reed's duties as a representative of the Communist Labor Party to the International and as a spokesman in Soviet Russia for the American revolutionary movement. To all of these duties he conscientiously devoted himself, but he was still a reporter and historian. He

wanted to know exactly what was happening. In the dead of
winter, the worst period of the year, the hardest winter Soviet
Russia had known, he went out into the country to see the
provincial towns and peasant villages. He went as far as the
Volga, talking with every one: with pretty girls; with specialists who complained over their tea about inefficiency; with a
jocular jailer, who said he could see no sense in eating vegetables
when there were nice fat dogs running around; with a peasant
girl, who lamented that she could bring no dowry to her husband; with peasants who blessed the Bolsheviks and peasants
who cursed them; with a horse-faced Englishman, who told him
in detail why Communism couldn't work. In Klin he attended
a meeting of the district soviet and went to the workers' theatre.
In Sverdlov he watched a trial. Often he drove from village to
village, talking with the peasants as the sleigh moved along the
rutted roads across the great white plain. He took down statistics, furnished by the bourgeois specialists, on the production of
wheat and potatoes, made notes on food rations, and recorded
the number of schools.

At last he came to the Volga. "Impressive for miles," he wrote
in his notebook. "Low abrupt banks. Wide meadows backed by
dark forests, as if setting stage for river. Snow-covered ice of
river. Fishing holes. Tracks across. The peasant sleighs. Far villages." In one of these villages a woman in a beautiful dress of
peasant linen gave him and his companions dinner. When they
thanked her, she bowed and said, "May it give you health." He
talked with her about religion, and she told him that, though
most of the older peasants still went to church, the younger people did not. Her husband praised the Communists, but he did
not belong to the party, for, he explained, he had a wife and
three children, and he could not make the sacrifices membership demanded. In a neighboring village a peasant complained
because he had had a horse confiscated. "This is a poor village,"
he said. "I do not own my own house. But I did own two horses,
and they called me bourgeois, and took one away." Another
peasant objected to the sovkhoz because the men employed
there worked only eight hours a day and had more food than

he. He had a son in the Red Army, but knew nothing of either Denikin or Kolchak.

Reed returned to Moscow, more impressed than ever by the vastness of the change the revolution was making in Russian life. Wherever there were factories, he had found the workers enthusiastic about the Soviet government, but the peasants were bewildered. The poorest peasants were, even in such a winter, better off than they had been before the October revolution, but they found it hard to adjust themselves to the new regime. Yet the new schools and the new medical centers were having their effect on old ideas, and Reed could see how swiftly the introduction of advanced methods of production might alter rural life. But it would be, he knew, a long and agonizing struggle.

In Moscow he found that the executive committee of the Communist International had worked out a program for the merging of the two American parties, to which the representative of the Slavic federations had agreed. A committee of six, three representing each party, was to call a convention, to which delegates were to be sent on the basis of membership in local units. The central committee elected by this convention would have control of the united party, including the federations.

Both parties had, in the meantime, been outlawed. On December 21, 1919, 249 foreign-born radicals, whose cases had been rushed through the Department of Labor without pretense of legal procedure, were deported on the *Buford*. On January 2, A. Mitchell Palmer's agents conducted simultaneous raids on Communist, Communist Labor, and Socialist meeting-places throughout the country, arresting more than ten thousand persons. Thirty-eight members of the Communist Labor Party, including Reed, and eighty-five members of the Communist Party were, three weeks later, indicted in Chicago. A man, who turned out to be a respectable owner of liberty bonds, was arrested in Beacon, New York, as John Reed, and Illinois officers hastened east with extradition papers.

It was, then, with the almost complete certainty of being sent to prison, that Reed planned to return to the United States. He was already under indictment in Chicago, and, as a matter of fact, most of the men who were indicted with him were, the following August, sentenced to from one to five years. In New York, moreover, his former colleagues on the *Revolutionary Age* were being brought to trial for having circulated the left-wing manifesto, of which he had been one of the authors. Nevertheless, when he went to greet Emma Goldman, who had arrived on the *Buford*, he was as buoyant as ever, full of enthusiasm for the revolution, and somewhat irritatingly contemptuous of her doubts. He told her a little of what he had seen, of the heroism and of the great achievements in the midst of civil war, and was grateful for what she could tell him of the movement in the United States and for the messages she brought from Louise Bryant. Promising to greet her friends in America for her, and to see her again in Moscow before very long, he rushed out of her room as impetuously as he had entered.

TWICE John Reed tried to make his way through the lines of Soviet Russia's enemies, and twice he failed. The first attempt was made through Latvia. On his way to the Red Army, he had to change at a junction. For a day and a night he waited in a dilapidated station, five miles from the nearest village. The windows in the waiting-room were broken, and the floor was coated with ice, for the water-pipes had burst. On the floor and on tables and benches, soldiers were lying, tossing and muttering in the delirium of typhus. Outside, on the station platform, peasants piled the bodies of three hundred soldiers who had grown tired on the march, fallen into the snow, and frozen. And yet, in another room of the station, soldiers, themselves like half-frozen skeletons, were cheering a Communist speaker.

The train he was expecting did not come, and soldiers warned him that it never would. The Red Army, they said, was retreating, and he could not possibly get through. At last an empty military train arrived, bound east, and Reed crawled into a box car, with two soldiers, a railroad worker, and a peasant woman. They built a fire, and, until the bottom of the car burned out, managed to keep comfortable.

It was an inglorious return, and, as soon as another plan could be devised, Reed made his second attempt. This time, hidden in the bunker of a Finnish ship bound for Sweden, he got as far as Abo, but there he was discovered. The Finnish authorities had, of course, no doubt as to his mission, but, to avoid international complications, they held him on the technical charge of smuggling, since he was carrying with him some funds as well as letters and propaganda. He was placed in solitary confinement in the police station in Abo.

It was early in March when he was arrested, and for the first month he was unable to communicate in any way with his friends in America. His letters to American diplomatic officials were undelivered or, if delivered, were not answered. A Finnish liberal, Madame Aino Malmberg, secured a lawyer for him, but she was no more successful than he in reaching the consul. She did manage to send word of Reed's arrest to an American reporter, and the New York papers of March 17 carried a brief story, but the State Department announced that it had received no information and had no reason to believe he had been seized.

Day after day Reed sat alone in his cell reading, or walked aimlessly about. Finally a stratagem occurred to him, and he suggested to Madame Malmberg that she should announce his death. On April 10 the papers in the United States carried a report that John Reed had been executed in Finland. The State Department was forced to investigate, and on April 15 it announced that it had definite information that he was alive. A few days later it gave out a statement that it would not interfere inasmuch as Reed had been arrested according to Finnish law. The Finnish government, it was reported, had discovered on his person sums of money and jewels worth 880,000 Finnish marks, as well as moving picture films, photographs, and pamphlets. He carried a seaman's identification card made out to James Gormley and forged passports and letters made out to Samuel Arnold, Jr.

Louise Bryant, who had doubted the stories of Reed's arrest, now began frantically to act on his behalf. Bainbridge Colby, Secretary of State, informed her that the department would, on her request, cable the legation at Helsingfors to assist Reed in getting a lawyer. She would have to pay all expenses, and the department would not guarantee reliability of counsel. After advancing funds to pay for cables, she hastened to get in touch with Reed's friends. There were many persons who, whatever their opinion of his politics, were unwilling to have him executed in Finland: Whigham and Hovey of the *Metropolitan*, Bourke Cockran, Senator McNary, Jane Addams, George Kirchwey, Fred Howe, Louis Post, Arthur Garfield Hays. Even Reed's uncle, General Burr, wrote a letter to the State Department.

By the end of April, the Finnish authorities decided to permit Reed to communicate with America, and on April 29, he wired Louise Bryant, "Nothing yet decided. Have everything necessary. Are you all right?" Four days later he wrote her a letter:

> Central Police Station
> Abo, Finland
> May 3, 1920.

Dearest Honey—

Last week a cable arrived from you, wanting to know about my case. So I know at least that you have heard of my arrest. This is what worried me very much—the idea that perhaps you knew nothing about me, and wondered where I was. I thought perhaps it would be as it was in 1918. For me it has been worse than that. I have heard absolutely not a word from you since I left home—except news of you from Emma and the other exiles, which proved that at any rate you were alive. I have been so fearfully worried—about your health, about whether you had anything to do, enough to eat, etc.—whether you were well or ill. You will never have an idea of what it has been to me—especially since I have been in here (now in the eighth week of solitary imprisonment).

Now about my case. I have sent you one letter, addressed to Croton, and two cables. At present I am in jail, waiting for something to happen. Up to now no charge has been laid against me, except that of smuggling. This case has been tried, the diamonds all confiscated, and I have been fined five thousand marks (about $250-$300). I have appealed. But this is not what keeps me in prison. It is the question of whether I have committed treason towards the Finnish state. It appears that there are "diplomatic negotiations" going on between the Finnish government and the United States government. Why, I do not know.

Now, honey, I want you *please not* to influence the American government to help me. I mean this very seriously. I wish this case to be decided entirely on its merits.

I am in good health—surprisingly good health—and almost all the time cheerful enough. But the thought of you drags at me sometimes until my imagination plays tricks, and I almost go crazy. Please, please write me about everything.

Don't send me any money—I have plenty. And *don't worry*—there's not the slightest danger. Please let mother know of my situation. You might send her one of these letters. I hate to ask you—but will you try to save my watch. That is all. I hope it won't be long before we see each other again. Spring is coming and I long for Croton.

Your loving

Jack.

Ten ɑays later he wrote her again, this time addressing the envelope to a friend.

Central Police Station
Abo, Finland
May 13.

For Louise Bryant

Dearest Honey—

Your dear letter of April 23rd arrived today. Evidently you have not yet received my two letters. I am not yet free, as you see, but on the other hand I am also not accused of anything. I am informed that the American government has demanded that I be surrendered to the American authorities, why I cannot understand. But I do not think the Finnish authorities can do this without accusing me, trying me, and finding me guilty. However, it is impossible to say what a bourgeois government cannot do.

I am sending you some money today. It seems terrible that you should have to meet all those burdens, and I have worried myself sick over your health.

I heard that you were planning to come here. If it is for the sake of helping me, I beg you not to do so. But if it is because you want to come abroad, and possibly to be with me in case I am delayed—and, of course, if you can find the money—do it by all means. But wait for a cable before you actually sail.

I am very well. Have given up smoking for the last two months here, and am allowed a little walk in the yard every day. The police master here has really been most friendly and generous to me. As for the American authorities, they have of course not been near me, or sent any word all the time I have been here. But I am thankful for that. I do not want any help from the authorities as regards myself.

I think I understand thoroughly the situation at home, and will know what to do.

I am all right, dearest, and except for the nervousness of doing nothing and being alone week after week, and worry about my honey, I am able to stand it indefinitely.

All my love, and greetings to all. Tell Horace [Liveright] the big chief [Lenin] thinks my book the best. Many compliments for yours.

                                                                    Jack.

By the fifteenth, Reed had had two more letters from Louise. He was surprised, he told her, that so many persons had become interested in his case, and he could scarcely believe her assertion that the Department of State was trying to secure his release. "I am informed by the Finns," he wrote, "that I am kept in prison at the request of the United States government." No representative of the government had ever been to see him, and only once had there been an inquiry, directed to his lawyer, about the progress of the case. "If I fail in all other ways to get a decision from the Finnish authorities, I shall probably try a hunger strike."

The threat of a hunger strike was effective, and four days later he was able to write Louise that he was to be released. "The Finns," he explained, "are asking the American minister, Magruder, to give me a passport. If he does—which is practically impossible—I shall start for Stockholm immediately, and from there, after learning the situation at home, I shall act accordingly. If he does not give me a passport, the Finnish government will give me notice to leave the country in twenty-four or forty-eight hours. The idea is, of course, if I then go to Sweden, I will be hustled to America without any opportunity to look around —more or less deported, in fact. So I have demanded, if I am to be told to leave the country, to go to Esthonia; I am asking a permit from the Esthonian government."

Whatever assurances Bainbridge Colby might give Louise Bryant, the government was apparently treating Reed as an enemy. William Hard, though he knew Reed but slightly, was one of the persons who acted in his behalf. After finding the Wilsonian liberals consistently evasive, he went to Bernard

Baruch. Baruch, who was about to leave Washington for New York, asked him who Reed was. On being assured that he was a dangerous radical but indubitably an American citizen, he went to the State Department, though it meant missing his train, and demanded action. He was told that the department would immediately request the Finnish government to see that Reed was protected.

Whether actually anything was done in Washington, even then, on Reed's behalf cannot be determined, but it seems likely that the State Department continued to work against him. On May 25, he learned that the Finnish authorities had given American agents access to his papers. Certain now that his passport would be refused, he withdrew the request he had made to Magruder, and asked Madame Malmberg to arrange for his return to Russia by way of either Reval or Bieloostrov. He also authorized her to act as his agent in the attempt to recover his papers from the government. Among the papers he listed letters from American exiles and Russians to friends in America, a preface in Lenin's handwriting to *Ten Days That Shook the World*, various photographs, a number of pamphlets, and the false passports.

As the days went on, and there was no sign of action, it became more and more difficult for Reed to remain patient. During the early weeks of his confinement, he had done much reading, but the amount of paper given him was so restricted that he could do no extensive writing. He did begin, on scraps of paper, a romantic prose-poem, called "The Ever-Victorious," and he made outlines for two novels. Again and again he had made notes for novels, but they had never been written. Now, in a Finnish prison, he amused himself by making another start. One of the novels was to be a story of New York politics, of a reformer, a boss, and a Socialist. It was not to be autobiographical, although the central character, a reporter who became disillusioned with reform and associated himself with the boss, was to be given many of Reed's experiences. The revolutionary movement was to be used as a foil to both the reformers and the boss.

The other novel was almost purely autobiography. Although the hero, Robin, was to be born in the Middle West and educated in a small college, his parents were obviously modeled after

Reed's: the father identifies himself with his son and lives in his life; the mother is described as "loving, narrow, maternal." After Robin is brought to New York, the outline becomes little more than a catalog of Reed's experiences. "Meets Steff. Gets job on magazine. Phillips, Siddall, Boyden, Nock. Dutch Treat. Harry Kemp comes with poem. . . . Brevoort. Hippolyte Havel. Henrietta Rodman. Mary Vorse . . . 42 Washington Sq. Seeger. Bobby Rogers. Red Lewis. Bobby Jones. Seeger lost in curious English poets. . . . Wash. Sq. Players. Prov. Players. . . . The coming of Gene O'Neill. . . . Robin in love with the doctor's wife—her salon. She rich, old. He poor. Conflict. He tries to leave. Wretchedness. Break . . . Death of Osgood. Death of Adams . . . Leo Stein's talk. . . . Long poem (mine) on the city. . . . *New Republic* . . . Harold Stearns. Randolph Bourne. Walter Lippmann . . . Gift-shops, guides, and village riff-raff. A scene in Frank Shay's book-shop. . . . Free-speech fight. Tannenbaum and unemployed—churches. . . . Haywood, Gurley. . . . Collapse of the I.W.W. Joining Socialists. Branch meetings, street speaking, Jim Larkin. Bayonne, the break with his paper. Free lancing, poverty, marriage. The war. Conscientious objector but registers. Not called. Russian revolution and the new Socialism. . . . Tortures, deportations, raids, soldier-mobs, fearful sentences. The raid on People's House. The Communist Party. . . . Peace and Bolshevism."

All this was exciting to look back on, in that dismal little cell, where Reed never undressed at night, where—despite his assurances to Louise Bryant—the food was meager and bad, where he waited and hope rose and fell. He also wrote one poem, which he called "A Letter to Louise":

> Rainy-rush of bird-song
> Apple blossom smoke
> Thin bells' water-falling sound
> Wind-rust on the silver pond
> Furry staring willow-wand
> Wan new grasses waking round
> Blue bird in the oak—
> Woven in my word-song.

White and slim my lover
Birch-tree in the shade
Mountain pools her fearless eyes
Innocent, all-answering.
Were I blinded to the spring
Happy thrill would in me rise
Smiling half-afraid
At the nearness of her.

All my weak endeavor
Lay I at her feet
Like a moth from oversea
Let my longing lightly rest
On her flower-petal breast
Till the red dawn set me free
To be with my sweet
Ever and forever.

But, as week after week passed by, and as freedom came close and drew away, impatience grew and any kind of concentration became impossible. After the good news of the middle of May, he heard nothing. There were, however, forces working for his liberation that he did not know about. The Soviet leaders, once they learned of Reed's imprisonment, began negotiations with the Finnish government, not relying on diplomatic letters, but proposing what amounted to an exchange of prisoners. The Soviets held two Finnish professors arrested for counter-revolutionary activities, and these they offered to exchange for Reed. (Lenin was reported as saying that he would gladly turn over a whole college faculty if he could get Reed released.) And apparently this proposal was more effective than whatever steps the State Department took, if, indeed, the United States government was not working for Reed's detention.

He wrote Louise:

May 30.

Dear Honey—

Why did your letters stop all of a sudden? I only got two. But probably you thought I would soon be out. However, here I still sit, going on the twelfth week of imprisonment. But the end is in sight. The Finnish government has already notified me that I shall not be tried, but turned loose. I asked the American minister here for a passport home. He did not reply—as he has refused to answer all communications from me. But he told a Finnish government official that he would on no circumstances give me a passport. Therefore, rather than be brutally deported, I have asked permission from the Esthonian government to allow me to go through Reval to Russia. Or at least Madame Malmberg has done it for me. I am given to understand that it will be done—the permission will be granted me; but for some strange reason no answer comes, although it is now *ten days* since I requested permission. And still I sit here, in the bright June weather, spending most of my time worrying about my honey and longing for her.

I shall return for the present to Russia. If you can come abroad, do so. Get ready, but don't start until later word from me! I shall send you much more definite instructions as soon as I leave here.

I have kept very well in prison, exercising, not smoking. (I quit three months ago.) Have been to the dentist and had all my teeth fixed. Have read many serious books, but almost crazy because I cannot write.

Don't forget the interest on Croton due August 1, and on Truro Sept. 26. Don't forget my watch.

Monday, May 31. Still no word from Esthonia.

Tuesday, June 1. Still no word. It seems to me as if I shall never get out. The worst is to keep on expecting release day after day. My mind is getting dull. Honey, the house ought to be rented.

Wednesday, June 2. Still not a whisper. It is dreadful to wait so, day after day—and after three months too. I have nothing to read, nothing to do. I can only sleep about five hours, and so am awake, penned in a little cage, for nineteen hours a day. This is my thirteenth week.

8 P.M.—Just this minute *word came!* I am to go to Reval on Saturday's boat from Helsingfors—or maybe I must wait until Tuesday. Anyway, *I'm going!* This is the last letter to my honey from this place. Wait for news from me, dearest.

Your loving

Jack.

On the seventh he telegraphed from Reval: "Passport home refused. Temporarily returning headquarters. Come if possible."

XXI

BY THE KREMLIN WALL

IN ESTHONIA fields were unplowed and factory chimneys smokeless. In Soviet Russia green crops were growing, and the factories were all at work. The people of Petrograd were not only better dressed and better fed than they had been when Reed left, three months before; they were stronger, happier, more confident. Bands played every afternoon in the parks, and thousands of people walked up and down or sat in little cafés drinking tea and coffee. The streets were clean, and the Nevsky—newly christened the October 25th Prospect—was being re-paved. At John MacLean Quay, formerly the English Quay, or at Jean Jaurès Quay, formerly the French Quay, it was possible to take small river-boats up the Neva to Smolny. And on the islands at the mouth of the Neva, where the millionaires and nobles had their summer villas, thousands of Petrograd workers were taking their vacations.

Reed went on to Moscow, where the public gardens blazed with flowers. The Kremlin walls had been repaired, and Moscow University, allowed to grow shabby since 1912, was being painted white. The theatres were open and crowded, and Reed heard Chaliapin in *Faust*. While he was in jail the civil war had begun again, with Pilsudsky and the Poles attacking in the Ukraine, and Wrangel and the last of the White Guard moving north from the Crimea; but the Red Army was winning victories on both fronts, and every one was optimistic.

Reed was not well. His arms and legs were swollen; his body was covered with sores, the result of malnutrition; and his gums had been attacked by scurvy. While Emma Goldman helped to take care of him, they argued together about the dictatorship of the proletariat. He was distressed by his two failures to reach the United States, but delighted with the change that had taken place in Russia. To her bitter criticisms, he replied with a heated defense of Soviet policy. Her mind had been set, he told her, in old-fashioned anarchist molds, and she could not recognize the revolution when she saw it.

In the warm summer days he quickly regained his good spirits, though he could not obliterate the effects of his imprisonment on his constitution. While he was convalescing, he wrote an article for the *Liberator*. "Just now it is a beautiful moment in Soviet Russia," he began. "Clear sunny day follows clear sunny day." After describing the atmosphere of Moscow and Petrograd, the sense of well-being and the new spirit of hope, he wrote: "And the children! This is a country for children, primarily. In every city, in every village, the children have their own public dining-rooms, where the food is better, and there is more of it, than for the grown-ups. Only the Red Army is fed so well. The children pay nothing for their food; they are clothed free of charge by the cities; for them are the schools, the children's colonies—land-owners' mansions scattered over the face of Russia; for them are the theatres and concerts—the immense, gorgeous state theatres crowded with children from orchestra to gallery. In their honor Tsarskoe Syelo—the Tsar's Village, the village of palaces—has been rechristened Dietskoe Syelo, the Children's Village; a hundred thousand of them spend the summer there, in relays. The streets are full of happy children."

He did not want to give a false impression: "This does not mean that all is well with Soviet Russia, that the people do not hunger, that there is not misery and disease and desperate, endless struggle. The winter was horrible beyond imagination. No one will ever know what Russia went through." And he went on to describe that winter, telling what he had seen in Moscow and Petrograd, on the Lettish front, in Serpukov. After telling about the Red Army and the labor armies, he was going on to describe his trip to the Volga, but he did not have time, and he sent the article as it was, unfinished.

Once he had recuperated, there was little time for writing, for he was needed to aid in preparations for the second congress of the Communist International. There were innumerable meetings to draw up plans, draft proposals, prepare appeals and proclamations, and Reed, as a member of the executive committee, was present at most of them. By the first of July delegates had begun to arrive. From all over the world they came, most of them traveling illegally, hiding on ships, passing through enemy lines at night, suffering frightful hardships. Some delegates never reached Russia, arrested or, one or two of them, killed. One American member of the I.W.W. crossed the Pacific and walked five hundred miles through the deserts and mountains of Manchuria to attend the congress.

Reed, taking a room in the hotel that was reserved for delegates and guests, began to make the acquaintance of his comrades. Learning that there was an American anarchist in a nearby room, he rapped on the door and walked in, calling, "Good morning, neighbor." The American, Owen W. Penney, looked up, and the first thing he noticed was the eyes, sparkling, smiling, sympathetic. It did not take Reed long to learn Penney's story. Born in the Middle West, the son of a miner, Penney had been in Europe all through the war, and had taken part in working-class struggles in half a dozen countries. Though an anarchist, he wanted to see what was happening in Russia, and he smuggled himself across the boundary from Germany.

Reed and Penney were friends by the time they went down together to breakfast, and Reed immediately began to point out the errors in anarcho-syndicalism, which he usually called absurdo-stupidism. Through Penney he met Paul Freeman, an Australian syndicalist, and the three of them spent hours together. In April Lenin had written *"Left-Wing" Communism: an Infantile Disorder* for the guidance of the congress. There was no English version in print, but Reed secured a translation in manuscript, going over it, sentence by sentence, with Freeman and Penney. The former was a Communist by the beginning of the congress and the latter by its close.

While he prepared for the congress, Reed was sending word to Louise Bryant by whatever means offered themselves. On the sixteenth of June he sent her one hundred dollars and gave her minute instructions for the trip to Russia. On the twenty-third he repeated his instructions, adding, "We shall not be separated another winter. It is beautiful here now, and everything is going well. Great events are to be expected. I can say no more now, except that I love you." And on the twenty-ninth another courier carried assurances that plans for her voyage and her entrance into Russia were practically completed.

On July 19, the congress opened in Petrograd with an address by Zinoviev, paying tribute to the martyrs of the revolution and describing the difference between the Second and Third Internationals. After his speech had been translated into German, French, and Italian, the presidium was elected. Kalinin greeted the congress in the name of the Russian workers and peasants, and Lenin, after a long ovation, spoke on imperialism, the situation of the world revolutionary movement, and the aims of the congress.

The mood of the congress was optimistic. The Red Army was driving back Pilsudsky's forces, and the Red Fleet was in the Caspian Sea. The Italian Socialists, the members of the German Independent Social Democratic Party, many French Socialists, and even members of the British Independent Labor Party favored affiliation with the Third International. The very composition of the congress gave hope. "It was remarkable," Reed wrote, "for the number of real proletarians, of actual workmen-fighters-strikers, barricade-defenders, and active leaders of the revolutionary nationalist movements in the backward and colonial countries. German Spartacists, Spanish syndicalists, American I.W.W.'s, Hungarian Soviet and Red Army leaders, British shop stewards and representatives of Clyde workers' committees, Dutch transport workers, Hindu, Korean, Chinese, and Persian insurrectionists, Irish Sinn Feiners and Communists, Argentinian dockers, Australian wobblies. All these people were not clear on Communism; they had violently divergent ideas about the dictatorship of the proletariat, parliamentarism, the need for a political party; but they were welcomed as brothers in revolution, as the best fighters of the working class, as comrades that were willing to die for the overthrow of capitalism."

On the first day of the congress there was a great demonstration in Petrograd. "Tremendous masses," Reed wrote, "flowed like a clashing sea through the broad streets, almost overwhelming with their enthusiastic affection the delegates as they marched from the Tauride Palace to the Field of Martyrs of the Revolution." On the steps of the old stock exchange, which had become a club for sailors, five thousand actors presented a pageant of the revolution from the Paris Commune to the worldwide triumph of the proletariat. Reed, watching it with the most intense excitement felt that one of his greatest dreams had come true. Here was the revolutionary art for which he had longed, since the Paterson pageant, seven years before, had given him his first glimpse of the possibilities of mass dramatic expression. "Why not write an article about it?" asked Fraina, who was sitting beside him. "An article!" Reed answered. "I'd like to write a book!" He might have written a book, tracing the winding road from Paterson to Petrograd, a book that would have summed up all that he felt about art and all that he felt about labor. It was all there, in the pageant before him, miraculously unified and terribly alive.

When the congress, after the preliminary session, moved to Moscow, crowds at every station greeted the special trains that carried the delegates. In Moscow itself three hundred thousand people—soldiers, workers, children, athletes—marched in honor of the congress. There was a great banquet at which Chaliapin sang and other artists performed. Delegates were housed, fed, given free access to theatres, and everywhere greeted with respect and affection. Soviet Russia, torn though it was by civil war, gave its best to the soldiers of world revolution.

When the congress reconvened in Moscow, on July 23, Reed, as soon as the order of business had been announced, rose and, in the name of twenty-nine comrades, proposed the placing of the question of the trade unions nearer the head of the list. "This is a serious problem," he said. "We must thoroughly discuss the trade union question and have time to consider everything related thereto." He also moved that, at least for the duration of discussion on this topic, English be made one of the official languages of the congress. Both motions were defeated.

While Zinoviev opened the discussion of the role of the Communist Party in the revolution, Reed looked about the great Andreyev Throne Room of the Imperial Palace in the Kremlin. It was an extraordinary gathering, and one that he was proud to belong to. He was enough of a poet to appreciate the color and romance and to feel the drama in the lives of these oppressed, police-hunted men and women who dared to plan the winning of a world. But it did not seem strange to him that he was here, for he had come by a path that, viewed in retrospect, seemed perfectly straight, and he felt himself at one with these workers of the nations.

The next day the composition of the various commissions was announced. There were to be five, and both the Communist Party and the Communist Labor Party were represented on each. Reed was appointed to both the commission on national minorities and the colonial question and the commission on trade union activities. Zinoviev served on the former, and Lenin, Kamenev, and Radek on the latter. During the next few days Reed was occupied with these two commissions, speaking frequently in their meetings.

On the twenty-sixth the congress as a whole took up the question of nationalist and colonial revolutionary movements. Reed, arriving late from the trade union commission, sent a note to Lenin, asking if he was to speak. Lenin replied, "Absolutely." From carefully prepared notes, he described the situation of the Negro in the United States, speaking of discrimination in every aspect of life. "As an oppressed and downtrodden people," he said, "the Negro offers to us a twofold opportunity: first, a strong race and social movement; second, a strong proletarian labor movement. . . . In both the northern and southern parts of the country the one aim must be to unite the Negro and the white laborer in common labor unions; this is the best and the quickest way to destroy race prejudice and develop class solidarity."

Soon every one at the congress knew John Reed as he walked, coatless and tieless and usually smiling, to his seat in the Kremlin. Many noticed and admired his broad shoulders, but some could see that his flesh was flabby and that he was not well. Although he spent as much time as he could in the sun, his face remained sallow, and there were new lines on his forehead and near the corners of his mouth. The forehead, underneath his disorderly hair, seemed broader now that his face had lost its good-natured pudginess. His mouth, when he was not grinning, was ordinarily rather gentle, but it could take a hard, straight line that his Greenwich Village friends would not have recognized. The eyes, though the touch of green in their brown was as confusing as ever, and though the light was as sharp and the eagerness as unmistakable, were startled and a little hurt.

He did not look healthy, and yet he was indefatigable. After spending all day at the congress, he was ready to devote half the night to talk. And the next morning he would be making vociferous speeches at the meeting of the commission on the trade union question. This question he wanted to discuss day and night, in the congress and out.

He became the spokesman in the commission for those who opposed the policy of working within the existing unions. The form of the unions in America and England, he argued, was such that they could not be used for revolutionary purposes even if the Communists did capture all the offices. He admitted that it was foolish to leave the unions so long as the masses were in them, but Communists should try, not to capture but to smash them, so that industrial unions could be built in their place. Europeans, who were familiar with a different kind of labor organization, failed, he insisted, to understand that in England and America unions were highly developed and developed in such a way as to restrain their members from revolutionary activity.

The theses prepared by the commission on the trade union question came to a vote on August 4, and there were very sharp and fundamental differences of opinion expressed by the delegates. Radek eloquently defended the resolutions of the majority, which the C.P. supported. Reed as eloquently attacked them. He contended that Communists could no more use the reactionary trade unions than they could the bourgeois state. The revolutionary crisis was advancing so swiftly that militant workers in the A.F. of L. were already looking for more effective organizations, and the masses of unorganized workers could not be brought into the reactionary unions. By entering the A.F. of L., Communists, instead of building their strength among the masses, would be isolating themselves. After Zinoviev had suggested that Reed was too optimistic, the theses proposed by Radek were adopted.

At the last business session, on August 6, Zinoviev announced the new executive committee, of which Reed was a member. The final meeting of the congress was held in the Moscow Opera House the next day. The delegates, members of the All-Russia Soviet Executive Committee, and leaders of the Moscow Soviet sat on the platform, and the great hall was filled with workers. After representatives of several countries had spoken, Zinoviev made the final speech, and Kalinin put the motion for adjournment. When the thousands of men and women had sung "The Internationale," and the applause was ceasing, the Italian delegates burst into one of their own revolutionary songs, and soon the entire throng was once more singing and shouting.

John Reed, as excited as he had ever been when he danced before the cheering section at a Harvard-Yale game, saw the chance, in these moments of wild enthusiasm, to carry out a cherished plan. Signaling to Paul Freeman, who was as tall as he, and to Owen Penney, he marched towards the smiling Lenin. Freeman grasped one leg and Reed the other, and Penney boosted. Before he knew what was happening, Lenin found himself high on Reed's and Freeman's shoulders, gazing down on a bewildered crowd. Ignorant of American customs, or perhaps disapproving, he protested, and, when protests did no good, kicked. They let him down, Reed, unabashed, joking at the bump on Penney's forehead.

For three weeks after the end of the congress Reed was occupied with meetings of the executive committee. The various applications for affiliation were carefully scrutinized, and the situation of the revolutionary forces in each country examined. The United Communist Party and the Communist Party were instructed to unite within the next two months—though actually it was almost a year before unification was achieved.

In the sessions of the E.C.C.I. Reed had an opportunity once more to debate the theses on trade unionism. "After a long and bitter fight," he reported to his comrades at home, "the executive committee made several amendments to their theses, which, although far from satisfactory to the objecting delegates, still made it possible for Communists in America to work for revolutionary industrial unionism and for the destruction of the reactionary American Federation of Labor." The revised theses did recognize that dual unionism might in some circumstances be necessary, and they recommended the supporting of such revolutionary unions as already existed, but they required Communists to join the regular trade unions and not to leave them unless they were forced to do so. Reed predicted that the next congress would adopt a different policy.

The whole concept of revolutionary industrial unionism had, of course, been implanted in Reed's mind at the time of his introduction to the class struggle in Paterson, and his observations of the A.F. of L. had convinced him that the I.W.W. was right. And now he was so deeply immersed in the struggle, so thoroughly pre-occupied with revolutionary tactics, that it seemed to him of supreme importance that the right approach to the trade unions should be adopted. So intense was his feeling that he was constantly involved, in the commission, in the congress, and in the meetings of the executive committee, in passionate debate. Zinoviev and Radek were the leaders of the other camp, and against Zinoviev in particular Reed developed some animosity. During one of the sessions of the executive committee, Reed peremptorily offered his resignation from the E.C.C.I. in protest against Zinoviev's decision on an organizational question. It was not, of course, a thing that a disciplined revolutionary would have done, and Reed was persuaded by his fellow-delegates to withdraw his resignation and offer his apologies to the committee.

At the end of August, a call came for members of the executive committee to go to the Congress of Oriental Nations at Baku. "An Appeal to the Enslaved Masses in Persia, Armenia, and Turkey" had been issued by the executive committee of the International in July. Describing the exploitation of the peasants and workmen of Persia, Mesopotamia, Anatolia, Armenia, Syria, and Arabia, the appeal challenged them to throw off the imperialist yoke. "Do not spare any effort," it concluded, "and let as many of you as possible come to Baku on September 1. Formerly you used to make pilgrimages across the desert to the Holy City; now cross mountains, rivers, and deserts to meet one another. . . . Let the congress show your foes in Europe, America, and in your own country that the time for slavery is over, that you have risen, and that you will conquer."

Reed was one of those assigned to go. On the twenty-sixth, just as he was making ready to leave, word came that Louise Bryant had reached Stockholm some time before and was on her way into Russia. He tried to make some arrangement for her to be sent after him to Baku, but the authorities refused to let a woman go through the zone of civil war. He left a note for her, explaining his absence, and naming persons in Petrograd and Moscow for her to see. "I am longing to see you," he wrote, "more than I can tell. It seems years. I am worrying about only one thing. I must soon go home, and it is awfully difficult to get out of here, especially for a woman. That is why I tried to get word to you to wait for me outside. But as soon as I found out that you were coming, I was glad that I was to see my honey sooner."

Baku, which the Soviets had lost in 1918, had been recaptured in the spring of 1920. On the Caspian Sea, across the Caucasus Mountains, it represented the farthest thrust of Soviet power into the Near East, the scene of the bitterest imperial struggle. To reach it, the delegates had to pass through the southern Ukraine, where the Red Army was battling with Wrangel's troops. They rode in an armored train, through the fertile Volga plains that Reed had seen deep with snow a few months before. From the window he could watch the peasants at their work, and then, as they came near the Caspian, there were glimpses of troops, and one or two guerrilla bands made futile raids against the train. And at last there was Baku, center of the richest oil deposits in the world, coveted by every power in Europe, an oriental city, an old Tartar city, being transformed by the world's newest great industry.

Two thousand men of the East, Turks, Persians, Armenians,

representatives of the Asiatic nationalities of Soviet Russia, even a few Hindus and Chinese, came to the congress, wearing their strange and colorful costumes. It was a dramatic, romantic scene, the kind of scene that John Reed loved. He was a member of the presidium and a speaker. Boyish in his open-necked white shirt, he stood before these bright-robed Orientals to tell them about American imperialism.

"I represent," he began, "the revolutionary workers of one of the greatest imperialist powers—the United States of America. You have not yet tasted American domination. You know and hate English, French, and Italian imperialists, but you probably think that 'free America' will rule better, will liberate the colonial peoples, will feed and protect them. But the workers and peasants of the Philippines, the peoples of Central America and of the islands in the Caribbean Sea—they know the meaning of the domination of 'free America.'"

After describing the conquest of the Philippines and explaining that formal emancipation would still leave American capitalists in control, after showing what had happened in Cuba, Haiti, and Santo Domingo, after telling what he had himself seen in Mexico, after depicting the sufferings of ten million Negroes, he asked the people of the Near East why they should expect better treatment from the United States. To the Armenians he pointed out that Cleveland Dodge, who administered Armenian relief, exploited the workers in his copper mines and, when they went on strike, drove them into the desert as ruthlessly as any Turk could have done. He spoke of the way relief had been used in Hungary to destroy the Soviets, and charged that American aid to the sufferers of the Near East would also be given only for the sake of advancing American interests.

"No, comrades," he said, "Uncle Sam never gives anything free of charge. He comes with a sack of hay in one hand and a whip in the other, and whoever believes his promises will pay in blood. . . . Don't trust American capitalists. There is but one road to freedom. Unite with the Russian workers and peasants, who overthrew their capitalists and whose Red Army conquers the troops of the foreign imperialists. Follow the red star of the Communist International!"

Radek, Zinoviev, and Bela Kun were the principal speakers. "The real revolution," Zinoviev said, "will blaze up only when the eight hundred million people in Asia unite with us, when the African continent unites, when we see that hundreds of millions of people are in the movement. We must kindle a holy war against the British and French capitalists. We must create a Red Army in the East, to organize uprisings in the rear of the British, to destroy every impudent British officer who lords it over Turkey, Persia, India, China." As the men of the East sprang to their feet, flourishing swords, spears, and revolvers, Reed, sitting at the front with the others of the presidium, could scarcely believe that this was not one of the dreams of oriental glamor with which *The Arabian Nights* had filled his boyhood.

With his gift for making himself understood by men whose language he did not know, Reed moved among the delegates and pieced together their romantic stories. He saw, of course, the practical difficulties of linking nationalist struggles with the proletarian revolution, but he knew that many of these two thousand delegates would go home to work patiently and heroically for the emancipation of the working class. He wished he could follow them, into the Orient that all his life he had wanted to know.

The congress ended, and the representatives of the International started back in their armored car to Moscow. As the train passed through the territory in which the fight against Wrangel was going on, it was attacked by bandits. The Red Army squad on the train repulsed the guerrillas and started in pursuit. Reed, begging for permission to go with them, was allowed to ride on the peasant wagon on which they mounted their machine guns. Up into the hills they went, laughing, good-natured boys like those in La Tropa. They were loath to return to the waiting train, and so was he.

He found Louise Bryant in Moscow. She had had to make the last stage of her trip disguised as a sailor, but she had come. To her he seemed older and sadder and strangely intense. She felt that he was tired and ill. But he was eager for her to see the new Russia, and they visited Lenin, Trotsky, Kamenev, Enver Pasha, and Bela Kun, saw the ballet and *Prince Igor*, went to the art galleries. There was still much for him to do, of course, meetings of the executive committee, special conferences, a report of the congress of the Comintern to write for the United Communist Party. At one time he dropped in at the Department of Foreign Affairs, where Nuorteva and Wilfred Humphries were working in the Anglo-American office. They asked him about Baku, and for two hours he talked to them, telling, with enthusiasm and drama, the story of the congress. "You should have seen the swords flash!" he said.

With Louise he talked about America, about the novel and the poetry he intended to write. He hoped that the active tasks of revolution could be left in other hands, that he might write, of and for the revolution of course, but write. But first there would be the final unification of the Communists to accomplish, and there was his indictment in Chicago. This he was determined to face, though Louise insisted that conviction was certain. When she urged him to stay in Russia and rest, he told her that that would be cowardly.

There was a touching letter from his mother that Louise had brought. He had written her from the Abo jail, the first letter he had been able to send to her in many months. "What you say about feeling selfish," she had replied, "makes me feel badly, dear. Don't ever feel like that. You are doing what you think is right—that is all any of us can do in this world—and if we don't do it, we're all wrong. Except for fear for your personal safety, the rest is all right in my eyes if you feel that it is."

It was a happy fortnight, despite Louise's alarm over Reed's health and her fear of the consequences if he returned to the United States. He was perfectly confident, very eager, very busy. On the morning of September 22, he went to Kamenev's office to see him, and found Clare Sheridan there, preparing to make a bust of the revolutionist. They spoke together briefly, and that night she wrote in her diary: "We were delayed in starting by John Reed, the American Communist, who came to see him on some business; a well-built, good-looking young man, who has given up everything at home to throw his heart and life into the work here. I understand the Russian spirit, but what strange force impels an apparently normal young man from the

United States? I am told by the Russians that his book, *Ten Days That Shook the World*, is the best book on the revolution, and that it has become a national classic and is taught in the schools."

THREE or four days later, Reed felt ill. He had always scorned to take any precautions against disease, laughing at Americans with their bug-powder and their fetish of sterilization. After all, he had been exposed to typhus in Serbian hospitals, on Russian trains, in barracks and in jails. Even now his illness, which the doctor diagnosed as influenza, did not seem serious. For a week Louise Bryant cared for him, and then, as he seemed to grow worse, asked for a consultation. The doctors, deciding that he had typhus, ordered his removal to the Marinsky Hospital.

Although he was in pain, his interest in the movement was undiminished. Louis Fraina brought him the stenographic record of his speeches in the congress. Having been translated from English into German and then from German into Russian, and finally translated back again into English, the speeches were fantastically garbled. Reed was distressed at the distortion of his ideas, and, unable to make the revisions himself, asked Fraina to put the text in shape. Until he actually lost consciousness, he was clear-headed, interested in what was going on, brave.

As it became apparent that his condition was serious, all the resources of the hospital were concentrated on the attempt to save his life: four doctors, two consulting physicians, an assistant surgeon, and an English-speaking nurse were in attendance. Santeri Nuorteva ransacked the city for the proper medicines, but they were hard to get. Indeed, as Robert Hallowell was to write, "His end might have been different if our State Department had not refused to allow medical supplies to go to Russia."

Into the great city, so busy with the tasks of revolution, too busy to think much of one more case of typhus, word went forth on the seventeenth of October that John Reed was dying. Wilfred Humphries and Santeri Nuorteva, hearing the report, hurried to the hospital. They came into the little room, and the doctor turned to them, saying that he was dead.

The body was taken to the Labor Temple, where for seven days it lay in state, guarded by soldiers of the Red Army. Louise

Bryant wrote to Mrs. Reed, telling of the illness and death. "He died on Sunday," she wrote, "but will not be buried until next Sunday, the twenty-fourth. He will be buried in the most honored spot in Russia, beside all the great heroes in the Kremlin. You know how honored he is here. . . . I feel very far away, but the Russians have been very kind to me. They have spared no effort to make things easier for me. And they loved Jack greatly, and they gave him every honor in their power. . . . We spoke often of home and of you and we thought how we could see you when we came back. We talked of long vacations when Jack could finish his history. He had a novel all planned out and many short stories . . ."

In America the revolutionary movement prepared its tributes. Even the kept press that he hated praised John Reed now that he was dead. Friends stopped each other on the street and talked about him. To the students of English 12, Copey, cursing the Bolsheviki, praised the courage and loyalty of his Jack Reed. There were many who talked about wasted talent, and some whose pat phrases concealed relief. But in Atlanta and Leavenworth, in Sing Sing and Cook County Jail, in hundreds of prisons, and in the hiding-places of an outlawed Communist movement, men shut their jaws tight.

During the week news came that Wrangel was retreating: the civil war was nearly over. The twenty-fourth was a gray day, with rain that was sometimes sleet and sometimes snow. The leaders of the Communist International and the Moscow Soviet and the handful of Americans in the city gathered in the Labor Temple. On the walls were flaming cartoons of the revolution. The coffin was covered with wreaths of artificial flowers—the tin wreaths Reed had found so hideous when he had watched, almost three years before, the burial of the revolutionary martyrs of Moscow. It was the best the struggling proletariat could do.

Through the streets of Moscow the procession moved to the Red Square, as Reed had marched to the funeral of the heroic workers and soldiers. Thousands of workers walked behind the coffin, and a band played, over and over, the funeral march of the revolution. At the grave by the wall of the Kremlin the great throng stood in the rain and sleet, while Bukharin, Kollontai, Radek, Reinstein, Murphy, and Rosmer spoke. To the Americans the speeches seemed hard and impersonal—except for the warmth of Alexandra Kollontai's tribute. For Bukharin and Radek and the others the death of John Reed was only an incident in the struggle for world revolution. He would have approved.

ACKNOWLEDGMENTS

WITHOUT the assistance of Louise Bryant, who placed at my disposal not only all of John Reed's papers but also her own notes regarding his life, this biography would have been almost impossible. The number of references to the Louise Bryant Collection in Appendix A is some measure of my indebtedness to her.

I am scarcely less indebted to John Stuart, who abandoned his own plan to write a biography of Reed, turned over to me all the material he had gathered, and for nearly a year devoted himself to research for this book. The book owes more than I can say to his faithful examination of newspaper and magazine files and to his resourceful investigation of all sorts of clues. It owes much, too, to his suggestions for the treatment of the material, and, though I have done the actual writing of the book, so that he is not to be held responsible for its faults, I am conscious of the extent to which his judgments have influenced and enriched the presentation.

To the individual members of the Harvard Alumni John Reed Committee and to the committee as a whole I am grateful for many kinds of assistance. It was this committee that made it possible for John Stuart to go to Paris, organize the material that Louise Bryant had so kindly offered to put at my disposal, and bring it back to this country. Its secretary-treasurer, Corliss Lamont, originally suggested my writing the book, and he has repeatedly helped and encouraged me.

A biography such as this, even though one individual retains responsibility, becomes a collective effort. Despite the considerable amount of documentary material available, the book would have been a bare outline if persons who knew John Reed had not come to my aid. More than one hundred and fifty of them did help me, and I gratefully list their names:

Jane Addams, G. W. H. Allen, Sherwood Anderson, William F. Avery, Roger Baldwin, George Gordon Battle, Bessie Beatty, Maurice Becker, George Biddle, Carl Binger, Frank Bohn, F. S. Boyd, Heywood Broun, Roger Burlingame, John G. Burr, Arthur P. Butler, David Carb, Kate Carew, Stuart Chase, Maximilian Cohen, Saxe Commins, Charles Townsend Copeland, William H. Daly,

Frank Damrosch, H. W. L. Dana, Francis W. Davis, Floyd Dell, Robert Dunn, T. S. Eliot, Joseph Ellner, Charles W. Ervin, Joseph Ettor, John Evans, F. D. Everett, George Falconer, Alice Withrow Field, Sara Bard Field, M. Eleanor Fitzgerald, Elizabeth Gurley Flynn, Martha Foley, Louis C. Fraina, Waldo Frank, Lewis Gannett, Arturo Giovannitti, H. J. Glintenkamp, Alan Gregg, Thomas N. Gregory, Alex Gumberg.

Robert Hallowell, Harry Hansen, Hutchins Hapgood, William Hard, Arthur Garfield Hays, Hugh H. Herdman, Paula Holladay, Frank M. Houck, R. S. Howard, Wilfred Humphries, Edward E. Hunt, Gustave A. Hunziker, Fannie Hurst, Agnes Inglis, Will Irwin, Ellis O. Jones, H. V. Kaltenborn, Francis F. Kane, John Kelley, Nicholas Kelley, John Kennard, Edna Kenton, Charles Kuntz, Alfred B. Kuttner, William S. Ladd, Sinclair Lewis, Sally Lewis, Paul Lieder, Edward Lindgren, Walter Lippmann, William Bross Lloyd, Herman Lorber.

Eadmonn MacAlpine, Percy MacKaye, Don Marquis, George H. Marsh, Edward S. Martin, George W. Martin, Lewis A. McArthur, Isaac McBride, Samuel Duff McCoy, Spencer Miller, Robert Minor, Richard Montgomery, Edward J. Morgan, Benjamin W. Morris, Charlotte Morton, Robert A. Morton, Scott Nearing, William Allan Neilson, Walter M. Nelson, Albert Jay Nock, Charles D. Osborne, Eric Parson, Jeannette D. Pearl, Waldo Peirce, Owen W. Penney, Marlen E. Pew, J. S. Phillips, W. T. Pickering, Amos Pinchot, Ernest Poole, Grace Potter, Lucien Price, Patrick Quinlan, Charles Recht, Boardman Robinson, Robert E. Rogers, Mrs. C. O. Rose.

Wheeler Sammons, Isidor Schneider, Howard Scott, Frank Shay, Lee Simonson, Herman Simpson, Harrison Smith, MacCormac Snow, Sigmund Spaeth, Louis Stark, Thomas Steep, Lincoln Steffens, George Stephenson, Alice Strong, Genevieve Taggard, Ida Tarbell, Graham Taylor, G. H. Tilghman, Berkeley G. Toby, Marie Tomsett, Carlo Tresca, John Kenneth Turner, Louis Untermeyer, Richard Van Buskirk, Mary Heaton Vorse, Mrs. David Wallerstein, Carl Walters, Helen Walters, Hathaway Watson, John Hall Wheelock, Albert Rhys Williams, Gluyas Williams, Bertram Wolfe, Berwick B. Wood, Charles Erskine Scott Wood, Francis C. Woodman, Hella Wuolojoki, Philip Wyman, Art Young, H. A. Osgood, Ruth Osgood.

Some of these persons gave more information than others, but all of them gave generously, and I thank them all. The reader may observe the absence from the list of certain names that appear frequently in the text. There were a few men and women who, though they were closely associated with Reed, refused, for reasons that seemed adequate to them, to help me. I mention the fact merely because it should be made clear that I did not intentionally neglect any possible source of information.

To some of the men and women I have listed I have a double debt, for they read portions of the manuscript: Frank Damrosch, Robert Dunn, Louis C. Fraina, Robert Hallowell, Edward E. Hunt, Samuel Duff McCoy, Boardman Robinson, Lincoln Steffens, Alice Strong, and Albert Rhys Williams.

My obligations to Robert Hallowell extend still further, for he gave me permission to reproduce his portrait of John Reed, painted for the Harvard Alumni John Reed Committee and now hung in Adams House at Harvard. His friendship, moreover, has been not only a personal satisfaction but an influence upon the book.

Special gratitude is also due Harrison Smith, who, in spite of his interest in another project for a biography of Reed, contributed his personal recollections and helped me to secure material that I needed.

I wish to thank Samuel Charniak, H. W. L. Dana, and Sergei Dinamov for gathering material in the Soviet Union, Lee Levenson for her faithful work in copying and recopying the manuscript, Nelson and Tillie Frank for scrutinizing the manuscript for errors of fact, and Robert G. Davis for his critical reading of the text.

If I have accidentally omitted any one from this list whose name belongs upon it, I offer apologies as well as thanks. There are those, very close to me, whose names I have consciously omitted, as they preferred; they know the magnitude of my debt and the warmth of my appreciation.

G. H.

Grafton, New York
January 1, 1936

APPENDIX A

Notes

Since it has seemed unwise to interrupt the pages of this biography with footnotes, I have listed below the principal sources for each chapter, and the careful reader will, I think, have little difficulty in discovering the authority for each statement. The sources are principally of three kinds: Reed's articles, published and unpublished; letters to and from him; and information given me in letters or interviews by persons who knew him.

The largest volume of material at my disposal was the collection preserved by John Reed's widow, Louise Bryant, which includes scores of manuscripts, more than a thousand letters to John Reed and more than a hundred from him, the notebooks that he kept in Mexico and Russia and many miscellaneous notes, pamphlets and newspapers that he had collected, scores of clippings related to him, and a variety of personal possessions. It was placed at my disposal through the generosity of Louise Bryant and with the cooperation of the Harvard Alumni John Reed Committee, which is its custodian. In these notes it is referred to as the L.B.C. All published works by John Reed mentioned in the text are listed in the bibliography (Appendix B).

Chapter I

For much of the information in this chapter I am indebted to H. H. Herdman, R. S. Howard, Dr. William S. Ladd, Miss Sally Lewis, Edward S. Martin, Lewis A. McArthur, Mrs. C. O. Rose, MacCormac Snow, Berwick B. Wood, Colonel Charles Erskine Scott Wood and especially Miss Alice Strong. Miss Strong, Mr. McArthur, and Elizabeth Gurley Flynn have helped me with copies of articles in Portland newspapers, and Richard G. Montgomery, in addition to giving me what information he could, appealed to others on my behalf.

Reed's description of Lee Sing's celebration of his birth is in an

unpublished manuscript in the L.B.C. Mrs. Alice Withrow Field secured for me information regarding Mrs. Green's ancestry. Obitu-
aries of Mr. Green appeared in the Portland *Oregonian* for Apr. 7
and Apr. 12, 1885. It is from that of the later date, written by T. B.
Merry, that I have quoted. There is also an account of Mr. Green's
life in H. W. Scott's *History of Portland* (Syracuse, N. Y., 1890).
Some of the information regarding C. J. Reed is taken from his obitu-
ary in the Portland *Oregonian* for July 3, 1912.

The second section of the chapter is based largely on Reed's autobiographical essay, "Almost Thirty," in the L.B.C. For comment on
the writing of this essay see Chapter XIII.

The essay, "The Best Camping Experience," is in the L.B.C.

Chapter II

A. P. Butler and F. C. Woodman, formerly masters of the Morristown School, and G. H. Tilghman, the present headmaster, have
given information on Reed's school activities. The Rev. Frank Damrosch, Jr. drew generously on his memories and lent a file of the
Morristonian. G. W. H. Allen lent his file of the *Rooster*. Letters
with useful information were received from Major John Kennard,
Roger Burlingame, and George Stephenson.

Much information has been derived from the *Morristonian*, and
all verse is quoted therefrom. The sentences by Reed are quoted
from "Almost Thirty." The story of the southern boy who influenced Reed was told me by Dr. Alan Gregg. G. H. Marsh gave me
the facts concerning C. J. Reed's appointment as United States
Marshal.

Chapter III

We have examined the files from 1906 to 1910 of the *Harvard
Crimson*, the *Harvard Monthly*, the *Harvard Advocate*, the *Lampoon*, and the *Harvard Illustrated Magazine*. We have also consulted
the university catalogs of the same period and the class albums. Some
information has been drawn from subsequent reports of the class of
1910.

This documentary material has been supplemented by letters from
or interviews with William F. Avery, Stuart Chase, Charles Townsend Copeland, Francis W. Davis, Alan Gregg, Robert Hallowell,
Edward E. Hunt, H. V. Kaltenborn, John Kelley, Nicholas Kelley,
Paul Lieder, Walter Lippmann, Percy MacKaye, George W. Martin, William Allan Neilson, Eric Parson, W. T. Pickering, Lucien
Price, Robert Emmons Rogers, Wheeler Sammons, Lee Simonson,

MacCormac Snow, Hathaway Watson, John Hall Wheelock, Gluyas Williams, and Philip Wyman.

Most of the passages in which Reed comments on Harvard are taken from "Almost Thirty." I have also drawn on another unpublished essay by him, "The Harvard Renaissance." Three different versions of this essay are in the possession of Edward E. Hunt, who lent them to me. There is a copy of the longest version in the L.B.C. The essay is discussed in Chapter V.

Robert Hallowell tells the story of Reed's proposal to write a book about Harvard in his article in the *New Republic* (Nov. 17, 1920). The account of the *Monthly* initiation is from Edward E. Hunt's "Friendly Faces" in the *Monthly* for March, 1917. (Hallowell told me about the poem Hunt read.) The description of the club system is from "The Harvard Renaissance." The bulletin from Concord is in the possession of Edward E. Hunt. Reed told the story of his meeting with William James in "A Reminiscence," in the *American Magazine* (Nov., 1911). In the same issue, in the department called "Interesting People," he has an article on Copeland. The words and music of *Diana's Debut* were published (Cambridge, 1910). The manuscripts of "Tit for Tat" and "The Last of the Pirates" and the letters from Steffens and Wood are in the L.B.C. The letters from which the adverse comments in the last paragraph are quoted were written in response to the Harvard Alumni John Reed Committee's appeal for funds.

CHAPTER IV

The story of Waldo Peirce's dive has become a legend. The account I have given is based upon a journal Reed wrote on the cattleboat (in the L.B.C.). This substantiates Peirce's own version of the adventure. Reed based a story on the incident, which he called "The Cattleboat Murder" (ms. in the L.B.C.). This was revised by Julian Street, and the revision, entitled "Overboard," appeared in the *Saturday Evening Post* for Oct. 28, 1911, as the work of Reed and Street. It is, naturally, the farthest removed from the facts of the three versions, but it is closer to the truth than some of the stories that have been circulated.

The account of the Spanish trip is derived from an unpublished article in the L.B.C., "A Dash Into Spain." Otherwise the chapter is based almost entirely on Reed's letters to his mother, father, and brother (in the L.B.C.) and to Alan Gregg (lent me by Dr. Gregg). This information has been supplemented by interviews with Waldo Peirce, Gluyas Williams, and H. W. L. Dana, and a letter from Kate Carew.

Chapter V

Steffens describes his relations with Reed in his *Autobiography*, especially pages 654-6. Reed pays tribute to Steffens in "Almost Thirty."

Reed's letters to Peirce were lent me by the latter. Other letters quoted in this chapter are in the L.B.C.

The description of Reed's wanderings about New York is based on a passage in "Almost Thirty." The list of plays is taken from a scrapbook in the L.B.C.

"The Harvard Radicalettes" was lent me by Edward E. Hunt.

The following persons gave, in interviews or letters, material used in this chapter: Robert Hallowell, Edward E. Hunt, Alfred Kuttner, Walter Lippmann, Percy MacKaye, Samuel Duff McCoy, H. A. Osgood, Ruth Osgood, Robert E. Rogers, Frank Shay, Lincoln Steffens.

The published poems, stories, and articles by Reed discussed in this chapter are listed in the bibliography. The unpublished ones are in the L.B.C.

Chapter VI

The story of the re-organization of the *Masses* is drawn from Art Young's *On My Way* (1928). Reed's draft of the statement of purpose is in the L.B.C. According to Max Eastman ("New Masses for Old," *Modern Monthly*, June, 1934), he gave Reed's statement the form in which it was published. Eastman speaks of Reed's connection with the magazine in a speech on John Reed reprinted in the *Liberator* for Dec., 1920.

Mabel Dodge's salon is described in Steffens' *Autobiography* and, in a fictional form that constitutes no disguise, in Carl Van Vechten's *Peter Whiffle* (1922) and Max Eastman's *Venture* (1927). Mabel Dodge Luhan's *Background* (1933) and *European Experiences* (1935) take her story only as far as her return to the United States in 1912.

Reed's arrest in Paterson is described in the New York *Times* and other papers of April 29, 1913. Reed described his arrest and imprisonment in "War in Paterson" (*Masses*, June, 1913) and conditions in the jail in "Sheriff Radcliff's Hotel" (*Metropolitan*, Sept., 1913).

The Paterson strike is described in *Industrial Relations* (64th Congress, 1st Session, Senate Document 415, 1916) Vol. III, 2411-2634. *Bill Haywood's Book* (1929) describes both the strike and the pageant, as does Mary Heaton Vorse's *A Footnote to Folly* (1935). Carlo Tresca, Elizabeth Gurley Flynn, Mary Heaton Vorse, Frederick Sumner Boyd, Ernest Poole, and Grace Potter gave information in interviews and letters. Tresca permitted us to read his unpublished autobiography. Susan Glaspell mentions the pageant in *The Road to the Temple* (1927). The printed program contains a synopsis of the pageant. John H. Steiger's *Memoirs of a Silk Striker* (Paterson, 1914) discusses the strike and the pageant in terms of complete hostility to the I.W.W.

There are brief references to John Reed's European trip in *The Autobiography of Alice B. Toklas* (1933) and Muriel Draper's *Music at Midnight* (1929). E. E. Hunt lent me a copy of a newspaper story about Reed's speaking to the Italian Socialists. Otherwise the material in the chapter is based upon Reed's letters to his mother and to Mr. Hunt. Mr. Hunt lent me the letters to him. Other letters quoted in this chapter are in the L.B.C.

CHAPTER VII

Floyd Dell's *Homecoming* (1933) and Alfred Kreymborg's *Troubadour* (1925) describe Greenwich Village in 1913 and mention Reed. Some of the material in the first section and the opening paragraphs of the second section is based on information given by F. S. Boyd, Waldo Frank, H. J. Glintenkamp, Don Marquis, and Lee Simonson. The interpretation of Reed's state of mind before going to Mexico owes much to "Almost Thirty."

The remainder of the chapter is entirely based on Reed's writings, except for a little information about Reed in El Paso and the Torreon campaign given by Thomas Steep. Most, but not all, of the material is included in *Insurgent Mexico*. The book is not, however, arranged in chronological order. I am giving, therefore, a chronological chart, with dates when they can be determined, and with the sources of information about each episode. The notebook referred to is the one Reed kept in Mexico, which exists, unfortunately incomplete, in the L.B.C.

Presidio and Ojinaga—*Insurgent Mexico*, "On the Border"; "Endymion" (*Masses*, Dec., 1916).

Chihuahua (Dec. 25–Jan. 1) *Metropolitan*, Feb., 1914, p. 72. Most of the material on Villa is in *Insurgent Mexico*, Part II; a little comes from Reed's article in the *World*, Mar. 1, 1914. Some of the impressions of Chihuahua and the entire account of the trip to the mines are found in the notebook. "Mac–American" (*Masses*, Apr., 1914) and the notebook describe New Year's Eve.

Jiminez (Jan. 1) and Magistral—*Insurgent Mexico*, Part II, and the notebook. *Insurgent Mexico* conceals what the notebook makes clear, that Reed made the trip with Mac.

Santa Maria del Oro (Jan. 6)—*Insurgent Mexico*, Part VI, chapters 2-3.

Las Nieves (c. Jan. 9) and La Cadena—*Insurgent Mexico*, Part I, and notebook.

Chihuahua (c. Feb. 1)

El Paso (Feb. 12 or earlier)—Dispatches to the *World*, Feb. 13-28; notebook; two unpublished mss. in L.B.C.—the account of the Hearst agent, called "In Short," and an untitled description of the detectives in El Paso. Mr. Steep remembers the trip into the desert.

Chihuahua (c. Feb. 23-28)—*World* dispatches.

Nogales (Mar. 2-4) *Insurgent Mexico*, Part V, and *World* dispatches, Mar. 4.

Chihuahua (c. Mar. 10) *Insurgent Mexico*, Part VI, chapter 1.

Campaign on Torreon (c. Mar. 17-28) *Insurgent Mexico*, Part IV, notebook, and *World* dispatches.

El Paso (Mar. 30)—*World* dispatches.

Throughout the chapter I have used many of Reed's phrases without interrupting the text by quotation marks. Steffens' views on Mexico are to be found in his *Autobiography*. Lippmann's letter to Reed is in the L.B.C. The second quotation is from Lippmann's article, "Legendary John Reed," in the *New Republic* for Dec. 26, 1914.

Chapter VIII

Reed's report of the Union Square meeting appeared in the New York *World* for Apr. 12, 1914. Pulitzer's editorial was in the *World* for Apr. 29.

Upton Sinclair describes the Denver newspaper story about Reed in *The Brass Check* (1920). Jane Addams and Harry Hansen gave information in letters about Reed's visit to Hull House.

The unpublished interview with Wilson is in the L.B.C., as are the letters from Wilson and Tumulty. The description of the meeting with Bryan is based on the opening paragraphs of Reed's article, "Bryan on Tour." (See Chapter XII.) These paragraphs were omitted from the printed article (*Collier's*, May 20, 1916), but appear in the version in the L.B.C. Congratulatory letters on the statement in the *Times* and the Ludlow article and the letters from Hovey and Steffens mentioned in the text are in the L.B.C.

Some information comes from interviews with F. S. Boyd and Mary Heaton Vorse.

Chapter IX

The narrative in the first section follows Reed's *Metropolitan* articles: "The Englishman" (Oct., 1914); "The Approach to War" (Nov.); and part of "With the Allies" (Dec.). A note appended to "The Traders' War" (*Masses*, Sept.) states: "This article is written by a well-known author and war correspondent who is compelled by arrangements with another publication to withhold his name." Internal evidence indicates that it is Reed's.

The description of the attempt to reach the French front is based on an unpublished manuscript in the L.B.C., "Shot at Sunrise," and on Robert Dunn's *Five Fronts* (1915). Reed's impressions of London are drawn from another unpublished manuscript in the L.B.C., "Rule, Britannia!" Some material in this section comes from "Notes on the War, by Our European Correspondent" (*Masses*, Nov.). A comparison of this article with "Rule, Britannia!" and "This Unpopular War" (*Seven Arts*, Aug., 1917) unquestionably establishes Reed's authorship.

The description of Reed's visit to Germany follows his articles in the *Metropolitan* for March and April, 1915. The interview with Liebknecht is described in the *Liberator*, Mar., 1919, and the *Revolutionary Age*, Feb. 1, 1919. Dunn's account of the visit to the German lines appears in *Five Fronts*.

Some material in the chapter has been derived from interviews with F. S. Boyd, Robert Dunn, Alfred Kuttner, Ernest Poole, Lee Simonson, Robert Rogers, and Mr. and Mrs. Carl Walters.

Chapter X

The first number of the *New Republic* was dated Nov. 7, 1914. Lippmann's article on Reed appeared in the issue of Dec. 26.

A copy of *Enter Dibble* was lent me by Edward E. Hunt.

There is a description of Roosevelt and Reed in Sonya Levien's "Col. Roosevelt in Our Office," *Metropolitan Bulletin* for May, 1916. This has been supplemented by information from Boardman Robinson, William Hard, and Marie Tomsett. The quotations are from Roosevelt's articles in the March and April (1915) *Metropolitan*.

President Hibben's letter of protest appeared in the *Post* for Mar. 2, 1915. In the account of the incident in his book, *Five Fronts*, Dunn omitted all mention of Reed's firing. Reed denied in his testimony at the *Masses* trial and in his testimony at the hearings of the Overman committee that he fired in the direction of the French lines. (See Chapters XVII and XVIII.)

Material on Reed's Boston lecture comes from Boston newspapers of March 4, 5, and 6, 1915, and from Dr. Alan Gregg.

CHAPTER XI

The chapter closely follows *The War in Eastern Europe*, supplemented by information from Boardman Robinson. A few details are taken from Reed's article, "This Unpopular War."

The section on Russia follows a long letter which Reed wrote to Carl Hovey from Petrograd on July 14, 1915 (in the L.B.C.) and an unpublished article (also in the L.B.C.) called "No Americans Need Apply!" All conversations are taken from the latter, in the course of which Reed remarked that, though of course he did not have a stenographic record of what was said, he was willing to vouch for the essential accuracy of his report.

The description of the Serbian Socialist is taken from "The World Well Lost" (*Masses*, Feb., 1916), and the account of the Standard Oil employee in Bucharest comes from "The Rights of Small Nations" (*New Republic*, Nov. 27, 1915). A few details concerning the treatment of the Jews are taken from Reed's article, "The Jew on the Eastern Front" in *The Book of the Exile* (1916). A few details of his visit to Constantinople are derived from an unpublished fragment in the L.B.C.

CHAPTER XII

The account of Reed's lecture at the Harvard Club comes from Boardman Robinson, Robert Hallowell, and H. W. L. Dana; the account of the lecture at Sing Sing from Spencer Miller, Jr. Sally Lewis, Sara Bard Field, Mr. and Mrs. Carl Walters, and others gave information on Reed's meeting with Louise Bryant. The Brooklyn *Eagle* for Feb. 18, 1916, reported the speech to the Intercollegiate Socialist Society; the New York *Telegraph* for Mar. 10, 1916, the speech to the Columbia Social Study Club; and the New York *Call* for Jan. 7, the speech to the Labor Forum. John Kenneth Turner repeated Reed's comment on Villa in a letter. Alfred Kuttner reported Reed's reaction to the Schmidt execution. The account of the Willard-Moran fight is contained in an unpublished manuscript in the L.B.C. The article on Bryan appeared in *Collier's* for May 20, 1916. A somewhat expanded version of the article, Reed's notes with Bryan's revisions, and the correspondence between them are in the L.B.C.

"Fog" did not appear in *Scribner's* until Aug., 1919, but, according to John Hall Wheelock, it was accepted in Oct. 1916. "Pygmalion" was bought by the *New Republic* but not published; it is included in *Tamburlaine*. Reed's plans for a workers' theatre can be gathered from various letters to and from him in the L.B.C. They were described to me in some detail by Miss Grace Potter. The quarrel between the artists and Max Eastman has been described by Mr. Eastman in his article, "New Masses for Old" (*Modern Monthly*, June, 1934). I have supplemented Mr. Eastman's account with information received from H. J. Glintenkamp.

Reed's conversation with W. A. Neilson is described in a letter Reed wrote Louise Bryant and in a letter from Mr. Neilson to me. The various letters and telegrams urging Reed to go to Mexico are in the L.B.C. The sources of the material on the Provincetown Players are: *The Provincetown Players: A Story of the Theatre*, by Helen Deutsch and Stella Hanau (New York, 1931); information from F. S. Boyd, Louise Bryant, Saxe Commins, Grace Potter, Robert Rogers, and Mary Heaton Vorse; articles in the Boston *Globe* for Aug. 13, 1916, the Boston *Journal* for Aug. 19, and the Boston *Post* for Sept. 10; Susan Glaspell's *The Road to the Temple* (New York, 1927). The manuscript of "The Eternal Quadrangle" is in the L.B.C., as are the manuscripts of all the unpublished stories mentioned in this chapter. Reed's Bayonne articles appeared in the *Tribune* for Oct. 28, 1916, and the *Metropolitan* for Jan., 1917. The account of the questions addressed to Hughes appeared in the Springfield *Republican* for Aug. 2, 1916; the appeal to Socialists in the New York *Times* of Oct. 28; Reed's own statement in the Minneapolis *News* for Oct. 19, and in other papers; a general statement of the group in the *Times* for Nov. 3.

The account of Reed's hospital experience is based upon his letters to Louise Bryant, a summary of the hospital records supplied by Dr. F. M. Houck, and information from Eric Parson, Carl Binger, and Walter Lippmann. "Hospital Notes" appeared in *Poetry* for Aug., 1917. "Two Rooms" was unpublished; the manuscript is in the L.B.C.

Chapter XIII

Reed's remarks to Whigham are quoted in Julian Street's "Soviet Saint" (*Saturday Evening Post*, Sept. 13, 1930). Art Young describes his experiences with the *Metropolitan* in *On My Way*, p. 261. The manuscripts of the articles on Gompers and the Second International are in the L.B.C. Grace Potter and Joseph Ellner furnished information about the peace meeting in Washington. Accounts of the hearings appeared in the newspapers of Apr. 13 and 15, 1917; see also *Volunteer and Conscription System* (Hearings before the House Committee on Military Affairs, Apr. 14, 1917). The letter on conscription appeared in the *Call* of Apr. 19. The unfinished poem is in the L.B.C. Reed described the Hunt's Point Palace meeting in the *Masses* for Aug., 1917. The Goldman-Berkman trial is described in Emma Goldman's *Living My Life* (1931) and in the newspapers of

July 4, 1917. A list of Reed's articles in the *Mail* appears in the bibliography. Information about the *Mail* was given by Arthur Garfield Hays and Sigmund Spaeth. Waldo Frank gave information on Reed's relations with the *Seven Arts*. "Almost Thirty" is in the L.B.C.

CHAPTER XIV

The report on Reed's examination for military service and a letter regarding his exemption are in the L.B.C. "A Letter from John Reed" (*Masses*, Nov.-Dec., 1917) describes the delay in Halifax. The voyage is described in two unpublished articles, "Across the War World" and "Scratch a Russian," in the L.B.C. The description of Stockholm appeared in a letter, sent to Robert Hallowell but intended for publication in the *Masses*, also in the L.B.C. The dispatch from Stockholm appeared in the *Call* for Sept. 9, 1917. The trip from Stockholm to Petrograd is described in "Red Russia—I. Entrance," an unpublished manuscript in the L.B.C.

The letter of Sept. 17 was a personal letter to Boardman Robinson. On the same day Reed sent an article, in the form of a letter to Mrs. Robinson. It is from this that the quotation regarding the revolutionary alignment is taken. Both are in the L.B.C. Mr. Francis describes his surveillance of Reed in his *Russia from the American Embassy* (1921). The trip to the northern front is described in Reed's article, "Red Russia—A Visit to the Russian Army," which appeared in the *Liberator* in two parts (Apr. and May, 1918). Reed told about the visit to Sestroretzk in "Factory Control in Russia" (*Voice of Labor*, Nov. 1, 1919). The article sent Robinson appeared in the *Call* for Dec. 26, 1917.

Some incidents in this chapter are drawn from the first three chapters of *Ten Days That Shook the World*. I have also followed Reed's notebooks, which are in the L.B.C. There are two fragments of notebooks, containing notes taken in late September and early October, and one complete notebook, covering in detail the trip to the northern front, the interview with Lianozov, the meeting at Obukhovsky Zarod, and a session of the Council of the Republic. There are parallel accounts of some of the events of this chapter in Bessie Beatty's *The Red Heart of Russia* (1918), Louise Bryant's *Six Red Months in Russia* (1918), and Albert Rhys Williams' *Through the Russian Revolution* (1921).

CHAPTER XV

The chapter follows Chapters III to IX of *Ten Days That Shook the World*, often using Reed's words. These chapters, in turn, follow Reed's notebooks, which are in the L.B.C. Some additional information is taken from his articles in the *Liberator:* "Red Russia—The Triumph of the Bolsheviki" (March); "Red Russia—Kerensky" (April); "Kerensky is Coming!" (July). The books by Bryant, Beatty, and Williams mentioned above have also been used, together with information from Bessie Beatty, Louise Bryant, Alexander Gumberg, and Albert Rhys Williams.

Chapter XVI

The first section draws on Chapters X, XI, and XII of *Ten Days That Shook the World* and, especially in the description of Moscow, on the notebooks in the L.B.C. The Bureau of International Revolutionary Propaganda is described by Reed in "Foreign Affairs" (*Liberator*, June, 1918), "How Soviet Russia Conquered Imperial Germany" (*Liberator*, Jan., 1919), and "Doctor Rakovsky" (*Revolutionary Age*, Jan. 25, 1919), and by Bryant and Williams in their books cited above.

Williams describes the Cirque Moderne meeting in his "The Spirit of Internationalism," in *One Year of Revolution* (1918). "Skeleton Report," dated Jan. 6, 1918, is in the L.B.C. Reed described the dissolution of the Constituent Assembly in "The Constituent Assembly in Russia" (*Revolutionary Age*, Nov. 30, 1918). Reed's speech before the All-Russian Congress of Soviets was quoted in an account of the session in *Izvestia* for Jan. 24, 1918. This account is translated in a footnote on pages 257-8 of Edgar Sisson's *One Hundred Red Days* (1931).

The appointment of Reed as consul to New York was announced in the New York papers for Jan. 31, 1918. Dosch-Fleurot's account of his conversation with Reed appeared in the New York *World*, Oct. 19, 1920. The *Call* editorial appeared Jan. 31, and Eastman's article in the *Call* Feb. 3, 1918. The cancellation of the appointment is rather obscure. Ambassador Francis testified regarding it in his appearance before the Overman Committee (*Brewing and Liquor Interests*, III, 965). Sisson's part is described in his book cited above. Alexander Gumberg states that his action was not suggested by Sisson, as Sisson maintains, but was undertaken on his own initiative.

Documents regarding Reed's stay in Christiania and the telegrams sent him by Bryant and Steffens are in the L.B.C. The "Introduction" dated Mar., 1918, is in the L.B.C. Except for three stanzas, which appeared in *Poetry* (Apr., 1919), "America, 1918" remained unpublished until it appeared in the *New Masses*, Oct. 18, 1935.

Some of the material in this chapter comes from Louise Bryant, Wilfred Humphries, Charles Kuntz, Robert Minor, Harrison Smith, Graham Taylor, and Albert Rhys Williams.

Chapter XVII

Reed's arrest on his arrival in New York was described in the papers of Apr. 29 and 30, 1918. Floyd Dell reported the first *Masses* trial in the *Liberator* for June. The accounts of Reed's New York speeches are taken from the newspapers, chiefly the *Call*. His speech in Boston was described to me by Robert Rogers, Harry Dana, and Lucien Price. His arrest in Philadelphia is recorded in the records of the trial (see Chapter XVIII), in the newspapers of June 2 and 3, and in the *Liberator* for July. The account of the Detroit meeting is based on information given by Agnes Inglis and Walter Nelson.

The correspondence regarding his attempts to recover his papers is in the L.B.C. Floyd Dell tells of Frank Harris' proposal in *Homecoming*, page 327; Reed's prospectus is in the L.B.C. Reed's letter to Steffens is reproduced on page 771 of *The Autobiography of Lincoln Steffens*. Steffens' reply is in the L.B.C. Art Young describes the trip to Terre Haute and Chicago in *On My Way;* Reed described his Cleveland experiences in an unpublished letter to the *Call*, lent me by Charles Ervin; the chief sources of material on Debs and the I.W.W. are, of course, Reed's two articles in the Sept. *Liberator.*

There is some correspondence regarding his resignation from the *Liberator* in the L.B.C. The letters from Haywood, Debs, and Wood are in the L.B.C. The Hunt's Point Palace meeting was reported in the papers of Sept. 14 and 15. Reed's statement appeared in the *Call* for Sept. 16.

The principal source of material for the description of Reed's testimony in the second *Masses* trial is the official transcript of the court stenographer's record. Reed's article, "About the Second *Masses* Trial," appeared in the *Liberator* for Dec. Art Young's *On My Way* and Floyd Dell's *Homecoming* describe the trial. Charles Recht not only permitted me to read his unpublished autobiography and gave me what information he could but also supplied the transcript of Reed's testimony at his own expense. Reed mentions the trial of the Russians in "About the Second *Masses* Trial," and there is an article on the subject, very possibly his, in the same issue of the *Liberator.*

Marlen Pew and Floyd Dell have supplied some of the information in this chapter.

Chapter XVIII

For some of the material on the Sisson documents I am indebted to Graham Taylor. Reed's letter to the *Public* appeared in the issue of Oct. 19, 1918. His letters to *Upton Sinclair's* are in the issues of

Aug. and Dec., 1918. Accounts of speeches are chiefly taken from the *Call*.

An account of Reed's speech in Brooklyn on Jan. 10, 1919, appears in the report of the Overman committee, Vol. II, pp. 2758-2761. This report (*Brewing and Liquor Interests and German and Bolshevik Propaganda, Report and Hearings of the Subcommittee on the Judiciary, United States Senate*, Washington, 1919) is the source of my account of the hearing. The testimony of Kennedy, Tunney, and Stevenson is in Volume II, beginning on page 2661. The testimony of all those who spoke on Russian conditions is in Volume III. Stanley Frost's article, one of a series on "American Bolsheviki" appeared in the New York *Tribune* for Mar. 27, 1919. The editorial, "One Man Who Needs the Rope," appeared in the Jacksonville (Florida) *Times-Union* for Feb. 24, 1919; a clipping of the editorial was lent me by Edward E. Hunt. Reed's letter to the *Times* was published in the *Revolutionary Age* for Apr. 12, 1919, and in the *Call* for Apr. 22.

The account of the Philadelphia trial is based on information from F. F. Kane, formerly Mr. Wallerstein's partner, Mrs. David Wallerstein, his widow, and Charlotte Morton, his secretary, and on the records of the trial, made available by Mr. Kane. Accounts of the trial appeared daily in the *Call*.

Some of the material in this chapter comes from interviews with or letters from Sherwood Anderson, Roger Baldwin, Maximilian Cohen, Paula Holliday, Alfred Kuttner, and Herman Lorber.

CHAPTER XIX

The Shaplen debate was reported in the *Call* for March 7, and a letter from Shaplen appeared in the issue of Mar. 8. Most of the documents involved in the rise of the left wing are to be found in the Lusk report (*Revolutionary Radicalism*, Albany, 1920). The files of the *Revolutionary Age* and the New York *Communist* and Louis C. Fraina's report to the Executive Committee of the Communist International (reprinted in *Red Radicalism*, exhibits collected by A. Mitchell Palmer, Washington, 1920) contain much material.

Fieldman's correspondence with Reed and drafts of Reed's articles are in the L.B.C., as are Reed's letters to and from Louise Bryant and his letters from his mother.

There is a large collection of reviews of *Ten Days That Shook the World* in the L.B.C. Wilfred Humphries and Louis Stark gave me information about Reed in Atlantic City. The left-wing conference is described in the Lusk report and in Fraina's report to the E.C.C.I. Helen and Carl Walters reported to me incidents of the weeks at

Truro. Susan Glaspell describes her conversation with Reed in *The Road to the Temple*, p. 302.

The three conventions are described in the Lusk report, the *Call*, James Oneal's *American Communism* (1927), *The American Labor Year Book*, Vol. III (1920), Fraina's report to the E.C.C.I., the *Communist Labor Party News* for Sept. and Oct., 1919, Max Eastman's "The Chicago Conventions" (*Liberator*, Oct., 1919), William Bross Lloyd's "Convention Impressions" (*Class Struggle*, Nov., 1919), and *Official Report of the Chicago Convention*, by John Reed and Benjamin Gitlow.

Information used in this chapter was supplied by Sherwood Anderson, Roger Baldwin, F. S. Boyd, Maximilian Cohen, Louis Fraina, Wilfred Humphries, Eadmonn MacAlpine, Scott Nearing, Jeannette Pearl, and Howard Scott.

The following chronological chart may assist the reader in following my account of the early period of Communism in the United States:

Nov. 7, 1918. Communist Propaganda League formed in Chicago.

Nov. 16, 1918. First issue of the *Revolutionary Age*, published by Local Boston of the Socialist Party.

Feb. 8, 1919. *Revolutionary Age* publishes program and manifesto of the left wing.

Feb. 15, 1919. Left wing organizes in New York City.

Mar. 2-6, 1919. First Congress of Third International in Moscow.

Apr. 19, 1919. First issue of New York *Communist*.

May 21, 1919. "The Socialist Task and Outlook," by Morris Hillquit, appears in New York *Call*.

May 24-30, 1919. National executive committee of Socialist Party meets in Chicago and expels 40,000 members.

June 21-24, 1919. Left-wing conference in New York City. Majority of delegates votes to work within Socialist Party. Minority, representing Slavic federations and Michigan Socialists, withdraws.

July 5, 1919. New York *Communist* combines with *Revolutionary Age*, which becomes national organ of left wing.

July 7, 1919. Slavic federations and Michigan Socialists issue call for Communist Party convention.

July 19, 1919. National organization committee (minority of left-wing conference, representing Slavic federations and Michigan Socialists) issues the *Communist* in Chicago.

July 26-27, 1919. New (unofficial) national executive committee, chosen in spring elections (declared illegal by existing national executive committee) meets in Chicago.

Aug. 23, 1919. Majority of national council of the left wing (elected at left-wing conference, June 21-24) joins Slavic federations

and Michigan Socialists in call for Communist Party convention.
Opposing minority resigns.

Aug. 30, 1919. National Emergency Convention of Socialist Party.
Left-wing delegates (including minority of national council of
the left wing) expelled and sympathizers withdraw.

Aug. 31, 1919. Left-wing delegates and sympathizers meet and proclaim their meeting to be true National Emergency Convention.

Sept. 1, 1919. Convention called by Slavic federations, Michigan
Socialists, and majority of national council of left wing forms
Communist Party.

Sept. 2, 1919. Left-wing delegates and sympathizers form Communist Labor Party.

May, 1920. The Communist Labor Party and a majority of the
Communist Party combine to form the United Communist
Party. A minority of the Communist Party calls itself the Com-
munist Party.

CHAPTER XX

George N. Falconer, Martha Foley, Don Marquis, Isidor Schneider, and Carlo Tresca have reported to me incidents of the three
weeks between Reed's arrival in New York and his departure for
Russia. The letters to Louise Bryant are in the L.B.C. An unfinished
article, in the L.B.C., describes Reed's arrival in Finland.

Angelica Balabonova describes Reed in Russia in an article, "John
Reed, Poet and Revolutionist," a translation of which is in the L.B.C.
Part of this article was reproduced in the souvenir program of the
John Reed memorial meeting, Oct. 17, 1921. An article in the New
York *World* of Aug. 11, 1921, based on information "from a source
that is beyond question as to authority," also dealt with the winter
of 1919–20. Most of my material, however, is drawn from Reed's
notebooks in the L.B.C. and from his article, "Soviet Russia Now,"
in the *Liberator* for Dec., 1920, and Jan., 1921. The notebooks
contain much more material than the article, especially the account
of the trip to the Volga.

In *Living My Life* (pp. 739-41), Emma Goldman speaks of Reed's
coming to see her soon after her arrival in Moscow in January. She
reports that he was planning to return by way of Latvia. In the
Liberator for Dec., 1920, he describes a trip to the Latvian front.
With no more evidence than Miss Goldman's statement, I have
assumed that this trip was part of an unsuccessful attempt to leave
Russia. Louise Bryant's correspondence with the State Department,
Reed's letters to her, and his letters to Madame Malmberg are in the
L.B.C. These are the principal sources for this episode. William
Hard described for me his conversation with Baruch. Eadmonn Mac-

Alpine reported the story of the exchange of prisoners, which he had heard from Reed in Russia.

The account of Reed's writings while in jail is based on a number of assumptions. One of the fragments of "The Ever-Victorious" is written on the back of a copy of a telegram sent from Abo, and the sheet is stamped with the prison seal. The notes for the two novels were, internal evidence shows, made after the fall of 1919. The chief reason for thinking they were made in Abo is that they are on the rather peculiar kind of squared paper on which all his prison letters were written. "A Letter to Louise" was written in the spring of 1920 and therefore presumably in Finland, though possibly after his return to Moscow.

CHAPTER XXI

Reed described his impressions of Moscow and Petrograd in June and July in his article for the *Liberator*. Emma Goldman speaks of Reed's return from Finland in *My Disillusionment in Russia* (1923), *My Further Disillusionment in Russia* (1924), and *Living My Life* (1931). Her statement that he felt his life had been needlessly jeopardized, made only in the latest of these three accounts, is not supported by information from other sources. The letters to Louise Bryant are in the L.B.C.

Jacob Rubin in *I Live to Tell* (1934) has stated that in June, 1920, Reed confessed to him that he was no longer a Communist. The events described in this chapter are sufficient refutation of this story, but doubt is also cast on it by: 1) the extremely questionable nature of much of the other material in the book; 2) the implausibility of Reed's making such a confession to Rubin, who was posing as a Bolshevik sympathizer, rather than to, say, Emma Goldman, who was opposed to the regime; 3) Rubin's ignorance of Reed's movements, as shown in his statement that Reed spent the summer in the Caucasus; 4) the unlikelihood of Reed's having made certain of the statements Rubin attributes to him, e.g., "In the United States I hated the capitalist system, but I was at liberty to get up on a street corner and express myself." The story would not even be worth bothering to contradict if it had not been given wide publicity by the Associated Press.

The account of the Comintern congress is based on Reed's article, "The World Congress of the Communist International," published in the *Communist*, #10 (no date), on the stenographic report, *Protokolle des II Kongresses der Kommunistischen Internationale* (Moscow, 1920), on *The Second Congress of the Communist International* (translations of reports in the Russian papers, published by the division of Russian affairs of the State Department, Washington,

1920), and on *Statutes, Theses, Etc. of the Communist International* (Chicago, 1923). Reed's speech on the Negro question is given in full in *The Second Congress of the Communist International*, pp. 151-4, and was commented upon in the New York *Tribune* for Nov. 27, 1920. Information regarding Reed's part in the congress was given me by Louis C. Fraina, Eadmonn MacAlpine, Owen W. Penney, and a delegate to the congress who does not wish to have his name revealed.

Translations of relevant portions of the official stenographic report of the Congress of Oriental Nations have been furnished me by friends. The incident of the return trip was described by Michael Gold in his column in the *Daily Worker* for Oct. 14, 1935. Louise Bryant describes the last month of Reed's life in her article, "Last Days with John Reed" (*Liberator*, Feb., 1921) and in her letter to Mrs. Reed, a copy of which was lent me by E. E. Hunt. The quotation from Clare Sheridan's diary is taken from her *Mayfair to Moscow* (1921), in which there is also a description of Reed's funeral. Emma Goldman describes the funeral in the works cited above, and Alexander Berkman in *The Bolshevik Myth* (1925). I am indebted for other information to Louis C. Fraina and Wilfred Humphries. The official medical report was printed in the New York *Call* for Nov. 3, 1920. Emma Goldman, Alexander Berkman, Marguerite Harrison (in *Marooned in Moscow*, 1921) and M. Schwartz (in an interview printed in the New York *Tribune* for Jan. 12, 1921) all mention the fact that Reed received the best medical attention that was possible under existing circumstances.

APPENDIX B

Bibliography

I. WORKS BY JOHN REED

1. Books and Pamphlets

Diana's Debut. Lyrics by J. S. Reed, music by Walter S. Langshaw. Cambridge: privately printed. 1910.

Sangar. Riverside, Conn.: Frederick C. Bursch. 1913.

The Day in Bohemia, or Life Among the Artists. Riverside, Conn.: privately printed. 1913.

Everymagazine, An Immorality Play. Words by Jack Reed, music by Bill Daly. New York: privately printed. 1913.

Insurgent Mexico. New York: D. Appleton and Company. 1914.

The War in Eastern Europe. New York: Charles Scribner's Sons. 1916. Abridged edition, *ibid.*, 1919.

Tamburlaine. Riverside, Conn.: Frederick C. Bursch. 1917.

The Sisson Documents. New York: Liberator Publishing Company. 1918.

Ten Days That Shook the World. New York: Boni and Liveright. 1919. New York: International Publishers. 1926. New York: Modern Library. 1935.

Daughter of the Revolution, edited by Floyd Dell. New York: Vanguard Press. 1927.

2. Plays

"Moondown," *Masses*, Sept., 1913.

"Freedom," in *The Provincetown Plays, Second Series* (New York, 1916) and *A Treasury of Plays for Men*, edited by Frank Shay (Boston, 1923).

"The Peace That Passeth Understanding," *Liberator*, Mar., 1919.

3. Poems

(Those marked with an asterisk are reprinted in *Tamburlaine*.)

"In Memoriam (Anson Hard Boulton)," *Morristonian*, Mar., 1905.

"The Storm at Midnight," *Morristonian*, Apr., 1905.

"The Violin," *Morristonian*, June, 1905.

"Twilight," *Morristonian*, Dec., 1905.

"Thermopylae," *Morristonian*, Dec., 1905.

"Sonnet to a Daisy (Apologies to Milton)," *Morristonian*, Jan., 1906.

"Diodotus' Speech in Defense of the People of Mytilene," *Morristonian*, Feb., 1906.

"Morning," *Morristonian*, Mar., 1906.

"To Thee," *Morristonian*, Mar., 1906.

"A Dedication," *Morristonian*, June, 1906.

"Lines to Tennyson," *Morristonian*, June, 1906.

"Lost," *Morristonian*, June, 1906.

"Guinevere," *Harvard Monthly*, July, 1907.

* "October," *Pacific Monthly*, Oct., 1907.

"Tschaikowsky," *Harvard Monthly*, Oct., 1907. (Reprinted in *Selected Poems from the Harvard Monthly, 1885–1910*, Cambridge, 1910.)

"Pan," *Morristonian*, Jan., 1908.

"The Tempest," *Harvard Monthly*, Jan., 1908.

"California," *Harvard Monthly*, Feb., 1908.

* "The Desert," *Harvard Monthly*, Apr., 1908.

"Night," *Pacific Monthly*, May, 1908.

"The West," *Harvard Advocate*, June 15, 1908.

"The Dancing Woman," *Harvard Monthly*, Oct., 1908.

* "Coyote Song," *Harvard Monthly*, Oct., 1908.

"The Sea-Gull," *Harvard Advocate*, Oct., 16, 1908.

"A Winter Run," *Harvard Illustrated Magazine*, Jan., 1909.

"The Sword Dance," *Harvard Monthly*, Feb., 1909.

"Dear Heart," *Harvard Monthly*, Mar., 1909.

"And Yet—," *Harvard Monthly*, Mar., 1909.

* "Forgotten" (Adapted from the French of Heredia), *Harvard Monthly*, May, 1909. Also *American Magazine*, Dec., 1911.

"Flowers of Fire" (Adapted from the French of Heredia), *Harvard Monthly*, May, 1909.

"De Profundo," *Harvard Monthly*, Oct., 1909.

"Melisande," *Harvard Monthly*, Nov., 1909.

"Score" (Words for song by J. W. Adams). Sheet music, Cambridge, 1909.

"Wanderlust," *Harvard Monthly*, May, 1910.

"Willamette," *Pacific Monthly*, July, 1910.

* "The Wanderer to His Heart's Desire," *American Magazine*, Aug., 1911.

* "The Foundations of a Sky-Scraper," *American Magazine*, Oct., 1911.

"Revolt," *International*, Jan., 1912.

* "The Slave" (Adapted from the French of Heredia), *American Magazine*, Feb., 1912.

"The Tenement Clothes Line," New York *Mail*, Apr. 24, 1912. (Reprinted in *The Day in Bohemia*.)

* "June in the City," *American Magazine*, June, 1912.

* "This Magazine of Ours," *American Magazine*, July, 1912.

* "The Wedding Ring," *American Magazine*, Aug., 1912.

* "Sangar," *Poetry*, Dec., 1912. (Published in booklet form by F. C. Bursch, Riverside, Conn., 1913. Reprinted in Monroe and Henderson, *The New Poetry*.)

* "Tamburlaine," *American Magazine*, Jan., 1913.

* "A Hymn to Manhattan," *American Magazine*, Feb., 1913. (Reprinted in *The Day in Bohemia*.)
* "Deep-Water Song," *Century*, Mar., 1913.
* "April," *American Magazine*, Apr., 1913.
* "A Song for May," *American Magazine*, May, 1913.
* "A Farmer's Woman," *Masses*, July, 1913. (Reprinted in *May Days*, edited by Genevieve Taggard.)
"Noon," *Collier's*, July 26, 1913.
"The Great Adventure," New York *Press*, Oct. 26, 1913.
* "Winter Night," *American Magazine*, Jan., 1914.
* "Love At Sea," *Masses*, May, 1916.
* "To Max Eastman," Hillacre Broadside, 1916 (?).
"Hospital Notes," *Poetry*, Aug., 1917.
"Proud New York," *Poetry*, Apr., 1919. (Reprinted in *Poetry*, Jan., 1921, and in Monroe and Henderson, *The New Poetry*.)
"Fog," Scribner's, Aug., 1919. (Reprinted in the *Liberator*, Dec., 1920, and in *May Days*, edited by Genevieve Taggard.)
"America, 1918," *New Masses*, Oct. 15, 1935.

4. Short Stories and Sketches

(Those marked with an asterisk are reprinted in *Daughter of the Revolution*.)

"A Typical Yankee Tale," *Morristonian*, Nov., 1904.
"The Transformation," *Morristonian*, Jan., 1905.
"Atlantis," *Morristonian*, May, 1905.
"The End of the World," *Morristonian*, Dec., 1905.
"The Tragedy of a Mild-Mannered Man," *Morristonian*, Jan., 1906.
"The Conspiracy," *Morristonian*, June, 1906.
"Bacchanal," *Harvard Monthly*, June, 1907.
"The Red Hand," *Harvard Monthly*, Apr., 1908.
"Infinities," *Pacific Monthly*, Oct., 1908.
"From Clatsop to Nekarney," *Harvard Monthly*, Dec., 1908.
"The Pharaoh," *Harvard Monthly*, Jan., 1909.
"The Singing Gates," *Harvard Monthly*, Feb., 1909.
"The Winged Stone," *Harvard Monthly*, Apr., 1909.
"In England's Need," *Harvard Monthly*, Jan. and Feb., 1910.
"East is East and West is West," *Harvard Monthly*, Oct., 1910.
"The Swimmers," *Forum*, Aug., 1911.
"Overboard" (in collaboration with Julian Street), *Saturday Evening Post*, Oct. 28, 1911.
"The Man from the Seine," *Century*, June, 1912.
"Monsieur Vidoq Steps Up," *Century*, Sept., 1912.
"The Dinner Guests of Big Tim," *American Magazine*, Dec., 1912.
* "Where the Heart Is," *Masses*, Jan., 1913.
* "A Taste of Justice," *Masses*, Apr., 1913.
"The Peripatetic Prince," *Smart Set*, June, 1913. (Reprinted in *The Smart Set Anthology*.)
* "Another Case of Ingratitude," *Masses*, July, 1913.
"Showing Mrs. Van," *Smart Set*, Dec., 1913.

* "Seeing is Believing," *Masses*, Dec., 1913.
* "Mac–American," *Masses*, Apr., 1914.
* "The Englishman. A War Correspondent's Wondering Observation," *Metropolitan*, Oct., 1914.
"The Cook and the Captain Bold," *Metropolitan*, Nov., 1914.
* "Daughter of the Revolution," *Masses*, Feb., 1915.
"The Barber of Lille," *Metropolitan*, July, 1915.
* "The Rights of Small Nations," *New Republic*, Nov. 27, 1915.
* "The World Well Lost," *Masses*, Feb., 1916.
* "The Capitalist," *Masses*, Apr., 1916.
* "Broadway Night," *Masses*, May, 1916.
* "The Head of the Family," *Metropolitan*, May, 1916.
"Dynamite," *Collier's*, Aug. 26, Sept. 2, 9, 16, 1916.
"The Last Clinch," *Metropolitan*, Nov., 1916.
* "Endymion, or On the Border," *Masses*, Dec., 1916.
"The Buccaneer's Grandson," *Metropolitan*, Jan., 1917.
"A Friend at Court," *Masses*, May, 1917.

5. ARTICLES

(Those marked with an asterisk are reprinted in *Insurgent Mexico;* those marked with two asterisks are reprinted in *The War in Eastern Europe.*)

"Immigrants," *Collier's*, May 20, 1911.
"The Involuntary Ethics of Big Business, A Fable for Pessimists," *Trend*, June, 1911.
"A Reminiscence," *American Magazine*, Nov., 1911.
"Charles Townsend Copeland," *American Magazine*, Nov., 1911.
"Frederick Muir," *American Magazine*, Apr., 1912.
"Joseph E. Ralph," *American Magazine*, Oct., 1912.
"War in Paterson," *Masses*, June, 1913.
"From Omaha to Broadway," *Metropolitan*, July, 1913.
"Sheriff Radcliff's Hotel," *Metropolitan*, Sept., 1913.
"With Villa in Mexico," *Metropolitan*, Feb., 1914.
"The Causes Behind Mexico's Revolution," New York *Times*, Apr. 27, 1914. (Reprinted as a pamphlet, June, 1914, by The American Association for International Conciliation, with an introduction by Professor John Bates Clark.)
* "With La Tropa," *Metropolitan*, Apr., 1914.
* "The Battle of La Cadena," *Metropolitan*, May, 1914.
* "Francisco Villa–The Man of Destiny," *Metropolitan*, June, 1914.
"What About Mexico?" *Masses*, June, 1914.
"If We Enter Mexico," *Metropolitan*, June, 1914.
* "With Villa on the March," *Metropolitan*, July, 1914.
"The Colorado War," *Metropolitan*, July, 1914.
* "Happy Valley," *Masses*, July, 1914.
* "The Battle," *Metropolitan*, Aug., 1914.
* "Jiminez and Beyond," *Masses*, Aug., 1914.
"The Traders' War," *Masses*, Sept. 1914. (Unsigned.)
* "Carranza–An Impression," *Metropolitan*, Sept., 1914.

* "El Cosmopolita," *Metropolitan*, Sept., 1914.
"The Approach to War," *Metropolitan*, Nov., 1914.
"Notes on the War," *Masses*, Nov., 1914. (Unsigned.)
"With the Allies," *Metropolitan*, Dec., 1914.
"German France," *Metropolitan*, Mar., 1915.
"The Worst Thing in Europe," *Masses*, Mar., 1915.
"In the German Trenches," *Metropolitan*, Apr., 1915.
"Back of Billy Sunday," *Metropolitan*, May, 1915.
** "Serbia Between Battles," *Metropolitan*, Aug., 1915.
** "At the Serbian Front," *Metropolitan*, Oct., 1915.
** "Breaking Into Bucovina," *Metropolitan*, Nov., 1915.
** "The Burning Balkans," *Metropolitan*, Dec., 1915.
"The Jew on the Eastern Front," in *The Book of Exile*, New York, 1916.
** "Constantinople The Great," *Metropolitan*, Jan., 1916.
** "Behind the Russian Retreat," *Metropolitan*, Mar., 1916.
** "Pinched in Poland," *Metropolitan*, May, 1916.
"Bryan on Tour," *Collier's*, May 20, 1916.
"The Mexican Tangle," *Masses*, June, 1916.
"Persecution of Mexican Refugees," *Masses*, June, 1916.
** "Holy Russia," *Metropolitan*, July, 1916.
"At the Throat of the Republic," *Masses*, July, 1916.
"Roosevelt Sold Them Out," *Masses*, Aug., 1916.
"The National Circus," *Metropolitan*, Sept., 1916.
"Industry's Miracle Maker," *Metropolitan*, Oct., 1916.
"Why They Hate Ford," *Masses*, Oct., 1916.
"An Heroic Pacifist," *Masses*, Nov., 1916.
Introduction to *Crimes of Charity*, by Konrad Bercovici, New York, 1917.
"Industrial Frightfulness in Bayonne," *Metropolitan*, Jan., 1917.
"Whose War?" *Masses*, Apr., 1917.
"Russia," *Masses*, May, 1917.
"The Myth of American Fatness," *Masses*, July, 1917.
"Militarism at Play," *Masses*, Aug., 1917.
"This Unpopular War," *Seven Arts*, Aug., 1917.
"One Solid Month of Liberty," *Masses*, Sept., 1917.
"News from France," *Masses*, Oct., 1917. (With Louise Bryant.)
"A Letter from John Reed," *Masses*, Nov.-Dec., 1917.
"Red Russia—The Triumph of the Bolsheviki," *Liberator*, Mar., 1918.
"Red Russia—Kerensky," *Liberator*, Apr., 1918.
"Red Russia—A Visit to the Russian Army," *Liberator*, Apr. and May, 1918.
"A Message to *Liberator* Readers," *Liberator*, June, 1918.
"Foreign Affairs," *Liberator*, June, 1918.
"Recognize Russia," *Liberator*, July, 1918.
"The Case for the Bolsheviki," *Independent*, July 13, 1918.
"Kerensky is Coming!" *Liberator*, July, 1918.
"John Reed vs. Maxim Gorky," *Upton Sinclair's*, Aug., 1918.
"How the Russian Revolution Works," *Liberator*, Aug., 1918.
"The Social Revolution in Court," *Liberator*, Sept., 1918.
"With Gene Debs on the Fourth," *Liberator*, Sept., 1918.
"On Intervention in Russia," *Liberator*, Nov., 1918.

"The Structure of the Soviet State," *Liberator*, Nov., 1918.

"The Second Day," in *One Year of Revolution*, New York, 1918.

"The Origins of Workers' Control in Russia," *Revolutionary Age*, Nov. 23, 1918.

"The Constituent Assembly in Russia," *Revolutionary Age*, Nov. 30, 1918.

"John Reed on the Bolsheviki," *Upton Sinclair's*, Dec., 1918.

"About the Second *Masses* Trial," *Liberator*, Dec., 1918.

"They are Still There!" *Revolutionary Age*, Dec. 11, 1918.

"Bolshevism in America," *Revolutionary Age*, Dec. 18, 1918.

Introduction to *Smoke*, by Ivan Turgenev, New York, 1919.

"How Soviet Russia Conquered Imperial Germany," *Liberator*, Jan. 1919.

"A White New Year," *Revolutionary Age*, Jan. 4, 1919.

"A New Appeal," *Revolutionary Age*, Jan. 18, 1919.

"The Background of Bolshevism," *Revolutionary Age*, Jan. 25, 1919.

"Doctor Rakovsky," *Revolutionary Age*, Jan. 25, 1919.

"Karl Liebknecht's Words," *Revolutionary Age*, Feb. 1, 1919.

"Our Own Black Hundred," *Liberator*, Feb., 1919.

"Great Bolshevik Conspiracy!" *Liberator*, Feb., 1919.

"The Latest from Russia," *Liberator*, Feb., 1919.

"Liebknecht Dead," *Liberator*, Mar., 1919.

"Workers' Control in America," *Revolutionary Age*, Mar. 15, 1919.

"Prinkipo and After," *Liberator*, Apr., 1919.

"On Bolshevism, Russian and American," *Revolutionary Age*, Apr. 12, 1919.

"The Blessings of Militarism," *Liberator*, May, 1919.

"Bolshevism—What It Is Not," *Liberator*, May, 1919.

"Why Political Democracy Must Go," New York *Communist*, May 8, 15, 24, 31, June 7, 14, 1919.

"The I.W.W. and Labor," New York *Communist*, May 31, 1919.

"The Tide Flows East," *Liberator*, June, 1919.

"Labor Is Not a Commodity," *Revolutionary Age*, July 5, 1919.

"Aspects of the Russian Revolution," *Revolutionary Age*, July 12, 1919.

"The Convention of the Dead," *Liberator*, Aug., 1919.

"Liar or Just Doesn't Know?" *Revolutionary Age*, Aug. 9, 1919.

"Shop Committees in Russia," *Voice of Labor*, Aug. 15, 1919.

"Hooray for the Constitution," *Voice of Labor*, Sept. 15, 1919.

"Communism in America," *Workers' Dreadnought* (London), Oct. 4, 1919.

"What's the Trouble with America?" *Voice of Labor*, Oct. 15, 1919.

"Factory Control in Russia," *Voice of Labor*, Nov. 1, 1919.

"Die Revolutionare Bewegung in Amerika," *Die Kommunistische Internationale*, #8 (Nov.–Dec., 1919), #9 (no date), #10 (no date).

"Die Industriearbeiter der Welt," *Die Kommunistische Internationale*, #13 (no date).

"The Negro Question." (Speech by John Reed at 2nd Congress of Communist International, printed in Moscow *Pravda*, Aug. 8, 1920; in *The Second Congress of the Communist International*, Washington, 1920.)

"The World Congress of the Communist International," *Communist*, #10 (no date).

"Soviet Russia Now," *Liberator*, Dec., 1920, Jan., 1921.

6. SIGNED NEWSPAPER REPORTS

"Rise of Bandit Villa," N. Y. *World*, Mar. 1, 1914.

"Torreon Is Captured in Terrific Battle," N. Y. *World*, Mar. 25, 1914.

"Whole Country Left a Waste," N. Y. *World*, Mar. 29, 1914.

"Madly Charging While Hundreds Died, Villa's Men Won Way to City," N. Y. *World*, Mar. 31, 1914.

"Mrs. Villa Is Told of Torreon's Fall and a Massacre," N. Y. *World*, Apr. 1, 1914.

"Saltillo and Monterey Next to be Attacked," N. Y. *World*, Apr. 4, 1914.

"Writer Once Jailed with I.W.W. Describes Meeting," N. Y. *World*, Apr. 12, 1914.

"Germany Has Shot Her Bolt," N. Y. *World*, Dec. 26, 1915.

"Bandit in Mountains Can Hold His Retreat," N. Y. *American*, Mar. 13, 1916.

"U. S. in Danger of Mountain Ambush," N. Y. *American*, Apr. 16, 1916.

"Why I Am for Wilson," New Orleans *States*, Sept. 27, 1916, and other papers.

"A City of Violence," N. Y. *Tribune*, Oct. 29, 1916.

"Whose War?" N. Y. *Call*, Mar. 18, 1917.

"The Most Tragic Incident I Saw in the War," N. Y. *World*, Apr. 22, 1917.

"The Fall of the Russian Bastile," N. Y. *Tribune*, Mar. 25, 1917.

"Why I Am Against Conscription," N. Y. *Call*, Apr. 19, 1917.

"Poisoner Waite Went to Death Chair With Sign of Neither Fear Nor Remorse," N. Y. *Mail*, May 25, 1917.

"25,000 May Refuse to Register for Conscription in New York," N. Y. *Mail*, June 1, 1917.

"Benny Leonard's Life Story," N. Y. *Mail*, June 1, 2, 3, 4, 5, 1917.

"Sees Failure of Irish Council," N. Y. *Mail*, June 6, 1917.

"Wealth, Beauty, War—Skylark," N. Y. *Mail*, June 7, 1917.

"Disease Greater Peril Than War to America's Army," N. Y. *Mail*, June 11, 1917.

"Macdougal Alley Trips to the Relief of War Horrors," N. Y. *Mail*, June 13, 1917.

"Great Excess War Profits Escape," N. Y. *Mail*, June 13, 1917.

"Big Business Has No Answer to Excess War Profit Plan," N. Y. *Mail*, June 14, 1917.

"Taxes for Deficits of the Poor While Rich Escape War Costs," N. Y. *Mail*, June 15, 1917.

"Rich Men Patriotic Until It Costs Money, Says Pinchot," N. Y. *Mail*, June 16, 1917.

"England's Excess Profits Tax Example for U. S. War Financing," N. Y. *Mail*, June 18, 1917.

"War Tax on All, Maxim's Plan," N. Y. *Mail*, June 19, 1917.

"Russian Sailors Declare Republic and Run Warship by Committee," N. Y. *Mail*, June 19, 1917.

"Senate Balks at High Tax on War Profits," N. Y. *Mail*, June 20, 1917.

"Public Opinion Forcing Senate to Profits Tax," N. Y. *Mail*, June 21, 1917.

"Senators Very Silent on Tax of War Profits," N. Y. *Mail*, June 22, 1917.

"Ten Senators Pledge Battle for 50% War Profit Tax," N. Y. *Mail*, June 23, 1917.

"Big Interests Unite to Fight Heavy Tax on Excess Profits," N. Y. *Mail*, June 25, 1917.

"Senate Gentle in Taxing Rich, Heavy on Poor," N. Y. *Mail*, June 28, 1917.

"Capital Swelters Under Stupefying Pressure of War," N. Y. *Mail*, July 3, 1917.

"Every U. S. Soldier to Have French Girl as 'Marraine,' " N. Y. *Mail*, July 5, 1917.

"Hoboken Waterfront Wide Open Strip for Late Merrymakers," N. Y. *Mail*, July 10, 1917.

"East Side Exiles Stirred by Russian Envoy's 'Welcome Home,' " N. Y. *Mail*, July 11, 1917.

"Woods Refuses to Allow Police to be 'Whitewashed,' " N. Y. *Mail*, July 14, 1917.

"Joy in Yaphank Over Building of Camp Upton," N. Y. *Mail*, July 16, 1917.

"Vast Plot Hides 'Higher ups' in Baff's Murder," N. Y. *Mail*, July 17, 1917.

"Make Profiteers Pay for War; No Stomach Tax, Says F. S. Howe," N. Y. *Mail*, July 19, 1917.

"Wilson Pardon Aids Suffrage," N. Y. *Mail*, July 19, 1917.

"John Reed Falls Down Hard on Beautiful Muckraking Story," N. Y. *Mail*, July 20, 1917.

"World of Strange Adventures Under Broadway Outdoes Movies," N. Y. *Mail*, July 21, 1917.

"Roumanian Soldier Finds His Way from Russian Front to America," N. Y. *Mail*, July 24, 1917.

"With the Poor in the City of Dreadful Night," N. Y. *Mail*, July 27, 1917.

"Sunken Gardens in Central Park Mere Plaything of the Rich," N. Y. *Mail*, July 27, 1917.

"Bowery Still Home of Nation's Masterless Men," N. Y. *Mail*, July 30, 1917.

"One Spot in New York Where Grass May be Used to Lie Upon," N. Y. *Mail*, July 30, 1917.

"Giddy Saratoga Throngs Forget All About War," N. Y. *Mail*, Aug. 2, 1917.

"Old Home Week for the Spirits Puts Lily Dale, N. Y., on the Map," N. Y. *Mail*, Aug. 3, 1917.

"Ed Martin is There Hovering," N. Y. *Mail*, Aug. 4, 1917.

"Spirit Controls at Lily Dale," N. Y. *Mail*, Aug. 6, 1917.

"Mrs. De Saulles, Ill, Taken from Cell to Sheriff's Home," N. Y. *Mail*, Aug. 7, 1917.

"Sicilian Duse Thrills East Side," N. Y. *Mail*, Aug. 8, 1917.

"John Al Raschid Reviews Night Scenes on the East Side," N. Y. *Mail*, Aug. 9, 1917.

"World Sick of War, Socialists Tell U. S.," N. Y. *Call*, Sept. 9, 1917.

"John Reed Cables the *Call* News of Bolshevik Revolt," N. Y. *Call*, Nov. 22, 1917.

"Bourgeoisie Forced Bolshevik Uprising, John Reed Says," N. Y. *Call*, Dec. 26, 1917.

"Bolshevik, Foes of All Imperialism," N. Y. *Call*, May 1, 1918.

"The Great Russian Offensive," N. Y. *Call*, July 27, 1918.
"Deportation–Where?" N. Y. *Call*, Mar. 30, 1919.

7. BOOK REVIEWS

The Upbuilders, by Lincoln Steffens. *Harvard Monthly*, Mar., 1910.
Who, Where, and Why is Villa? by A. Margo. *Masses*, May, 1917.
Glad of Earth, by Clement Wood. *Masses*, May, 1917.
The Labor Movement in Japan, by Sen Katayama. *Liberator*, Mar., 1919.
Bolshevism, by John Spargo. New York *Tribune*, May 3, 1919.

8. MISCELLANEOUS

Rooster, 1904–05, 12 issues. Unsigned jokes and verse.
Lampoon, 1906–11, vols. 52-61. Unsigned jokes and verse; may be identified
   from indexes in bound volumes.
Harvard Monthly, 1910, vol 49. Editorials, initialed.
Masses, 1913–17, vols. 4-9. Editorial and other notes, initialed.
"The Bolsheviki," letter to *The Public*, Oct. 19, 1918.
"The Dead and the Living," extract from letter, *Liberator*, Feb., 1921.

II. WORKS ABOUT JOHN REED

1. BOOK

One of Us, lithographs by Lynd Ward and narrative by Granville Hicks,
New York, 1935.

2. ARTICLES

Anonymous, "Insurgent Reed," *Metropolitan Bulletin*, July 15, 1916.
Anonymous, "John Reed," *Communist*, #10 (no date).
Balabonova, Angelica, "John Reed, Poet and Revolutionist," Souvenir Program
   of the John Reed Memorial, Oct. 17, 1921.
Beer, Thomas, "Playboy," *American Mercury*, June, 1934.
Bernard, Elmer H., "Storm Boy," *Harvard Graduates' Magazine*, Mar., 1934.
Brown, Rose, "John Reed's Youth," Moscow *Daily News*, Oct. 17, 1935.
Bryant, Louise, "Last Days with John Reed," *Liberator*, Feb., 1921.
Dell, Floyd, Introduction to *Daughter of the Revolution*, New York, 1927.
Dell, Floyd, "John Reed: Revolutionist," New York *Call*, Oct. 31, 1920.
Dinamov, Sergei, "The Literary Method of John Reed," *Literature of the
   World Revolution*, #4, 1931.
Dosch-Fleurot, Arno, "*World* Man Tells of Reed in Russia," New York
   World, Oct. 19, 1920.
Dos Passos, John, "Jack Reed," *New Masses*, Oct., 1930.
Eastman, Max, "John Reed," *Liberator*, Dec., 1920.
Frost, Stanley, "John Reed–Revolution as a Sport," New York *Tribune*, Mar.
   27, 1919.
Gilebaux, Henri, "John Reed," *Russian Press Review*, Oct. 29, 1920.
Gold, Michael, "John Reed and the Real Thing," *New Masses*, Nov., 1927.

Hicks, Granville, Introduction to *Ten Days That Shook the World*, New York, 1935.

Hicks, Granville, "John Reed," *New Masses*, Dec., 1932.

Hicks, Granville, "John Reed," *Soviet Russia Today*, Oct., 1935.

Hunt, Edward Eyre, "Prophets of Rebellion," *Outlook*, Mar. 8, 1925.

Hunt, Edward Eyre, "Stelligeri—A Footnote on Democracy," in *Essays in Memory of Barrett Wendell*, Cambridge, 1926.

Karsner, David, "John Reed and Billy Williams: Two Portraits," New York *Call* Oct. 24, 1920.

Lippmann, Walter, "Legendary John Reed," *New Republic*, Dec. 26, 1914.

Mason, Gregory, "Reed, Villa, and the Village," *Outlook*, May 6, 1925.

Minor, Robert, "John Reed," *The Red Album*, Cleveland, 1921.

Monroe, Harriet, "Two Poets Have Died," *Poetry*, Jan., 1921.

Pass, Joseph, "John Reed—Revolutionary Symbol," *Daily Worker*, Oct. 24, 1931.

Reinstein, Boris, "John Reed," *Die Kommunistische Internationale*, #14 (no date).

Robinson, Boardman, "A Memory," *Liberator*, Feb., 1921.

Steffens, Lincoln, "The Boy from Oregon," *The Partisan*, Dec., 1933.

Steffens, Lincoln, "John Reed," *Freeman*, Nov. 3, 1920. (Reprinted as pamphlet, with introduction by Clarence Darrow, Chicago, 1921.)

Street, Julian, "A Soviet Saint: The Story of John Reed," *Saturday Evening Post*, Sept. 13, 1930.

Tudbury, Moran, "Young Immortals: John Reed," *College Humor*, Apr., 1932.

Varine, "John Reed," *Bulletin Communiste*, Nov. 11, 1920.

3. Books Mentioning John Reed

Beatty, Bessie, *The Red Heart of Russia*, New York, 1918.

Berkman, Alexander, *The Bolshevik Myth*, New York, 1925.

Brewing and Liquor Interests and German and Bolshevik Propaganda, 66th Congress, 1st session, Senate document 62, Washington, 1919.

Bryant, Louise, *Six Red Months in Russia*, New York, 1918.

Dell, Floyd, *Homecoming: an Autobiography*, New York, 1933.

Deutsch, Helen, and Hanau, Stella, *The Provincetown: a Story of the Theatre*, New York, 1931.

Draper, Muriel, *Music at Midnight*, New York, 1929.

Dunn, Robert, *Five Fronts*, New York, 1915.

Eaton, W. P., *The Theatre Guild: the First Ten Years*, New York, 1929.

Farson, Negley, *The Way of a Transgressor*, New York, 1936.

Francis, David R., *Russia from the American Embassy, April, 1916–November, 1918*, New York, 1921.

Glaspell, Susan, *The Road to the Temple*, New York, 1927.

Goldman, Emma, *Living My Life*, New York, 1931.

Goldman, Emma, *My Disillusionment in Russia*, New York, 1923.

Goldman, Emma, *My Further Disillusionment in Russia*, New York, 1924.

Hard, William, *Raymond Robin's Own Story*, New York, 1920.

Harrison, Marguerite, *Marooned in Moscow*, New York, 1921.

Harrison, Marguerite, *There's Always Tomorrow*, New York, 1935.

Haywood, William D., *Bill Haywood's Book*, New York, 1929.

Hillquit, Morris, *Loose Leaves from a Busy Life*, New York, 1934.

Kreymborg, Alfred, *Troubadour: an Autobiography*, New York, 1925.

Mayer, Edwin Justus, *A Preface to Life*, New York, 1923.

Parry, Albert, *Garrets and Pretenders*, New York, 1933.

Revolutionary Radicalism, Its History, Purpose and Tactics (Report of the Joint Legislative Committee Investigating Seditious Activities), Albany, 1920.

Rubin, Jacob H., *I Live to Tell*, Indianapolis, 1934.

Sheridan, Clare, *Mayfair to Moscow*, New York, 1921.

Sisson, Edgar, *One Hundred Red Days*, New Haven, 1931.

Steffens, Lincoln, *Autobiography*, New York, 1931.

Steiger, John N., *The Memoirs of a Silk Striker*, Paterson, 1914.

Stein, Gertrude, *The Autobiography of Alice B. Toklas*, New York, 1933.

Taggard, Genevieve (editor), *May Days, An Anthology of Verse from Masses-Liberator*, New York, 1925.

Towne, Charles Hanson, *This New York of Mine*, New York, 1931.

Vorse, Mary Heaton, *A Footnote to Folly*, New York, 1935.

Williams, Albert Rhys, *Through the Russian Revolution*, New York, 1921.

Young, Art, *On My Way*, New York, 1928.

INDEX